In the Hands of a Chef

In the Hands of a Chef
of a Chef

❧ COOKING WITH JODY ADAMS ☙

JODY ADAMS *and*
KEN RIVARD

June 2007
Jody Adams

WILLIAM MORROW
75 YEARS OF PUBLISHING
An Imprint of HarperCollins *Publishers*

HarperCollins books may be purchased for educational, business, or sales promotional use. For information please write: Special Markets Department, HarperCollins Publishers Inc., 10 East 53rd Street, New York, NY 10022.

FIRST EDITION

Printed on acid-free paper

Library of Congress Cataloging-in-Publication Data

Adams, Jody.
In the hands of a chef : cooking with Jody Adams / Jody Adams and Ken Rivard.
p.   cm.
ISBN 0-688-16837-X
1. Cookery.   2. Cookery, International.   I. Rivard, Ken, 1951–   II. Title.

TX714 .A422   2002
641.5—dc21
2001032946

02   03   04   05   06   QW   10 9 8 7 6 5 4 3 2 1

FOR OLIVER AND ROXANNE

Contents

Acknowledgments

T*he collaborative nature of cooking* first drew me into my mother's kitchen and later to restaurants. My success as a chef is the result of many partnerships, and what keeps me going back to the kitchen is not just the food—it's working side by side with other people. There is always more to learn. I would like to extend my thanks to my parents, Tom and Po Adams, who taught me to celebrate food; to my sisters, Ginny and Eliza, my first kitchen partners; to my first teachers, Gordon Hamersley, Nancy Verde Barr, Lydia Shire, and Susan Regis; to my sous-chefs, past and present, for giving me a rock to stand on—Petal Joseph, Ruth-Anne Adams, Frank Vasello, and Laura Brennan; to the kitchen and service staffs at Rialto, whose commitment to what we do makes us successful every day; to my partners, Michela Larson and Karen Haskell, who insisted I write this book and then, as always, supported the process to the end; to Dick Friedman, one of my biggest fans; to Gary Sullivan, who in recent years has taught me the true meaning of service; to our customers, whose vigilance and appreciation remind me why we are here; and to all the producers and purveyors whose exceptional raw ingredients make my job possible.

No cookbook is ever written alone. Doe Coover, our agent, deserves special thanks for her abiding optimism and for helping us to conceptualize the book, both times around. Justin Schwartz earned our respect for believing in our ship; Harriet Bell, for her insight and confidence that our vessel would actually someday sail into port; Pam Krueger, our ever-diligent recipe tester, kept us honest. Thanks to Ellen Silverman for her spectacular photographs; and to Karen Ferries for her patient incorporation of changes to the text. Valerie and Ihsan Gurdal and their staff at Formaggio Kitchens, who endured endless questions about their spices, seasonings, cheeses, and other specialty ingredients; Nan Niland, Ralph Helmick, Anne Fabiny, and Larry Cohen—no one should ever underestimate the importance of friends or volunteer palates; to my patient husband, Ken, enormous love and gratitude—he gave me a voice and chased me for two and a half years to get things just right; without him, it never would have happened. (To my wife, Jody: it takes two to tango—Ken.) Finally, thank you, Oliver and Roxanne, uninhibited critics, enthusiastic diners, sources of the magic and love that keep us afloat.

Introduction

❦

The shortest route I know to human happiness is cooking. The immediacy of mincing garlic, stripping kale, or searing fresh sea scallops takes me away from my ordinary cares and, however briefly, narrows my responsibility to just the radish or the sprig of rosemary in front of me. The vivid red appeal of a fresh tomato sauce is a kind of satisfaction in itself. As a chef with a restaurant to run, I'm aware that the bottom line is my customers' satisfaction with the food that appears on their tables. But as a cook, especially a cook at home, these other pleasures are as important as the consumption of the meal. They're a kind of built-in bonus that comes with "handmade" food.

Cookbooks these days seem less and less inclined to celebrate this essential truth. One type of book offers an antidote to our overscheduled lives, promising to compress kitchen time to the minimum. Another tempts (or overwhelms) us with elaborate restaurant-style preparations and presentations. This book argues for a third category—artisanal home food. Good food made from scratch. This category finds its inspiration in regional cooking, mostly European, in the type of dishes that used to be prepared for family dinners. Although some of the recipes in this book are both fast and simple. I'm announcing my intention up front: to seduce you into spending more time, not less, in your kitchen.

The distinctive feature of artisanal cooking is its being handmade, of taking fresh raw ingredients through a series of steps to a finished state. With everything from sea urchin roe sushi to Mexican duck fajitas available in grocery stores today, artisanal cooking is clearly no longer a necessity, but some of us choose to do it anyway. Some aspects of experience are worth keeping in your own hands, and few are as hands-on or as immediately satisfying as cooking. This book is an invitation to place yourself in my hands and, I hope, experience why I'm so passionate about my particular patch of territory.

None of the recipes in these pages belongs to the juggle-four-oranges-in-the-air-while-fanning-the-squabs-with-your-foot school of cooking. When you need technique, I explain what to do. When you need to know how something should look or taste, I tell you. Many of the recipes do require some time, if not necessarily your constant attention. But when I ask you to invest time in a dish, there is always a reward in the depth of flavor.

Each of these recipes is something we do at my house, even if from time to time a more elaborate variation of the dish is served at Rialto. Although this is not a restaurant cookbook, it does contain a chapter of signature preparations, "A Mile in a Chef's Shoes"—including, most notably, Soupe de Poisson and Roasted Marinated Long Island Duck with Green Olive and Balsamic Vinegar Sauce. These are far and away my most frequently requested recipes. You *can* make them in your own kitchen, with less effort than you might think. You are, presumably, already a passionate eater; my goal is to turn you into a passionate cook.

The Kitchen in My Head

ike every cook, I'm the product of a constellation of culinary influences—my mom, cooking classes, numberless cookbooks, memorable meals, travel, work experience, and the chefs who employed me. Even after I became a chef, with the freedom to explore my own instincts, it took a few years before everything I'd learned shook itself into some kind of coherence: what I call "the kitchen in my head." The practical result is that I have great confidence in my food. I love what I cook, whether at work or at home.

Most of my cooking life has revolved around a fascination for high-quality ingredients and figuring out the best ways of handling them. Although as a child I accompanied my mother on infrequent trips for baked goods or chicken at Italian shops on Federal Hill in Providence, these were exhilarating exceptions that proved the rule—most food came prepackaged, from the supermarket. It wasn't until I was a teenager, living in England during one of my father's sabbaticals, with opportunities for travel to France and Italy, that I came to see an alternative to the supermarket model. In addition to the Oxford market with its stalls of vendors, there were the butcher shops with enameled trays of freshly killed rabbits, gleaming livers, and the occasional calf's head. It soon became something of an obsession with me to visit markets wherever we traveled. When we returned to Providence, my mother and I began shopping regularly on Federal Hill. To this day, museums drain me after an hour or two, but I can wander through farmers' markets all day and return home with my finds, energized for cooking.

Part of the allure of ingredients (and, by extension, markets) for me is simple sensual pleasure. Stacks of leeks, white, bulbous, and gleaming, bundled red and white radishes, and the circus-tent stripes of delicata squash all grab my eye as I pass by. Purple-top turnips beg to be lifted, hefted, and judged heavy or light for their size; a flat of local strawberries or tomatoes stirs the same thing in me that used to be reached only by a new box of crayons, a visceral urge to touch and smell before using.

Noting variations in the color and heft in turnips, rutabagas, and celery root is practical as well as aesthetic. Visual and tactile differences between the same vegetables offer clues to water, starch, and sugar content, which affect how you cook them. Summer garlic is sweet and forgiving; if you turn your back on winter garlic, it burns. A turnip that feels light for its size will taste bitter and may have a spongy texture. In my cooking classes, I've found that home cooks who are already familiar with technique are often surprised to see how much their food improves when they apply a little more attention and discernment to choosing their ingredients, regardless of whether the ingredient is a Hubbard squash or a chicken leg.

As a restaurateur, I know the vendors and in many cases the actual producers of the particular raw ingredients I buy. When you know the people growing or harvesting your ingredients, you treat the ingredients with greater respect. I've squished through the Wellfleet tidal flats where my friends Patrick and Barbara Woodbury devote themselves to raising perfect clams: they can tell the health and quality of a clam with a simple tap. In thirteen years of business with them, I have never had so much as a clam with a cracked shell. How could I not treat their clams with respect (and ensure that my cooks do the same)? With the resurgence of farmers' markets across the country, it is now possible for home cooks to form the same type of relationship with vendors that until recently had been the exclusive domain of people in the food business.

With the Federal Hill neighborhood and its Italian markets only a short drive from my house, and the immigrant Portuguese neighborhood also close by, it was probably fated I'd learn cooking technique by studying Europe's regional cuisines. Regional cooking is really no more than the collective knowledge of the people who live where particular ingredients are most accessible. This usually means home cooks, because that's "where the rubber meets the road" in terms of culinary experience—the family dinner table. What works sticks around, and becomes part of the local cooking tradition. Technique enters the picture for me not as something isolated, valued in itself, but as a series of steps that arise in a particular place with local ingredients. My first exposure to technique came through the regional food of Italy, later followed by that of France and Spain, and eventually the farther reaches of the Mediterranean. First comes the *what*—the ingredients—then comes the *how*—the way of making the most of ingredients. Technique is all about distilling knowledge of what works into steps that I can reproduce at home or teach in classes or do at Rialto. The process of searing seafood, for example, is much more understandable when it's embedded in the story of how people in Normandy like to treat their scallops. Seen this way, technique and ingredients are partners, dependent on each other, in a dance that transforms raw ingredients into a finished dish.

For the first part of my career, as the chef of Michela's in Boston, I specialized in carefully researched dishes based on regional Italian food. This had the obvious advantage of giving me, a new chef, a framework. When writing a menu, for example, and thinking about new seafood entrées, I had someplace to go. Instead of having to ponder the terrifyingly open-ended question of, "OK, let's see, we need a few fish dishes—what can I do?" I could take a page from the experience of cooks in Tuscany or Puglia. But over time, I found myself less and less bound to the idea of reproducing dishes exactly as they might be cooked in their place of origin. By the time I left Michela's, I had come to regard regional cuisine as a resource (one among several), a library of particular techniques and ingredient combinations that might be visited for inspiration. What about all the wonderful ingredients indigenous to New England—and not found in France? I am grateful for my grounding in regional cuisine, perhaps the way a jazz musician appreciates his classical training—it all gets put to use. But my cooking now, at Rialto, is looser. I rely on my instincts more (that kitchen in my head). I'm willing to let my cooking be inspired by dishes I've tasted while traveling, but not dominated by them, and I always try to take my first cue from what's best in the markets accessible to me. Who knows where my instincts will take me? Probably France or Italy or Spain, but some items on my menu found their inspiration in Tunisia or Guatemala—or just around the corner in Maine.

How to Use This Book

Cooking isn't magic—except to those who can't cook. Success may not be instant, but it is almost always certain, especially with practice. Every recipe in this book has been tested at least twice, once by me and once by my friend and recipe tester Pam Krueger. Pam is not a culinary professional, she's a home cook, and as we worked our way through this manuscript, she encountered many new taste combinations and more than one unfamiliar technique. When she didn't understand a recipe, we rewrote the recipe to answer her concerns; we talked about potential pitfalls and how to avoid them, and we tried to incorporate as much of this information into the recipes as possible, often testing recipes another third time. In the course of this process, we discovered a few guidelines for increasing your chances for a happy experience in the kitchen.

This book is about my taste and experience, the places my hands and palate naturally go, and I encourage you to follow me there—even if it's not your first instinct. The idea of a particular dish is often more forbidding to home cooks than the actual preparation or taste of the dish itself. For instance, there is a recipe for Rabbit Soup with Garlic and Peppers (page 58). Try making the recipe with rabbit, as it's written, instead of automatically substituting chicken. You may discover tastes you never knew you had. While writing this book, I farmed out recipes to friends, watching to see which (if any) of the preparations survived beyond the OK-we'll-make-it-once-for-you-because-you're-our-buddy stage. My friends were often surprised that they liked previously unfamiliar dishes like brandade and roast goose, but I was not. Even more satisfying to me was how much they liked making the food.

Read each recipe through before making a shopping list. Some of the recipes have several components; cooking all of them for the first time can be quite challenging. The Roasted Marinated Long Island Duck with Green Olive and Balsamic Vinegar Sauce, for example, explains how to roast the duck as well as make a duck stock and use the stock to make a green olive sauce. If you want to try everything your first time out of the gate, by all means go for it, but if not, your pleasure (or that of your guests) in a slow-roasted duck will make up for your reservations about skipping the sauce. A dish that you can comfortably make in an hour or an hour and half is no fun to make if you try to compress it into forty-five minutes. When you have time, with slow-roasting under your belt, you can try the stock and sauce.

A good carpenter never blames his tools for poor work, but it is difficult to do great work with poor tools. Investing in a few heavy-bottomed pots, decent knives, and a sharpening steel will more than repay the cost of their initial outlay. Almost every other piece of equipment is optional, but knives and a couple of serious pots are essential. It is almost impossible to sauté properly in a pan that won't conduct heat evenly. By the same token, knives that can't hold a sharp edge (which can be restored before each use by a few good strokes on the steel) make chopping and slicing a dangerous chore, instead of the pleasure it should be.

Finally, have fun. If you can't find a particular herb (or you *really, really* like an alternative), feel free to make substitutions; if a particular substitution is problematic, I'll warn you. This book should enhance your confidence, not tear it down. I want the recipes to contribute to your overall store of happiness, not deplete it. Make it your business to cook just *a little* beyond your abilities and you will soon find yourself in the lamentable position of all great cooks—wishing you had more time in your life to spend in the kitchen.

Starters and Small Bites

ॐ

My favorite style of entertaining is to invite guests for around four o'clock on a Sunday afternoon, which allows plenty of time for everyone to hang out and catch up before sitting down at the table. I usually offer one—at most, two—homemade dishes for nibbling with wine, and everyone is encouraged to serve himself. Little treats—whether called tapas, canapés, or meze—encourage guests to slow down and savor the moment, especially if it's on a cocktail napkin right in front of them.

My repertoire of predinner food falls into two categories—items I prepare ahead and those that can be done while friends are standing around relaxing with a glass of wine. With the exception of Grilled Clams on the Half-Shell with Garlic Crostini—they absolutely have to go on the grill at the last minute—all these recipes in this chapter can be made in advance if inviting friends into your kitchen makes you uncomfortable.

This chapter is one of the few places in the book where I indulge in deep-frying. Health-conscious friends who would never order (or make at home) anything deep-fried feel free to try Goujonettes of Sole if they know they're only going to consume a few mouthfuls. People love small tastes of fried things, especially if there is a sauce to go with them.

Supplement whatever you've chosen to make with simple items like olives or cheeses or breads. My aim here isn't to replace any of these—just to expand your repertoire into the memorable, the special. If you're the sort of person who can't bear to serve anything unless it's homemade, of course, feel free to do so—and invite me over.

Smoked Salmon Rolls with Arugula, Mascarpone, Chives, and Capers

A visit to Peck's, the famed food emporium in Milan, inspired this dish. I came across a display of their torta cheeses—bricks of cheese layered with different ingredients, including one with smoked salmon and mascarpone. The combination is fabulous. Mascarpone's subtle sweetness doesn't overwhelm the flavor of delicate smoked salmon. The bundles can be done a day ahead, minus the arugula, and kept refrigerated. Before serving, push 3 arugula leaves into the top of each roll. You can elevate the rolls from finger food to a full appetizer by using a more elaborate presentation. Arrange 4 rolls each atop portions of a simple arugula salad and accompany with Parchment Bread (page 21).

MAKES 24 HORS D'OEUVRES OR 6 APPETIZER SERVINGS

5 ounces mascarpone (about ⅔ cup)
2 tablespoons capers, rinsed
2 tablespoons minced fresh chives
1 teaspoon freshly squeezed lemon juice
Kosher salt and freshly ground black pepper
¾ pound smoked salmon, cut into 24 thin slices,
   2 to 3 inches on the short side (presliced salmon
   is fine)
48 small tender arugula leaves

1. Mix the mascarpone with 1 tablespoon of the capers, 1 tablespoon of the chives, and the lemon juice. Season with salt and pepper.

2. Lay the salmon slices out on a cutting board so that they're all arranged with a short side facing you, with plenty of space above and below each slice. (If necessary, fill and roll the slices in batches.)

3. Put a spoonful of the mascarpone mixture on the narrow end of one slice. Lay 2 arugula leaves, fanned slightly apart, across the mascarpone, so that the tips of the leaves will project several inches from one end of the roll, and roll up the salmon. Stand the roll upright, the arugula leaves pointing upward, on a platter large enough to hold all 24 rolls. Repeat the process with the remaining slices. Cover and refrigerate until serving.

4. Remove from the refrigerator, sprinkle with the remaining 1 tablespoon each capers and chives, and serve.

Grilled Clams on the Half-Shell with Garlic Crostini

Grilling clams turns into culinary theater—everyone soon gathers around to investigate the aroma of the clams sizzling in a little olive oil seasoned with white pepper. The clams can be opened several hours in advance as long as they're kept chilled and covered, and care is taken not to spill any of their juice, called "liquor."

MAKES 40 HORS D'OEUVRES

1 to 2 cups kosher salt
40 littleneck clams (3½ to 4 pounds), scrubbed
Freshly ground white pepper (if you only have pre-ground white pepper, substitute freshly ground black pepper)
About 1 cup extra virgin olive oil
1 loaf rustic bread, cut into twenty 1½-inch-thick slices
6 garlic cloves, peeled

1. Prepare a fire in a grill with both hot and medium sections (see page 265). A grill is hot when you can hold your hand near the cooking surface for no more than a count of 2 before having to pull it away. For the medium section, you should be able to hold your hand near the cooking surface for at least a count of 4 before having to pull it away.

2. Cover a large platter with a ½-inch layer of kosher salt, to hold the clams without tipping after opening. Open the clams (see box), setting each clam in its half-shell on the platter.

The clams will cook—and stay moist—in their own juice, so preserve as much of this flavorful liquid while opening them as possible. Sprinkle the clams with white pepper and drizzle each with about ½ teaspoon olive oil—don't measure, just drizzle lightly.

3. To make the crostini, brush the bread slices lightly with olive oil. Place on the medium part of the grill and grill until toasted, a minute or two on each side—watch them carefully so they don't burn. Rub the grilled slices with the garlic and sprinkle with salt. Cut the crostini in half crosswise so you have 40 pieces.

4. Using tongs, place the clams, in their shells, on the hot grill. Watch for the liquor and olive oil to boil. Allow the clams to boil until they're just cooked—depending on the temperature of the grill, this may be only a minute. Err on the side of underdoneness; if they're a shade underdone, you can always put them back on the grill for a few seconds. Transfer the clams back to the platter. Serve the clams and crostini immediately.

HOW TO OPEN A CLAM

The easiest way to learn how to open a clam is to ask the shucker at a raw bar to demonstrate the technique—it's not really difficult, just difficult to describe. Once you've mastered the technique, you can open clams with almost any knife, but using a clam knife, with its sturdy, blunt-edged blade, is the easiest and safest way to learn. Hold the clam on a folded towel in the palm of your hand; the towel prevents the clam from slipping while protecting your hand. The hinge of the clam should point toward your wrist, the outer rim of the clam toward your fingers. Keeping the clam level so as little juice as possible spills during opening, work the thin side of the blade into the outer rim of the clam between the edges of the shells. This is usually just a matter of placing the knife edge against the seam and squeezing the blade into the clam. Once the knife blade is between the shells, a simple twist of the blade will pry the shells apart. Carefully detach the meat from the upper shell with the knife. Twist off the top shell and discard. Place the clam in its half-shell on a platter spread with kosher salt so the shell doesn't tip.

Goujonettes of Sole with Rémoulade Sauce

These tasty strips of sole are named for their resemblance to *goujons*, tiny members of the minnow family, which the French love to dredge in flour and fry whole. Goujonettes are prepared the same way, then served with lemon or a flavored mayonnaise. You can prepare a lovely presentation of the sole on a platter, but I have to admit that this is one of my favorite friends-hanging-out-in-the-kitchen dishes. Goujonettes are perfect right out of the pan and everyone loses whatever inhibitions he may have had about using his fingers to dip the tasty strips of sole into a bowl of rémoulade.

MAKES 36 HORS D'OEUVRES

1 pound fresh skinless sole fillets
½ cup milk
¼ cup unbleached all-purpose flour
2 tablespoons semolina flour
Kosher salt and freshly ground black pepper
4 cups vegetable oil for deep-frying
1 bunch flat-leaf parsley for garnish
1 recipe Rémoulade (page 14), chilled

1. Remove any skin, bones, or cartilage from the fish fillets. Slice the fish into "goujonette" strips about 1 inch wide and 4 inches long.

2. Pour the milk into a shallow bowl. Mix the flours together on a plate. Dip the fish strips in the milk and then season with salt and pepper. Roll in the flour mixture and lay out on a tray. Refrigerate until ready to use.

3. Preheat the oven to 200°F. Line a sheet pan with paper towels and put in the oven.

4. Heat the oil in a deep pot to 350°F. Use a deep-fry thermometer to check the temperature. Carefully lower 4 or 5 goujonettes into the oil (put each in individually, or they'll stick together) and deep-fry until they are golden brown on the outside and cooked through, 3 to 4 minutes. As they finish cooking, transfer them to the sheet pan in the oven. Continue until all the sole is cooked.

5. Serve on a warm platter garnished with the parsley. Offer the bowl of rémoulade sauce on the side.

Mayonnaise—and Variations

Homemade mayonnaise will be a culinary epiphany if you've never made it before, both from the standpoint of taste and the sense of astonished accomplishment that goes along with making it. There are literally dozens of variations with different herbs and flavorings to transform the basic recipe into a memorable sauce. I've listed a few of the classics below. The convention in making mayonnaise is to use 1 cup of oil for each egg yolk. My version halves the amount of oil, resulting in a richer flavor and texture. Please use only absolutely fresh eggs, and allow all of the ingredients to come to room temperature before beginning the recipe.

Homemade mayonnaise will keep for 4 to 5 days in the refrigerator. Keep in mind that the flavor of fresh herbs may fade after a day or two, although the mayonnaise will remain usable for some time longer.

MAKES A GENEROUS ½ CUP

1 extra-large egg yolk
½ teaspoon Dijon mustard
2 teaspoons freshly squeezed lemon juice
¼ cup vegetable oil
¼ cup extra virgin olive oil
Kosher salt and freshly ground black pepper

1. In a small bowl, beat the egg yolk with the mustard and lemon juice. Whisk in the vegetable oil, one drop at a time. This will establish the all-important emulsion; after you've made an emulsion with the vegetable oil, you can then begin adding the olive oil in a thin, steady stream, continuing to beat all the while. If it seems as though the olive oil isn't being incorporated into the emulsion, stop adding oil, and keep beating. If it seems as though the emulsion still isn't incorporating the oil, beat a drop or two of water into the mixture to loosen it. Then resume adding the oil.

2. Season with salt and pepper. If the mayonnaise seems too thick, beat in a drop or two of water. Cover and refrigerate until ready to serve.

Aïoli

Aïoli is a traditional French sauce of mayonnaise flavored with minced garlic. Although some versions call for a bit of potato as a thickener, I prefer to keep things simple—just mayonnaise and garlic. As a condiment for soups, fish, and vegetables, aïoli is ubiquitous in southern France and coastal Italy. There's even a French dish called a grand aïoli, composed of various cooked vegetables served with aïoli for dipping. To make aïoli, simply mince and then mash 2 cloves of garlic with a pinch of salt until they form a paste, then beat into the basic mayonnaise.

Rouille

Rouille is a peppery condiment used to top the floating croutons in the Provençal *soupe de poisson* (fish soup), but there's no reason you can't use it with other seafood dishes. I particularly like it with cold seafood salads. Some versions of rouille include potatoes or bread crumbs to provide the sauce with body; my favorite is this version, based on mayonnaise. Mince and then mash 2 cloves of garlic with a little salt until they form a paste. (Or use more or less garlic according to taste.) Beat the garlic paste, 4 teaspoons paprika, and ¼ teaspoon cayenne pepper into the basic mayonnaise.

Rémoulade

Rémoulade is another classic French condiment, with a bracing flavor of anchovies, cornichons, capers, and herbs. Although it is traditionally served with seafood, I also like it with cold pork or lamb. I never make less than a cup of rémoulade, and those are the quantities I list here. Make a double recipe (1 cup) of the basic mayonnaise. Combine ½ cup finely chopped fresh flat-leaf parsley; 2 tablespoons finely chopped tarragon; 2 garlic cloves, minced; 1 shallot, minced; 2 tablespoons capers, rinsed and coarsely chopped; 2 tablespoons finely chopped cornichons; and 4 anchovy fillets, rinsed and minced, and blend well, then mix into the mayonnaise. Add 1 tablespoon freshly squeezed lemon juice and season with kosher salt and freshly ground black pepper. Taste, and adjust the seasoning as necessary, adding more lemon juice (up to 2 tablespoons in all) a teaspoon at a time. (Makes about 1¼ cups.)

Herbal Mayonnaise

Add 2 to 4 tablespoons of finely chopped fresh herbs to the basic mayonnaise. Tarragon, basil, chervil, thyme, and dill all make delicious additions.

Goat Cheese Terrine with Dried Figs and Hazelnuts

This is a jewel-like composed terrine made with two different types of goat cheese, hazelnuts, dried figs, and sweet sherry. Don't skimp on the quality of the ingredients. Nothing is cooked or altered in any way, so the ingredients should be the best available. Buy a high-quality fresh goat cheese that has some goat in the taste and don't skimp on the figs. Turkish figs, especially from Ismir, are still plump with residual moisture and are often sticky with the reduced sugar sap of their own juices. If you can't find Turkish figs, substitute the plumpest dried figs you can find. The grape leaves provide a slightly tart, dramatic wrapping, but they can be omitted if you prefer. The terrine will keep for several days refrigerated.

MAKES TWELVE 2-OUNCE SERVINGS

¼ **pound high-quality dried figs, preferably Turkish**

¼ **cup sweet sherry, such as Pedro Jiménez**

5 grape leaves preserved in brine (available in jars in the Middle Eastern section of your grocery store), rinsed and drained

1 pound fresh goat cheese, divided into 5 equal portions

¼ **pound aged goat cheese (such as Coach Farm Aged Brick or Bûcheron), crumbled**

½ **cup hazelnuts, toasted and coarsely chopped**

1. Remove the stems from the figs and slice the figs crosswise into ¼-inch slices. Put into a bowl and pour the sherry over them. Allow them to steep for 30 minutes, then drain if there's any remaining liquid.

2. Line a 6 × 3-inch loaf pan with plastic wrap, letting several extra inches drape over the sides (there should be enough so that once the pan is filled, the overhanging plastic wrap can be folded over to cover the top completely). The plastic wrap makes it easy to unmold the ter-

rine after chilling; if you're using a metal pan that isn't nonreactive, the wrap also prevents the metal from interacting with the cheese mixture.

3. Line the sides and bottom of the pan with grape leaves, allowing a couple of inches of leaves to drape over the sides so that after the terrine is filled, the leaves can be folded back over the top. Spread 1 portion of the fresh goat cheese over the bottom of the pan and top with half of the aged goat cheese. Lay half the figs over the cheese, top with another portion of fresh cheese, and cover with half the hazelnuts. Top with another portion of fresh goat cheese and then the remaining aged cheese. Lay the remaining figs over the cheese, top with another layer of fresh goat cheese, and cover with the remaining hazelnuts. Finish with a final layer of fresh goat cheese. Fold the grape leaves back over the terrine, followed by the plastic wrap. Tap the pan several times on the counter to release any air bubbles. Refrigerate for 4 hours to set.

4. Invert the terrine onto a platter. The terrine should easily come out of the pan once it's chilled. Carefully peel away the plastic wrap, so you don't tear the grape leaves. Cut a slice from the terrine with a knife so the inside is visible. Present the terrine and end slice on a small platter.

TOASTING NUTS AND SEEDS

Spread the nuts on a single layer on a sheet pan and toast in a 350°F oven until golden and aromatic, about 10 minutes. Keep a close watch while they toast—a minute or two of neglect is all it takes to burn them.

Seeds should be toasted on top of the stove to minimize the risk of burning. Cook them in a dry pan, tossing constantly, just until they become aromatic, 3 to 4 minutes. Immediately transfer them to a cool plate. Always grind seeds after toasting.

Venetian Duck Liver and Porcini Pâté

On my first visit to Northern Italy, I was struck by how often there were only two antipasto choices: a smooth liver pâté or some sliced prosciutto. These seemed to make up the antipasti selection in every small restaurant I visited. They were strategic choices for family-run businesses where every dollar counted: prosciutto was a dependable option for conservative clients, while more adventurous diners could try the house pâté—which also gave the kitchen an opportunity to shine without investing in costlier ingredients.

This pâté is based on several with raisins I tried in Venice. I use the livers reserved from Rialto's roasted duck entrée, but you can substitute chicken livers; duck livers simply increase the richness.

MAKES TWENTY-FOUR 2-OUNCE SERVINGS

¼ cup currants

1 cup plus 2 tablespoons Marsala

2½ pounds fresh duck livers (available from many butchers; substitute chicken livers if necessary)

Kosher salt and freshly ground black pepper

2 tablespoons extra virgin olive oil

1 pound (4 sticks) plus 2 tablespoons unsalted butter, at room temperature

2 large shallots, minced

3 garlic cloves, minced

1 ounce dried porcini, reconstituted in warm water (see page 271) and finely chopped (soaking liquid saved)

5 anchovies, rinsed and finely chopped

¼ cup finely chopped fresh sage plus 1 bunch sage for garnish

½ cup cornichons

½ cup small pickled onions

½ cup Dijon mustard (optional)

DO AHEAD: The pâté needs to chill for at least 6 hours before serving, and it will keep for up to 5 days in the refrigerator.

1. Put the currants in a small bowl, add 2 tablespoons of the Marsala, and set aside to plump.

2. Meanwhile, clean the livers of all sinew and veins. Season with salt and pepper. Heat 1 tablespoon of the olive oil and 1 tablespoon of the butter in a large sauté pan over medium heat. As soon as the butter stops foaming, add the livers, and sear on both sides. Don't crowd the pan; cook the livers in batches if necessary. By the time the livers are lightly seared, they should be cooked to medium-rare. Drain in a colander and allow to cool.

3. Heat the remaining 1 tablespoon olive oil with 1 tablespoon of the butter in a sauté pan over medium heat. Add the shallots and garlic and cook until tender, 2 to 3 minutes. Add the porcini, porcini soaking liquid, and the remaining 1 cup Marsala and cook until the liquids have reduced to a glaze, about 9 minutes. Let cool to room temperature.

4. Put the cooled livers in the food processor and process to a paste. Add the Marsala reduction, the anchovies, and sage. Pulse 3 times.

Add the remaining 1 pound butter, 1 stick at a time, processing until completely incorporated. Transfer the liver paste to a bowl. Fold in the currants, with the Marsala they were soaking in, and season with salt and pepper.

5. Line a 6 × 3-inch loaf pan with plastic wrap, letting several inches drape over the sides, so that you can fold it back over the pâté once the pan is filled. Pour the pâté into the pan. Tap the pan several times on the counter to remove any air bubbles. Fold the plastic wrap over the top and refrigerate for at least 6 hours.

6. To serve, carefully lift the pâté out of the terrine and invert it onto a platter. Peel away the plastic wrap. Garnish with the bunch of sage and a small handful of the cornichons and onions. Offer the remaining pickles on the side, along with the mustard, if desired.

Walnut Breadsticks

Pizza dough lends itself to quick homemade breadsticks and crackers (never throw away left-over dough for this reason). These breadsticks incorporate chopped walnuts and fresh herbs, but you can play with a wide array of other ingredients. Fiery-food lovers can sprinkle the dough with red pepper flakes or cayenne pepper. Finely chopped cooked bacon, prosciutto, ricotta salata, crumbled feta, and chopped olives are also good. I've even rolled cooked lentils into the dough. Pick only a couple of ingredients for any one batch of breadsticks or their tastes begin to muddle. Keep the quantity of any add-ins down to a cup per half-pound of dough and chop them quite fine, so the breadsticks don't fall apart.

MAKES ABOUT 24 BREADSTICKS

About 2 tablespoons extra virgin olive oil
½ recipe Pizza Dough (page 123), cut into 4 pieces
    and allowed to rest at room temperature for 30
    minutes
Flour for rolling out the dough
1 cup walnuts, toasted and finely chopped
2 tablespoons finely chopped fresh herbs (such as
    basil, parsley, thyme, tarragon, etc.)
¼ cup freshly grated Parmesan
Kosher salt and freshly ground black pepper

1. Preheat the oven to 400°F. Rub a large sheet pan with a light coating of olive oil, 2 to 3 teaspoons.

2. Roll out each piece of pizza dough on a lightly floured surface into a rough rectangle 4 to 5 inches wide and about 8 inches long. Rub each rectangle of dough with a teaspoon of the olive oil. Sprinkle each one with ¼ cup of the walnuts, 1½ teaspoons of the herbs, 1 table-spoon of the cheese, and salt and pepper. Roll over the ingredients with the rolling pin to press them into the dough.

3. Slice the dough lengthwise into ¾-inch-wide strips. Grasp a strip of dough by both ends and give it 4 or 5 twists while stretching it, until it's about 10 to 12 inches long. Set the twisted strip down on the sheet pan. (If the dough seems to be stretching only in the middle, lay the strip down and do a couple of mini-stretches in the thicker spots to even things out before you twist the dough.) Repeat the process with the remaining dough. You should get about 2 dozen breadsticks.

4. Bake until crisp and golden, about 10 minutes. Allow the breadsticks to cool completely before serving. They'll keep overnight in a tightly sealed container. Don't refrigerate or they'll become soggy.

Rosemary-Parmesan Crackers

The crisp puffiness of these delicate crackers tempts people to pick them up, and they give off a wonderful aroma of garlic and rosemary. They won't last long. Any of the items used to flavor breadsticks (see page 19) can be sprinkled on top of the crackers just before baking, as long as you do it in moderation. The aim is an extremely light cracker with a hint of seasoning.

MAKES 40 TO 50 CRACKERS

About 3 tablespoons extra virgin olive oil
½ recipe Basic Pizza Dough (page 123), cut into
    4 pieces, rolled into balls, and allowed to rest
    at room temperature for 30 minutes
Flour for rolling out the dough
½ cup finely chopped fresh rosemary
10 to 12 garlic cloves, finely chopped
1 cup freshly grated Parmesan
Kosher salt and freshly ground black pepper

1. Preheat the oven to 400°F. Rub two sheet pans with a light coating of olive oil, 2 to 3 teaspoons apiece.

2. Roll out each ball of dough on a lightly floured surface into a round as thin as possible, about ⅛ inch thick. Transfer to the sheet pans. Rub each round with a teaspoon of the olive oil. Sprinkle each one with 2 tablespoons of the rosemary, a quarter of the garlic, and ¼ cup of the cheese, and season with salt and pepper.

3. Using a pizza cutter, slice each round of dough into 10 to 12 thin wedges. Bake until crisp and golden, about 15 minutes. Allow to cool before serving. They'll keep overnight in a tightly-sealed container. Don't refrigerate or they'll become soggy.

Parchment Bread

These are large, dramatic wafer-thin crackers adapted from the traditional Sardinian flatbread called *carta di musica* (the name means "sheet music"). I like to serve Parchment Bread as a simple starter, matched only with a bowl of good olives, or as a base for salads, where it absorbs the flavors but remains crisp.

If you don't have a pizza stone or baking tiles, you can bake the crackers on a baking sheet dusted with cornmeal.

MAKES EIGHT 8-INCH ROUND CRACKERS

1 cup unbleached all-purpose flour, plus additional for rolling out the dough
½ cup semolina flour
½ teaspoon kosher salt
About ¾ cup warm water
Cornmeal for dusting

DO AHEAD: You can prepare the dough up to 3 days in advance. Follow the recipe through Step 1 and refrigerate the dough until you're ready to finish the recipe.

1. Mix the flour, semolina, and salt in a mixing bowl. Gradually add just enough warm water to form a dough. The object is to add enough water to make a solid, quite soft mass of dough (softer, say, than pizza dough), but not so much that the dough becomes sticky rather than tacky. Knead the dough until it becomes elastic and smooth, about 3 minutes. Form it into a ball, wrap it in plastic wrap, and let it rest for at least 2 hours. (Refrigerate the dough if allowing it to rest for longer than 2 hours.)

2. Place a pizza stone or unglazed baking tiles on the center rack and preheat the oven to 450°F.

3. After the dough has rested (bring to room temperature if chilled), unwrap it, divide it into 8 equal pieces, and shape each one into a ball. Cover with a towel and let rest for 10 minutes.

4. Using plenty of flour to prevent the dough from sticking to the rolling surface, roll each ball into a very thin circle 8 to 9 inches across. You should be able to read through the dough.

5. One at a time, transfer the parchment bread circles to a pizza peel dusted with cornmeal and slide them onto the pizza stone or tiles in the oven. Add only as many circles as will fit comfortably on the stone or tiles without touching, and bake for about 1 minute on each side, or until golden and crispy; they're easy to turn over with a pair of tongs. Remove from the oven and let cool. Repeat until all the circles are cooked. Parchment bread can be stored for about 3 days in an airtight container. Don't refrigerate or they'll become soggy.

Brandade de Morue

Morue is the French word for salt cod, the equivalent of the Italian *baccalà*, Spanish *baccalao*, or Portuguese *bacalhau*. Originally fresh cod was salted and partially dried to preserve it during the long trip from the Atlantic fisheries to European seaports. Salt cod ranges from quite firm to pliable in texture, but regardless of its texture, it becomes quite soft after soaking. Brandade is a Provençal dish in which olive oil and usually garlic (and sometimes potatoes and cream) are blended with shreds of the fish resurrected from its salted state.

Transforming salt cod into the ambrosial purée of brandade is quite easy and satisfying out of all proportion to the effort involved. The spectacular finished product bears no resemblance to its dried origins, especially when you add a little cream and potato to smooth out the texture. Spread on croutons, it's a delicious hors d'oeuvre (see page 24). You can also heat it with some chopped roasted red peppers and a little olive oil or cream for a pasta or gnocchi sauce.

MAKES ABOUT 3 CUPS

1 pound center-cut salt cod (the thickest part of the fillet)
1 medium baking potato (6 ounces)
5 tablespoons extra virgin olive oil
4 garlic cloves, minced
4 shallots, minced
1 cup heavy cream
Kosher salt and freshly ground black pepper
1 to 2 tablespoons freshly squeezed lemon juice

DO AHEAD: Soak the cod, following the instructions in Step 1.

1. Soak the salt cod in the refrigerator for 12 hours, or longer if needed, in a large bowl of cold water, changing the water 3 or more times. When ready, the cod should not be completely salt-free, or it will lack its distinctive flavor. It should taste a bit more salty than a fish that you've seasoned and cooked with salt.

2. Preheat the oven to 450°F.

3. Bake the potato until tender, about 50 to 60 minutes. As soon as the potato comes out of the oven, split it in half, scoop out the steaming flesh, and rice it. If you don't rice the potato while it's still warm, it will turn into a gummy mess.

4. While the potato is cooking, drain and rinse the salt cod, then put it into a medium pot and cover with cold salted water. Bring to a boil. Reduce the heat and simmer until the fish is cooked through, about 10 minutes. Allow to cool in the liquid.

5. Heat the olive oil in a small saucepan over moderate heat. Add the garlic and shallots and cook until soft, about 4 minutes. Add the cream and simmer for about 7 minutes, to reduce slightly. Remove from the heat.

6. Drain the cod and pat dry with paper towels. Remove the skin and bones, then put it into a food processor and pulse a few times to break it into coarse pieces. With the machine running, add the garlic-cream mixture in a steady stream. Transfer the cod to a medium bowl, add the potato, and stir until everything's mixed well. Season with salt and pepper and 1 tablespoon of the lemon juice. The saltiness of soaked salt cod varies quite a bit, so taste the brandade and add more salt and/or lemon juice if necessary, adding additional lemon juice only ½ teaspoon at a time and mixing thoroughly. If not using the brandade immediately, cover and refrigerate it. It will keep for up to a week.

Brandade Croutons

The French regard brandade de morue, the seasoned purée of salt cod, as a special treat. It used to be served as a reward on Saturday for having endured the self-denial of a Friday fast. For those unfamiliar with its flavor, it is a delicious mystery.

When tomatoes are in season, add a slice of tomato between the brandade and the toast. A wedge of marinated artichoke heart or a strip of peeled roasted red pepper works well on top. A side bowl of mixed olives offers a sharp, briny contrast to the unctuous creaminess of the cod purée. Other optional garnishes are rinsed capers, sliced scallions, or cherry tomato halves.

MAKES 20 TO 25 HORS D'OEUVRES

4 tablespoons chopped fresh flat-leaf parsley, plus several sprigs for garnish

3 cups Brandade de Morue (page 22), at room temperature

1 loaf French bread, cut into ½-inch-thick slices and toasted

1. Preheat the oven to 400°F.

2. Mix the chopped parsley with the brandade. Place a mound of brandade atop each slice of toast. Set the toasts on a sheet and bake until the brandade is warmed through.

3. Arrange the toasts on a platter, garnish with sprigs of parsley, and serve.

Green Olive Tapenade

apenade is easy to make and infinitely adaptive. I use it both as a condiment and as an hors d'oeuvre. The recipe below produces a tapenade with undiluted olive flavor—just the way I like it when I want to complement a main dish like Monkfish and Clam Bourride (page 218). But when I'm serving tapenade as an hors d'oeuvre, I might add another seasoning or two, such as a couple of teaspoons of chopped fresh thyme, more garlic, a pinch of hot red pepper flakes, or several minced sun-dried tomatoes. My favorite olives for tapenade are Provençal Lucques, beautiful pale green olives with pointed tips and a mild flavor, but Picholine, manzanilla, or cracked green Greek olives all make fine alternatives, with different nuances in flavor. Tapenade keeps for several weeks in the refrigerator.

MAKES 1 CUP OR 20 TO 25 HORS D'OEUVRE SERVINGS

1 cup pitted green olives (about 1 to 1¼ pounds unpitted; see box)

3 anchovies, rinsed

1 tablespoon capers, rinsed

½ garlic clove, minced

1 to 2 tablespoons extra virgin olive oil

1 loaf French bread, cut into ½-inch-thick slices and toasted

1. Combine the olives, anchovies, capers, and garlic in a food processor and pulse to a rough paste, adding the olive oil as necessary. Transfer to a serving bowl and place in the center of a platter.

2. Arrange the slices of toast around the tapenade and serve.

HOW TO PIT A LOT OF OLIVES

Smashing whole olives with the side of a chef's knife works fine for small amounts of olives, but to pit olives in quantity, you need a more efficient method. Cover a cutting board with a kitchen towel (this prevents the olives from rolling all over the place). Spread as many olives as will fit in a single layer on the towel. Cover with a second kitchen towel, then bash the olives once or twice with a heavy skillet. A quick glance beneath the towel will tell you if you need to hit them again—the pits and flesh should separate easily.

Purchase about 1¼ pounds of whole small green olives to make 1 cup of pitted olives. You can buy slightly less if you're using a larger, fleshier variety like manzanillas.

Spiced Bagna Cauda

The name bagna cauda *comes* from *bagno caldo*, Italian for "hot bath," referring to the warm dipping sauce served with raw vegetables in the Piedmont section of Italy. I've departed from the traditional version by lightly roasting some of the vegetables first instead of serving them raw, a step that adds considerably to the depth and complexity of their flavor.

MAKES 12 TO 16 HORS D'OEUVRES OR 4 APPETIZER SERVINGS

¾ cup extra virgin olive oil

½ cup thinly sliced garlic

12 anchovies, rinsed and finely chopped

2 tablespoons unsalted butter

Pinch of hot red pepper flakes

½ pound Jerusalem artichokes

½ small celery root (about ½ pound)

½ pound cauliflower

Kosher salt and freshly ground black pepper

1 large yellow pepper, roasted (see page 99), peeled, stemmed, and seeded, and cut into quarters

1 large red pepper, roasted (see page 99), peeled, stemmed, and seeded, and cut into quarters

8 scallions, trimmed

1 tablespoon freshly squeezed lemon juice

1 large fennel bulb, trimmed of stalks and tough outer layers, cut lengthwise in half, cored, and thinly sliced crosswise

4 celery stalks from the heart, peeled and cut lengthwise in half

1 lemon, cut into 4 wedges

4 sprigs flat-leaf parsley for garnish

DO AHEAD: Trim the Jerusalem artichokes, celery root, cauliflower, peppers, and scallions and refrigerate until ready to roast. Keep the Jerusalem artichokes and celery root in a non-reactive container, covered with water into which you've squeezed the juice of half a lemon to prevent discoloration.

1. Preheat the oven to 400°F.

2. Heat ½ cup of the olive oil with the garlic over medium heat until the garlic becomes tender and aromatic, a couple of minutes. Add the chopped anchovies, butter, and pepper flakes and remove from the heat. Cover to keep warm, allowing the ingredients to steep until the sauce is needed.

3. Peel and trim the Jerusalem artichokes, and cut into 2-inch chunks. Do the same with the celery root. Break the cauliflower into uniform pieces. Toss the Jerusalem artichokes, celery root, and cauliflower in a large bowl with the remaining ¼ cup olive oil. Season with salt and pepper. Spread the vegetables on a sheet pan (save the olive oil) and roast until tender and beginning to brown, 15 to 20 minutes. Give them a toss after 10 minutes so they cook evenly.

4. While the vegetables are roasting, toss the peppers and scallions in the bowl with the leftover olive oil. Add them to the sheet pan for the last 5 minutes of roasting.

5. Season the bagna cauda with salt and the lemon juice. Arrange the roasted vegetables in the center of a large platter, then surround them with the sliced fennel and celery sticks. Pour the sauce (reheat if necessary) over the vegetables, garnish the platter with the lemon wedges and parsley sprigs, and serve.

Socca Crêpes with Spinach and Herb Filling

Socca *are rustic crêpes sold* by vendors in Nice's open-air markets and in workingmen's cafés. Made of chickpea flour, alone or in combination with wheat flour, they're traditionally cooked over wood fires on large flat copper pans called *plaques*, some a couple of feet wide, and cut into wedges for individual servings. The flavor has a cozy, toasty quality that places it within the realm of comfort food. This recipe makes thinner mini-socca, about 6 inches in diameter, and although they're usually eaten plain, I've taken the liberty of adding a filling. An herbed mixture of spinach and feta with garlic goes well with the rustic socca flavor.

Socca are actually quite easy and fairly quick to prepare, but if you're making them for the first time, you might want to make them ahead to spare yourself any anxiety. This recipe makes enough batter for about 20 hors d'oeuvre-sized socca, so you can afford to mess up a few and still have more than enough to complete the dish. A nonstick sauté pan makes a fine substitute for a crêpe pan, as long as it has sloping sides (making it easier to pick up an edge and flip the socca over).

MAKES 16 HORS D'OEUVRES

SOCCA
2 cups chickpea flour (available in health food stores and good Italian markets)
1¼ cups water, plus more if needed
3 extra-large eggs, lightly beaten
¼ cup extra virgin olive oil
2 teaspoons kosher salt
1 teaspoon freshly ground black pepper

Extra virgin olive oil for cooking the crêpes

FILLING
¼ cup extra virgin olive oil
5 garlic cloves, finely chopped
1 pound flat-leaf spinach, trimmed of thick stems, washed, and dried
Kosher salt and freshly ground black pepper
½ cup chopped fresh flat-leaf parsley
¼ cup chopped fresh oregano
¼ cup chopped fresh mint
¼ cup chopped fresh cilantro
½ pound feta cheese, crumbled

2 tablespoons extra virgin olive oil

DO AHEAD: The socca can be made a day or two in advance, tightly wrapped, and refrigerated until ready to use.

1. Combine the flour, water, eggs, ¼ cup of olive oil, salt, and pepper in a large bowl and beat well. Allow the batter to sit for 30 minutes.

2. Stir the batter, then check the consistency. It should be the consistency of traditional wheat flour crêpe batter, that is, the thickness of heavy cream. If the batter is too thick, add more water, 1 tablespoon at a time. (You will have about 3 cups of batter.)

3. Heat 1 teaspoon olive oil in a small nonstick sauté pan over medium heat. Ladle about 2 tablespoons of batter into the hot pan, then quickly tilt the pan to make a thin even circle of batter about 6 inches across. Cook the socca until it just starts to color, about 30 seconds, then carefully peel it away from the pan (it should come free easily), flip it, and cook the other side, adding more oil as needed. Transfer to a plate and repeat with the remaining batter. Stack the socca as they finish cooking so they don't dry out. You should end up with around 20 crêpes. Select the best 16 and set the remainder aside for another use (hint: with powdered sugar, jam, or honey for breakfast tomorrow). If you're making the socca ahead, let the stack cool completely, then wrap tightly in plastic wrap and refrigerate until you're ready to use them.

4. To make the filling, heat ¼ cup of olive oil and garlic in a large sauté pan over medium heat until the garlic becomes aromatic, 1 to 2 minutes. Add the spinach, cover, and cook until wilted. Season with salt and pepper. Drain, if necessary, and let cool. Add the chopped herbs and crumbled feta to the spinach, mixing well.

5. Lay the 16 socca on a counter. Imagine each socca as a clock face and distribute the spinach mixture evenly among the socca, placing it in the upper right quadrant of each crêpe (between 12 o'clock and 3 o'clock). Fold each crêpe in half (along the 3 o'clock–9 o'clock axis), then in half again so it's folded in quarters.

6. Preheat the oven to 200°F. Place a platter in the oven.

7. Heat a large sauté pan over medium-high heat. Add the olive oil. Add the folded crêpes and cook, turning once, until golden brown and crisp on each side, 3 to 5 minutes. You may have to do them in two batches. Transfer to the warm platter as you finish them. Serve warm or at room temperature.

Stocks and Soups

❦

Anyone who makes soups on a regular basis eventually becomes interested in stocks, because stocks mean better soups. With stocks, you can also make risotto, braise meats, and prepare reduction sauces. When I don't have homemade stock in the freezer, I use high-quality canned low-sodium chicken broth to braise vegetables; my husband uses it for risotto. But for a special meal where I want to use the best ingredients I can get my hands on, I prefer homemade stock. This chapter teaches you to make three basic stocks—chicken, fish, and lobster—all you'll need for even the fanciest dishes in this book.

The soup recipes range from the simple to the complex. Orzo in Chicken Broth with Many Greens and Asiago is a one-two-three recipe; Lobster, Corn, and Smoked Fish Chowder is almost instant (provided you have the ingredients on hand), whereas Roasted Tomato and Farro Soup simmers for the better part of an hour. Fresh Tomato Soup with Seared Eggplant Sandwiches is a whimsical reworking of a couple of tried-and-true classics; other selections will probably be new to you, like Fresh Green Pea Soup with Shaved Radicchio and Pistachios or Clam and White Bean Soup with Fennel, Anchovy, and Lemon. Whether you're looking for a formal first course, a hearty entrée, or just comfort in a bowl, you'll find it here.

Chicken Stock

This simple, straightforward recipe makes a rich stock with a clean flavor. As a base for soups, sauces, or braising liquids, it beats the pants off anything that you can buy in a can. The quality of your ingredients, however, will make a significant impact on the final product. This recipe calls for 5 pounds of chicken parts; make sure that includes *at least* 1 pound of legs and thighs, preferably more. Even better if the parts come from organic free-range chicken. If you have a really large stockpot, and the freezer space, the quantities are easily doubled.

If you have a leftover duck or goose carcass, especially one with shreds of meat still attached to it, you can substitute it for an equal amount of chicken parts to make duck or goose stock. Goose stock makes an exquisite risotto (see page 174). Since most of us only have either of these fowl around after roasting them, the likelihood is that you'll have leftover carcasses, mostly bones. I roast two geese on Christmas Day and then make stock from the carcasses and as many odd scraps as I can find after dinner. If, however, you cook only one goose or duck, make up the difference with a package of chicken legs or thighs. The stock will still have a pronounced flavor of goose or duck.

Homemade chicken stock will keep for 5 days refrigerated; boil refrigerated stock before using it if it is older than a day or two. Refrigerate the stock for several hours before freezing. Frozen stock will keep for up to 6 months; boil before using.

MAKES 3 QUARTS

4 bay leaves

4 sprigs flat-leaf parsley

2 sprigs thyme

1 teaspoon black peppercorns

5 pounds chicken parts—backs, necks, and/or wings, etc., with at least 1 pound legs and/or thighs

2 medium carrots, coarsely chopped

2 celery stalks, coarsely chopped

2 medium onions, coarsely chopped

1. Pile the bay leaves, parsley, thyme, and peppercorns in the middle of a piece of cheesecloth and tie into a bundle. Set aside.

2. Rinse the chicken parts under cold running water. Put into a stockpot and add just enough water to come ½ inch below the top of the chicken parts (the bones will settle down during cooking). Bring to a boil. Reduce the heat to a simmer and add the vegetables and bundle of herbs. Move the pot toward you so it sits 2 inches off the center of the burner. This will cause the fat and impurities to collect at the edge of the pot closest to you, making it easier to skim them off. Simmer for 1½ hours, skimming occasionally.

3. Pour the stock through a fine strainer into another large pot or container. Refrigerate. After the stock has cooled, skim off the fat that has accumulated on the surface. Refrigerate or freeze the stock until ready to use.

HOMEMADE CHICKEN STOCK VERSUS CANNED BROTH

I use homemade chicken stock almost exclusively. Some butchers and specialty food stores sell frozen chicken and veal stocks; in my limited experience with them, I've found them to be reasonably good, but quite expensive. The real question is, can you substitute canned broth for chicken stock in recipes?

The answer is a qualified "yes." Canned broths tend to be highly salted, unlike my homemade stock (did you notice—no salt?) If a recipe requires the stock to be reduced (cooked down), the saltiness will intensify, which is why I recommend using only a low-sodium canned broth. Secondly, canned broth doesn't have the body of homemade stock, with its high collagen content from the chicken bones. In soups or some braises, this isn't a problem, but when making sauces that call for the chicken stock to be substantially reduced, you cannot substitute an equivalent amount of canned broth for stock. Start with twice as much broth as homemade stock called for in the recipe and then reduce it by half before proceeding. That is, simmer the canned broth until the amount that remains is the same as the amount of homemade stock called for in the recipe. In any recipe that calls for stock, I indicate whether an equivalent amount of high-quality low-sodium canned chicken broth can be substituted or if it needs to be reduced first.

Fish Stock

Fish stock is simple to make, takes far less time than poultry stock, and freezes well. Roasting the bones is actually easier than sautéing them, and it increases the depth of flavor. When the time comes to make a seafood soup or risotto, you'll be glad you invested an hour in this.

Homemade fish stock will keep for 5 days refrigerated; boil refrigerated stock before using it if it is older than a day or two. Refrigerate stock for several hours before freezing. Frozen stock will keep for up to 6 months; boil before using.

MAKES 3 QUARTS

5 pounds fish bones, and the heads, from white-fleshed fish such as cod, haddock, or flounder

¼ cup vegetable oil

3 sprigs flat-leaf parsley

2 sprigs thyme

3 bay leaves

1 teaspoon black peppercorns

2 leeks, white part only, trimmed of roots and tough outer leaves, thinly sliced crosswise and swirled in a bowl of cold water to remove any grit

1 small onion, thinly sliced

1 medium carrot, thinly sliced

2 celery stalks, thinly sliced crosswise

1 small fennel bulb, trimmed of stalks and tough outer layers, sliced in half lengthwise, cored, and thinly sliced crosswise

¼ pound mushrooms, cleaned and coarsely chopped

2 cups dry white wine

1. Using kitchen shears, remove the eyeballs and gills from the fish heads. Put the bones in a large pot and rinse under cold running water for at least 30 minutes. Drain.

2. Preheat the oven to 450°F.

3. Spread the fish bones in a large roasting pan and pat dry with paper towels. Drizzle with 2 tablespoons of the vegetable oil and toss well. Roast for 30 minutes, or until all the bones are golden brown.

4. Meanwhile, pile the parsley, thyme, bay leaves, and peppercorns in the middle of a piece of cheesecloth and tie into a bundle. Set aside.

5. Heat the remaining 2 tablespoons vegetable oil in a large stockpot over medium-high heat. Add the leeks, onion, carrot, celery, fennel, and mushrooms. Cook until lightly browned, about 10 minutes.

6. Add the bones to the stockpot, along with the cheesecloth bundle, white wine, and enough water to come ½ inch below the bones. Bring to a boil, then lower the heat to a simmer. Move the pot toward you so it sits 2 inches off the center of the burner. This will cause the fat and impurities to collect at the edge of the pot closest to you, making it easier to skim them off. Simmer for 30 minutes, skimming as necessary.

7. Pour the stock through a fine strainer into another large pot or container. Refrigerate. After the stock has cooled, skim off the fat that has accumulated on the surface. Refrigerate or freeze the stock until ready to use.

Lobster Stock

Every year, my extended family manages to get together for one weekend in Barnstable, on Cape Cod, and one night is dedicated to a fixing a lobster dinner. I save the lobster bodies to make stock. After allowing it to cool, I pour the finished stock into ice cube trays and freeze it. The next day, I empty the cubes into freezer bags. Then, for the next six months, I have cubes of lobster stock I can add to soups or use to make quick butter sauces for sautéed seafood.

Homemade lobster stock will keep for 5 days refrigerated; boil refrigerated stock before using it if it is older than a day or two. Refrigerate the stock for several hours before freezing. Frozen stock will keep for up to 6 months; boil before using.

MAKES 3 QUARTS

3 sprigs flat-leaf parsley

2 sprigs tarragon

3 bay leaves

1 teaspoon black peppercorns

¼ cup vegetable oil

2 leeks, white part only, trimmed of roots and tough outer leaves, thinly sliced crosswise, and swirled vigorously in a bowl of cold water to remove any grit

1 small onion, thinly sliced

1 medium carrot, thinly sliced crosswise

1 small fennel bulb, trimmed of stalks and tough outer layers, cut in half lengthwise, cored, and thinly sliced crosswise

2 celery stalks, thinly sliced crosswise

5 pounds lobster bodies, rinsed and coarsely chopped

2 tablespoons tomato paste

2 cups dry white wine

½ cup brandy

16-ounces (2 cups) canned whole tomatoes, with their liquid

1. Pile the parsley, tarragon, bay leaves, and peppercorns in the middle of a piece of cheesecloth and tie into a bundle. Set aside.

2. Heat 2 tablespoons of the vegetable oil in a large sauté pan over medium-high heat. Add the vegetables and cook until they brown, about 15 minutes. Transfer the vegetables to a stockpot.

3. Add the remaining 2 tablespoons oil to the sauté pan. Add the lobster bodies and cook until they brown, about 20 minutes, tossing occasionally. If necessary, cook them in a couple of sauté pans or do them in batches.

4. Add the tomato paste to the pan and cook for 3 minutes. Take the pan off the heat and add the wine and brandy. Return the pan to the heat and stir to deglaze. Transfer everything to the stockpot.

5. Add the tomatoes to the stockpot, then add enough water to come ½ inch below the top of the contents of the pot. Add the cheesecloth bundle. Bring to a boil over high heat, then lower the heat to a simmer. Move the pot

toward you so it sits 2 inches off the center of the burner. This will cause the fat and impurities to collect at the edge of the pot closest to you, making it easier to skim them off. Simmer for 1 hour.

6. Pour the stock through a fine strainer into another large pot or container. Refrigerate. After the stock has cooled, skim off the fat that has accumulated on the surface. Refrigerate or freeze the stock until ready to use.

Chilled Smooth Corn Soup with Tomatoes, Avocado, and Lime

This is an August recipe, a summer finale, when local corn is at its peak. I can't think of another recipe that squeezes more flavor out of corn than this one. Even the stripped cobs are put to use. This is one case where you should absolutely stick to the times given in the recipe, cooking the kernels briefly in as little water as possible in order to preserve their freshness. The result is an intense creamy hit of corn with absolutely no cream. Smoked bluefish, homemade salsa, and crème fraîche give the soup a little counterpoint and bring your palate back to that wonderful summer corn flavor.

MAKES 4 SERVINGS

6 ears corn, husked

1 small white onion, cut into ¼-inch-thick slices

Kosher salt and freshly ground black pepper

1 tablespoon extra virgin olive oil

1 medium leek, white part only, trimmed of roots and tough outer leaves, thinly sliced crosswise, and swirled vigorously in a bowl of cold water to remove any grit

1 shallot, thinly sliced

1 ripe avocado

½ cucumber

1 small tomato, peeled (see page 55), seeded, and chopped into ¼-inch dice

2 tablespoons diced (¼-inch) red onion

1 to 2 tablespoons freshly squeezed lime juice

2 ounces smoked bluefish (substitute smoked salmon if bluefish is unavailable), skin and any bones removed, cut into ¼-inch dice

¼ cup crème fraîche or yogurt

2 tablespoons chopped chives

DO AHEAD: This soup needs to chill before it is served. Typically I make it the night before,

then finish the garnishes before serving. If you're pressed for time, chill the soup in a shallow bowl in your freezer.

1. Use a sharp knife to strip the corn kernels from the cobs. Set the kernels aside. Cut each cob into 4 pieces.

2. Put the cobs into a pot, along with the sliced onion. Add enough water to barely cover. (If you use too much water, the stock will taste thin.) Season with salt and pepper. Bring to a boil, then lower the heat to a simmer and cook for 35 minutes. Discard the cobs.

3. Meanwhile, heat the olive oil in a sauté pan over medium heat. Add the leek and shallot and cook until tender, 6 to 8 minutes. Add the corn kernels, season with salt and pepper, and cook until they just start to soften, about 2 minutes. Do not overcook, the corn should still taste fresh. Remove from the heat and set aside until the corn broth finishes cooking

4. Add the sautéed vegetables to the corn broth and simmer for 5 minutes. Strain the broth into a bowl and purée the solids in a blender, adding just enough of the broth to make a thick soup. Push the soup through a medium strainer, then chill for at least 3 hours. (You will have about a quart of soup.)

5. Peel the avocado, remove the pit, and chop the flesh into ¼-inch dice. Peel, seed, and chop the cucumber into ¼-inch dice. Mix the tomato, avocado, cucumber, and diced onion together. Toss with salt, pepper, and lime juice to taste.

6. Taste the soup and adjust the seasoning if necessary. Distribute the fish evenly among four chilled bowls. Ladle the soup into the bowls. Add a spoonful of the chopped vegetable salad and a spoonful of crème fraîche to each, sprinkle with the chives, and serve immediately.

Chilled Grilled Tomato Soup with Spicy Lobster and Corn Salad

More often than not in August, our refrigerator contains a jug of gazpacho. This is a traditional recipe, using grilled tomatoes for added flavor. In Spain, gazpacho is often served with an array of little garnishes—scallions, croutons, minced onion—enabling diners to customize the dish. I've added a lobster and corn salad that elevates a simple soup into an elegant summer lunch. If lobster seems too extravagant, simply make the corn salad.

Without the other salad and lobster garnish, this makes about 4 cups of gazpacho; the recipe easily doubles for larger portions or more servings.

MAKES 4 TO 6 SERVINGS

SOUP
16 plum tomatoes (about 3 pounds)
Kosher salt and freshly ground black pepper
⅓ cup plus ¼ cup extra virgin olive oil
¼ cup ½-inch chunks crustless day old white bread
3 tablespoons high-quality red wine vinegar
½ red pepper, peeled with a vegetable peeler, stemmed, seeded, and cut into chunks
½ green pepper, peeled with a vegetable peeler, stemmed, seeded, and cut into chunks
1 cucumber, peeled, seeded, and cut into chunks
½ small red onion, chopped into ½-inch dice
½ celery stalk, peeled and chopped into ½-inch dice
1 garlic clove, minced
1 serrano pepper, stemmed, seeded, and thinly sliced
2 tablespoons chopped fresh flat-leaf parsley
2 tablespoons chopped fresh basil

LOBSTER AND CORN SALAD
2 ears corn, husked and kernels stripped off with a sharp knife (about 1½ cups)

7 ounces freshly cooked lobster meat, cut into ½-inch pieces
¼ cup shelled fava beans, long-blanched (see Fava Notes, page 88) and peeled (optional)
1 scallion, trimmed and thinly sliced
1 serrano pepper, stemmed, seeded and thinly sliced
1 tablespoon chopped fresh basil
1 tablespoon red wine vinegar
3 tablespoons extra virgin olive oil, plus extra for garnish
Kosher salt and freshly ground black pepper
4 sprigs flat-leaf parsley for garnish

DO AHEAD: With the exception of combining the salad ingredients, everything in this dish can be prepared a day ahead. Steam the corn, prepare the soup, and gather the individual salad components. Cover everything tightly and refrigerate.

1. Preheat a medium fire in a grill. A grill is medium when you can hold your hand near the cooking surface for no longer than a count of 4 before you have to pull it away. You can use a broiler instead, but I prefer the smokier flavor from the grill.

2. Slice the plum tomatoes lengthwise in half. Toss with salt and pepper and ¼ cup of the olive oil. Grill, cut side down, until charred, 4 to 5 minutes. Flip and repeat on skin side. Allow to cool, then remove the skin and seeds.

3. Mix the bread with the vinegar and the remaining ⅓ cup olive oil in a small bowl. Let sit for 10 minutes.

4. In a food processor, combine the grilled tomatoes, red and green peppers, cucumber, onion, celery, garlic, serrano pepper, parsley, and basil and pulse until puréed. Add the soaked bread and purée again. Transfer to a bowl and chill for at least 30 minutes.

5. Bring a small pot of salted water to a boil. Prepare a bowl of ice water. Add the corn to the boiling water and blanch for 1 to 2 minutes. Drain and shock in the ice water. Drain again and blot dry with a paper towel.

6. Mix the corn with half the lobster meat, the favas, the scallion, serrano pepper, and basil in a medium bowl. Toss with the wine vinegar and olive oil. Season with salt and pepper. The flavors should be bright and pronounced.

7. Ladle the soup into chilled bowls. Put a spoonful of the corn salad in the center of each bowl. Scatter the remaining lobster on top of the salads. Garnish each with a sprig of parsley. Drizzle with extra virgin olive oil and serve.

Orzo in Chicken Broth with Many Greens and Asiago

Orzo *means "barley" in Italian,* but it's actually a small rice-shaped pasta, one of the many tiny pastina that are generally added to soups. I make this soup when I want to take care of myself but don't have an enormous amount of energy. After you've cleaned and chopped the greens there is little to do except heat everything together and then curl up somewhere with a steaming bowl of comfort.

MAKES 4 TO 6 SERVINGS

Kosher salt

½ pound orzo pasta

6 cups Chicken Stock (page 31) or high-quality canned low-sodium chicken broth

1 cup dry sherry

2 cups lightly packed flat-leaf spinach, trimmed of thick stems, washed, and coarsely chopped

4 scallions, trimmed and thinly sliced

2 cups lightly packed arugula, rinsed thoroughly, drained, and coarsely chopped

1 cup coarsely chopped watercress leaves

½ cup coarsely chopped fresh flat-leaf parsley

1 teaspoon freshly squeezed lemon juice

Freshly ground black pepper

½ cup grated Asiago

1. Bring a large pot of water to a boil and season with salt. Add the orzo and stir constantly until the water returns to a boil. Cook until the orzo is tender but still offers some resistance when you bite it, about 8 minutes.

2. Meanwhile, bring the chicken broth and sherry to a boil in a large saucepan. Lower the heat and simmer for 10 minutes. Add the spinach, scallions, arugula, watercress, and parsley and cook until tender, only a minute or two. Add the lemon juice and season with salt and pepper.

3. Add the orzo to the broth. Serve in warm bowls, sprinkled with the grated Asiago.

Fresh Green Pea Soup with Shaved Radicchio and Pistachios

On first impression, sweet peas and bitter radicchio may seem more like adversaries than partners, but what a pairing they make in soup. This is one of those dishes where the flavor seems to rock back and forth between two balanced camps—the sweet and the sharp—making a compulsively flavorful soup. A creamy impression of fresh sweet peas and nutty pistachios gradually yields to a bitter crunch of radicchio that wipes the slate clean, preparing your palate for the next spoonful.

MAKES 4 TO 6 SERVINGS

Kosher salt

4 cups fresh or frozen peas

2 tablespoons unsalted butter

2 leeks, white part only, trimmed of roots and tough outer leaves, sliced thinly crosswise, and swirled vigorously in a bowl of cold water to remove any grit

Freshly ground black pepper

6 cups Chicken Stock (page 31) or high-quality canned low-sodium chicken broth

1 cup raw pistachios

1 cup light cream

1 small head radicchio, washed, dried, and thinly sliced crosswise

1. Bring a medium saucepan of salted water to a boil. Meanwhile, fill a second pot with ice water. Add the peas to the boiling water and cook until just tender, about 1 minute. Drain and plunge them into the ice bath to cool. Drain and set aside.

2. Melt 1 tablespoon of the butter in a small sauté pan over medium heat. Add the leeks, season with salt and pepper, and cook until tender, about 8 minutes. Add the peas and chicken stock and simmer for 2 minutes. Purée the mixture in a food processor or blender. Strain through a fine sieve and set aside.

3. Grind the pistachios in two batches: Put ½ cup of the nuts in a blender or food processor and pulse until they form a powder. Watch closely—if you process them too long, they will become a paste. Transfer to a small saucepan and repeat with the second batch.

4. Stir the cream into the pistachios and simmer over low heat for 1 minute. Season with salt and pepper. Keep warm.

5. Melt the remaining 1 tablespoon butter in a large sauté pan over high heat. Add the radicchio, season with salt and pepper, and cook until tender, about 5 minutes.

6. Ladle the pea soup into warm bowls. Swirl some of the warm pistachio cream into each portion, top with the radicchio, and serve immediately.

Fresh Tomato Soup with Seared Eggplant Sandwiches

This dish shows how even old standbys can sometimes be reworked so they become vivid and fresh again. Tomato soup and old-fashioned eggplant Parmesan are too predictable. But an open-faced sandwich of eggplant slices with pesto and mozzarella—that would get me to sit up and pay attention. And what if we serve it in a rich tomato broth jazzed up with some garlic and onions? The soup tastes wonderful and the black stripe of eggplant against the brilliant red soup attracts the eye. Where did this dish come from? Not any one place, but bits and pieces of the puzzle are assembled from all over Italy.

MAKES 4 SERVINGS

About ½ cup extra virgin olive oil

2 medium onions, chopped into ¼-inch dice

4 garlic cloves, finely chopped

Kosher salt and freshly ground black pepper

4 pounds ripe plum tomatoes, coarsely chopped

1 teaspoon sugar

1 beautiful eggplant (about 10 ounces), sliced ½ inch thick into 8 slices

2 cups water

½ cup chopped fresh basil, plus 4 leaves for garnish

¼ cup Pesto (page 44)

Four ¼-inch-thick slices fresh mozzarella (about 2 ounces)

Four ½-inch-thick slices rustic bread, about the same size as the eggplant slices

1. Heat 2 tablespoons of the olive oil in a large soup pot over medium heat. Add the onions and garlic, season with salt and pepper, and cook until tender, 7 to 8 minutes. Add the tomatoes and sugar, lower the heat, and cook for 25 minutes.

2. While the tomatoes are cooking, season 8 eggplant slices with salt and pepper. (If you have more than 8 slices, set the remainder aside for another use or discard.) Heat 2 tablespoons of the olive oil in a large sauté pan over medium-high heat. Add the eggplant slices and sear on each side until golden brown and cooked through. Remove from the heat and let cool.

3. Add the water to the tomatoes and bring to a boil, then lower the heat to a simmer and cook for 5 minutes. Purée in a blender and strain through a fine sieve. Return the tomato soup to the pot, add the chopped basil, and simmer for 5 minutes.

4. Preheat the oven to 375°F.

5. Spread the eggplant slices with the pesto. Put a slice of mozzarella on 4 of the slices. Top with the remaining 4 eggplant slices, pesto side down, to make "sandwiches."

6. Brush the bread with about 2 tablespoons of the olive oil and place on a small baking sheet.

Toast in the oven until golden brown. Top each slice with an eggplant sandwich and continue heating until the cheese begins to melt.

7. While the sandwiches are heating, reheat the tomato broth.

8. Place an eggplant sandwich in the bottom of each warm bowl. Pour the tomato broth around the sandwiches. Drizzle with olive oil, garnish with the basil leaves, and serve immediately.

Pesto

Although the Fresh Tomato Soup recipe calls for only ¼ cup of pesto, it hardly seems worth the effort to make less than a cup. The remainder always disappears into sandwiches, crostini, or pasta within a few days. Toward the end of basil season, I make a double batch without the cheese and freeze it in plastic containers the size of baby food jars, topping each portion with a light covering of olive oil; it will keep for 3 months frozen. Allow it to thaw in the refrigerator, then stir in the cheese.

MAKES ABOUT 1 CUP

2 cups lightly packed basil leaves
¾ cup extra virgin olive oil
2 garlic cloves, minced and then mashed with a
     pinch of salt to a paste
¼ cup pine nuts, toasted
¼ cup freshly grated Parmesan
2 tablespoons freshly grated Pecorino Romano
Kosher salt

1. Put the basil leaves in a food processor. With the motor running, add the oil in a thin steady stream and process until the basil is finely chopped, about 1 minute. Add the garlic and pine nuts and process for another 20 seconds, or until the pine nuts are finely chopped but not a paste.

2. Transfer the pesto to a bowl. Stir in the cheeses. Taste and season with salt as necessary.

Summer Squash and Onion Soup with Toasted Almonds

Quite a few Junes and Julys had to pass before I finally figured out that the key to enjoying summer squash is to move it from main character to supporting role in a dish. The flavor of summer squash is too fragile to carry the load when the whole show rests on its shoulders. But in a light soup, with some complementary ingredients, summer squash shines. Finely diced, the squash adds color, texture, and a mild but distinctly summery flavor to chicken stock. Ginger and savory (or thyme) enhance its flavor rather than cover it up. Sweet onions, sherry, and almonds (a Spanish combination) contribute depth without overwhelming it. The broken angel hair pasta cooks quickly and adds substance before the freshness of the vegetables simmers away.

MAKES 6 TO 8 SERVINGS

2 tablespoons unsalted butter

4 medium sweet onions (Vidalia or Walla Walla, for example), thinly sliced

2 garlic cloves, minced

1 teaspoon minced fresh ginger

Kosher salt and freshly ground black pepper

½ cup dry sherry

6 cups Chicken Stock (page 31) or high-quality canned low-sodium chicken broth

2 ounces angel hair pasta, broken into 2-inch lengths

2 pounds mixed summer squashes (zucchini, yellow summer, and pattypan are all good choices), scrubbed and chopped into ¼-inch dice

1 tablespoon chopped fresh savory or thyme

¼ cup sliced almonds, toasted

¼ cup freshly grated Parmesan

1. Melt the butter in a large sauté pan over medium heat. Add the onions, garlic, and ginger, season with salt and pepper, and cook until golden, about 20 minutes.

2. Add the sherry and reduce by half, only a minute or two. Add the chicken stock, pasta, and squash. Bring to a boil and cook until the pasta and squash are just cooked, about 3 minutes. Season with salt and pepper.

3. Add the savory and ladle the soup into warm bowls. Sprinkle with the almonds and cheese and serve immediately.

Clam and White Bean Soup with Fennel, Anchovy, and Lemon

This satisfying soup is another instance of a European classic crashing into the New England seacoast and ending up better for the experience. The dish began life as an Italian bean soup loaded with fennel. But I already loved steaming fresh Wellfleet clams with fennel, and it was only a matter of time before the clams and beans were introduced. The beans lend the soup a luscious quality that recalls a cream chowder, but in this case it's without either cream or pork fat.

MAKES 4 TO 6 SERVINGS

½ cup dried medium white beans (navy or cannellini), picked over for stones and broken beans, and rinsed

½ cup extra virgin olive oil

1 medium white onion, chopped into ½-inch dice

1 small carrot, chopped into ½-inch dice

½ celery stalk, chopped into ½-inch dice

1 fennel bulb, trimmed of stalks and tough outer layers, cut in half lengthwise, cored, and chopped into ½-inch dice

6 garlic cloves, chopped

1 teaspoon fennel seeds

4 bay leaves

3 cups Fish Stock (page 33) or 2 cups Chicken Stock (page 31) plus 1 cup bottled clam juice

1 teaspoon chopped fresh thyme

Kosher salt and freshly ground black pepper.

2 anchovies, rinsed and finely chopped

1 teaspoon minced lemon zest

40 littleneck clams (3½ to 4 pounds), scrubbed

1 cup dry white wine

¼ cup chopped fresh basil

1. Put the beans in a medium saucepan, cover with 2 inches of water, and bring to a boil, then turn off the heat. Let sit uncovered for 1 hour. Drain.

2. Heat ¼ cup of the olive oil in a large saucepan over medium heat. Add the onion, carrot, celery, and fennel, and cook until tender and beginning to brown, about 8 minutes. Add two-thirds of the garlic, the fennel seeds and bay leaves, and cook 2 minutes.

3. Add the drained beans, stir well, and then add water to cover by 2 inches. Bring to a boil, reduce the heat to a simmer, and cook for 1 hour.

4. Add the fish stock and continue cooking until the beans are tender, about 30 minutes. The mixture should still be quite soupy by the time the beans are done; if not, add more water as necessary. Stir in the thyme and season with salt and pepper. Keep warm below a simmer.

5. Heat 2 tablespoons of the olive oil in a large sauté pan over medium heat. Add the remain-

ing garlic and cook for 3 minutes. Add the anchovies, lemon zest, clams, and white wine, cover, and cook until the clams have opened, about 5 minutes. Discard any clams that don't open.

6. Add the clams and the steaming liquid to the beans and stir in the basil. Taste and add salt and pepper if necessary. Ladle into warm bowls, drizzle with the remaining 2 tablespoons olive oil, and serve immediately.

Lobster, Corn, and Smoked Fish Chowder

very home cook needs the first-course equivalent of a little black dress—convenient and provocative at the same time. This is a rich, astonishingly quick appetizer soup that leaves you wanting more. The classic chowder trio of seafood, salt pork, and milk metamorphoses into chunks of lobster and corn kernels suspended in an aromatic base of smoked trout and cream. Using homemade lobster or fish stock gives it a depth of flavor unusual in a soup that cooks so briefly. The ingredients shouldn't come together until the last moment, when they're heated for just a few minutes, so don't assemble the chowder until you're ready to serve it.

MAKES 4 SERVINGS

Kosher salt

One 1-pound lobster (or ¼ pound freshly cooked lobster meat)

1 tablespoon unsalted butter

2 ears corn, husked and kernels stripped off with a sharp knife (about 1½ cups)

2 shallots, finely diced

1 garlic clove, minced

2 cups light cream

2 cups Lobster Stock (page 34) or Fish Stock (page 33) or 1 cup clam juice plus 1 cup water

2 ounces smoked trout, skin and any bones removed, broken into small pieces

Freshly ground black pepper

2 tablespoons chopped fresh chives for garnish

1. If you're using a live lobster, set a steaming rack in a large pot big enough to hold the lobster. The rack should sit at least 2 inches off the bottom of the pot (support it on ramekins if necessary). Add 1 inch of salted water to the pot and bring to a boil. Set the lobster on the rack, cover, and steam for 10 minutes. Let cool.

2. When the lobster is cool enough to handle, crack open the shell and remove the meat from the tail and claws. Cut the meat into ½-inch pieces. Cover and refrigerate.

3. Melt the butter in a medium saucepan over medium-low heat. Add the corn and cook until it starts to soften, about 2 minutes. Add the shallots and garlic and cook for 3 more minutes until aromatic. Add the cream and lobster stock and heat through. Add the lobster and smoked trout and heat until warmed through. Season with salt and pepper.

4. Ladle the chowder into warm bowls, sprinkle with the chopped chives, and serve.

Stilton and Watercress Soup

Too many cheese soups are weighty, gloppy affairs. This recipe produces a lighter soup with a smooth, creamy body infused with the spectacular flavor of Stilton cheese. Stilton's unique taste easily justifies its position as England's only name-protected cheese, so don't make the mistake of substituting any old blue cheese for the genuine article.

MAKES 4 TO 6 SERVINGS

2 tablespoons unsalted butter

2 medium leeks, white part only, trimmed of roots and tough outer leaves, thinly sliced crosswise, and swirled vigorously in a bowl of cold water to remove any grit

Kosher salt and freshly ground black pepper

2 baking potatoes, peeled, cut into quarters, and placed in a bowl with water to cover

4 cups Chicken Stock (page 31) or high-quality canned low-sodium chicken broth

2 bunches watercress, tough stems removed, washed and coarsely chopped

1 cup heavy cream

3 ounces Stilton (If Stilton is unavailable, substitute French Fourme d'Ambert or Italian Gorgonzola *naturale,* also called "aged" Gorgonzola—not *dolce,* or "sweet," Gorgonzola)

GARNISHES (OPTIONAL)

12 very thin slices peeled and cored apple (keep covered with lightly salted water)

4 to 6 small sprigs watercress, large stems removed

2 to 3 teaspoons chopped walnuts

1. Melt the butter in a large heavy saucepan over medium heat. Add the leeks, season with salt and pepper, and cook until tender, about 8 minutes.

2. Remove the potatoes from the water and add them to the saucepan. Add the chicken stock, season with salt, and bring to a boil. Lower the heat and simmer until the potatoes are fork-tender, about 20 minutes. Add the watercress and simmer until it's tender but still green, 3 to 4 minutes.

3. Carefully purée the soup in a food processor. Pour the purée through a coarse strainer into a clean pan. Heat the soup over medium heat until hot. Add the cream and Stilton, stirring constantly until the cheese has melted. Taste and adjust the seasonings.

4. Ladle the soup into warm bowls. If using the garnishes, float a few slices of apple and a sprig of watercress atop each portion. Sprinkle with the chopped walnuts, and serve immediately.

Mussel Soup over Polenta with Saffron, Tomatoes, and Garlic

Mussels are the harried cook's friend. The simple process of steaming them with white wine, garlic, and a few herbs produces a broth so intensely flavorful that you can just adjust the seasonings and call it a day—with a great soup. If saffron and tomatoes are on hand, you have the makings of one of the Mediterranean's storied flavor combinations, and the basis of dozens of different fish stews. Perhaps because this takes so little effort, and happens so quickly, slices of grilled rustic bread are more often associated with this type of soup than polenta. Why make more work? But polenta adds a dimension that bread does not. Bread is a pleasant companion; polenta elevates the dish with its own flavor and texture. Mussels are extremely perishable and should be eaten within a day of cooking, but the exquisite broth will last for a couple of days if refrigerated.

MAKES 4 TO 6 SERVINGS

POLENTA
2 cups water
Kosher salt
½ cup coarsely ground cornmeal
½ teaspoon hot red pepper flakes
2 tablespoons freshly grated Pecorino Romano

2 tablespoons extra virgin olive oil

SOUP
½ cup extra virgin olive oil
1 large red onion, thinly sliced
4 garlic cloves, thinly sliced
Kosher salt
Pinch of saffron
½ teaspoon hot red pepper flakes
48 mussels, scrubbed and debearded
6 ripe plum tomatoes, peeled (see page 55),
    seeded, and chopped into ¼-inch dice
1 cup dry white wine
3 cups Fish Stock (page 33) or 2 cups Chicken
    Stock (page 31), plus 1 cup bottled clam juice

½ cup chopped fresh flat-leaf parsley
Freshly ground black pepper

1. Bring the water to a boil in a medium heavy saucepan over high heat. Add ½ teaspoon salt, then add the polenta in a slow, steady stream through your fingers, whisking constantly so it doesn't clump up. If you get any lumps, mash them against the side of the pot with a wooden spoon and keep stirring. Lower the heat to a simmer and cook, stirring frequently, until the polenta is thick and shiny and begins to pull away from the sides of the pan, about 30 minutes. Regulate the heat as necessary so the mixture doesn't boil over or cook too quickly.

2. When the polenta is done, stir in the hot pepper flakes and cheese. Season with salt as necessary. Pour the polenta into a glass or ceramic loaf pan. Allow to cool uncovered in the refrigerator until chilled and firm, at least 30 minutes.

3. When the polenta is cold, cut it into 4 or 6 equal triangular portions, depending on how many you want to serve. Cover and refrigerate until ready to use.

4. Preheat the oven to 200°F.

5. Heat 2 tablespoons of olive oil in a medium sauté pan over medium-high heat. Add the polenta, top side down, and sear until golden brown, about 5 minutes. Flip and cook on the second side until golden brown and heated through, about 3 minutes. Put the polenta into shallow ovenproof soup bowls and keep warm in the oven.

6. Heat ½ cup of olive oil in a large sauté pan over medium heat. Add the onion and garlic, season with salt, and cook until tender, about 5 minutes. Add the saffron, red pepper flakes, mussels, and tomatoes, then add the wine, cover, and cook until the mussels open, 4 to 5 minutes. Divide the mussels among the soup bowls, discarding any mussels that haven't opened, and return to the oven.

7. Add the fish stock to the sauté pan and bring to a boil. Add the parsley and season with salt and pepper as necessary. Pour the soup over the mussels and polenta and serve immediately.

Oliver's Chicken Stew

I *have a special fondness for* this recipe; I wrote it several months after our first child was born, while I was still the sous-chef at Hammersley's Bistro in Boston. I'd go to the market in the morning before work and buy a chicken, a bunch of leeks, a bunch of carrots, and a head of celery. They'd go into a pot with some lemon and tarragon and chicken stock and everything would cook together for forty-five minutes. Later, Ken, who worked at home, would strip the meat off the bones, reduce the stock, and return everything to the pot along with some pasta. The result is thicker and richer than ordinary chicken soup. Then he'd purée some of the stew for Oliver. The two of them had dinner for the next three days.

Food writer Sheryl Julian published the recipe in the *Boston Globe* ten years ago and I suddenly found myself with a fan club. People stopped me in the street to tell me they'd made Oliver's Chicken Stew. For years, when I'd pass through the dining room to check on things, new clients would introduce themselves by assuring me that they made my chicken stew. Once or twice a year someone still calls Rialto and says she's lost the recipe and could I please send her a copy. The ingredients are standard French chicken soup, but my own theory is that the recipe is successful because it's uncomplicated and it tricks people into making a rich chicken stock. Poaching the chicken and vegetables in stock makes it possible to remove the chicken before it overcooks, while the meat is still tasty. Reducing the poaching liquid intensifies the flavor, making a rich soup even more concentrated.

MAKES 6 TO 8 SERVINGS

CHICKEN STEW

1 free-range chicken (about 3 pounds), washed

8 cups Chicken Stock (page 31) or high-quality canned low-sodium chicken broth

Kosher salt

5 medium carrots, peeled and sliced ¾ inch thick on an extreme diagonal

5 celery stalks, peeled and sliced ¾ inch thick on an extreme diagonal

4 medium leeks, white part only, trimmed of roots and tough outer leaves, sliced ¾ inch thick on an extreme diagonal, and swirled vigorously in a bowl of cold water to remove any grit

Bouquet garni: 1 bay leaf plus a few sprigs parsley, tied together with kitchen twine

1 teaspoon chopped fresh thyme

4 garlic cloves, smashed

Freshly ground black pepper

½ cup stellini (tiny star pasta)

3 tablespoons unsalted butter, at room temperature

1 tablespoon freshly squeezed lemon juice, or more to taste

1 tablespoon chopped fresh tarragon

¼ cup coarsely chopped fresh flat-leaf parsley

GARNISH

4 thick slices crusty Italian bread

¼ cup extra virgin olive oil

½ cup freshly grated Parmesan

1. Place the chicken breast side down in a large deep soup kettle. Add the stock and 4 teaspoons salt (or, if using canned stock, first taste, then add salt as needed). Bring to a boil and skim the surface thoroughly. Lower the heat and add the carrots, celery, leeks, bouquet garni, thyme, and garlic and season with pepper. Adjust the heat so the water barely bubbles. Poach the chicken for 15 minutes, then flip it over and continue poaching until cooked through, about 25 minutes. Lift the chicken out of the pot, transfer to a large plate, and allow to cool.

2. Taste the vegetables. If they're tender, strain the stock into a large saucepan, setting the vegetables aside. If they're not yet tender, transfer them with the stock to the saucepan. Discard the bouquet garni. Set the stock over medium-high heat and let it simmer steadily until the liquid reduces by half, about 20 minutes.

3. While the stock is reducing, put a medium saucepan of salted water on to boil for the pasta. As soon as the chicken is cool enough to handle, remove the skin and pull the meat off the bones. Discard the skin and bones and shred the meat into large pieces. Set the meat aside, covered, in a warm place.

4. When the water comes to a rapid boil, add the pasta. Cook until it is tender but still has some bite, about 5 minutes. Drain and set aside.

5. When the chicken stock is reduced, whisk in the butter, then add the lemon juice and tarragon. Taste for seasoning and add more lemon, salt, and pepper if necessary. Add the vegetables, chopped parsley, and pasta to the broth. (Sometimes if I know there are going to be leftovers, I set aside what won't be consumed before I add the pasta to the remainder. That way the pasta doesn't absorb the liquid in what will be leftovers.) Keep warm over low heat.

6. Brush the bread with the olive oil and either toast or grill until golden. Sprinkle each slice of toast with 2 tablespoons of the Parmesan.

7. Set 1 cheese toast in each of four deep dinner plates. Distribute the chicken over the toast. Ladle the broth, vegetables, and pasta over the chicken and serve.

Roasted Tomato and Farro Soup

*F*arro is an ancient grain* that was for thousands of years a staple throughout the Mediterranean. The Romans, who recognized that its large hard kernels made poor flour, used it to make a savory porridge, a dish still served for good luck at the weddings of modern Romans. Farro's creamy texture makes it an excellent addition to soup, and Umbrian cuisine includes several soups thickened with farro. Although not yet as available as Arborio rice, it's becoming more and more common in specialty food stores or even well-stocked Italian groceries.

This soup is a great transition from light summer cooking to the heartier fare of the approaching cooler weather. You can make this dish any time of the year by substituting canned tomatoes for fresh ones, but roasted fresh tomatoes add a depth to the soup's flavor unavailable the rest of the year.

Cull through the cheese drawer in your refrigerator for leftover rinds of grating cheese. Throw them in while the soup is cooking; they add body and flavor. Remove any undissolved pieces before serving.

MAKES 4 TO 6 SERVINGS

---

3 tablespoons extra virgin olive oil

2 ounces sliced pancetta, cut into ¼-inch dice

2 celery stalks, peeled and chopped into ¼-inch dice

1 small onion, chopped into ¼-inch dice

1 medium leek, white part only, trimmed of roots and tough outer leaves, chopped into ½-inch dice, and swirled vigorously in a bowl of cold water to remove any grit

Kosher salt and freshly ground black pepper

2 garlic cloves, minced

1 cup farro

3 bay leaves

1 tablespoon chopped fresh thyme

1 teaspoon dried oregano

4 cups Chicken Stock (page 31) or high-quality canned low-sodium chicken broth

2 cups water

Leftover cheese rinds (see headnote; optional)

4 pounds ripe plum tomatoes, cut lengthwise in half

GARNISH

4 ripe plum tomatoes, peeled (see box), seeded, and cut into ½-inch dice

2 peperoncini or hot cherry peppers, thinly sliced and seeded

2 tablespoons fresh basil leaves cut into thin strips

¼ cup freshly grated Parmesan (optional)

Extra virgin olive oil

1. To make the soup base, heat 2 tablespoons of the olive oil in a large heavy pot over medium heat. Add the pancetta and cook until the fat starts to render, 2 to 3 minutes. Add the celery, onion, and leek and season with salt and pepper. Cook, stirring occasionally, until tender, about

7 minutes. Add the garlic, farro, bay leaves, thyme, and oregano and stir. Add the chicken stock and water; the liquid should cover the ingredients by ½ inch. Season again with salt and pepper, and add the optional cheese rinds.

2. Cook uncovered until the farro is tender, *not* mushy, about 20 minutes. If the liquid evaporates below the level of the farro, add more water. When the farro is done, the soup base should be thick but not pasty.

3. Meanwhile, preheat the broiler. Toss the split plum tomatoes with the remaining 1 tablespoon olive oil and season with salt and pepper. Arrange the tomatoes cut side down on a sheet pan and broil until they're browned and tender, about 15 minutes. Put the tomatoes through a food mill to get rid of their skins and seeds, or purée them in a food processor, then strain the purée to remove the skin and seeds.

4. Add the tomato purée to the soup base and cook over medium heat for 20 minutes. Taste and adjust the seasonings. Remove the bay leaves and any cheese rinds.

5. Ladle the soup into warm bowls. Garnish each bowl with the diced tomatoes, peperoncini, and basil. Add a light grating of Parmesan, if desired, and then drizzle each serving with extra virgin olive oil.

HOW TO PEEL TOMATOES

In a perfect world, tomatoes would be skinless, but until then it's up to you to peel them. Begin by bringing a pot of unsalted water to a boil. The pot should be large enough to hold as many tomatoes as you're going to peel. While the water heats, fill a bowl with ice water. Cut a shallow X in the base of each tomato, just deep enough to break the skin without slicing into the flesh. Blanch the tomatoes in boiling water for a scant 10 seconds, long enough to loosen the skins without cooking the flesh. Using a slotted spoon, immediately transfer the blanched tomatoes to the bowl of ice water. Let them cool for a minute, then remove them—the skin will have curled back at the site of each X and peels away easily.

Escarole Soup with Mushrooms and Little Meatballs

E*scarole soup used to be* a mainstay on the menus of family-run Italian immigrant restaurants, as familiar as pasta with red or white sauce, and with good reason. Hearty green leaves with real flavor in a delicious beef broth with meatballs—on a cold rainy day, what could warm you faster? The primary hurdle to making escarole soup at home is that few of us keep beef stock on hand, and canned alternatives have little to recommend them. They taste artificial and unacceptably salty. My solution is to sweat the escarole with some sautéed aromatic vegetables and mushrooms, then to add chicken stock. My kids love discovering the marble-sized meatballs hiding among the floating strands of escarole. This is a fairly thick soup; if you like more broth, increase the chicken stock to 8 cups.

MAKES 4 TO 6 SERVINGS

MEATBALLS

1 tablespoon extra virgin olive oil

1 shallot, minced

1 garlic clove, minced

Kosher salt and freshly ground black pepper

½ pound ground veal

1 extra-large egg

2 tablespoons freshly grated Parmesan

2 tablespoons chopped fresh flat-leaf parsley

¼ cup unbleached all-purpose flour

BROTH

2 tablespoons extra virgin olive oil

1 medium carrot, peeled and chopped into ¼-inch dice

1 celery stalk, peeled and chopped into ¼-inch dice

1 leek, white part only, trimmed of roots and tough outer leaves, finely chopped, and swirled vigorously in a bowl of cold water to remove any grit

½ pound mushrooms, finely chopped

1 garlic clove, finely chopped

Kosher salt and freshly ground black pepper

1 head escarole, coarsely chopped and rinsed thoroughly to remove any grit

6 cups Chicken Stock (page 31) or high-quality canned low-sodium chicken broth

1 tablespoon chopped fresh sage

1 tablespoon chopped fresh thyme

¼ cup freshly grated Parmesan, plus more for serving

1. To make the meatballs, heat 1 tablespoon of olive oil in a small sauté pan over medium heat. Add the shallots and garlic, season with salt and pepper, and cook until tender about 3 minutes. Let cool.

2. Combine the remaining meatball ingredients except the flour in a bowl, add the shallots and garlic, and mix. Test the mixture by forming a small amount into a ball and frying it. Taste, and adjust the seasonings in the meat mixture as necessary. Dust your hands with flour and form the mixture into meatballs the size of marbles (about ½ teaspoon). Cover and refrigerate at least 15 minutes.

3. To make the broth, heat 2 tablespoons of olive oil in a soup pot over medium heat. Add the carrot, celery, leek, and mushrooms, and season with salt and pepper. Cook for 5 min-utes or until tender. Add the garlic and esca-role, cover, and cook for 5 minutes. Add the chicken stock and herbs and cook, uncovered, for an additional 10 minutes. Taste and adjust the seasonings.

4. Add the meatballs to the soup and poach for 5 minutes. Ladle the soup into warm bowls, sprinkle with the grated Parmesan, and serve. Offer additional cheese on the side.

Rabbit Soup with Garlic and Peppers

T*his rustic dish is a* great introduction to cooking rabbit. The rabbit is seared, then simmered slowly in a garlicky soup broth. The meat is easily stripped from the bones after the rabbit is cooked. Rabbit is a natural partner to garlic and pepper, both sweet and hot. All the different peppers in this recipe—paprika, freshly ground black pepper, sweet red peppers, and hot red pepper flakes—weave together to make a hearty, peasant-style soup.

MAKES 6 TO 8 SERVINGS

One 3-pound rabbit
Kosher salt and freshly ground black pepper
½ cup extra virgin olive oil
½ pound chorizo sausages pricked with a fork (so they don't split)
3 medium onions, chopped into ¼-inch dice
3 red peppers (about ½ pound each), peeled with a vegetable peeler, stemmed, seeded, and cut into ½-inch strips
2 cups peeled garlic cloves (see Note) (about 2 heads or 25 cloves)
1 tablespoon paprika
4 bay leaves
1 tablespoon chopped fresh thyme
½ teaspoon hot red pepper flakes
8 cups Chicken Stock (page 31) or high-quality canned low-sodium chicken broth or more as needed
2 cups cooked chickpeas (see page 230) or canned chickpeas, rinsed well
2 tablespoons dry sherry
6 ripe plum tomatoes, peeled (see page 55), seeded, and chopped into ¼-inch dice (or one 15-ounce can diced tomatoes)
½ cup chopped fresh flat-leaf parsley

1. Season the rabbit all over with salt and pepper. Heat the olive oil in a large Dutch oven or soup pot over medium heat (the pot should be large enough to hold the rabbit and sausage in a single layer). Add the rabbit and sausage and brown on both sides, about 5 minutes per side. Transfer to a plate and set aside.

2. Add the onions to the pot, season with salt and pepper, and cook until lightly browned, about 10 minutes. Lower the heat if the onions are cooking too fast. Add the peppers, season with salt and pepper, and cook until the peppers just begin to soften, about 3 minutes. Add the garlic, paprika, bay leaves, thyme, and red pepper flakes and cook for 1 minute.

3. Add the chicken stock and bring to a boil. Lower the heat to a simmer, then return the rabbit and sausage to the pot. Cover and cook for 1 hour.

4. Flip the sausage and rabbit so they cook evenly, add the chickpeas, and cook for another 30 minutes or so, adding more stock if needed. When done, the rabbit should be just about falling off the bone.

5. Remove the rabbit and sausage from the pot. When it is cool enough to handle, shred the

rabbit meat off the bones. Slice the sausage into ½-inch diagonal pieces. Remove the bay leaves and discard. Season the soup with salt and pepper.

6. Return the meat to the pot. Heat the soup to warm everything through. Add the sherry, tomatoes, and parsley and simmer for 5 minutes.

7. Ladle the soup into warm bowls and serve.

NOTE: To peel the garlic, blanch the unpeeled cloves in boiling water for 15 seconds, then shock in ice water and drain. The skins should slide off easily.

Salads

❧

Salad ingredients are the ultimate individualists. They may be tossed in the same bowl, but they never really blend together, and anything more than a few ingredients risks sinking the whole enterprise. The central point of salad is for a few items to stand out from the crowd while you balance texture, size, color, and acidity. By restricting the focus, it's easier to appreciate in-season tomatoes, corn that you've just stripped off the cob, high-quality sherry vinegar, and fresh herbs.

Roughly half the recipes of this chapter are based on leafy greens tossed with homemade vinaigrettes. But the addition of one or two other elements—edible flowers, deviled eggs, a mint infusion, fried onions, or a wide variety of herbs—ensures that each is distinctly different. Typically I offer leafy salads after a main course, where they serve as a breather before dessert. But one of green salad's charms is its ability to become a side dish, main course, or even the slightly sweet finale to a meal.

The remaining salads are all iconoclasts, sharing only their individuality. Panzanella, a traditional Italian bread salad, and Grilled Onion and Parsley Salad with Black Olives and Pomegranate Seeds are worlds apart in taste and texture. Both are comfortable as side dishes, salad courses, or even the basis of a lunch entrée. Roasted Pear and Radicchio Salad and Beet and Spinach Salad are composed of separately prepared elements artfully arranged on individual plates, unified only by a sauce or dressing. Either can serve as a formal prelude to a main course or stand alone as the centerpiece of a light lunch.

Local Lettuces with Sherry Vinaigrette and Edible Flowers

Fancy garnishes are guilty until proven innocent in my book, but I make an exception for edible flowers—they actually add to the flavor of a salad. Nasturtiums have an appealing pepperiness; chive blossoms taste almost as you would imagine, with an unexpected sweetness; in fact, the flowers of most herbs have a faint flavor of the herb itself. Johnny-jump-ups, pansies, and rose and marigold petals are also edible, as well as squash and zucchini blossoms. Young dandelion flowers (and their greens) are delicious, but their bitter flavor makes them more appropriate for a salad with stronger flavors. A salad with herbs and baby lettuces is ideal for other edible flowers because it doesn't need a strong vinaigrette, which would overwhelm the flowers' mild flavor. Flowers for eating should only be purchased from a grocer, produce dealer, or organic farmer—not a florist.

MAKES 4 SERVINGS

1 teaspoon minced shallot

1 teaspoon Dijon mustard

1 tablespoon sherry vinegar

1 tablespoon balsamic vinegar

½ cup extra virgin olive oil

Kosher salt and freshly ground black pepper

6 cups lightly packed baby lettuces, washed and dried well

¾ cup mixed herb leaves (e.g., chervil, parsley, basil, mint, chives, and thyme), stems removed as necessary, large leaves of mint and basil chopped in half

4 small radishes, cut into ⅛-inch matchsticks

2 ounces organic edible flowers or flower petals (nasturtium blossoms, pansies, johnny-jump-ups, etc.; see headnote)

1. Whisk the shallot, mustard, and vinegars together in a small bowl to form an emulsion. Continue whisking while adding the olive oil in a thin, steady stream until it is completely absorbed and the vinaigrette is smooth. Season with salt and pepper.

2. Toss the lettuces in a large bowl with the herbs. Add enough vinaigrette for a light coating and toss gently until everything is dressed. (You may have a little vinaigrette left over, depending on the size and shape of your greens.) Taste, then season with salt and pepper if necessary.

3. Arrange the salad on chilled plates. Sprinkle each serving with radish sticks and flowers. Serve immediately.

PREMIUM OIL AND VINEGAR

The effort of seeking out edible flowers can be defeated by a poor-quality oil or vinegar. Although you could spend a fortune on balsamic vinegar or single-estate extra virgin olive oil, delicious brands of both are available in specialty food stores for only a modest increase over the price of mass-produced brands. They make a palatable difference. My table olive oil is an extra virgin from Greece; I buy it in gallon cans. I also usually have a single half-liter bottle of more expensive French or Italian oil that I use to treat myself. You can buy exceptional sherry vinegar for less than ten dollars a bottle, and while the citizens of Modena may dismiss your balsamic vinegar bought for the same price, your guests won't.

Bibb Lettuce with Creamy Mustard Dressing and Herb-Stuffed Eggs

This is an old-fashioned salad, not unlike something my grandmother would have made (minus the garlic) on a warm summer evening.

MAKES 4 SERVINGS

4 extra-large eggs

2 tablespoons Mayonnaise (page 13)

1 tablespoon plus 1 teaspoon Dijon mustard

2 tablespoons finely chopped fresh flat-leaf parsley

1 tablespoon minced fresh chives

1 teaspoon finely chopped fresh tarragon

1 teaspoon freshly squeezed lemon juice

Kosher salt and freshly ground black pepper

4 garlic cloves, peeled

½ cup heavy cream

3 tablespoons extra virgin olive oil, plus some for toasting the bread

1 small shallot, minced

2 tablespoons red wine vinegar

Eight ½-inch-thick slices French bread

1 head Bibb lettuce, separated into leaves

2 celery stalks, peeled and thinly sliced on the diagonal

1. Put the eggs in a small saucepan and cover with cold water. Bring the water to a boil over high heat. Remove the saucepan from the heat and allow the eggs to cool in the water for 25 minutes; drain.

2. Peel the eggs and cut in half lengthwise. The yolks should still be bright yellow and slightly soft in the very center. Scoop out the yolks and push them through a fine-mesh strainer into a bowl. Add the mayonnaise, 1 teaspoon of the mustard, the herbs, and lemon juice and mix well. Season with salt and pepper. Spoon the herbed yolks into the whites. Cover and refrigerate.

3. Meanwhile, put the garlic in a small saucepan and cover with 1 inch of water. Season with salt and bring to a boil, then reduce the heat to a simmer and cook until the garlic is very soft, about 10 minutes. Drain the garlic, rinse, and drain again. Return the garlic to the pan and add the cream. Bring to a boil, lower the heat to a simmer, and cook until thickened, about 6 minutes. Season with salt and pepper. Transfer cream and garlic to a blender, add 3 tablespoons of the oil, and purée until smooth.

4. Whisk the remaining 1 tablespoon mustard, the shallot, and vinegar together in a small bowl. Whisk in the puréed cream mixture. Season with salt and pepper.

5. To make the croutons, brush the slices of bread with the olive oil and toast until golden brown and crisp. Season with salt and pepper.

6. Toss the lettuce in a large bowl with the celery and dressing. Season with salt and pepper. Distribute the salad among four chilled plates. Put half an egg on each crouton. Set 2 croutons on each salad and serve.

Minted Romaine Salad with Grapes, Ricotta Salata, and Toasted Almonds

My friend and teacher Nancy Verde Barr first introduced me to the Italian technique of steeping mint in vinegar and water, then using the liquid to add a bold mint flavor to salad. A steeping period as short as 30 minutes will give the vinaigrette a substantial mint kick, but if you have the inclination, you might try it for a couple of hours, or even overnight to see just how intense the flavor can become.

In my repertoire of salads, this one is a rare exception in that my favorite time to serve it is out of season, in the winter. In New England, there is no local table grape industry, so I buy them out of season in a supermarket; mint is available year-round (but not in my backyard). The salad makes a bright and refreshing contrast to root vegetables, like a summer day that has suddenly wandered into the middle of February.

MAKES 4 SERVINGS

¼ cup red wine vinegar

2 tablespoons water

½ cup plus 2 tablespoons coarsely chopped fresh mint

1 small shallot, minced

¾ cup extra virgin olive oil

Kosher salt and freshly ground black pepper

1 large head Romaine lettuce, leaves separated, washed, and dried

1 small red onion, sliced paper-thin, soaked in ice water for 30 minutes (to remove bitterness), drained, and dried

½ pound seedless grapes, washed and cut in half

½ cup sliced almonds, toasted

¼ pound ricotta salata, thinly sliced

1. Combine vinegar, water, and 2 tablespoons of the chopped mint in a small nonreactive saucepan. Bring to a simmer, then remove from the heat, and let steep for 30 minutes.

2. Strain the vinegar into a small bowl and discard the mint. Add the shallot. Whisk in the oil in a thin, steady stream. Season with salt and pepper.

3. Mix the Romaine leaves in a large bowl with the remaining ½ cup mint, the red onion, and grapes. Add the vinaigrette and toss well. Taste, then season with salt and pepper if necessary.

4. Arrange the salad on chilled plates, top with the toasted almonds and slices of ricotta salata, and serve.

Arugula and Portobella Mushroom Salad

This is a poor man's version of the classic Italian salad of porcini mushrooms sliced paper-thin and dressed with extra virgin olive oil, lemon juice, and black pepper. Portobellas aren't as noble as porcini, but they're more readily available and a lot less expensive. They have their own admirable flavor, and their meaty texture almost equals that of porcini. This salad makes a fine appetizer, accompaniment for a Tuscan-Style Sirloin with Parmesan, Lemon, and Truffle Oil (page 263), or end-of-the-meal salad. If you chance upon a batch of fresh porcini and are feeling flush, by all means replace the portobellas with their more aristocratic cousins.

Examine the portobella cap carefully before you buy it. It should feel firm, not spongy, and the edges of the cap should be still be intact, not dry or cracked. Slice it as thin as possible with a sharp knife or, if its blade is very sharp, a mandoline.

MAKES 4 SERVINGS

1 head endive, separated into leaves (about
   12 leaves)
4 cups lightly packed arugula, washed and dried
1 large portobella mushroom cap (3 to 4 ounces),
   cleaned and sliced paper-thin
1 tablespoon freshly squeezed lemon juice
6 tablespoons extra virgin olive oil
Kosher salt and freshly ground black pepper
2 ounces Parmesan, shaved with vegetable peeler

1. Put the endive leaves, arugula, and mushrooms in a bowl. Drizzle the lemon juice over the salad, add the olive oil, season with salt and pepper, and toss well. Taste, then adjust the seasonings if necessary.

2. Arrange the salad on chilled plates, sprinkle with the Parmesan shavings, and serve.

Escarole, Romaine, and Capocollo Salad with Anchovy Dressing and Fried Onions

This is a hearty country-style combination of escarole and romaine that bears a distant relation to Caesar salad—similar ingredients, but much different handling, with crispy fried onions replacing the textural crunch of a Caesar salad's croutons. I like to use capocollo instead of prosciutto because it's fattier, a little less refined, which is just right for the strong flavors of this dish.

Take the time to fry the onions; the salad just isn't the same without the irresistible crispy topping. They can be made several hours in advance without any loss of flavor or texture, and they're intended to be served at room temperature, not warm.

MAKES 4 SERVINGS

1 garlic clove, minced and then mashed with a
   pinch of salt to make a paste
½ teaspoon minced shallot
5 anchovies, rinsed and coarsely chopped
½ teaspoon Dijon mustard
2 tablespoons red wine vinegar
½ cup extra virgin olive oil
Kosher salt and freshly ground black pepper
4 cups vegetable oil for deep-frying
½ cup unbleached all-purpose flour
¼ cup semolina flour
1 medium white onion, sliced paper-thin
8 leaves Romaine lettuce, washed, dried, and cut
   crosswise into 3-inch-wide strips
8 escarole leaves, washed thoroughly, dried, and
   cut crosswise into 1-inch-wide strips
3 ounces thinly sliced capocollo, cut into ¼-inch-
   wide strips
2 ounces shaved pecorino Romano

1. Combine the garlic, shallot, anchovies, and mustard in a small bowl. Whisk in the red wine vinegar to make an emulsion. Add the extra virgin olive oil in a thin, steady stream, whisking constantly until the vinaigrette is smooth and emulsified. Season with salt and pepper.

2. Heat the vegetable oil in a small deep pot to 350°F. Use a deep-fry thermometer to check the temperature.

3. Toss the flours together in a large bowl. Add the onion and toss until coated. The onion will separate into rings, which is fine. Fry the onions, a handful at a time, until golden brown, 2 to 3 minutes. Scoop out and drain on paper towels. When all the onions are done, season with salt.

4. Toss the Romaine, escarole, and capocollo together in a large bowl. Add the vinaigrette and toss again. Taste, then season with salt and pepper if necessary.

5. Arrange the salad on chilled plates. Top each with some pecorino shavings and a small handful of fried onions, and serve.

Avocado and Chipotle Shrimp Salad with Tequila Shooters

Chipotle peppers and a host of south-of-the-border seasonings put a Mexican spin on this adults-only shrimp and avocado salad. But when I wanted a wild over-the-top accompaniment, I remembered an old Martha Stewart trick of hollowing out cucumber sections to make sake glasses. A little salt transforms the cucumbers into shot glasses for tequila shooters. Make sure you eat this in the shade.

MAKES 4 SERVINGS

1 European (seedless) cucumber, washed
¼ cup freshly squeezed lime juice
½ cup plus 1 tablespoon tequila
2 teaspoons sugar
1 garlic clove, minced
2 jalapeño peppers, stemmed, seeded, and minced
½ cup extra virgin olive oil
Kosher salt and freshly ground black pepper
2 canned chipotle chiles in adobo, finely chopped, with their sauce
2 ripe avocados
8 extra-large shrimp (about ¾ pound), peeled and deveined
1 cup halved cherry tomatoes
1 small red onion, chopped into ¼-inch dice
1 tablespoon chopped fresh mint
2 tablespoons chopped fresh cilantro, plus 4 sprigs for garnish
1 lime, cut into quarters

1. Trim the ends of the cucumber, then cut it crosswise into quarters. Using a melon baller or a small spoon, scoop the flesh out of each piece, leaving ¼-inch-thick walls and a ½-inch bottom. Cover and refrigerate until needed.

2. Whisk together the lime juice, 1 tablespoon of the tequila, ½ teaspoon of the sugar, the garlic, and jalapeños in a small bowl. Whisk in ¼ cup plus 2 tablespoons of the olive oil in a slow, thin stream. Season with salt and pepper.

3. Mix the chipotle chiles with 1 teaspoon of the sugar and 1 tablespoon of the vinaigrette in a small bowl. Add the shrimp and toss well. Cover and marinate for 1 hour in the refrigerator. Refrigerate the rest of the vinaigrette.

4. When you're ready to finish the dish, peel, pit and cut each avocado into 8 slices.

5. Heat the remaining 2 tablespoons olive oil in a large sauté pan over medium heat. Season the shrimp with salt, then add to the pan and cook for about 5 minutes on each side, or until just cooked through. Remove the pan from the heat and let cool.

6. When the pan has cooled, add the tomatoes, red onion, and herbs to the shrimp, along with ¼ cup of the vinaigrette. Season with salt and toss well (do this in the pan so you don't lose any of the shrimp's cooking juices).

7. Arrange 4 slices of avocado on each plate. Sprinkle the avocado with salt and pepper and drizzle with the remaining vinaigrette. Spoon the salad on top, putting 2 shrimp on each plate. Dip the tops of the cucumber into salt if desired. Fill each one with 2 tablespoons of the tequila.

8. Stand a cucumber shooter next to each salad, garnish each salad with a wedge of lime and a sprig of cilantro, and serve.

Fingerling Potato, Fig, and Tarragon Salad

This salad was born out of one of those what-do-we-have-in-the-larder nights when there seemed to be a little of this and a little of that. Adding the figs was taking a chance—figs and tarragon?—but they're wonderful. The extra sweetness is welcome in a cold salad, and they add a little more textural contrast. A great companion to grilled fish or chicken.

MAKES 4 SERVINGS

1½ pounds fingerling potatoes (if fingerlings are unavailable, substitute other small new potatoes), scrubbed and cut lengthwise in half

6 bay leaves, preferably fresh

2 garlic cloves, finely chopped

Kosher salt and freshly ground black pepper

1 teaspoon Dijon mustard

3 tablespoons red wine vinegar

½ cup extra virgin olive oil

1 celery stalk, peeled and chopped into ¼-inch dice

12 dried figs, preferably Turkish, stems removed and cut lengthwise into quarters

1 small red onion, chopped into ¼-inch dice

2 tablespoons chopped fresh flat-leaf parsley

1 tablespoon chopped fresh tarragon

¼ cup chopped pitted green olives

1. Put the potatoes in a saucepan and add cold water to cover by ½ inch. Add the bay leaves and garlic, season with salt and pepper, and bring to a boil. Reduce the heat to a simmer and cook until the potatoes are just tender, about 10 minutes. Remove from the heat and allow the potatoes to cool in the water. Drain, removing and discarding the bay leaves.

2. Whisk the mustard and red wine vinegar together in a small bowl to form an emulsion. Continue whisking while slowly adding the olive in a thin, steady stream. Season the vinaigrette with salt and pepper.

3. Just before serving, combine the potatoes, celery, figs, red onion, parsley, tarragon, and olives in a large bowl, add the vinaigrette, and toss to coat. Taste, season with salt and pepper if necessary, and serve.

Panzanella—Fried Bread Salad with Roasted Peppers, Capers, and Toasted Garlic

Panzanella, Italian bread salad, is one of the reasons to save your stale bread during the summer months, when other salad ingredients are at their peak. As Americans, we often reduce the life cycle of bread to two stages—fresh and throw-it-away. But in cultures where bread is baked locally, the cycle extends from one day of baking to the next, and it may last for as long as a week. As a loaf becomes progressively firmer, it can be grilled or toasted, rubbed with olive oil to make crostini or bruschetta, or fried in olive oil for delicious croutons. Here the croutons absorb the flavor of the olive oil and add crunch to the finished salad.

MAKES 4 SERVINGS

½ cup extra virgin olive oil, plus more if needed

20 garlic cloves, peeled

Kosher salt and freshly ground black pepper

2 cups 1-inch crustless bread cubes

1 large red onion, cut into ¼-inch-thick slices

5 large red peppers, roasted (see page 99), peeled, stemmed, seeded, and cut into 1-inch-wide strips

2 anchovies, rinsed and finely chopped

1 tablespoon capers, rinsed

¼ cup balsamic vinegar

1 cup chopped fresh flat-leaf parsley

½ cup chopped fresh basil

1 ounce Pecorino Romano shavings

DO AHEAD: Roast and peel the peppers. Peel the garlic; wrap it tightly in several layers of plastic wrap and refrigerate so it doesn't dry out.

1. Heat the olive oil in a large sauté pan over low heat. Add the garlic cloves, season with salt and pepper, and cook until tender and golden, about 15 minutes. Remove the garlic from the pan with a slotted spoon, and set aside.

2. Increase the heat to medium. Add the bread to the pan and sauté until golden brown on all sides, 4 to 5 minutes. Transfer the bread to a large bowl.

3. Add the onion to the pan and cook until tender, about 5 minutes. Add to the bread.

4. Add the garlic, roasted peppers, anchovies, and capers to the bowl. Toss well. Season with salt and pepper. Add the balsamic vinegar, parsley, basil, and, if necessary, additional olive oil, season with salt and pepper, and toss again. Taste, and adjust the seasonings as necessary.

5. Arrange the salad on chilled plates, top with the pecorino shavings, and serve.

Roasted Pear and Radicchio Salad with Gorgonzola Cream and Toasted Hazelnuts

*P**ears and blue cheese, especially* Stilton, Roquefort, or Gorgonzola, are a combination that seems to continually reinvent itself. The new wrinkle here is radicchio. The combination works well as an appetizer or a great end-of-the-meal salad because it mimics a fruit and cheese course. Be sure to use Gorgonzola *dolce,* the sweet, softer style of the cheese, not the firmer aged cheese known as Gorgonzola *naturale.*

MAKES 4 SERVINGS

2 ripe but firm Bosc pears

Kosher salt and freshly ground black pepper

1 large head radicchio, washed, dried, and cut into quarters

6 tablespoons plus 2 teaspoons extra virgin olive oil, plus additional for oiling the baking sheet

1 cup heavy cream

2 ounces Gorgonzola *dolce*, cut into small pieces

2 ounces watercress, washed, dried, and trimmed of thick stems

2 tablespoons plus 1 teaspoon balsamic vinegar

About 2 ounces (¼ cup) hazelnuts, toasted and coarsely chopped

1 shallot, peeled, sliced paper-thin, soaked in ice water for 30 minutes (to remove bitterness), drained, and dried

1. Preheat the oven to 450°F.

2. Cut the pears in half and remove their cores. Place the pears and radicchio in a large bowl, season with salt and pepper, and toss with 3 tablespoons of the olive oil. Place the pears and radicchio cut side down on a well-oiled baking sheet. Roast on the bottom rack of the oven until the radicchio is tender and brown around the edges, 10 to 15 minutes. Remove the radicchio and set aside. Continue cooking the pears until tender and caramelized to a deep golden brown on the cut side, an additional 15 to 20 minutes.

3. Put the cream in a small saucepan and set it over medium heat—place the pan slightly off center so that as the cream heats, the foam and fat will accumulate against the side of the pan. Simmer, skimming the foam frequently, until the cream reduces by one-quarter, about 3 minutes. Lower the heat and whisk in the cheese until completely melted. Don't let the mixture boil, or it will break; lower the heat if necessary. Season with salt and pepper, remove from the heat, and keep warm.

4. Divide the sauce among four warmed plates. Gently toss the pears, radicchio, and watercress with 2 tablespoons of the balsamic vinegar and 3 tablespoons of the olive oil. Arrange atop the sauced plates.

5. Toss the hazelnuts and sliced shallots with the remaining 1 teaspoon balsamic vinegar and 2 teaspoons olive oil. Spoon the hazelnuts and shallots over the salads and serve.

Grilled Onion and Parsley Salad with Black Olives and Pomegranate Seeds

Everyone knows that herbs are flavorings, but what about herbs as vegetables in their own right? The concept isn't as farfetched as it might seem. Sorrel is known primarily as an herb in this country, but in Europe, especially in France, it's often cooked and served as a sauce. Fennel clearly straddles the line, and in Italy, arugula is sometimes used as a seasoning, as well as a green. Eva Sommaripa, whose farm in Westport, Massachusetts, is the source of many of the high-quality herbs we use at Rialto, encouraged me to broaden my perspective on herbs many years ago, especially when thinking of salad greens. As Eva's friends can attest, she is nothing if not persuasive. I put herbs on everything and often feature an herb salad on my menu.

Like the Middle Eastern tabbouleh, this salad uses parsley leaves as a primary ingredient. After you've made it once or twice, try substituting basil leaves or chives for half of the parsley for a much different effect.

MAKES 4 SERVINGS

2 large sweet onions (Vidalia or Walla Walla, for example), sliced ½ inch thick

⅓ cup extra virgin olive oil

Kosher salt and freshly ground black pepper

Leaves from 1 bunch flat-leaf parsley

¼ cup pitted Niçoise olives

¼ cup pomegranate seeds

3 tablespoons balsamic vinegar

1. Prepare a medium fire in a grill. You should be able to hold your hand near the grilling surface for a count of 4 before having to pull it away.

2. Toss the onions with 2 tablespoons of the olive oil and season with salt and pepper. Grill until lightly charred and tender, 8 to 10 minutes per side. Be careful not to burn the onions. If you can cook with the top of your grill down, the time will be somewhat shortened. Transfer the onions to a plate and let them cool to room temperature.

3. Toss the onions with the remaining olive oil, the parsley, olives, pomegranate seeds, and vinegar. Season with salt and pepper and serve.

Tomato and Grilled Mushroom Salad with Mustard Vinaigrette

*T*he summer when I was fifteen, we left England, where my father was taking his sabbatical, for two wonderful weeks in the ancient walled town of Flavigny, in Burgundy. Most nights we ate at a small bistro where each meal began with a large plate of perfectly ripe peeled tomatoes sprinkled heavily with chopped parsley. Our server whisked together a simple tableside vinaigrette of mustard, red wine vinegar, and extra virgin olive oil. As an adult, I tried for many years to duplicate the flavor of what my memory told me was a basic one-two-three recipe, but I could never get it to work out. Several years ago, I found myself nibbling a sample of curly parsley from my mother's herb garden when I suddenly realized that I was tasting the missing ingredient. When we turned up our noses at curly parsley in the '80s in favor of flat-leaf, or "Italian," parsley, as it's sometimes called, we eliminated a flavor from our palette. This salad needs the sharper taste of the curly variety to taste right, at least to me.

This dish is actually two salads, although I love them together when I can get my hands on good tomatoes and mushrooms simultaneously. A loaf of bread, a couple of nice cheeses, and you have a great summer meal.

MAKES 4 SERVINGS

½ **pound assorted mushrooms large enough to slice or chop and grill (portabellas, cremini, and/or large white mushrooms)**
1 **garlic clove, minced**
½ **cup plus 2 tablespoons extra virgin olive oil**
2 **teaspoons chopped fresh thyme**
Kosher salt and freshly ground black pepper
2 **tablespoons Dijon mustard**
2½ **tablespoons red wine vinegar**
1 **pound ripe beefsteak tomatoes, peeled (see page 55)**
¼ **cup finely chopped fresh curly parsley**
1 **shallot, sliced paper-thin, soaked in ice water for 20 minutes (to remove bitterness), drained, and patted dry**
1 **ounce aged sheep's milk or goat cheese, grated**

1. Prepare a medium fire in a grill. You should be able to hold your hand near the grilling surface for a count of 4 before having to pull it away.

2. To prepare the mushrooms, cut large mushroom caps, such as portabellas, into 1-inch-thick slices. Cut other mushrooms into 2-inch pieces. The point is to cut them so they'll cook fairly speedily while leaving them large enough not to fall between the bars of the grill. (Use a grill basket if you have one.) Toss the mushrooms with the garlic, 2 tablespoons of the oil, and the thyme. Season with salt and pepper. Grill, turning once, until tender and slightly charred, about 6 minutes. Set aside.

3. Whisk the mustard and red wine vinegar together in a small bowl to form an emulsion. Whisk in the remaining ½ cup olive oil in a thin, steady stream until it is completely absorbed. Season with salt and pepper.

4. Remove the stems and cut the tomatoes into slices ½ inch thick.

5. Arrange the tomatoes in overlapping rows on a platter. Season with salt and pepper. Spoon two-thirds of the vinaigrette over the tomatoes and sprinkle with the chopped parsley. Arrange the grilled mushrooms over the tomatoes. Distribute the shallots over the top and drizzle with the remaining vinaigrette. Sprinkle with the grated cheese and serve.

Beet and Spinach Salad with Goat Cheese and Grilled Fresh Figs

Beets and *chèvre, fresh goat* cheese, are a solid combination, but simply not interesting enough by themselves. Figs and spinach add just enough interest to enliven the salad without overwhelming it. Many chèvres are pleasant enough but almost as nondescript as cream cheese. Try to find one with some chalky tartness that can offer a counterpoint to its mildly sweet partners, beets and figs.

MAKES 4 SERVINGS

4 small beets, washed, greens trimmed to an inch

2 orange quarters (wash the orange before slicing)

Kosher salt

1 teaspoon grated orange zest

¼ cup balsamic vinegar

1 teaspoon crushed toasted anise seeds

1 teaspoon Dijon mustard

1 teaspoon minced shallots

½ cup plus 1 tablespoon plus 1 teaspoon extra virgin olive oil

Freshly ground black pepper

8 fresh figs, cut lengthwise in half

3 cups lightly packed baby spinach leaves

¼ pound fresh goat cheese

1 tablespoon capers, rinsed

1. Put the beets in a saucepan large enough to accommodate them in a single layer. Squeeze the juice from the orange quarters into the pan. Add the rinds and enough water to cover the beets by an inch. Season with salt, cover, and bring to a boil. Lower the heat to a simmer and cook until the beets are tender, about 45 minutes. Allow the beets to cool in the cooking liquid.

2. Drain the beets, then remove the skins and stems by rubbing them with an old kitchen towel. Cut each beet into 8 wedges. Place the wedges in a large bowl and toss with the orange zest and 1 tablespoon of the balsamic vinegar.

3. Whisk together the anise seeds, mustard, and shallots with the remaining 3 tablespoons balsamic vinegar in a small bowl. Add ½ cup of the olive oil in a thin, steady stream, whisking constantly, until the vinaigrette is smooth and completely blended. Season with salt and pepper.

4. Preheat a grill pan over high heat (or use an outdoor grill, if you prefer). Brush the grill pan with 1 teaspoon of the olive oil. Toss the figs with the remaining 1 tablespoon olive oil. Grill cut side down until browned and tender, only a minute. Remove from the heat and toss with 1 tablespoon of the vinaigrette.

5. Add the spinach and the remaining vinaigrette to the bowl with the beets. Toss well, then arrange on four plates. Crumble the goat cheese over the beets, garnish with the grilled figs, and capers and serve.

Four Vegetable Starters,

23 SIDES, AND A FEW THINGS FOR THE PANTRY

Vegetables were a marginal attraction for me, an enhancement for the culinary centerpiece of meat or fish, until I studied the food of southern France, Italy, and Spain, where appreciation for fresh seasonal produce approaches a near-spiritual reverence. As opportunities to travel came my way, I began to understand why other cultures lavish such care on their vegetables. If you live in an environment where animal protein is historically scarce, you exercise your creativity on what *is* available. If winter means you have to work your way through a cellar full of turnips and potatoes, you become adept at purées and gratins and roasting in order to stave off monotony. The reappearance of tender greens in the spring is a welcome relief, and the ripening of tomatoes cause for celebration.

My approach to vegetables is to think seasonally, buy locally, and fill in the gaps with the best global produce available during the winter. From late spring through the fall, I cook with whatever looks best at the local farmers' market. In the winter, when of necessity I need to shop indoors, I go to one of the really good produce or whole foods stores near to me.

My shopping at farmers' markets is motivated by far more than a nostalgic fondness for a European lifestyle. Farmers' markets are supplied by small farmers, and these producers are responsive to consumers in ways that large wholesalers are not. Heirloom tomatoes or peaches are far more likely to show up in a farmers' market than a grocery store. Before I decided to include recipes for squash blossoms in this book, I asked the zucchini vendor in my market whether she'd sell me zucchini blossoms. "How many do you want?" She was already selling them to other customers who ordered them in advance. As a chef, I'm accustomed to having suppliers try to oblige me, but in farmers' markets, ordinary consumers find that vendors are eager to form the same type of sustaining relationships with them.

The recipes in this chapter offer you a broad range of seasonal choices. Warm Spring Vegetable Salad with Favas, Green Beans, Peas, and Radicchio, Warm Asparagus Spears with Aged Gouda, and Slow-Roasted Tomatoes are spring and summer treats, as are Simple Favas with Butter and Leek, Artichoke, and Fennel Strudel. (It's unlikely that fava beans will ever show up in my New England farmers' market, but they do put in a seasonal appearance in my local whole-foods grocery store.)

Crisp Shredded Potato Pancakes, Winter Vegetable Gratin with Cranberries and Chestnuts, a variety of roasted vegetable recipes, and highly seasoned purées and mashes provide an antidote to cold-weather tedium. Broccoli rabe, ordinary broccoli, and a selection of hardy leafy greens keep a green thread alive in your culinary repertoire through the winter months. Braised Escarole with Parmesan Crust is the dish to make when you just can't stand another gray February day. By the time you've cooked your way through these, the first spring asparagus should be just around the corner.

Braised Leeks and Shiitakes Wrapped in Pancetta

*O*nce you taste leeks braised in a little white wine and chicken stock, you'll never go back to braising them in water. Here the braised leeks are stuffed with a couple of sautéed shiitakes, then wrapped with pancetta to hold everything together. There's a final sauté to seal the bundles. The finished leeks deserve their own course as an appetizer. Almost all of the steps in this dish can be done a day ahead and the bundles refrigerated overnight. Save the final sauté until just before serving.

MAKES 4 APPETIZER SERVINGS

4 large leeks (white part needs to be 6 inches long after trimming)

2 tablespoons extra virgin olive oil

8 medium shiitakes, stems removed and discarded or saved for stock

Kosher salt and freshly ground black pepper

1 garlic clove, finely chopped

1 cup Chicken Stock (page 31) or high-quality canned low-sodium chicken broth

¼ cup dry white wine

1 sprig thyme

¼ teaspoon finely chopped fresh rosemary

8 thin slices pancetta (3 to 4 ounces)

1. Trim the roots off each leek. Cut off the green tops and any tough outer leaves. Slice each leek lengthwise, leaving a 2-inch section of the base intact. Holding the base tightly, swish each leek vigorously in a pot of cold water, spreading the leaves apart, then rinse under cold running water to dislodge any sand or grit trapped between the leaves. Shake off excess water.

2. Heat the oil in a large sauté pan over medium heat. Add the mushroom caps, season with salt and pepper, and cook, turning once, until tender, about 3 minutes per side. Transfer the mushrooms to a plate and set aside.

3. Add the leeks to the pan and sear all over until lightly browned. Season with salt and pepper. Add the garlic and cook until it becomes aromatic, about a minute. Add the stock, wine, thyme, and rosemary, lay a piece of foil over the leeks, and then cover with a lid. Reduce the heat to low and simmer until the leeks are tender, 30 to 40 minutes. Remove the leeks from the liquid and cool; reserve the braising liquid.

4. Insert 2 shiitakes between the halves of each leek, like a sandwich. Wrap 2 slices of the pancetta around each leek in a spiral, to secure the shiitakes and bind the leek halves together.

5. Place the pancetta-wrapped leeks in a large nonstick sauté pan and cook over medium heat, using tongs to turn the leeks, until the pancetta is browned all over and the leeks are warm. Serve drizzled with the braising liquid.

Warm Asparagus Spears with Aged Gouda and Sherry Vinaigrette

*A*sparagus are finger food in my family, like corn on the cob or clams on the half-shell, and in the spring when they first appear in the markets, we eat as much as we can. Unless the spears are pencil-thin, I peel the stalks; unpeeled thick spears have an unpleasant "stemmy" flavor and are tough. Although we often eat steamed asparagus dressed with a little good olive oil, this recipe calls for blanching the asparagus, then giving it a quick roast. Roasting brings out a nutty quality in the vegetable's flavor, well matched with the aged Gouda that is sprinkled on just before serving.

MAKES 4 APPETIZER SERVINGS

2 pounds asparagus
Kosher salt
2 tablespoons extra virgin olive oil
Freshly ground black pepper

VINAIGRETTE
¼ teaspoon minced shallot
½ teaspoon Dijon mustard
1 tablespoon sherry vinegar
¼ cup extra virgin olive oil
Kosher salt and freshly ground black pepper

1 tablespoon minced shallots
2 ounces aged Gouda, sliced paper-thin
¼ cup chervil sprigs

1. Preheat the oven to 400°F.

2. If the asparagus are large, snap the fibrous portion off the root end of the stems, then peel the remaining stem. If the asparagus are pencil-thin, simply snap off the ends.

3. Bring a large pot of water to a boil. Prepare a large bowl of ice water. Season the boiling water generously with salt, add the asparagus, and cook until bright green and tender (the time will depend on the thickness of the asparagus). Plunge the asparagus into the ice water to stop the cooking. Drain thoroughly.

4. Toss the asparagus with the olive oil and season with salt and pepper. Arrange on a sheet pan in a single layer. Roast until hot, 4 to 5 minutes.

5. Meanwhile, make the vinaigrette: Whisk the shallot, mustard, and sherry vinegar together in a small bowl. Continue whisking while you add the olive oil in a smooth, steady stream until thoroughly incorporated. Season with salt and pepper.

6. Remove the asparagus from the oven and toss with the vinaigrette and the 1 tablespoon shallots. Divide among four warmed plates. Arrange the cheese on and around the asparagus, sprinkle with the chervil sprigs, and serve.

EASY ASPARAGUS OPTIONS

Here are three possible additions, to be used either alone or in combination.

⌐ Slice 4 large mushrooms as thin as you can. Toss them in the vinaigrette with the asparagus.

⌐ Drizzle 1½ teaspoons truffle oil over each plate of asparagus before adding the Gouda.

⌐ After garnishing with chervil, sprinkle 1½ teaspoons edible flowers over each plate.

I particularly like chive flowers because their violet color makes a striking contrast against the green of the asparagus.

Curried Squash Fritters

Delicata squash, with its pumpkin-like flavor, is an ideal candidate for fritters. Delicata rings have the added charm of resembling doughnuts. Unfortunately, their season is limited on the East Coast, and some people find peeling their nubbly skin a pain in the neck, so you may want to use butternut squash instead, more widely available and nearly as tasty.

2 to 2½ pounds small delicata squashes or
   1 butternut squash of the same weight
½ cup unbleached all-purpose flour
¼ cup cornstarch
1 tablespoon curry powder
1 extra-large egg white, chilled
½ cup cold beer or ice water
4 cups vegetable oil for deep-frying
Kosher salt
1 lime, cut into quarters

1. Peel the squash. If using delicatas, you may want to use a paring knife instead of a vegetable peeler; don't worry about getting every bit of skin out of the squashes' ridged surfaces. Slice the delicatas crosswise ¼ inch thick. Use a paring knife to remove the seeds at the center of each ring. If using a butternut squash, split the squash lengthwise and scoop out the seeds. Cut each half crosswise into ¼-inch-thick slices.

2. Mix the flour, cornstarch, and curry powder in a medium bowl. Beat the egg white with the beer in a small bowl. Whisk the wet ingredients into the dry until just mixed. If you overbeat the batter, the fritter coating will be tough. Cover and refrigerate for 20 minutes.

3. Preheat the oven to 200°F. Line a sheet pan with paper towels and put it in the oven.

4. Heat the vegetable oil in a deep pot over medium heat to 350°F. Use a deep-fry thermometer to check the temperature. Dip a slice of squash into the batter and then carefully lower it into the hot oil. Repeat until you have 6 slices of squash in the pot. The squashes will bob to the surface of the oil. Fry, turning once, until the batter is crisp and the squash is tender, about 2 minutes per side. As the fritters finish cooking, transfer them to the towel-lined sheet pan in the oven. Continue frying the squash slices in batches until they are all cooked.

5. Place the fritters on a warm platter, sprinkle with salt, and garnish with the lime wedges. Serve immediately.

Braised Artichokes with Anchovies, Capers, and Lemon Zest

Braising artichokes is easy. The most demanding aspect of the recipe is trimming them beforehand, and with baby artichokes even that step is made simple because it's unnecessary to remove the chokes. Hot or cold, braised artichokes make a dramatic appetizer or side dish. This recipe is based on an Italian preparation I was once served by my friend and fellow restaurateur Charlie Robinson. The strong, acidic flavors of lemon and capers balance the artichokes' natural bitterness. Serve them as a warm accompaniment to Seared Lamb Steaks with Balsamic Vinegar and Red Pepper Marinade (page 278), Roast Leg of Lamb with Mustard Crumbs (page 282), or Braised Veal Shanks with Flageolets and Preserved Lemon (page 266).

An appealing feature of braised artichokes is that the entire dish can be prepared several days in advance, only improving in flavor as the seasonings interact. Allow the artichokes to cool in the cooking liquid, then refrigerate. Any leftovers make a delicious addition to risotto or use them, along with their braising liquid, as the base of a simple sauce for pasta.

MAKES 4 APPETIZER SERVINGS

2 pounds baby artichokes (about 24) or 4 larger
    artichokes (about ½ pound each)
2 lemons, cut in half, for trimming the artichokes
⅔ cup extra virgin olive oil
1 small onion, chopped into ½-inch dice
Kosher salt to taste
2 garlic cloves, finely chopped
½ cup dry white wine
4 anchovies, rinsed and finely chopped
2 tablespoons capers, rinsed
2 teaspoons grated lemon zest
6 sun-dried tomato halves, sliced into very thin
    strips
2 teaspoons freshly squeezed lemon juice
½ teaspoon hot red pepper flakes
3 bay leaves
1 teaspoon dried oregano

1. Following the instructions on page 85, trim the artichokes, placing each one in acidulated water as you finish trimming it. If using larger artichokes, cut them into quarters.

2. Combine the oil and onion in a large nonreactive sauté pan over medium heat and sauté the onion until translucent, 3 to 4 minutes. Add the garlic and cook until it releases its perfume, another minute or so; season with salt.

3. Drain the trimmed artichokes and add them, along with the remaining ingredients, to the pan. Add enough water to just cover the artichokes, about 1 cup. Season with salt. Cover and simmer until the artichokes are tender when pierced with a knife. Check after 20 minutes; remove the bay leaves and discard. Larger artichokes may take 30 to 40 minutes. Serve the artichokes drizzled with some of the braising juices.

HANDLING AND TRIMMING ARTICHOKES

I remember learning to eat artichokes as a child and thinking it was one of the strangest things I'd ever seen. *You put the leaf in your mouth and scrape the flesh off it with your teeth?!* How bizarre, and what a strange flavor! Of course, as my daughter, Roxanne, demonstrates, dipping each leaf into a bowl of lemon butter is its own reward. When I grew older and learned that it was necessary to prune the crown, snap off the tough leaf ends, and trim the stem at the base of the artichoke before you could actually think about cooking it, the trimming procedure seeming fitting in a Byzantine sort of way. You wouldn't expect that anything you ate by scraping it across your teeth would be prepared by a simple *peeling,* would you?

Trimming artichokes involves several simple but necessary steps that appear to discard a major portion of the vegetable. Don't worry. You're not removing anything edible. The point of trimming an artichoke is to make it easy to reach the edible parts. Baby artichokes, about 1¼ ounces each, require less trimming than larger ones, which range from 8 ounces to well over a pound. Bigger is not necessarily better. Baby artichokes haven't had time to outgrow their youthful tenderness, and more of the vegetable is edible. The "choke," the thistle-like center of the artichoke, is edible in a cooked baby artichoke; in an adult, it must be removed as part of the trimming process.

Artichokes will discolor easily during trimming, from contact with a carbon-steel knife or from prolonged exposure to air. You can remedy this by using a knife with a stainless steel blade and rubbing the cut spots with a lemon half. Cut-and-rub is a habit worth cultivating. If you're not going to use the trimmed artichokes immediately, keep them covered with acidulated water (water containing lemon juice) until you need them. Two lemons will suffice for trimming 2 pounds of artichokes (3 to 4 medium-sized ones or 24 babies). They'll yield enough juice for 2 quarts of acidulated water, with enough lemon left over for rubbing the cut surfaces as you trim.

Cooked artichokes can be refrigerated in oil. After several days, the oil will take on the flavor of artichokes, a nice touch for vinaigrettes. Never reach into a jar of oil with your bare fingers to remove an artichoke (or any other vegetable). Bacteria from your skin will rapidly spoil the oil.

TO TRIM LARGE ARTICHOKES

1. Scrub 2 lemons, then cut them in half. Combine the juice of 1½ of the lemons with 2 quarts cold water in a large bowl. Add the squeezed rinds to the water. Save the remaining lemon half to use during trimming.

2. One at a time, lay each artichoke on its side. Using a chef's knife, make a straight cut across the "crown," or top of the artichoke. Don't be shy: The top quarter of the artichoke is mostly prickly leaf ends, and you're not sacrificing anything by whacking it off. Depending on the size of the artichoke, this can amount to an inch or two. Rub the trimmed leaves with lemon.

3. Gently snap back the tough upper portion of each outer leaf, leaving the meaty part of the leaf still attached. Continue working around the artichoke until all the tough leaves have been snapped and the remaining leaves are pale green and tender.

4. Trim the tough skin around the base of the artichoke. Pare the skin off the stem and trim the tip (leave most of the stem intact). Rub the entire artichoke with the lemon.

5. If the recipe calls for artichoke quarters, cut each artichoke lengthwise into quarters and remove the choke. Rub the quarters all over with the lemon.

6. As you finish each artichoke, place it in the bowl of lemon water. Trimmed artichokes can be stored, refrigerated, in acidulated water, for 24 hours.

TO TRIM BABY ARTICHOKES

1. Prepare a bowl of acidulated water with 2 lemons as directed above.

2. One at a time, trim ½ inch off the crown of each artichoke and snap off any tough or scarred outer leaves, until only pale green leaves remain. Trim away the tip of the stem and peel the stem itself. As you finish each artichoke, rub the cut spots with the lemon half to prevent the flesh from turning brown or cover with acidulated water until ready to use. The choke of a baby artichoke is edible after cooking, so you don't need to remove it.

Creamed Corn with Squash Blossoms and Scallions

My *paternal grandmother was a* primly delicate little woman who declined to eat with her fingers. She made stripping the kernels off an ear of corn at one's plate without causing the kernels or cob to fly across the table appear to be simply one of those skills that any well-mannered Philadelphia lady was assumed to know. In her kitchen (*not* at the table) she taught me to rub the back of a knife against the stripped cob to extract the hidden "corn milk." Her own creamed corn was an exercise in simplicity—corn, butter, cream, salt, and pepper. You don't have to really do too much more than that, especially with today's super-sweet varieties of corn, but if you have a garden with zucchini vines and their blossoms, or a vendor in your local farmers' market who will sell you the blossoms, then this recipe is a treat.

MAKES 4 SIDE-DISH SERVINGS

6 ears corn

2 tablespoons unsalted butter

1 small onion, finely diced

Kosher salt and freshly ground black pepper

16 squash blossoms, stamens removed

½ cup crème fraîche

2 tablespoons finely chopped fresh basil

2 to 3 scallions, trimmed and thinly sliced

1. Husk the corn and strip the kernels off the cobs. Rub the dull edge of a knife down the stripped cobs to extract the corn "milk." Set aside.

2. Heat 1 tablespoon of the butter in a large sauté pan over medium heat. Add the onion, season with salt and pepper, and cook until tender, about 5 minutes. Add the corn kernels and corn milk. Cook until the corn is tender, 3 to 4 minutes. Transfer 1 cup of the corn to a food processor and purée. Return the corn purée to the pan and stir everything together. Set aside.

3. In a second large sauté pan, melt the remaining 1 tablespoon butter over high heat. Add the squash blossoms, season with salt and pepper, and sear until wilted and golden on both sides, about 3 minutes per side. Transfer the blossoms to the pan with the corn.

4. Lower the heat to medium. Add the crème fraîche, basil, and scallions, season with salt and pepper, and cook over medium heat until heated through. Serve immediately.

Simple Favas with Butter

This is both the simplest and most luxurious recipe in this book. The fresh flavor of favas transcends their humble origin as a bean, but the effort involved in shelling and peeling them makes them the caviar of shell beans. As a result, a dish composed exclusively of favas is a rare luxury. One of the great joys of visiting the eastern Mediterranean is the popularity of fava bean purée, a gastronomic delight that is almost always too labor-intensive to think about doing here. Save this preparation for really good friends, to accompany a wonderful roasted meat dish like rack of spring lamb. Then again, you could just eat them all yourself.

MAKES 4 SIDE-DISH SERVINGS

2 tablespoons unsalted butter

1½ to 2 cups shelled fava beans, long-blanched (see Fava Notes, page 88) and peeled (about 3 pounds in the pod)

Kosher salt and freshly ground black pepper

Melt the butter in a large sauté pan over medium-high heat. When the foam subsides, add the favas, season with salt and pepper, and toss until heated through. Serve immediately.

FAVA NOTES

Fava beans are usually sold in their large plump pods. You can count on getting ½ to ¾ cup of beans for each pound of fava pods. (If you get more, consider yourself lucky.) Unlike other beans, which have only to be shelled, favas need to be blanched and then peeled, which makes them quite labor-intensive. The only exception to this is very young favas, no larger than, say, navy beans. Personally, I find it soothing to peel them while listening to tango or opera. The ubiquitous popularity of favas in Mediterranean countries can only be a sign of a saner, slower approach to life. Still, you needn't commit to listening to the entire production of *Aïda* to enjoy them. A small portion of favas, with their bright green color and distinctive flavor, makes a welcome component in vegetable stews or one of several ingredients in a pasta sauce.

THE SHORT BLANCH ‹s Before you can peel favas, you have to shuck them. Snap the stem end off the pod and peel away the "thread" down one of the seams. You can then snap the pod open by running your thumb along the seam. Shovel the beans out of the open pod with your thumb. The individual beans will still be covered with a thick green membranous skin and need to be blanched to loosen the skin. Blanch the favas in salted boiling water for 1 minute, then plunge them into a bowl of ice water to stop the cooking. After draining the beans, you can either pinch the skin off with your fingers or use a paring knife. I pinch off a piece of the skin near the thick end of the bean, then squeeze from the other end so the fava pops out of the hole. After the membranes are removed, the favas are ready (at last!) to be treated like any other raw vegetable.

After a few beans, you will become quite practiced at this technique. I suggest putting on a good tango CD. Your fingers will seem to work by themselves as you imagine yourself spinning across the floor in a Buenos Aires dance hall.

THE LONG BLANCH ‹s The problem with the traditional shuck-blanch-peel method is that afterward you've still got to cook them, which means another blanching or braising or whatever. I've found that you can save yourself a step if you extend the blanching time—in other words, you precook them in their membranes. Although you still need to peel them, they will require little additional cooking. Fava beans vary in size, and large ones take longer to cook than small ones. Let them boil for 3 minutes, then scoop one out of the water, peel it, and taste. If it no longer tastes raw, they're done. Plunge them into ice water, then drain and peel. If they're not done, let them cook for another 30 seconds and try again.

I use the long-blanch method 90 percent of the time when I'm cooking favas. If I'm going to add them to a dish that will then continue to braise for another 8 to 10 minutes, I use the short blanch.

Favas and Fiddleheads with Garlic and Pancetta

*T*his is a pretty dish that not only tastes good but, with two shades of intense green, seems just the ticket for celebrating the springtime arrival of local greens, especially fiddleheads from New Hampshire and Maine. After relying for several months on root vegetables and imported greens, I can't wait to begin putting fresh local produce back on the table. The availability of fiddleheads, bright green curls of baby fern, limited to only a few weeks in late spring and early summer, makes this a once-a-year combination. The earthy, fecund flavor of fiddleheads takes well to the meaty taste of pancetta. It seemed natural to me to mix them with favas (even if they are from California), another item commonly paired in Italy with pancetta or prosciutto.

MAKES 4 SIDE-DISH SERVINGS

½ pound fiddlehead ferns, trimmed of any split, broken, or dirty stems

Kosher salt

2 ounces thinly sliced pancetta, cut into ½-inch pieces

2 tablespoons extra virgin olive oil

2 garlic cloves, thinly sliced

1 cup shelled fava beans, long-blanched (see Fava Notes, page 88) and peeled (about 2 pounds in the pod)

Freshly ground black pepper

1 tablespoon freshly squeezed lemon juice

1. Drop the fiddleheads into a bowl of room-temperature water. Swirl with your hand to remove the brown papery parts.

2. Bring a large pot of salted water to a boil. While it's heating, prepare a bowl of ice water. Add the fiddleheads to the boiling water and blanch until tender, 7 to 8 minutes. Drain and immediately plunge the fiddleheads into the ice water to stop the cooking; drain thoroughly.

3. Heat a large sauté pan over medium-high heat. Add the pancetta and cook until it begins to render its fat and get crispy, about 4 minutes. Add the olive oil and garlic. Cook until the garlic is aromatic, just a minute. (If it starts to sizzle as soon as it hits the pan, lower the heat so it doesn't burn.) Add the favas and fiddleheads, season with salt and pepper, and cook, stirring occasionally, until they're heated through. Drizzle with the lemon juice and serve immediately.

Warm Spring Vegetable Salad with Favas, Green Beans, Peas, and Radicchio

T*his dish builds on one* of my favorite Italian vegetable combinations, a warm salad of radicchio and blanched peas. I've simply taken it several steps further by adding two other spring arrivals, favas and thin green beans. Bring a large pot of salted water to a boil and blanch the vegetables in sequence, transferring them to a bowl of ice water as they finish cooking. The salad is dressed with a cream and lemon vinaigrette, which may sound unusual but is a great match with the vegetables. Please don't skip the favas—they add a wonderful element in both taste and texture. You can cut down on serving-day preparation time by blanching the vegetables a day ahead. Refrigerate in resealable plastic bags, then assemble the salad just before serving.

MAKES 4 SIDE-DISH SERVINGS

¾ cup extra virgin olive oil

1 large red onion (about ½ pound), sliced ¼ inch thick

2 large heads radicchio, washed, dried, cored, and cut crosswise into ½-inch-wide strips

Kosher salt and freshly ground black pepper

½ pound thin green beans, trimmed and blanched in boiling salted water until just cooked, about 4 minutes

½ pound fresh peas, shelled and blanched in boiling salted water until just cooked, 1 to 3 minutes, depending on their size

1½ to 2 cups shelled fava beans, long-blanched (see Fava Notes, page 88), and peeled (about 3 pounds in the pod)

¼ cup coarsely chopped fresh flat-leaf parsley

2 tablespoons chopped fresh thyme

1 teaspoon finely chopped fresh rosemary

1 teaspoon grated lemon zest

3 to 4 tablespoons freshly squeezed lemon juice

¼ cup light cream

1. Heat ¼ cup of the olive oil in a large sauté pan over medium-high heat. Add the onion and cook until translucent, about 3 minutes. Turn the heat to high, add the radicchio, and sear until browned. Season with salt and pepper and cook for 4 minutes. Lower the heat to medium, add the green beans, peas, and favas, and cook until just heated through. Season with salt and pepper and add the parsley and thyme. Remove from the heat and arrange on a platter.

2. In a medium bowl, whisk together the rosemary, lemon zest, 3 tablespoons lemon juice (if you like tart vinaigrettes, use more), and the remaining ½ cup olive oil. Whisk in the cream. Season with salt and pepper.

3. Drizzle the vinaigrette over the vegetables and serve. (If you're going to have leftovers, dress only the portion you are serving, and store the remaining vegetables and vinaigrette separately in the refrigerator.) Serve at room temperature.

Fiery Garlicky Greens

I can't tell whether my taste buds have become desensitized or broccoli rabe has become milder over the years. My first taste of broccoli rabe more than twenty-five years ago struck me as both wonderful and shockingly bitter. I still love it, but it no longer seems as strong. I recently came across a recipe written some ten years ago advising readers to blanch broccoli rabe for a full five minutes in order to remove the bitterness. When my husband cooks it, he often skips the blanching altogether or simply braises the rabe in a covered pan with a little water for a couple of minutes. By the time the rabe has finished cooking, the water's gone—and the rabe tastes fine.

The traditional matches for broccoli rabe include raisins, pine nuts, garlic, and hot red pepper flakes. In this recipe, I've paired it with other sharp greens that can stand up to hot red pepper flakes. The greens are delicious served cold as well as hot, so they make a great picnic dish.

MAKES 4 SIDE-DISH SERVINGS

Kosher salt

1½ pounds broccoli rabe, washed and trimmed of tough or split stems

⅓ cup extra virgin olive oil

8 garlic cloves, sliced paper-thin

½ pound chicory, washed and chopped crosswise into 2-inch sections

½ pound arugula, washed

½ to ¾ teaspoon hot red pepper flakes

DO AHEAD: The broccoli rabe can be blanched ahead of time. Just be sure to plunge it into cold water to stop the cooking, then drain and refrigerate until ready to use.

1. Bring a large pot of salted water to a boil. Blanch the broccoli rabe for 3 minutes, then plunge it immediately into an ice bath to stop the cooking. Drain and set aside.

2. Combine the olive oil and garlic in a large sauté pan over medium-low heat and cook until the garlic is just golden around the edges, 8 to 10 minutes. Do not let the garlic burn. Remove the garlic from the pan and set it aside.

3. Increase the heat to high, add the broccoli rabe and chicory, and cook until the chicory has wilted. Add the arugula, season with salt, and add red pepper flakes to taste. Cook until the arugula wilts, stirring frequently. It will only take a minute or two, so don't take your eye off the pan, or the arugula will overcook. Return the garlic to the pan, stir, and serve immediately.

Leek, Artichoke, and Fennel Strudel

This versatile phyllo pastry roll is stuffed with an aromatic combination of leeks, artichokes, fennel, potatoes, and goat cheese. With phyllo, an amateur can look like a professional, and the final dish is adaptable to however you want to serve it. The roll of strudel can be cut into portions appropriate for side dishes for four or an entrée for two.

You can prepare as much or as little of this dish ahead as you wish, short of the final baking. You can cook the vegetables a day ahead and then assemble the strudel before baking. The strudel can even be completely assembled and refrigerated overnight until ready to bake.

MAKES 4 SIDE-DISH SERVINGS OR 2 ENTRÉE SERVINGS

½ pound Red Bliss potatoes, scrubbed
Kosher salt
¼ cup extra virgin olive oil
2 large leeks, white part only, trimmed of roots and tough outer leaves, sliced ¼ inch thick crosswise, and swirled vigorously in a bowl of cold water to remove any grit
2 small fennel bulbs, trimmed of stalks and tough outer layers, cut lengthwise in half, cored, and thinly sliced crosswise
Freshly ground black pepper
½ pound trimmed baby artichokes (about 1¼ pounds, untrimmed; see page 85), cut into quarters (if baby artichokes are unavailable, substitute a 9-ounce package frozen artichoke hearts, thawed)
6 small or 4 large garlic cloves, finely chopped
½ teaspoon fennel seeds
½ teaspoon ground coriander
1 teaspoon chopped fresh thyme
½ teaspoon chopped fresh rosemary
½ cup dry white wine
½ cup water
1 cup chopped fresh flat-leaf parsley
2 teaspoons freshly squeezed lemon juice
About 2 ounces (½ cup) freshly grated Parmesan

About 5 ounces (1 cup) crumbled feta cheese
8 sheets phyllo dough
½ stick unsalted butter, melted

1. Chop the potatoes into ¼-inch dice. Put into a small pot, add cold water to cover by 1 inch, and season with salt. Bring to a boil. Reduce the heat and simmer until the potatoes are tender, about 10 minutes. Drain and let cool.

2. While the potatoes are cooking, heat the olive oil in a large sauté pan over medium heat. Add the leeks and fennel and season with salt and pepper. Cook for 5 minutes until they begin to get tender. Add the artichokes, garlic, fennel seeds, coriander, thyme, and rosemary and cook until the leeks and fennel are tender, 5 to 7 minutes. (If using frozen artichoke hearts, wait to add them until the next step.)

3. Add the wine and water. Continue cooking, stirring occasionally, until the artichokes are tender and the liquid has evaporated, about 8 minutes. Add the potatoes and toss well. Let cool.

4. Preheat the oven to 350°F.

5. Add the parsley, lemon juice, Parmesan, and feta cheese to the vegetables and toss well. Taste for seasoning and adjust as necessary.

6. Lay a sheet of phyllo dough out on the counter with a long edge toward you. Brush with a thin coat of melted butter. Carefully position a second sheet of phyllo atop the first and brush it with a teaspoon of melted butter. Continue until you have a stack of 4 phyllo sheets. Arrange half of the vegetables in a narrow mound running along the bottom edge of the phyllo stack. Roll up tightly. Brush the log with 1 teaspoon butter. Repeat to make a second log.

7. Trim the ends of the logs, then cut each log into 4 pieces. Set on a buttered baking sheet. Bake until golden brown, about 45 minutes.

8. Arrange on a platter, or place 2 pieces on each of four warm plates.

NOTE: Frozen artichoke hearts can be substituted for fresh baby artichokes if the latter are unavailable. Do not use marinated artichokes (the kind that come in a jar)—their taste is too sharp. Add the artichokes in Step 3, after most of the water has evaporated. Since frozen artichoke hearts are already cooked, they only need to be in the pan long enough to warm. Allow the rest of the liquid to evaporate and continue with the recipe.

Braised Escarole with Parmesan Crust

Escarole intimidates people. People who think nothing of sautéing spinach or Swiss chard shy away from it. Its coarse fibrous leaves seem just too strange to mess with, which is unfortunate, because braising melts the plant's fibers into a silky, spinach-like consistency. I particularly like to pair braised escarole with bold-flavored meat dishes, like Roasted Marinated Long Island Duck with Green Olive and Balsamic Vinegar Sauce (page 316) or Roast Leg of Lamb with Mustard Crumbs (page 282).

MAKES 4 SIDE-DISH SERVINGS

1 large head escarole

¼ cup extra virgin olive oil

Kosher salt and freshly ground black pepper

1 medium white onion, thinly sliced

2 garlic cloves, chopped

2 teaspoons chopped fresh rosemary

2 teaspoons chopped fresh sage

1 teaspoon grated lemon zest

1 cup Chicken Stock (page 31) or high-quality canned low-sodium chicken broth

¼ cup dry white wine

½ cup freshly grated Parmesan

¼ cup fresh bread crumbs

DO AHEAD: The escarole can be braised several days ahead and refrigerated until you are ready to serve it, which can be quite convenient if you're serving it with something else that requires your attention. If braising ahead, omit the crust of cheese and bread crumbs. To reheat, first bring it to room temperature, then put it in a 375°F oven for 10 minutes. Remove from the oven, top with the crust ingredients, and return to the oven until the crust browns, about 15 minutes.

1. Preheat oven to 325°F.

2. Cut the escarole lengthwise into quarters, wash thoroughly (see box), and pat completely dry.

3. Heat 3 tablespoons of the olive oil in a large ovenproof sauté pan or flameproof gratin dish over medium heat. (It's important to use a shallow pan with low sides so excess moisture can evaporate as the dish cooks.) Sear the escarole until browned and season with salt and pepper. Transfer to a plate.

4. Reduce the heat to medium-low, add the remaining 1 tablespoon olive oil, onions, and garlic to the pan, and cook until the onion is tender, about 10 minutes.

5. Return the escarole to the pan and add the herbs, lemon zest, chicken stock, and wine. Bring to a boil and cook for 10 minutes, or until the liquid is reduced to a third of its original volume. Cover the escarole with a piece of foil, transfer to the oven and braise for 30 minutes, or until it is tender and the liquid has been absorbed.

6. Take the pan out of the oven and increase the oven temperature to 400°F. Remove the foil and sprinkle the cheese and crumbs over the top of the escarole. Return the pan to the oven and bake until a golden brown crust forms, about 15 minutes. Serve immediately.

HOW TO CLEAN ESCAROLE

Nothing ruins a dish of escarole faster than the sudden awareness that it is still gritty. Extra pains must be taken to clean escarole when the heads are simply quartered or halved before cooking (individual leaves are easy to rinse). Begin by letting the cut-up escarole rest for a minute in a large pot filled with warm water. The warm water relaxes the escarole, allowing the sand trapped between the leaves at the base of each section to rinse free. Slide your fingers between the leaves as far as they will go toward the base without breaking the leaves and shake vigorously. Repeat with each section, then change the water and wash the escarole again. Inspect the base of each section for any remaining grit. If necessary, rinse again so they're completely clean. Drain and pat dry.

Braised Eggplant and Red Peppers with Honey and Spices

I *began experimenting with toasted spice* seeds about fifteen years ago, after encountering them in Middle Eastern dishes. At first glance this dish might be mistaken for ratatouille, but the toasted mustard, coriander, and cumin seeds move it into a more exotic culinary zone. Because the dish is good hot or cold, it, works well on picnics or as a complement to grilled meats (no running between outdoor grill and kitchen).

On a technical note, eggplant is a sponge for oil. If you broil it, as indicated below, you can give it a great color without having to use as much oil as you would to get the same effect by sautéing. Secondly, the skin of Japanese eggplant is much more delicate than that of its Italian or American counterpart. You don't need to peel it before cooking.

I like including leftovers on a plate of Middle Eastern dishes served at room temperature. With some high-quality Greek or Armenian whole-milk yogurt, a few olives, hummus, and pita, it's all I need for lunch.

MAKES 4 SIDE-DISH SERVINGS OR ENOUGH SAUCE FOR 1 POUND PASTA

½ teaspoon mustard seeds

½ teaspoon coriander seeds

¼ teaspoon cumin seeds

4 Japanese eggplants (about 1 pound), sliced on a diagonal about 1 inch thick

6 tablespoons extra virgin olive oil

Kosher salt and freshly ground black pepper

1 medium onion, chopped into ¼-inch dice

2 red peppers, peeled with a vegetable peeler, stemmed, seeded, and chopped into 1-inch pieces

4 garlic cloves, minced

1 teaspoon minced fresh ginger

½ cup cherry tomatoes, cut in half

½ cup water

1 tablespoon chopped fresh mint

2 tablespoons chopped fresh flat-leaf parsley

1 tablespoon honey

1 tablespoon red wine vinegar

1. Toast the mustard, coriander, and cumin seeds in a small dry pan over low heat until they start to pop, 3 to 5 minutes; do not allow to burn. Remove from the heat. When the seeds are cool, grind them in a spice mill or crush them into a powder with a mortar and pestle.

2. Preheat the broiler. Toss the eggplant slices in a large bowl with 3 tablespoons of the olive oil. Season with salt and pepper. Arrange the eggplant slices in a single layer on a sheet pan and broil until golden brown, about 5 minutes. Flip the pieces and broil for 5 minutes on the other side, or until golden brown. Set aside.

3. Heat the remaining 3 tablespoons olive oil in a large heavy-bottomed sauté pan over medium heat. Add the onion and red peppers and cook until tender, about 7 minutes. Season with salt

and pepper. Add the garlic and ginger and continue cooking until they release their perfume, a couple of minutes. Add the eggplant, tomatoes, and water. Cover with a tight-fitting lid, lower the heat, and simmer for 10 minutes.

Taste and adjust the salt and pepper if necessary.

4. Stir in the mint, parsley, honey, and red wine vinegar. Remove from the heat. Serve hot or at room temperature.

Roasted Red Saffron Peppers with Mint and Chiles

A *Spanish* tapa, *one of those* elegant little dishes designed to accompany aperitifs, gave me the idea for this dish, which tastes as bright as its wonderful hue. You can find saffron and peppers in one combination or another all along the Mediterranean shoreline of Spain and France, but the sherry vinegar is a distinctly Spanish touch. This is a great dish to prepare at the end of the summer, when red peppers are cheap and you've fired up the charcoal grill. The smoky flavor from grilling the peppers makes the dish all that much richer.

Serve the peppers as a side dish with grilled chicken or pork, or chop them up and use as a relish with the same food, served cold. The peppers will keep for up to a week if refrigerated.

MAKES 4 SIDE-DISH SERVINGS

¼ cup extra virgin olive oil

1 medium onion, cut into ¼-inch-thick slices

2 garlic cloves, chopped

¼ teaspoon hot red pepper flakes

½ teaspoon paprika, preferably Spanish

¼ teaspoon saffron

4 red peppers, roasted (see box), peeled, stemmed, seeds and membranes removed, and sliced into 1-inch-wide strips

2 tablespoons sherry vinegar

Kosher salt and freshly ground black pepper

2 tablespoons chopped fresh mint

DO AHEAD: Roast, peel, seed, and slice the peppers, then refrigerate them until you're ready to finish the recipe. If you're preparing the dish a day ahead, omit the mint until just before serving.

1. Heat the oil in a large sauté pan over medium heat. Add the onion and cook until tender, about 10 minutes. Add the garlic, red pepper flakes, paprika, and saffron and cook until the garlic releases its perfume, a couple of minutes.

2. Add the peppers and sherry vinegar. Season with salt and pepper, turn the heat to low, and cook for another 3 minutes. Stir in the mint and serve.

HOW TO ROAST PEPPERS

MAKES AS MANY AS YOU LIKE.

Roasted red peppers are one of the few pantry staples in our house whose versatility approaches that of roasted garlic. When puréed, they flavor and thicken soups and sauces. They make great sandwiches, especially with mozzarella, roast beef, or cured Italian meats. And a few roasted peppers are halfway to one of my favorite dishes, Panzanella (page 71).

The recipes in this book call for roasted red (or yellow) peppers, but you can apply the technique to any pepper with a thick layer of flesh. Peppers with thin walls don't have enough flesh left after peeling to make roasting them worthwhile. Take care when charring the peppers not to take them beyond the black-and-barely-blistered stage, or you'll burn the flesh as well as the skin.

Roasted peppers will keep for 4 to 5 days if tightly wrapped and refrigerated. Covered in olive oil in an airtight container and refrigerated, they will last for 2 weeks. Always use a fork or tongs to remove them from the container, to avoid introducing bacteria from your skin into the oil.

1. Preheat the broiler or prepare a hot fire in a grill.

2. Set the peppers on a rack close to the heat. Broil or grill the peppers on one side until their skins begin to blister and blacken, then turn and repeat, turning as necessary, until the peppers have blackened all over. Depending on the size of the peppers, the process will take 10 to 20 minutes.

3. Put the peppers in a paper bag, close the bag, and allow to cool. As the peppers cool down, moisture will condense between the flesh of the peppers and their charred skins, making them easy to peel.

4. As soon as they're cool enough to be handled, remove the peppers from the bag and rub off their skins with a kitchen towel or your fingers. Their skins should slip off easily. Some people like to peel them under cool running water, but I prefer the messier method I've described; peeling them under water seems to remove some of the roasted flavor. Remove the stems, seeds, and membranes with a paring knife. If not using immediately, refrigerate them in a nonreactive container. (If you like, cover them with extra virgin olive oil for longer keeping.)

Sweet-and-Sour Shallots

A *companion dish of onions, shallots,* and even garlic is common with main courses in Italy and France. I'm indebted to Boston chef Laura Brennan for introducing me to the recipe I've adapted here. The shallots are browned in butter, then cooked in seasoned chicken stock, balsamic vinegar, and port, which reduces to a rich golden glaze. Serve the shallots as a warm side dish or a room-temperature condiment for meat. Leftovers with some goat cheese make an excellent pizza topping.

MAKES 4 SIDE-DISH SERVINGS

2 tablespoons unsalted butter

12 large shallots (or 12 cipolline or 24 pearl onions), peeled

Kosher salt and freshly ground black pepper

¼ cup port

¼ cup balsamic vinegar

2 tablespoons honey

2 bay leaves

1 teaspoon chopped fresh thyme

¼ teaspoon fennel seeds

1 cup Chicken Stock (page 31) or high-quality canned low-sodium chicken broth

1. Melt the butter in a large sauté pan over medium heat. As soon as the butter stops foaming, add the shallots, season with salt and pepper, and brown all over. Lower the heat as necessary so the butter doesn't burn.

2. Add the remaining ingredients and continue cooking until the shallots are tender and the liquids have reduced to a glaze, about 20 minutes. Pay close attention so you don't overreduce the sauce. Remove the bay leaves and serve the shallots warm or at room temperature.

Wild Mushroom Fricassee

A *wild mushroom fricassee is a* woodsy, rustic take on sautéed mushrooms. The distinct textures, flavors, and appearance of the different fungi come through in the completed dish instead of dissipating into a general "mushroomy" flavor. The fricassee makes a great side dish with game, but you can also combine it with gnocchi or spaetzle for a fine entrée, especially for vegetarians, if you substitute light cream for the chicken stock. One of my favorite uses for the fricassee (omitting the chicken stock altogether so the mixture is drier) is in Roasted Potatoes Stuffed with Wild Mushrooms and Truffled Eggs (page 301).

MAKES 4 SIDE-DISH SERVINGS

1½ pounds assorted mushrooms (portabellas, oyster, shiitakes, or chanterelles), cleaned, shiitake stems discarded

3 to 5 tablespoons unsalted butter

Kosher salt and freshly ground black pepper

2 cups Chicken Stock (page 31) or 4 cups high-quality canned low-sodium chicken broth, reduced to 2 cups (see page 32)

3 shallots, minced

4 garlic cloves, minced

½ cup dry Marsala

1 teaspoon chopped fresh thyme

1. Chop the mushrooms into pieces 2 to 3 inches long, as necessary: I like to leave wild mushrooms as whole or as large as is practical, especially the really beautiful ones like morels and chanterelles.

2. Sauté the mushrooms in batches, each type individually. Heat 1 tablespoon of the butter in a large sauté pan over medium heat. As soon as it stops foaming, add the first batch of mushrooms and season with salt and pepper. If you add the mushrooms before the butter stops foaming, the pan won't be hot enough to sear. Don't crowd the pan—if you cook too many mushrooms at once, they tend to steam instead of sear. Sauté the mushrooms until they are tender and their juices have evaporated, then transfer to a plate. Add another tablespoon of butter to the pan and, as soon as it stops foaming, add the next batch of mushrooms. Continue until you've cooked all the mushrooms, adding a tablespoon of butter to the pan before each new batch.

3. While the mushrooms are cooking, bring the chicken stock to a simmer in a saucepan over medium heat and simmer until it reduces to 1 cup, about 15 minutes.

4. After removing the final batch of mushrooms from the pan, lower the heat to medium. Add ½ tablespoon butter to the pan, along with the shallots and garlic (do not wait for the butter to foam), and cook until the shallots are tender, about 3 minutes. Return all the mushrooms to the pan, add the Marsala and thyme, and cook until the Marsala has reduced by half.

5. Add the chicken stock to the mushrooms, simmer and reduce to make a slightly soupy sauce. Taste and adjust the seasoning as necessary. Serve immediately.

Orange Beets

I use this recipe more than any other for preparing beets. The orange flavor is so light it's almost undetectable—until you take it away. Served warm, these beets make a simple side dish, but they can just as well be the jumping-off point for a cold beet salad or a startling addition to risotto.

If skinning beets seems too messy for the last minute before serving, make the beets ahead, then reheat them in a little extra virgin olive oil or butter.

MAKES 4 SIDE-DISH SERVINGS

2 oranges, washed and quartered

1 small onion, chopped into ½-inch dice

1 teaspoon coriander seeds

4 bay leaves

1 tablespoon fennel seeds

6 medium beets, washed and greens trimmed to an inch

Kosher salt and freshly ground black pepper

1. Squeeze the orange quarters to release their juice into a large nonreactive saucepan that will hold the beets in a single layer. Add the rinds and all the remaining ingredients, seasoning with salt and pepper. Add enough water to cover the beets by an inch. Cover and bring to a boil, then reduce the heat to a simmer and continue cooking until the beets are tender. Depending on the size of the beets, they'll take from 45 minutes to an hour to cook. Allow the beets to cool slightly in the cooking liquid.

2. As soon as the beets are cool enough to handle, remove the skins and stems (see box). Cut into slices or quarters, season with salt and pepper, and serve immediately.

ON PEELING COOKED BEETS

Disposable surgical gloves are a godsend when it comes to preparing beets. You can work while the beets are still warm because the gloves provide a layer of insulation, and the latex surface has enough "grab" that you can just rub the skins and stems off. No need for a knife. Since they also protect your hands from staining, you don't have to peel the beets under running water, a technique that robs them of flavor. Surgical plastic gloves are available at hardware or kitchen equipment stores. A kitchen towel—an old one, so you don't care if it stains—also makes a fine tool for rubbing the skins off beets (or roasted peppers).

The French, recognizing the virtues of beets as well as their vices, have the right idea when it comes to beets. French shoppers can purchase beets already cooked and peeled—and preserved in Cryovac. All flavor and no mess.

Celery Root Purée

Most people first come to know celery root (also called celeriac) as a crunchy salad ingredient, perhaps in celery root rémoulade, a French preparation of celery root matchsticks in a mayonnaise sauce flavored with mustard. It also makes a wonderful purée. For those unfamiliar with celery root's taste ("what *is* this?") the identity of the purée is a pleasant dinner revelation. Butter and cream enhance the flavor instead of overwhelming it. You can extend celery root with potatoes, but I'd rather save my money for the unadulterated dish. It's unmatched with pork and apples as a cold-weather combination.

Celery root's knobby exterior is more easily skinned with a sharp paring knife than a vegetable peeler. Keep cut celery root in water acidulated with a little lemon juice (see page 84) so it doesn't discolor.

MAKES 4 SIDE-DISH SERVINGS

4 tablespoon unsalted butter

1 small onion, sliced ¼ inch thick

Kosher salt and freshly ground black pepper

1 celery root (about 1 pound), peeled and diced into
   1-inch cubes

2 garlic cloves, minced

1½ cups Chicken Stock (page 31) or high-quality
   canned low-sodium chicken broth

1 small apple, peeled, cored, and cut into
   8 wedges

Up to ¼ cup heavy cream (optional)

2 tablespoons freshly squeezed lemon juice

1. Heat 2 tablespoons of the butter in a heavy saucepan over medium heat and sauté the onions until lightly browned, 10 to 15 minutes. Take care not to burn them. Season with salt and pepper. Transfer the onions to a bowl.

2. Add the remaining 2 tablespoons butter to the saucepan, increase the heat to medium-high, and sear the celery root until lightly browned on all sides. Turn the heat to low. Add the garlic, return the onions to the pan, and season with salt and pepper. Add the chicken stock and apple pieces, cover, and cook until the celery root is tender enough to purée and the stock has reduced to a glaze, about an hour.

3. Purée the celery root. The texture should resemble mashed potatoes. For a smoother texture add the optional cream. Add the lemon juice. Taste for seasoning, add more salt and pepper, if necessary, and serve.

Glazed Carrots in Honey and Orange Juice with Black Sesame Seeds and Mint

I *picked up some black sesame* seeds at a Middle Eastern market one October and after putting them on the shelf at home promptly forgot about them. A few weeks later, I was desperately scavenging through our larder for *something* that would qualify our meal of chicken and rice as an official Halloween dinner, and I chanced on the black sesame seeds. The rest was simple luck, fresh carrots in the refrigerator, and a thriving stand of mint on the edge of our yard that hadn't yet realized the season was over. The combination of mint, citrus, and sesame evokes an eastern Mediterranean harmony, while the sesame seeds' color makes a striking visual impression.

MAKES 4 SIDE-DISH SERVINGS

1 pound small carrots

1 tablespoon vegetable oil

Kosher salt and freshly ground black pepper

1 tablespoon finely chopped fresh ginger

1 garlic clove, finely chopped

1 tablespoon chopped shallots

2 tablespoons honey

½ cup freshly squeezed orange juice

1 tablespoon soy sauce

¼ cup water

1 teaspoon sesame oil

1 tablespoon chopped fresh mint

1 teaspoon black sesame seeds (available in Middle Eastern markets and health food stores)

1. Peel the carrots and cut into 2-inch lengths on the diagonal. If the carrots are thicker than your finger, first slice them in half lengthwise, before sectioning them.

2. Heat the oil in a medium sauté pan over high heat and sear the carrots until lightly browned. Season with salt and pepper. Turn the heat to low, add the ginger, garlic, and shallots, and cook until tender, 5 to 7 minutes.

3. Add the honey, orange juice, soy sauce, and ¼ cup water. Cover the pan and continue cooking, tossing occasionally, until the carrots are tender and the liquids have reduced to a glaze, about 30 minutes.

4. Remove from the heat and toss with the sesame oil, mint, and sesame seeds. Taste for seasoning and adjust the salt and pepper. Serve immediately.

Skordalia—Garlic Mashed Potatoes

In its homeland of Greece, skordalia blurs the distinctions between sauce and condiment, between condiment and side dish, between hot and room-temperature food. Whatever it is, skordalia can become an addictive replacement for ordinary mashed potatoes. The dominant flavors are of potato, olive oil, raw garlic, and vinegar; the combination is at once sensual and primitive.

Don't try to take shortcuts by using a food processor instead of ricing the potatoes and then whipping in the garlic and oil by hand. The potatoes will turn gummy instead of remaining starchy, and the garlic will taste too strong.

MAKES 4 SIDE-DISH SERVINGS

2 pounds baking potatoes, peeled and cut into
    large pieces
Kosher salt
4 garlic cloves, minced and then mashed with
    ¼ teaspoon salt to a paste
½ cup plus 2 tablespoons extra virgin olive oil
5 teaspoons champagne vinegar (or high-quality
    white wine vinegar)
Freshly ground black pepper

1. Put the potatoes in a saucepan, add cold water to cover by 1 inch, season with salt, and bring to a boil. Reduce the heat and simmer until the potatoes are tender, about 20 minutes. Be careful not to overcook them, or they will become waterlogged.

2. Drain, return the potatoes to the pan, and cook over medium heat tossing a few times until dry, about 5 minutes.

3. While the potatoes are still warm, push them through a ricer into a large bowl. (Don't let them cool, or they'll be too gummy to push through the ricer.) Beat in the garlic and olive oil. Add the vinegar and season with salt and pepper to taste. Serve warm or at room temperature.

Versatile Buttermilk Mashed Potatoes

Buttermilk contributes a lightly acid contrast to the rich influence of butter and cream in these straightforward mashed potatoes, but use whole milk if that's what you want. Mashed potatoes are among the most adaptable of all side dishes. Two short variations follow the master recipe. We like the lemony mashed potatoes with braised lamb or with grilled tuna; when we're having steak, we usually opt for the roasted garlic version.

MAKES 4 SIDE-DISH SERVINGS

2 pounds baking potatoes, peeled and cut into large pieces
Kosher salt
⅓ cup heavy cream
⅓ cup buttermilk
4 tablespoons unsalted butter at room temperature, cut into 4 pieces
Freshly ground black pepper

1. Put the potatoes in a medium saucepan, add cold water to cover by 1 inch, season with salt, and bring to a boil. Reduce the heat and simmer until the potatoes are tender, about 20 minutes. Be careful not to overcook them, or they will become waterlogged.

2. Drain, return the potatoes to the pan, and cook over medium heat, tossing a few times until dry, about 5 minutes.

3. While the potatoes are still warm, crush them with a potato masher. Alternatively, you can push them through a ricer into a bowl; just don't let them cool, or they'll be too gummy to push through the ricer.

4. Combine the cream and buttermilk in a small saucepan over medium heat. Heat just to the point of scalding; do not boil. Whisk the butter and the scalded cream mixture into the potatoes. Season with salt and pepper. Serve immediately.

Lemon Mashed Potatoes

Add 1 tablespoon grated lemon zest to the saucepan when heating the cream and buttermilk. Whisk 2 teaspoons freshly squeezed lemon juice into the potatoes along with the butter and the cream mixture in Step 4. If you're inclined to want more lemon flavor, increase the amounts of lemon zest and lemon juice cautiously. A subtle taste of lemon can become an overpowering one quite quickly. The only downside to adding lemon to mashed potatoes is that the taste soon fades. If you want to restore the lemon flavor in leftovers, whisk in freshly squeezed lemon juice just before serving.

Roasted Garlic Mashed Potatoes

For a strong flavor of raw garlic, go to Skordalia (page 106), but for a subtler, sweeter garlic flavor, mash ¼ cup Roasted Garlic (page 119) into a paste. Whisk the paste into the potatoes after adding the butter in Step 4.

Sweet Potato Mash

Sweet potatoes are a deliciously sugary tuber that puts in a brief appearance around Christmas. Maybe if they weren't usually served drowned in syrup, they wouldn't disappear for the rest of the year. Mashed sweet potatoes are just the right complement for pork and chicken, and leftovers can be used to thicken soup. A sweet potato mash also requires far less fat to bring up the flavor than conventional potatoes, an advantage if you're watching your weight. I've included orange juice in my recipe to provide an acidic citrus accent rather than to sweeten an already sugary vegetable. If you're unfamiliar with the selection and care of sweet potatoes, please read Sweet Potato Notes following this recipe.

MAKES 4 SIDE-DISH SERVINGS

3 orange sweet potatoes (about 2 pounds), scrubbed

4 tablespoons unsalted butter at room temperature, and cut into 4 pieces

¼ cup freshly squeezed orange juice

½ teaspoon minced fresh ginger

Kosher salt and freshly ground black pepper

1. Preheat the oven to 400°F.

2. Set the potatoes in a roasting pan. Roast until they're very soft and the tips are beginning to darken, about 1 hour.

3. Either wait until the potatoes are cool enough to handle with your bare hands, or use a dish towel to hold them. Cut them in half and scoop the flesh into a food processor. Add the butter, orange juice, and ginger; purée until smooth. Season with salt and pepper. Serve immediately.

SWEET POTATO NOTES

In recent years, finding true sweet-fleshed sweet potatoes has become a little more complicated than it used to be. Chances are just about any fresh tuber labeled "sweet potato" will in fact be one, but there are a few facts to bear in mind when making your selection. Sweet potatoes are often available in several different varieties, in a range of colors from pale orange to a deep red-orange. As a rule of thumb, the deeper the color, the sweeter the potato.

In many parts of the country, especially the South, people use the terms "sweet potato" and "yam" interchangeably. The vegetable that appears in a can of "candied yams" is an orange sweet potato. Nevertheless, sweet potatoes and true yams are two entirely different vegetables. Real yams are bigger, harder, and have darker skins than sweet potatoes, and they are not at all sweet. They are a vital staple in many parts of Africa and Latin America, both as a thickener for soups and stews and as a dish in their own right. It used to be that yams were sold only in markets catering to Latin and African populations, but now both kinds of tubers are often found in well-stocked produce departments. True yams have a bland flavor, which makes them a great foil for hot, spicy sauces, but a poor substitute in sweet potato recipes, which depend on a sweet-fleshed tuber.

Supermarket labeling is often inaccurate. If you're undecided as to whether to purchase a particular orange tuber for a recipe, ask if it's sweet. There are no sweet yams.

Whatever their color, sweet potatoes bruise more easily than regular potatoes and care should be taken in their handling. Use the same criteria for purchasing sweet potatoes as you would regular potatoes. They should be firm, without bruises, soft spots, or "eyes." Store them as you would regular potatoes (i.e., no refrigeration) in a cool, dry place with plenty of air circulating around them, but bear in mind that they have a much shorter storage life than potatoes—use them within a few days of purchase.

Crisp Shredded Potato Cakes with Crème Fraîche

You could probably walk from Paris to Krakow and never stray beyond hailing distance of a home where potato pancakes are eaten. If the citizens of any region eat potatoes, there's a good chance they have a recipe for potato pancakes. My two favorites are pommes Anna and rösti, from France and Switzerland respectively. For pommes Anna, several layers of thinly sliced potatoes overlap to build up the cake; rösti, on the other hand, are fashioned from one thin crisp layer of matchstick potatoes.

The potato cakes in this recipe are based on rösti. No flour or eggs are used to bind the potatoes; the starch in the potatoes themselves holds the pancakes together. The flavors of butter and potatoes come through slightly more strongly than they would otherwise. Besides serving these as a side dish, I sometimes use them as an exquisitely crisp base for a stew, or pair them with smoked salmon for brunch.

MAKES 4 SIDE-DISH SERVINGS

2 baking potatoes (approximately 1 pound)
Kosher salt and freshly ground black pepper
8 tablespoons (1 stick) unsalted butter, clarified
   (see page 111)
¼ cup minced white onion
¼ cup crème fraîche
2 tablespoons minced fresh chives

DO AHEAD: The potatoes can be peeled a few hours ahead of time, but do not shred them. Shredding releases the starch necessary to bind the potato cake together as it cooks; if the potatoes are shredded in advance, the starch will drain away in the water. Keep the whole peeled potatoes covered with water in a large bowl; pat dry before shredding.

1. Peel the potatoes. Shred them lengthwise on a grater or mandoline, using the "large" option, so that you produce the longest possible shreds. Season with salt and pepper.

2. Heat 2 tablespoons of the clarified butter in a 9-inch nonstick sauté pan over medium-high heat. Spread a quarter of the potatoes evenly in the pan. (This should produce a thin layer only a few shreds thick.) Sprinkle 1 tablespoon of the minced onion over the potatoes. Cook, uncovered, on the first side until golden brown, 3 to 4 minutes. Reduce the heat to medium if it seems as if the potatoes are starting to burn. As the grated potatoes cook, they'll stick together in a pancake. Don't disturb the potato cake until you're pretty sure it's cooked. Flip the cake and cook on the second side until golden brown, another 3 to 4 minutes. Transfer to a platter and keep warm in a low oven. Repeat to make 3 more cakes.

3. Top each potato cake with a tablespoon of crème fraîche, sprinkle with the chives, and serve immediately.

CLARIFIED BUTTER

Many of the recipes in this book ask you to sauté or fry ingredients in fat—olive oil, vegetable oil, or butter. Fat acts as a medium to transfer heat from the surface of the hot pan to the irregular surface of the food. By conducting heat into all the minuscule nooks and crannies in the surface of meat and vegetables, fat helps them to brown evenly (which is why it's so hard to brown things well in a nonstick skillet with no fat). In high-temperature frying, however, not all fats are created equal; some work better than others. The milk solids in whole butter, for example, burn at high temperatures, turning black and contributing an acrid flavor to whatever is being cooked. If you want to use butter for high-temperature frying, you've got to get rid of butter's milk solids first—you've got to clarify it. Clarified butter is pure butterfat, unlike regular whole butter, which also contains water and whey, as well as milk solids.

To make clarified butter, begin by bringing at least 1 stick of butter to a simmer in a small pan over low heat. Let it simmer slowly for 15 minutes. The butter should be barely moving. If it seems too active, lower the heat. A foamy layer of milk solids will gradually accumulate on the surface, and a layer of whey will sink to the bottom of the pan. Skim off the milk solids with a spoon. When all the milk solids have been removed, carefully decant the clear butterfat into a container, leaving behind the layer of whey. A stick of butter (¼ pound) will yield almost ½ cup clarified butter. It will easily keep for several weeks in the refrigerator, but it must be tightly covered, or it will absorb the odors of other stored food. Clarified butter can be frozen for 5 or 6 months.

Roasted Vegetables with Fresh Herbs and Pomegranate Seeds

The dominant flavors in this dish come from the caramelization of the vegetables themselves, brought into sharp focus by a mixture of fresh herbs sprinkled on the dish *after* the roasting. Vegetables roasted with herbs take on the flavor; if the herbs—especially distinctive herbs like sage and rosemary—are added later, they stand apart, like little bright lights of flavor drawing attention to the main attraction. The pomegranate seeds in this dish contribute both tartness and visual appeal—my kids love them.

MAKES 4 SIDE-DISH SERVINGS

1 medium red onion, skin on, cut lengthwise into quarters

1 medium sweet potato, peeled and cut lengthwise into quarters

4 small Red Bliss potatoes, washed and cut in half

4 medium beets, trimmed of greens, scrubbed, and quartered

4 small white turnips, peeled and cut in half

1 small acorn or dumpling squash, halved, seeded, and cut into eighths

2 heads garlic, cut in half across the cloves

¼ cup extra virgin olive oil

Kosher salt and freshly ground black pepper

2 tablespoons chopped mixed fresh herbs (flat-leaf parsley, rosemary, sage, and thyme)

¼ cup pomegranate seeds

1. Preheat the oven to 350°F.

2. Toss the onion, potatoes, beets, turnips, squash, and garlic with the olive oil and season with salt and pepper. Arrange in a single layer on a shallow baking pan and roast for 30 minutes. The vegetables will cook at slightly different rates—the squash and potatoes will cook the fastest; the beets will take longest. After 30 minutes, remove any vegetables that have become golden brown and tender. Keep them warm atop the stove as the remainder continues cooking. Check every 10 minutes after the first 30 minutes have elapsed. The total cooking time will be between 1 hour and 1 hour and 15 minutes.

3. When all the vegetables are done, slip the skins off the beets (see page 103), if desired. Remove the skin from the onion. Arrange the vegetables on a warm platter and sprinkle with the fresh herbs and pomegranate seeds. Serve immediately.

Roasted Spicy Curried Broccoli and Cauliflower

Even when not cooked to death, boiled broccoli and cauliflower taste insipid to me. But roasting, ah, . . . roasting is another story. Roasted, these vegetables actually taste as if they're meeting other ingredients halfway. I can't stand boiled broccoli with cheese sauce, but roasted broccoli dusted with a little Parmigiano-Reggiano is a ticket to culinary heaven. A complex, nut-like flavor emerges in roasted cauliflower that is completely absent in the boiled vegetable. Roasting elevates cauliflower to a partner with curry, instead of simply a medium for a creamed curry sauce.

MAKES 4 SIDE-DISH SERVINGS

1 pound broccoli
1 pound cauliflower
1 small red onion
3 garlic cloves, finely chopped
1 tablespoon curry powder
¼ teaspoon hot red pepper flakes
6 tablespoons extra virgin olive oil
Kosher salt

1. Preheat the oven to 325°F.

2. Using a sharp paring knife, cut the flowerets from the stems of the broccoli. Peel the stems and cut into 3-inch lengths. If the stems are more than an inch thick, split them lengthwise. Cut the cauliflower into small flowerets. Peel the onion and cut into ½-inch-thick slices.

3. Put the vegetables into a bowl and toss with the garlic, curry powder, red pepper flakes, and olive oil. Season with salt.

4. Arrange the vegetables in a single layer in a roasting pan and place in the middle of the oven. After 20 minutes, toss the vegetables so they will cook evenly. Continue roasting until all the vegetables are tender and browned, about another 20 minutes. Serve.

Winter Vegetable Gratin with Cranberries and Chestnuts

I f we ever decide to sell our house, I'll have this gratin warming in the oven when prospective buyers drop by. The aroma of baking pears, celery root, and potatoes with cream and cheese generates an irresistible atmosphere of comfort. A specialty of the French alpine region of Savoie, gratins were designed to take advantage of the heat of a cooling bread oven. Thinly sliced autumn and winter vegetables would be layered in a shallow ceramic or glazed earthenware dish, covered with heavy cream or broth, and baked uncovered at a low temperature until the liquid was completely absorbed. This gratin could serve as the main course of a meal for 6, or more as a side dish.

I've made some adjustments, using a deeper baking dish than usual and cutting the typical 4 cups of cream back to 2 since most of us won't have the opportunity of working off the previous night's dinner by milking a herd of cows or setting off on an alpine trek the next morning.

MAKES 8 TO 10 SIDE-DISH SERVINGS

SPECIAL EQUIPMENT: A 3-quart baking dish is essential for this recipe. You need at least 1½ inches of space between the top of the vegetables and the rim of the dish. This is to accommodate the 4½ cups of liquid that are added after the gratin is constructed, as well as the layer of plastic wrap and foil that need to be pressed down on top of the gratin.

5 tablespoons unsalted butter

4 large leeks, white part only, trimmed of roots and tough outer leaves, thinly sliced crosswise, and swirled vigorously in a bowl of cold water to remove any grit

Kosher salt and freshly ground black pepper

4 Bosc pears, peeled, cored, and cut into ½-inch-thick slices (or see the variation that follows)

3 large potatoes, peeled and sliced ⅛ inch thick

2 tablespoons chopped fresh sage

1 celery root (about 1 pound), peeled and sliced ⅛ inch thick

2 cups grated Gruyère cheese (6 to 8 ounces)

1½ cups cooked and peeled chestnuts (see page 244); if you can't get chestnuts, substitute 1 cup coarsely chopped toasted walnuts

1 fennel bulb, trimmed of stalks and tough outer layers, cut lengthwise in half, cored, and cut crosswise into ¼-inch-thick slices

1 pound winter squash (butternut, buttercup, or Hubbard), peeled and sliced ⅛ inch thick

1 cup dried cranberries, soaked in ¼ cup warm water

2½ cups milk

2 cups cream

1. Preheat the oven to 350°F.

2. Heat a large nonstick sauté pan over medium heat. Add 2 tablespoons of the butter. When it

has melted, add the leeks and cook until they begin to brown, about 5 minutes. Season with salt and pepper and transfer to a plate.

3. Wipe the pan clean with a paper towel, then heat 2 more tablespoons butter over medium heat. As soon as it melts add the pears and sauté until they begin to brown, about 5 minutes. Remove from the heat.

4. Rub the bottom and sides of a 3-quart baking dish with the final tablespoon of butter. Layer half the potatoes in the bottom of the dish. Season with salt, pepper, and a sprinkle of the sage. As you add each subsequent layer, season it the same way. Use all of the leeks for the next layer, followed by all of the celery root. Top with 1 cup of the cheese. Sprinkle with the chestnuts, then use the fennel, squash, cranberries, and pears for the subsequent layers. Finish with the remaining potatoes. Pour the milk over the top of the gratin. Press a layer of plastic wrap against the potatoes, then follow it with a layer of aluminum foil, tucking the foil around the edges so it both sits on the gratin and is fastened snugly to the dish. The plastic wrap will prevent the potatoes from drying out.

5. Bake for 30 minutes. Remove the dish from the oven. Carefully peel back a corner of the foil and plastic wrap and pour the cream over the top of the gratin, then replace the wrap and foil. Bake for 30 minutes longer.

6. Remove the foil and plastic wrap. The tip of a sharp knife should easily penetrate the gratin without any resistance; if the vegetables are still somewhat firm, cook for another 15 minutes and test with a knife again. Sprinkle the gratin with the remaining 1 cup cheese and bake for an additional 15 minutes, or until the cheese has formed a golden crust.

7. Allow the gratin to cool for 10 minutes before serving.

Gratin with Caramelized Pears

If you love pears, you can prepare a spectacular variation on this gratin by substituting a topping of roasted caramelized pear halves in place of the layer of sautéed pears. Peel 8 Bosc pears, cut them in half, scoop out the cores, and toss with 3 tablespoons extra virgin olive oil. Season with salt and pepper. Lay the pears cut side down on an oiled baking sheet. Bake at 450°F until they are tender and the cut sides are a deep caramelized brown, about 30 minutes. Refrigerate until ready to use (you can prepare them a day ahead).

Prepare the gratin, omitting the layer of sautéed pears. While the gratin is baking, allow the caramelized pear halves to come to room temperature. After adding the final cup of cheese in Step 6, top with pear halves and return to the oven for 10 minutes, then run it under the broiler for another 3 minutes to bring up the color in the pears.

Glazed Turnips with Chestnuts and Prunes

Turnips and chestnuts and prunes, oh, my. At various times, I've matched each of these ingredients with duck. To bring all of them together in the same duck preparation would seem like inviting jealous suitors to dinner on the same night, an invitation to a fight. But without the duck's powerful attraction, the turnips and chestnuts and prunes discover they have quite a bit in common, especially with the help of a Madeira glaze. Be sure to reduce the liquid in the pan to just a glaze, or the dish will taste unfinished.

When buying turnips, select those that feel dense and heavy for their size, whether small or large. The fresher the turnip, the heavier it feels. In the spring and fall, this isn't a problem because young turnips between 4 and 6 ounces are readily available at farmers' markets and high-quality produce departments. In the late fall and winter, however, the only available turnips tend to be larger—and older. Avoid turnips that are spongy, feel light, or are heavily scarred from knocking around in storage.

This recipe easily doubles or triples, if you're considering serving it at a holiday meal. Leftovers reheat well. You can also chop them coarsely and mix with an equal amount of bread crumbs for an impromptu stuffing for chicken or Cornish game hens.

MAKES 4 SIDE-DISH SERVINGS

2 tablespoons unsalted butter

4 small purple-top turnips (about 1½ pounds), peeled and cut into quarters

8 chestnuts, cooked and peeled (see page 244)

Kosher salt and freshly ground black pepper

1 shallot, minced

1 tablespoon sugar

4 sage leaves

½ cup Madeira

1 cup Chicken Stock (page 31) or high-quality canned low-sodium chicken broth

½ cup pitted prunes

2 tablespoons chopped fresh flat-leaf parsley

DO AHEAD: The turnips can be peeled a few hours in advance, but keep them covered with water. If exposed to air, they'll discolor.

1. Melt the butter in a large sauté pan over medium-high heat. When the foam subsides, add the turnips and chestnuts. Season with salt and pepper. Cook, stirring occasionally, until they begin to caramelize, about 5 minutes.

2. Add the shallot, sugar, and sage, toss to coat the turnips, and cook for 3 minutes. Add the Madeira and cook for 3 more minutes or until it has reduced by half. Remove the chestnuts and set aside. Add the chicken stock, lower the heat to medium, and cook until the turnips are tender, 8 to 10 minutes. Watch the pan carefully. By the time the turnips are done, the liquid should have reduced to a glaze. If not, remove the turnips and continue reducing the liquid until only a glaze remains, then return the turnips to the pan.

3. Return the chestnuts to the pan. Add the prunes. Stir until everything is heated through. Sprinkle with the parsley and serve.

Slow-Roasted Tomatoes

I remember when Dean & DeLuca, a New York gourmet store, introduced sun-dried tomatoes from San Remo almost twenty years ago. No other single food product in my experience has been embraced with such enthusiasm or proven so enduring.

Sun-dried tomatoes piqued my interest in other techniques for preserving tomatoes, especially slow-roasting and slow-braising (see the next recipe). Unlike that of their sun-dried cousins, the flesh of tomatoes roasted in the oven for several hours at a low temperature is still juicy; something of their freshness still lingers. "SDT"s are like dried porcini—they need to be restored or used in a medium that will restore them. Slow-*roasted* tomatoes are like prunes—they're fine as they are. Their texture reminds me of the strawberries in strawberry jam. In fact, one of my husband's favorite breakfasts is slow-roasted tomatoes spread on toasted Italian bread, with a little salt. We use them in pasta and salads, as a side dish for a picnic with bread and cheese, as a topping for pizza, and as a special addition to baked fish dishes.

After making the recipe once or twice, try fine-tuning the cooking time according to the water content of the particular batch of tomatoes and the texture you prefer in the finished product. One caveat: Unlike slow-braising, which can improve the flavor of winter tomatoes, this technique depends on ripe, high-quality tomatoes. What you put in is what you will get out, only more concentrated. Slow-roasted tomatoes have a shorter shelf life than either sun-dried or slow-braised tomatoes. They will last for about a week in the refrigerator.

MAKES 2 CUPS

12 plum tomatoes or 2 pints cherry tomatoes
2 tablespoons extra virgin olive oil
½ teaspoon sugar
½ teaspoon kosher salt
¼ teaspoon freshly ground black pepper
1 teaspoon chopped fresh thyme

1. Preheat the oven to 250°F.

2. Cut the tomatoes in half lengthwise. Toss the tomatoes in a bowl with the remaining ingredients.

3. Arrange cut side up in a single layer on a rack sitting in a shallow roasting pan. Roast plum tomatoes for about 4 hours, cherry tomatoes for about 2 hours. Begin checking after half the cooking time, then every 30 minutes. They're done when the edges have curled and the skin has wrinkled, but they should still be juicy at heart. Let cool, then refrigerate in a tightly sealed container. (Do not store in oil.)

Slow-Braised Tomatoes

U nless you live in a greenhouse, there will inevitably come a time when the quality of the tomatoes available to you takes a dip. Tomato salads are out of the question, but what do you do when you want tomatoes for a sauce or soup, or to add to braising liquids for hearty winter meat dishes? You can rely on high-quality canned tomatoes or, for a more intense flavor, try these slow-braised tomatoes. They're a great way to concentrate flavor in winter tomatoes. Food writer and cookbook author Nancy Verde Barr first introduced me to the Italian technique of slowly braising tomatoes in oil. Her stovetop version is more rigorous and authentic than mine. At Rialto, we braise the tomatoes in the oven—we can make more in a single batch and they require less attention. Slow-braising produces a more unctuous tomato than slow-roasting, better suited to soups, sauces, and braises, where you want concentrated tomato flavor, but texture isn't an issue. Store slow-braised tomatoes in their cooking oil in the refrigerator, where they will last for 2 weeks. (Note: The oil tastes fabulous and is reusable.) Never insert your bare fingers into the storage container, or you risk contaminating the oil with bacteria from your skin.

MAKES 4 TO 5 CUPS

¼ cup extra virgin olive oil, plus approximately
   ½ cup for braising
1 large white onion, cut into ½-inch dice
6 garlic cloves, smashed
18 basil leaves
⅛ teaspoon hot red pepper flakes
24 ripe plum tomatoes or 48 ripe cherry tomatoes
2 teaspoons sugar
1 teaspoon kosher salt

1. Preheat the oven to 250°F.

2. Heat ¼ cup olive oil in a large sauté pan over medium heat. Add the onion and garlic and cook, stirring occasionally, until tender, about 5 minutes. Remove from the heat, add the basil leaves and red pepper flakes, and stir well.

3. Cut the tomatoes in half lengthwise. (Leave cherry tomatoes whole.) Toss the tomatoes with the sugar and salt.

4. Place the tomatoes cut side down in a roasting pan that will hold them in a single layer. (If you don't have a large enough pan, use an additional roasting pan and more olive oil.) Spoon the onion mixture over the tomatoes. Add enough olive oil to come halfway up the tomatoes, about ½ cup.

5. Roast until the tomatoes are tender, but not falling apart, about 3 hours (about 1 hour for cherry tomatoes). Stir once, gently, during the braising. Let cool; then refrigerate, covered, in their oil.

Roasted Garlic

Although this recipe calls for two heads of garlic, I often double or triple the amount, especially if I know that I've got a brutal schedule coming up in the next week. Sauce, soup, or stock instantly acquires depth with the addition of roasted garlic. Also, since everyone ought to have as part of her culinary repertoire a raft of respectable quick meals, the combination of roasted and fresh garlic, olive oil, and herbs, with or without high-quality canned tomatoes, makes a homemade pasta sauce of which you can be proud. Roasted garlic will keep, covered and refrigerated, for 4 to 5 days.

MAKES ABOUT ½ CUP

2 tablespoons extra virgin olive oil
Kosher salt and freshly ground black pepper
2 large heads garlic

1. Preheat the oven to 350°F.

2. Grease a small roasting pan, pie plate, or baking dish with 1 tablespoon of the olive oil. Season the oil with salt and pepper.

3. Cut the garlic heads in half across the cloves, so you end up with a top and bottom cross-section of each head. Place cut side down in the pan. Drizzle with the remaining 1 tablespoon olive oil and season with salt and pepper. If the garlic seems dry (see box on following page), add 2 tablespoons water. Roast until the garlic is tender and the cut sides are golden brown, 40 to 50 minutes.

4. Squeeze the heads gently, and the individual cloves should slide right out of the skin.

SEASONAL GARLIC

The water content of garlic varies considerably from one season to the next. From late spring through the fall, it's easy to find garlic that's sweet and juicy. By New Year's Day, however, produce departments are filling their shelves from stocks of stored garlic. Not only do some dried-out cloves appear in the heads, but the usable garlic is often harsher, more concentrated than in the warmer months, so I adjust recipes accordingly. I might use less in a dish that calls for sautéed garlic. When roasting garlic in the winter, I always add a couple of tablespoons of water to the pan so the garlic rehydrates as it cooks.

Pizza, Tarts, and Crostatas

※

This chapter, which might easily have been called Savory Crusts I Have Known and Loved, opens with my favorite Neapolitan flatbread—pizza. For me, pizza begins and ends with the crust. The topping may be interesting, but if it isn't sitting on a rich, yeasty crust that's both chewy and complex, all is for naught. The real difference between a good and a great crust isn't effort—it's time. Great crusts result from a slow second rising, which few commercial pizza makers take time to do. The recipe for Basic Pizza Dough shows you how to do it. Once you've got the crust down, you can play with any of the other pizza recipes.

In Italy, pizza is primarily considered a snack, and it's in that spirit that I present these recipes. Thinking of pizza as a snack allows you to use richer ingredients than you might otherwise, because the intention is to serve small portions, something to take the edge off an appetite or whet it for things to come. Smoked Salmon Pizza with Mascarpone and Capers and Five-Cheese Pizza with Caramelized Onions are both quite rich, ideal for serving with drinks or as appetizers. At the opposite end of the spectrum is a pizza with very thin crust and ingredients that act more as seasonings than the usual toppings, Crispy Prosciutto and Parsley Pizza.

Pizzas are always made with a yeasted dough. Tarts, on the other hand, can be made with a variety of crusts. I've included three tart recipes that demonstrate a range of flavor and effort; an

Alsatian Tarte Flambée made with smoked bacon, onions, and cheese; a simple Tomato, Basil, and Parmesan Tart that would feel at home anywhere south of the Vaucluse; and a recipe that has its origins in the eastern end of the Mediterranean—individual Phyllo Tarts with Smoky Eggplant, Bulgur, and Roasted Red Peppers.

A pair of contrasting *crostatas* closes the chapter. *Crostata* is a generic Italian term for pie, sweet or savory; it may be baked in a standard pie plate or free-form. Made with pastry dough and filled with a mixture of precooked vegetables, savory crostatas are often topped with cheese or a custard mixture. A Spring Vegetable Crostata illustrates the light style, while the Caramelized Squash, Pear, and Blue Cheese Crostata is a heartier cold-weather dish. By the way, making a crostata is a great technique for transforming leftover vegetables into a different dish altogether.

Basic Pizza Dough

Y ou can make good pizza dough in a few hours. Great dough, one whose crust will make people sit up and wonder if they've been eating cardboard all their lives, requires a little extra time, but almost no extra effort. A memorable pizza crust will almost always have been made from dough that has had the benefit of an extended second rising, usually stretched out over 6 to 8 hours. This second rising allows the gluten fibers greater time to develop, resulting in a chewier crust. The long second rising also eliminates the raw quality that crust made from "quick" dough sometimes seems to have. A good crust tastes mature, like a well-made bread, good enough to stand on its own, instead of just serving as a vehicle for the topping.

I always let my dough rise slowly the second time. The minor inconvenience of planning ahead is more than offset by the superior flavor of the finished pizza crust. If I'm going to make pizza on Saturday, I prepare the dough Friday night and let it rise once at room temperature. Then I punch the dough down and throw it into the refrigerator. By chilling the dough, I slow the second rising way down, so it takes place over 6 to 8 hours. On Saturday morning, the dough is ready. I leave the dough in the refrigerator if I'm going to use it that night. If I've made extra, I wrap it tightly in several layers of plastic wrap and freeze it. Frozen pizza dough lasts for a month.

Most pizza dough recipes are vague when it comes to the size of the pizza that the dough will make, as well as the thickness of the crust. I make thin-crust pizzas, meaning the dough is about $\frac{3}{16}$ inch thick. But you don't have to worry about measuring this. If you roll a pound of pizza dough into two 12-inch pizzas, the dough will be the right thickness. You can even roll the dough out into two 16-inch pizzas, in which case the crust will be really thin, an effect that works particularly well when you're topping the dough with only a few ingredients, or with items that you don't want to cook too long, or when you're using the dough for homemade crackers.

MAKES 1 POUND—ENOUGH FOR FOUR 8-INCH OR TWO 12-INCH THIN-CRUST PIZZAS OR TWO 16-INCH VERY-THIN-CRUST PIZZAS

¾ cup warm water

½ package yeast (scant 1 teaspoon)

1 tablespoon kosher salt

3 tablespoons extra virgin olive oil

1½ to 1¾ cups unbleached all-purpose flour, plus more as needed

1. To proof the yeast, put 2 tablespoons of the warm water in a large bowl, stir in the yeast, and let it rest. After a few minutes, bubbles should begin to form, demonstrating that the yeast is alive and active. If nothing happens after 10 or 15 minutes, discard the mixture and start over with fresh yeast.

2. Add the remaining ½ cup plus 2 tablespoons water, the salt, and 2 tablespoons of the olive

oil to the yeast mixture and mix well. Use a wooden spoon to stir in 1½ cups flour ½ cup at a time. After incorporating the final ½ cup flour, the dough should be too stiff to stir; if not, gradually add the remaining ¼ cup. Transfer the dough to a clean board and knead until smooth and elastic, about 7 minutes. You can sprinkle the dough with a little flour if it's too sticky to knead, but try to use as little as possible: The more flour you use, the denser the dough will be; the less flour, the lighter the dough, and hence the crisper the crust. Try to work with dough that's still a little tacky.

3. Rub a large bowl with the remaining 1 tablespoon olive oil. Put the dough in the bowl, then flip it so that it's completely coated with oil. Cover with a damp towel and allow to rise until doubled in bulk. Depending on the yeast and flour, this can take anywhere from 1 to 2 hours.

4. *For a quick dough (for use within an hour or so),* punch it down after the first rising, then cut it into 2 or 4 pieces, depending on how many pizzas you intend to make, and roll the pieces into balls. Cover the balls with a towel and let rise again at room temperature until double in bulk, about 45 minutes; as soon as the dough finishes the quick second rising, it's ready to use. *For a slow second rising,* punch the dough down after the first rising, cover with the towel, and refrigerate for 6 to 8 hours.

5. After the second rising, the dough is ready to use. Either proceed with one of the pizza recipes or wrap the dough tightly in plastic wrap and refrigerate. Or, if not using within a day, put the wrapped dough in a plastic bag and freeze it; allow frozen dough to thaw in the refrigerator. All dough should be at room temperature before using.

Pizza Tools

A *pizza stone and a pizza* peel, the wide wooden paddle used to move pizza in and out of the oven, will make your experience more satisfying. Pizza stones come in a variety of sizes and shapes. I own two rectangular ones, the largest that will fit on my oven racks. Each stone will hold one 16-inch pizza or two or more smaller ones. The circular stones seem to hold only one pizza, unless you're making very small ones.

About half an hour before the pizza is ready to bake, I preheat my oven to 500°F, giving the stones time to warm. The stones provide an even source of direct heat for the entire bottom surface of the dough, producing a crisp crust. Several large unglazed tiles (referred to as "unsalted" or quarry tiles in the trade), available at many home renovation stores, are an inexpensive alternative.

Pizza peels are available in home versions with a short handle. They're an inexpensive accessory that can help avert a disastrous spill. If you don't have a peel, assemble your pizzas on an upside-down sheet pan dusted with cornmeal or a rimless cookie sheet, then slide them off the sheet onto the pizza stone.

Baking Pizzas—One at a Time or All at Once?

All of my pizza recipes call for a pound of pizza dough. Because most people don't own multiple pizza stones, or a stone large enough to accommodate more than one pizza at a time, the recipes usually suggest rolling out the dough, topping the crust, and baking each pizza individually. While one pizza bakes, you prepare the next. This works if you're adding pizza to an array of hors d'oeuvres, or if your gatherings tend to be the loose sort of affairs where everyone gravitates to the kitchen.

But what if you want to serve your pizza all at once, say, as a separate course at the type of dinner when guests aren't supposed to stroll into the kitchen as each pizza finishes?

My preference is to make a single large pizza, rolling the dough into whatever irregular shape strikes my fancy—oblong or roughly oval, sometimes with a weird extension or two. Everyone loves the *"rustica"* just-tossed-off look when it arrives at the table, hot and ready for slicing. If your heart is set on serving individual pizzas, dispense with the pizza stone altogether. Instead, bake all the pizzas at once on sheet pans dusted with cornmeal. What you lose in crispiness, you gain in convenience. A third solution is to choose a recipe like the Smoked Salmon Pizza, in which all the crusts are baked first, then the topping added. Keep the crusts warm on top of the oven (don't pile them up or cover them—they'll get soggy), top all of them at the same time, and serve.

Fig and Taleggio Pizza with Sage and Honey

*I*n *this fortuitous dish, a* couple of different ideas find expression in a single recipe. Ever since I tasted Gorgonzola drizzled with honey at Checchino restaurant in Rome, I'd thought about experimenting with a honey and cheese combination on an appetizer pizza. Instead of Gorgonzola, which struck me as a little too pungent, I opted for Taleggio, a soft-ripening, washed-rind cheese from Lombardy. Figs, a traditional partner with Taleggio, made a good addition to the combination. Use an amber honey whose character will contribute something besides simple sweetness—I like "autumn honey," a deep, almost black honey that begins appearing in New England farmers' markets in October.

MAKES FOUR 8-INCH THIN-CRUST PIZZAS

1 recipe Basic Pizza Dough (page 123) at room temperature
Flour for rolling out the dough
Cornmeal for dusting
4 teaspoons extra virgin olive oil
12 ounces fresh ricotta
Kosher salt and freshly ground black pepper
12 ounces Taleggio, trimmed of rind and cut into ½-inch cubes
12 large fresh figs (or dried figs, soaked in water at least 30 minutes, drained, and patted dry), cut into quarters
32 medium sage leaves
¾ cup freshly grated Parmesan
1½ to 2 tablespoons high-quality honey

DO AHEAD: Make the dough.

1. Place a pizza stone on the bottom rack of the oven and preheat the oven to 500°F.

2. Cut the pizza dough into 4 equal pieces and roll into balls. Cover loosely with plastic wrap and let rest for 20 minutes.

3. Using plenty of flour, roll a dough ball into a circle about 8 inches in diameter. Push the crust together to thicken it slightly around the edge for a rim. Or, if you want to use your hands instead of a rolling pin, first press the ball flat with your palm. Starting at the center of the disk, use your fingertips to stretch the dough, working outward; try to maintain an even thickness as you work. Leave the dough a little thicker around the edge to form a rim.

4. Transfer the circle to a peel or sheet pan sprinkled with cornmeal. Dimple the dough with your fingertips so it doesn't puff up during baking. Brush 1 teaspoon of the olive oil over the dough or rub it on with your fingertips, leaving a ½-inch border around the edge.

5. Season the ricotta with salt and pepper. Spread one-quarter of the ricotta over the dough, leaving a ½-inch border. Distribute one-quarter each of the Taleggio, figs, and sage leaves evenly over the pizza. Sprinkle with one-quarter of the Parmesan.

6. Slide the pizza onto the pizza stone and bake for 12 to 15 minutes, or until the crust is crispy, the topping bubbly and brown. While the first pizza is baking, prepare the second.

7. Remove the pizza from the oven with the peel, or slide it onto a sheet pan, and transfer to a cutting board. Place the second pizza in the oven. Cut the finished pizza into 4 slices, place in a plate, drizzle with honey, and serve. Start working on the third pizza, and repeat the process until you've finished all 4 pizzas.

Five-Cheese Pizza with Caramelized Onions and Truffle Oil

As a young cook, I used to make pizza Margherita, the traditional combination using tomatoes, basil, and mozzarella. Over time I experimented, adding other cheeses to the mozzarella and omitting the tomatoes. Eventually I ended up with this pizza, which I called a Margherita Bianca. Some years later I read that the original pizza was named after Queen Margherita of Savoy and the topping reflected the colors of the Italian flag—green, white, and red. Somewhat sheepishly, I changed the name to this one, and vowed to be more scrupulous about my treatment of traditional culinary terms in the future. Regardless of the name, you can't beat this combination of mozzarella, Asiago, fresh ricotta, ricotta salata, and Parmesan. Caramelized onions offer a nice counterpoint to the richness of the cheese. An optional drizzle of truffle oil adds a final luxurious touch.

MAKES FOUR 8-INCH THIN-CRUST PIZZAS

3 tablespoons plus 1 teaspoon extra virgin olive oil

2 large onions, thinly sliced

Kosher salt and freshly ground black pepper

1 recipe Basic Pizza Dough (page 123), at room temperature

Flour for rolling out the dough

Cornmeal for dusting

12 ounces fresh ricotta

1 tablespoon chopped fresh oregano

4 ounces fresh mozzarella, cut into ¼-inch slices

4 ounces ricotta salata, cut into ½-inch dice

½ cup grated Asiago

½ cup freshly grated Parmesan

1 to 2 tablespoons white truffle oil (optional)

DO AHEAD: Make the dough and caramelize the onions.

1. Heat 2 tablespoons of the oil in a large sauté pan over medium heat. Add the onions, season with salt and pepper, and cook, stirring occasionally, until translucent, 3 to 5 minutes. Reduce the heat to low and continue cooking, stirring occasionally, until the onions are golden, caramelized, and sweet, 30 to 40 minutes. Do not let them cook too fast, or they'll dry out and burn rather than caramelize; add a little water if they look too dry. Let them cool before using.

2. As the onions draw close to finishing, place a pizza stone on the bottom rack of the oven and preheat the oven to 500°F.

3. Cut the dough into 4 equal pieces and roll into balls. Drape with plastic wrap and let rest for 20 minutes.

4. Using plenty of flour, roll a dough ball into a circle about 8 inches in diameter. Push the crust together to thicken it slightly around the edge for a rim. Or, if you want to use your hands instead of a rolling pin, first press the ball flat with your palm. Starting at the center of the disk, use your fingertips to stretch the dough, working outward; try to maintain an even thickness as you work. Leave the dough a little thicker around the edge to form a rim.

5. Transfer the circle to a peel or a sheet pan sprinkled with cornmeal. Dimple the dough with your fingertips so it doesn't puff up during baking. Brush 1 teaspoon of the olive oil over the dough or rub it on with your fingertips, leaving a ½-inch border around the edge.

6. Season the fresh ricotta with salt and pepper. Spread one-quarter of the ricotta over the dough, leaving the border uncovered. Top with one-quarter each of the onions and oregano. Distribute one-quarter of each of the remaining 4 cheeses over the dough.

7. Slide the pizza onto the pizza stone and bake for 12 to 15 minutes or until the crust is crispy, the topping bubbly and brown. While the first pizza is baking, prepare the second.

8. Remove the pizza from the oven with the peel, or slide it onto a sheet pan, and transfer to a cutting board. Place the second pizza in the oven. Cut the finished pizza into 4 slices, place on a plate, drizzle with truffle oil, if using, and serve. Start working on the third pizza, and repeat the process until you've finished all 4 pizzas.

Smoked Salmon Pizza with Mascarpone and Capers

These pizzas make an easy first course because the crusts are baked ahead, then the toppings added, making it easy to serve four individual pizzas at the same time. Mascarpone is the gourmand's cream cheese and a great partner for smoked salmon. Think of this as the most heavenly lox and cream cheese you've ever eaten.

MAKES FOUR 8-INCH THIN-CRUST PIZZAS

1 recipe Basic Pizza Dough (page 123), at room temperature
Flour for rolling out the dough
Cornmeal for dusting
4 teaspoons extra virgin olive oil
¾ to 1 pound mascarpone (1½ to 2 cups)
Kosher salt and freshly ground black pepper
1 pound thinly sliced smoked salmon
2 tablespoons capers, rinsed
2 tablespoons minced fresh chives
4 lemon wedges

DO AHEAD: Make the dough.

1. Place a pizza stone on the bottom rack of the oven and preheat the oven to 500°F.

2. Cut the pizza dough into 4 equal pieces and roll into balls. Drape with plastic wrap and let rest for 20 minutes.

3. Using plenty of flour, roll a dough ball into a circle about 8 inches in diameter. Push the crust together to thicken it slightly around the edge for a rim. Or, if you want to use your hands instead of a rolling pin, first press the ball flat with your palm. Starting at the center of the disk, use your fingertips to stretch the dough, working outward; try to maintain an even thickness as you work. Leave the dough a little thicker around the edge to form a rim.

4. Transfer the circle to a peel or a sheet pan sprinkled with cornmeal. Dimple the dough with your fingertips so it doesn't puff up during baking. Brush 1 teaspoon olive oil over the dough or rub it on with your fingertips.

5. Slide the pizza onto the pizza stone and bake for 10 to 12 minutes, or until crispy and golden brown. While the first crust is baking, roll out the second and brush with oil.

6. Remove the crust from the oven with the peel, or slide it onto a sheet pan, and keep warm, uncovered, on top of the oven. Place the next circle of dough in the oven. Start working on the third ball of dough, and repeat the process until you've finished all 4 crusts. Don't stack or cover the finished crusts—they'll get soggy.

7. Spread each warm crust with one-quarter of the mascarpone, leaving a ½-inch border. Season with salt and pepper. Arrange one-quarter of the salmon on top of each pizza and then sprinkle with the capers, chives, and additional pepper. Garnish each pizza with a lemon wedge, and serve.

Crispy Prosciutto and Parsley Pizza

The original Roman or Neapolitan approach to pizza was to fashion a very thin crust in an extremely narrow oval, perhaps four or five times as long as it was wide, to be served to a group of diners on a long thin plank. The pizza was sliced crosswise into pieces that could be folded in half for convenient eating. The topping was often no more than olive oil and a dense dusting of rosemary or oregano, sometimes pared with minimalist shavings of mushrooms or other vegetables, anchovies, prosciutto, or another meat. The point was the brick-baked crust, with just enough topping for a snack to tide you over until you went home, where the really serious eating occurred.

MAKES TWO 10 × 20-INCH VERY-THIN-CRUST PIZZAS

⅓ cup extra virgin olive oil

4 garlic cloves, thinly sliced

Kosher salt and freshly ground black pepper

1 recipe Basic Pizza Dough (page 123), at room temperature

Flour for rolling out the dough

Cornmeal for dusting

1½ cups coarsely chopped fresh flat-leaf parsley

½ cup grated Fontina

¼ cup grated Asiago

8 thin slices prosciutto

DO AHEAD: Make the dough.

1. Place a pizza stone on the bottom rack of the oven and preheat the oven to 500°F.

2. Heat the olive oil in a small sauté pan over low heat. Add the garlic, season with salt and pepper, and cook until tender, about 5 minutes. Take care not to let it burn. Let cool.

3. Cut the pizza dough into 2 equal pieces and roll into balls. Drape with plastic wrap and let rest for 20 minutes.

4. Using plenty of flour, roll one ball of dough into a rough rectangle about 10 inches wide and 20 inches long (or as long a shape as will fit on your pizza stone or sheet pan). If the dough begins to contract as you try to roll it out, let it rest for 10 minutes to relax, then try rolling it again. Pinch the dough lightly around the edge to form a rim.

5. Transfer the dough to a peel or sheet pan sprinkled with cornmeal. Dimple the dough with your fingertips so it doesn't puff up during baking. Spread a tablespoon of the garlic oil and half the garlic over the dough. Then sprinkle half the parsley over the dough. Season with salt and pepper. Sprinkle half of each cheese over the parsley.

6. Slide the pizza onto the stone or place the sheet pan in the oven, and bake until the crust is starting to turn brown and crispy, about 5 minutes. Top with half the prosciutto and bake for an additional 5 minutes, or until the prosciutto is starting to crisp. Remove from the oven, transfer to a serving plate, and cut into 8 slices.

7. Drizzle the pizza with a teaspoon of the garlic oil and serve. Repeat the procedure with the second ball of dough and the remaining ingredients.

Tarte Flambée with Caramelized Onions, Smoked Bacon, and Creamy Cheese

*C*ontrary to what its name might lead you to expect, this tart isn't flambéed. The "flaming" refers to the burnt edges of this thin Alsatian flatbread, made from pizza dough and strewn with onions and bacon. In the original version, the raw ingredients were tossed over the dough with a little cheese and cooked rapidly in the hot brick oven of the town baker. Somewhere along the line—presumably in more prosperous times—a dollop of rich cheese was thrown into the mixture. Taking the time to caramelize the onions and crisping the bacon beforehand transforms the tart into an even richer, more luxurious dish.

MAKES FOUR 10-INCH TARTS

3 tablespoons plus 1 teaspoon extra virgin olive oil

2 large onions, thinly sliced

Kosher salt and freshly ground black pepper

8 to 12 strips meaty smoked bacon

6 ounces (about ⅔ cup) fromage blanc (or soft cream cheese, if fromage blanc is unavailable)

3 ounces (⅓ cup) mascarpone

3 ounces (⅓ cup) crème fraîche

2 tablespoons unbleached all-purpose flour, plus extra for rolling out the dough

1 recipe Basic Pizza Dough (page 123), at room temperature

Cornmeal for dusting

DO AHEAD: Make the dough and caramelize the onions.

1. Heat 2 tablespoons of the oil in a large sauté pan over medium heat. Add the onions, season with salt and pepper, and cook, stirring occasionally, until the onions are translucent, 3 to 5 minutes. Reduce the heat to low and continue cooking, stirring occasionally, until the onions are golden, caramelized, and sweet, 30 to 40 minutes. Do not let them cook too fast, or they'll dry out and burn rather than caramelize; add a little water if they look too dry. Let them cool before using.

2. While the onions are caramelizing, cook the bacon in a second large sauté pan over medium heat just until it starts to become crispy but some of the fat still remains. Transfer to a rack and allow to cool.

3. Cut the bacon crosswise into ½-inch-wide strips. Mix the fromage blanc, mascarpone, crème fraîche, and flour together. Season with salt and pepper.

4. Place a pizza stone on the bottom rack of the oven and preheat the oven to 500°F.

5. Cut the pizza dough into 4 equal pieces and roll into balls. Drape with plastic wrap and let rest for 20 minutes.

6. Using plenty of flour, roll one of the balls of dough into a circle 10 to 11 inches in diameter. Push the crust together to thicken it slightly around the edge for a rim. Transfer the circle to a peel or sheet pan sprinkled with cornmeal. Dimple the dough with your fingertips so it doesn't puff up during baking. Brush 1 teaspoon of the olive oil over the dough or rub it on with your fingertips, leaving a ½-inch border around the edge.

7. Spread one-quarter of the cheese mixture evenly over the dough. Then spread one-quarter of the onions evenly over the cheese. Distribute one-quarter of the bacon over the onions.

8. Slide the tart onto the stone and bake for 12 to 15 minutes, or until the bacon is crispy, the cheese bubbles, and the crust is a deep golden brown. While the first tart is baking, prepare the second.

9. Remove the tart from the oven with the peel, or slide it onto a sheet pan, and transfer to a cutting board. Place the next tart in the oven. Cut the finished tart into 4 slices, place on a plate, and serve immediately. Start working on the third tart, and repeat the process until you've finished all 4 tarts.

Phyllo Tarts with Smoky Eggplant, Bulgur, and Roasted Red Peppers

I *love layering flavors and textures* in tarts—crispy, creamy, or crunchy, salty, sweet, or hot. The smoky flavor in this tart comes from Aleppo pepper, available in the Middle Eastern section of many supermarkets and in specialty markets. If you can't find it, you can substitute a combination of hot red pepper flakes and paprika.

Prepare the bulgur and eggplant a day in advance if you like. Baked phyllo becomes soggy as it absorbs moisture from the air, especially in humid environments. If you bake the tarts within a few hours of serving, they should be fine; any longer, and you may need to crisp them for a few minutes in a 400°F oven. This is a great item to serve when some of your guests don't eat meat.

MAKES FOUR 5 × 6-INCH TARTS

6 tablespoons extra virgin olive oil

1 medium onion, chopped into ¼-inch dice

¼ cup coarse bulgur wheat, rinsed

Kosher salt and freshly ground black pepper

¼ cup finely chopped walnuts

3 ounces feta, crumbled

2 medium eggplants (about 1¾ pound total)

2 garlic cloves, minced and then mashed with a
    pinch of salt to a paste

2 tablespoons red wine vinegar

4 scallions, trimmed and sliced paper-thin

¼ cup finely chopped fresh flat-leaf parsley

2 tablespoons finely chopped fresh mint

1 teaspoon Aleppo pepper (or ¼ teaspoon hot red
    pepper flakes plus ½ teaspoon paprika)

4 sheets phyllo dough

4 tablespoons unsalted butter, melted

½ cup grated Asiago

1 red pepper, roasted (see page 99), peeled, seeded,
    stemmed, and cut into ¼-inch strips

1. Heat 2 tablespoons of the olive oil in a large sauté pan over medium heat. Add the onions and cook until tender, about 10 minutes. Add the bulgur, ½ teaspoon salt, and ¾ cup water. Cover, reduce the heat to low, and cook until all the water has been absorbed, about 10 minutes. Let cool, then season with salt and pepper and stir in the walnuts and feta.

2. Preheat the broiler. Put the eggplants on a baking sheet pan and poke them several times with a fork so they don't explode while cooking. Place the pan under the broiler. Turn the eggplants as the skin blackens so they cook evenly. Broil until they are thoroughly blackened and the flesh is very tender, 12 to 15 minutes. Let cool.

3. As soon as the eggplants are cool enough to handle, cut them in half lengthwise and scoop out the flesh. Discard the skin. Finely chop the flesh. Mix the eggplant with the garlic, red wine vinegar, the remaining ¼ cup olive oil, the scallions, parsley, mint, and Aleppo pepper. Season with salt.

4. Preheat the oven to 425°F. Line a sheet pan with parchment paper.

5. Lay a sheet of phyllo dough on the counter. Keep the others from drying out by covering with plastic wrap. Brush the sheet with a thin layer of melted butter. Fold the sheet crosswise in half. Brush again with a thin layer of butter. Fold crosswise in half again, brush with butter, and then fold in half again, so you have a rectangle, measuring about 5 × 6 inches. Place the folded phyllo on the parchment-lined sheet pan. Repeat with the remaining sheets of phyllo.

6. Cover each phyllo rectangle with one-quarter of the bulgur mixture. Cover the bulgur with the eggplant mixture and then sprinkle with the Asiago. Garnish the tops with crisscrossing strips of roasted red pepper.

7. Bake the tarts until the phyllo is golden brown, 20 to 25 minutes. Allow to cool for 5 minutes before serving. They're also good at room temperature.

Spring Vegetable Crostata

Many savory crostatas depend on root vegetables for substance. This recipe takes the dish in a lighter direction with tender spring vegetables—blanched scallions, fresh peas, and wilted lettuce. Although cooked lettuce is almost unheard of in this country, it's delicious with cream or a rich cheese like mascarpone. Make sure the other vegetables are thoroughly cooked, since the crostata spends only enough time in the oven for the pastry to bake and the custard to set. Once you learn this basic technique, try experimenting with equivalent amounts of beet greens, escarole, string beans, or other soft vegetables of your choice.

MAKES 4 TO 6 APPETIZER SERVINGS

12 ounces mascarpone (1½ cups)

3 extra-large egg yolks

Kosher salt and freshly ground black pepper

¼ cup chopped fresh flat-leaf parsley

2 tablespoons chopped fresh tarragon

2 tablespoons chopped fresh savory or thyme

2 teaspoons freshly squeezed lemon juice

1 cup fresh peas

12 medium asparagus spears, tough ends snapped off, stems peeled, and cut on the diagonal into 2-inch lengths

2 tablespoons unsalted butter

1 bunch scallions, trimmed and cut on the diagonal into 2-inch lengths

1 head Boston lettuce, cut into 8 wedges, washed, and dried well

1 recipe Basic Pastry Dough (page 343), chilled

3 tablespoons freshly grated Parmesan

1. Mix the mascarpone with the egg yolks in a medium bowl and season with salt and pepper. Stir in the herbs and lemon juice. Cover and refrigerate.

2. Bring a large pot of salted water to a boil. While the water heats, prepare a large bowl of ice water. As soon as the water boils, add the peas and blanch for 1 minute. Scoop a pea out of the boiling water and plunge it into the ice water to stop the cooking. Taste it. If it's tender, scoop out the remaining peas and put them in the ice water; if it's not quite done, let the others cook for another 30 seconds before removing them.

3. Add the asparagus to the boiling water and blanch for 3 minutes. Test an asparagus stalk. Depending on their size, the asparagus may need to cook for as much as another minute. When tender scoop out of the boiling water and plunge into the ice water. Drain the vegetables and spin or pat dry.

4. Heat the butter in a large sauté pan over medium-low heat. Add the scallions, season with salt and pepper, and cook until tender, about 4 minutes. Add the lettuce, season with salt and pepper, cover, and cook until the lettuce is wilted and tender, about 3 minutes. Uncover the pan, increase the heat to medium-high, and cook off any water, about 1 minute. Remove from the heat and let cool.

5. Place the pastry dough on a lightly floured surface and roll it into a 16-inch circle, about ⅛ inch thick. Fold it into quarters, transfer it to a sheet pan lined with parchment paper, and unfold. Spread the cool scallion-lettuce mixture over the pastry, leaving a 2-inch border. Arrange the peas and asparagus over it. Pull up the edges of the pastry and gently fold them over the vegetables into a rim. Pleat the dough as necessary but do not crimp. Place the crostata in the refrigerator and chill for 30 minutes.

6. Preheat the oven to 375°F.

7. Remove the crostata from the refrigerator and pour the mascarpone mixture over the vegetables. Sprinkle with the Parmesan. Bake for 35 to 40 minutes, or until the crust is golden brown and crisp.

8. Let rest for 5 minutes, then cut into wedges and serve.

Caramelized Squash, Pear, and Blue Cheese Crostata

*O*n Sunday nights, Boston chef Gordon Hammersley used to emulate a practice of French family restaurants. In place of the formal Hammersley's Bistro menu, he offered a shorter selection of economical "Sunday Suppers." It was a great deal all around. Patrons loved the lowered prices and the almost theatrical suspense of never knowing exactly what would be on the menu. As a sous-chef then, I couldn't have asked for a better crash course in menu writing. Crostatas evolved into something of a personal specialty with me, as a way of using seasonal ingredients in a rustic, efficient way. Caramelized squash and pears with blue cheese was at the top of my list of favorite fillings. In this case, the pears and squash are sautéed and glazed to save time, but the recipe is a good template for just about any combination of slow-roasted root vegetables, especially carrots or beets, or sweet potatoes, whose natural sugars caramelize during roasting.

MAKES 4 ENTRÉE SERVINGS

1 recipe Basic Pastry Dough (page 343), chilled

6 tablespoons extra virgin olive oil

2 pounds orange winter squash such as butternut, delicata, or Hubbard, peeled, seeded, and cut into ¼-inch-thick slices

Kosher salt and freshly ground black pepper

¼ cup sugar

1 teaspoon ground allspice

4 ripe pears, peeled, cored, and cut into eighths

2 tablespoons sherry vinegar

2 leeks, white part only, trimmed of roots and tough outer leaves, thinly sliced crosswise, and swirled vigorously in a bowl of cold water to remove any grit

⅓ pound (5 ounces) Gorgonzola (or your favorite high-quality blue cheese, such as Great Hill Blue or Stilton), crumbled

1. On a lightly floured surface, roll the dough into a 16-inch circle, about ⅛ inch thick. Line a sheet pan with parchment paper. Fold the dough into quarters, transfer it to the sheet pan, and unfold. Cover with plastic wrap and refrigerate for 30 minutes.

2. Heat 2 tablespoons of the olive oil in a large sauté pan over medium-high heat. Add the squash slices, season with salt and pepper, and cook until the squash is tender and golden brown, about 6 minutes. Sprinkle with 2 tablespoons of the sugar and the allspice. Toss until the sugar has melted and caramelized on the squash. Remove from the heat and set aside.

3. Heat 2 tablespoons of the olive oil in a second large sauté pan over medium-high heat. Add the pears and cook until golden and tender, about 12 minutes. Sprinkle with the remaining 2 tablespoons sugar and toss until the sugar has melted and caramelized on the pears. Add the vinegar and season generously with pepper. Set aside.

4. Heat the remaining 2 tablespoons olive oil in a medium sauté pan over medium heat. Add the leeks, season with salt and pepper, and cook until tender, 5 to 6 minutes. Let cool.

5. Preheat the oven to 375°F.

6. Remove the pastry circle from the refrigerator. Spread the cooked leeks on the circle, leaving a 2-inch border. Alternate the squash and pears over the leeks spoke fashion. Pull up the edges of the crust and gently flip them over the filling to form a wide, rustic edge. Pleat the dough as necessary but do not crimp.

7. Bake the tart until the crust is crisp and golden brown, 40 to 45 minutes. Sprinkle the blue cheese over the top of the tart and bake for an additional 5 minutes.

8. Let rest for 5 minutes, then cut into wedges and serve.

Pam's Tomato, Basil, and Parmesan Tarts

S ome combinations—crust, tomatoes, basil, a little cheese, and olive oil—seem to transcend cultural limitations. Everyone who encounters the ingredients seems somehow compelled to combine them in similar ways. My good friend—and recipe tester—Pam Krueger introduced me to these tarts.

This version uses basic unsweetened pastry dough, but you can clearly apply the same combination to puff pastry, phyllo, or even pizza dough; you'll need about 12 ounces of dough. The recipe easily doubles or triples. Time is your only limitation.

MAKES FOUR 3 × 4-INCH TARTS

1 recipe Basic Pastry Dough (page 343), chilled
½ cup freshly grated Parmesan
24 beautiful basil leaves
8 ripe plum tomatoes, sliced ½ inch thick
2 shallots, minced
2 garlic cloves, minced
Kosher salt and freshly ground black pepper
2 tablespoons extra virgin olive oil

DO AHEAD: Make the dough.

1. Line a sheet pan with parchment paper. Divide the dough into 4 equal pieces and shape into disks. Roll each disk into a rough 6 × 4-inch rectangle, about ¼ inch thick, on a floured surface. Transfer the dough to the sheet pan. Drape with plastic wrap and refrigerate for 30 minutes.

2. Preheat the oven to 425°F.

3. Remove the dough from the refrigerator and sprinkle with half the cheese. Lay 6 basil leaves on each rectangle. Toss the tomatoes with the shallots and garlic and season with salt and pepper. Lay the tomatoes, overlapping them, atop the basil leaves. Drizzle with the olive oil. Sprinkle with the remaining cheese.

4. Bake for 25 minutes, or until each crust is crisp and golden brown and the tomatoes are soft. Serve hot or at room temperature.

Mostly Pasta,

WITH A TASTE OF GNOCCHI, POLENTA, AND RISOTTO

Italians have a culinary genius for transforming ordinary starches into sensual treasures. In goes flour, potatoes, cornmeal, or rice; out comes pasta, gnocchi, polenta, or risotto. None of these skills is difficult to learn, unless you forswear the use of all kitchen machines.

This chapter includes instructions for making gnocchi, polenta, and a single risotto, but the emphasis is on pasta. Preparing pasta dough and rolling it out with nothing more than a rolling pin is a true skill, and people who are good at it are a wonder to behold, but I suggest an easier route. Mix the dough with a food processor, then employ an inexpensive hand-cranked pasta machine to knead and roll the dough into sheets of fresh pasta. At home, you can roll your pasta sheets far thinner (and make more delicate ravioli) than boutique pasta stores can. Pappardelle and tagliatelle, lasagna made with fresh noodles, exquisitely delicate ravioli, and a variety of "hand-folded" pasta dishes like *fazzo-letti* (handkerchiefs) or *nidimi* (little nests) flow from the ability to make fresh noodles.

Being able to make your own fettuccine or pappardelle can also come in handy with leftovers. The remains of any dish of braised meat can be transformed into a new meal by being used as a sauce for fresh pasta.

All of the recipes in this chapter cultivate your ability to pay attention. Italians have taught us to eat pasta a little chewier than we used to. Risotto is supposed to have a little resistance left in the grains; potato gnocchi are done when they're cooked through with just a hint of resilience in them. You have to taste and make a judgment. Timings like "*3 to 5 minutes*," "*about 10 minutes*," etc., should be taken as guides, not inflexible rules. With a little experience, you can sense when things are nearing completion. The process is akin to grilling a steak and relying on an instant-read digital thermometer. If you press the steak with your finger each time you take a reading, after a while you'll be able to tell from how the meat feels whether it's time to remove it from the grill. The same is true of these dishes. Learn to judge doneness by how the pasta or gnocchi feels in your mouth; use times only as a general guideline.

Master Recipe—Fresh Pasta

T*he rewards of making fresh* egg pasta are far out of proportion to the amount of effort required. The task is made easy with the use of a food processor and an inexpensive manual pasta machine. Here are a few tips to make your first experience rolling the dough a little easier.

- Don't skip the first few passes through the widest setting of the rollers. This kneads the dough, developing the gluten and helping it become more elastic.

- If the dough sticks to the rollers, dust it with a little flour.

- If a small tear appears in the dough, patch the tear and roll the dough through the same setting of the pasta machine again. For larger tears, wad the sheet into a ball, flatten it with your palm, and start again, beginning with the widest setting of the rollers. Tears may occur if the dough is sticking to the rollers or you're rolling too fast.

- You should be able to roll a small piece of dough from start to finished sheet in about 10 minutes. Try not to work more slowly than this, or the dough will start to dry out while you're rolling it.

- You can roll out fresh pasta a day ahead of cooking. Make a stack of sheets, layering them between parchment paper dusted with semolina flour. (Semolina is a little coarser than regular flour and keeps everything from sticking.) Put the stack on a tray and refrigerate, covered with plastic wrap, until you're ready to cut the pasta. I generally prefer not to use made-ahead pasta for ravioli, because it's harder to seal than dough that you've just finished rolling. If you do want to use dough you've made in advance, be sure to moisten the ravioli sheets with a little water around the pockets of filling to get a good seal.

MAKES 1 POUND

2 cups unbleached all-purpose flour, plus extra for rolling

3 extra-large eggs

1. Put the flour in the bowl of a food processor. Beat the eggs in a bowl with a fork. With the food processor running, add the beaten eggs in a steady stream. Process until the dough comes together and is smooth and elastic, about 4 minutes. If the dough seems sticky, add a little more flour. Put the ball of dough in a bowl and cover with plastic. Let rest for 20 minutes.

2. Divide the dough into 6 pieces. Cover 5 of the pieces with plastic. Flatten the remaining piece of dough slightly with your hand, dust it with flour, and crank it through a manual pasta machine with the rollers set at their maximum distance apart, the #1 setting. Fold the dough in thirds as though you were folding a business letter and run it through the machine again, feeding the narrow side into the rollers. Repeat the process of folding and rolling 4 or 5 more times. This process kneads the dough and prepares it for the next step of thinning it. Don't hesitate to sprinkle the dough with flour as necessary as you continue running it through the machine; you don't want it to stick to the rollers.

3. Gradually roll the dough to the desired thinness, narrowing the distance between the rollers with each pass of the dough. If the dough tears, just patch it together and roll it through the same setting again, a little more slowly this time. If the dough sticks to the rollers, sprinkle it with flour. (You will soon get the feel for the right speed and the proper level of moisture to keep the dough rolling efficiently.) After you've rolled the dough through the #6 setting, it should be thin enough to cut into any string pasta. For ravioli, the dough should be rolled slightly thinner. If you have an older machine there may be only one more setting; otherwise, the machine may go up to #9. For ravioli, roll the dough through #7 if that's your highest setting, or through #8. (I never use #9—the dough becomes too delicate to handle easily.)

4. Let the dough dry for 5 to 10 minutes before cutting it into noodles. Ravioli should be prepared while the dough is still moist. Transfer the cut noodles to a board or a sheet pan covered with a towel lightly dusted with flour.

Using a Half-Recipe of Fresh Pasta

Once in a while I only need one ½ pound of fresh pasta dough (a half-recipe). If I know I'll use the remainder within a few days, I simply make the full pound of dough and roll out half for whatever I'm making, saving the rest as a tightly wrapped ball in the refrigerator. It will keep for up to 4 days; after that, the gluten starts to break down. If I only want to make ½ pound of pasta, I follow the recipe, using 1 cup flour, 1 extra-large egg, 1 extra-large egg yolk, and 1 tablespoon water; I divide the dough into 3 balls instead of 6. A third alternative is simply to buy ½ pound of pasta dough and roll it out yourself. The pasta store near me, in addition to a variety of noodles and ravioli, sells fresh dough, uncut sheets, and even ravioli molds and pastry wheels.

On Cutting Pasta

~ Before cutting noodles, allow the sheets to dry (not on top of each other) on floured kitchen towels for 5 to 10 minutes. Wait just until the dough is no longer sticky before cutting—but not too long, or the dough will break when you try to run it through the cutters. After cutting, pile the noodles in soft bundles on floured towels or cutting board. It's OK if they dry out before cooking.

~ If making ravioli, use each sheet as soon as you finish rolling it, leaving the other pieces of dough tightly wrapped. Using the dough while it is still moist helps to make a good seal. Place cut ravioli on a tray lined with a towel dusted with semolina flour. Completed ravioli can sit out for several hours before cooking or be refrigerated overnight, tightly covered or wrapped in plastic. They can also be frozen; Put them on a flour-dusted tray in the freezer. As soon as they're hard, transfer to a freezer bag. They'll keep for a month.

FETTUCCINE OR TAGLIATELLE
Tagliatelle and fettuccine are essentially the same noodle, about ⅜ inch wide, with different names depending on the region: It's fettuccine in the south of Italy, tagliatelle in the north.

LASAGNA
Roll out sheets of pasta through the #6 setting. The recipes for lasagna and for nidimi call for various sizes of squares and rectangles, so cut as directed in the individual recipe.

PAPPARDELLE
Pappardelle is a wide hand-cut noodle, often seen with tiny zigzag edges. Lay a sheet of pasta on a floured surface and use a pastry wheel (which will give it the zigzag edge) or a sharp knife to cut ¾-inch-wide noodles.

RAVIOLI
After making the master recipe for Fresh Pasta, divide the dough into 5 pieces. Roll each piece into a sheet of pasta 20 inches long (it doesn't have to be exact) and 5 inches wide. Lay a sheet horizontally on a flat, floured work surface in front of you. To understand where the filling goes, imagine folding the sheet in half lengthwise and then cutting it crosswise to make 8 square ravioli, about 2½ inches on a side. Place 8 spoonfuls of filling on the dough in a single row along the side nearest you. Fold the pasta over. Cut between the pockets of filling with a pastry wheel. Press the air out of the individual ravioli with your fingertips, working outward from the filling, and seal the edges by pressing on them with your fingertips or using the back of a fork (kids like doing this).

If the dough is no longer moist when you're making the ravioli, brush the empty space around the filling with water before folding the dough. This will help make the seal stick. Transfer the finished ravioli to a sheet pan covered with a kitchen towel dusted with flour. A pound of pasta dough will make approximately 40 ravioli.

Linguine with Salsa Cruda

A *sauce of uncooked tomatoes is* one of late summer's culinary payoffs, the reward for waiting for locally grown tomatoes to arrive, whether from your own garden or the nearest farmers' market. Since the components retain their distinctive flavors instead of blending together, the dish is only as good as its poorest ingredient—don't skimp on the quality of olive oil or substitute second-rate tomatoes. This is a dish of sharp, contrasting flavors with lots of heat. If you want to tone things down, substitute spinach for the arugula and cut back on the serrano peppers.

MAKES 4 ENTRÉE SERVINGS

Kosher salt
1 pound high-quality dried linguine
¼ cup extra virgin olive oil
4 garlic cloves, finely chopped
4 serrano peppers, stemmed, seeded, and thinly sliced (use less for a milder sauce)
3 tablespoons capers, rinsed
10 ripe medium tomatoes, peeled (see page 55), seeded, and chopped into ½-inch dice
2½ cups arugula, rinsed thoroughly, drained, and coarsely chopped
Freshly ground black pepper
2½ ounces Pecorino Romano shavings

1. Bring a large pot of water to a boil. Season with salt. Add the linguine and stir so that the strands don't stick together. (If the pot isn't large enough for the linguine to lie flat, either break the strands in half or hold one end of the pasta bundle while the other end softens in the boiling water, then release the pasta into the water.) Cover the pot if necessary to bring the water back to a boil. Cook for 1 minute, then stir again. Continue to check periodically to make sure the strands aren't sticking together, and cook until the pasta is tender but still offers a little bit of resistance when you bite into it. Begin checking for doneness 7 or 8 minutes after it has returned to a boil.

2. Meanwhile, heat the oil in a large saucepan over medium heat and add the garlic, peppers, and capers. Cook until the garlic is tender, about 3 minutes. Remove from the heat.

3. When the linguine is done, use a measuring cup to scoop out ¼ cup pasta water and set it aside. Drain the pasta, transfer it to a large warm bowl, and add the tomatoes.

4. Add the reserved pasta water to the saucepan and bring to a boil. Pour the mixture over the pasta, add the arugula, and toss well. Taste, then add salt and pepper if necessary. Serve immediately, offering the pecorino shavings on the side.

Pappardelle with Smoked Mussels, Shrimp, Yellow Peppers, and Black Olives

In its home region of Tuscany, pappardelle is often served with game sauces. Tuscans think of these wide noodles as standing up to the big-bodied flavors of wild mushrooms, duck, and rabbit. Seafood, typically lighter fare, is associated with linguine or spaghetti. I've taken some liberties here by bringing seafood together with these noodles, but the combination of smoked mussels, roasted peppers, and black olives makes this a bold sauce with a lot of texture.

Traditional thinking holds that sauces with olive oil adhere to dried pasta better than fresh noodles, which are preferred with cream sauces and meat ragouts. While I generally go along with this, seafood sauces seem more problematic, with a little more room for personal choice. Squid and clams seem happiest, to my taste, with linguine, but I prefer fresh noodles with two of the three seafood sauces I've included in this chapter.

MAKES 4 ENTRÉE SERVINGS

½ cup extra virgin olive oil

1 small red onion, cut into ¼-inch dice

2 garlic cloves, minced

2 yellow peppers, roasted (see page 99), peeled, seeded, stemmed, and cut into ¼-inch-wide strips

3 plum tomatoes, peeled (see page 55), seeded, and cut into ¼-inch-wide strips

½ teaspoon chopped fresh marjoram

¼ teaspoon hot red pepper flakes

2 tablespoons chopped pitted black olives

24 medium shrimp (about 1 pound), peeled, deveined, and split lengthwise

½ pint smoked mussels

1 recipe Fresh Pasta (pages 142–43), cut into pappardelle (see page 144)

DO AHEAD: Roast and peel the peppers, peel the shrimp, and peel the tomatoes a day in advance. Wait, however, until the day of serving to chop the tomatoes, so they don't dry out.

1. Put a large pot of water on to boil.

2. Meanwhile, heat the olive oil in a large sauté pan over medium-high heat. Add the onion and cook until tender, 3 to 5 minutes. Add the garlic and peppers and cook for 3 minutes. Add the tomatoes, marjoram, and red pepper flakes, and cook for 5 minutes. Add the shrimp, olives, and mussels and cook until the shrimp are just cooked through, 3 to 4 minutes. Keep warm.

3. Season the boiling water with salt, add the pappardelle, and stir so that the strands don't stick together. Cover the pot if necessary to bring the water back to a boil. Cook for 1

minute, then stir again. Continue to check periodically to make sure the strands aren't sticking together, and cook until the pasta is tender but still offers a little bit of resistance when you bite into it, about 3 minutes. Before draining the pasta, use a measuring cup to scoop out ¼ cup of the pasta water. Set it aside.

4. Pour the pasta into a colander, then transfer the pasta to a large warm bowl. Pour the sauce over it and toss well. If the sauce is too thick to coat the pasta, add a little of the reserved pasta water to thin it, then toss again. Serve immediately.

Cornmeal Pappardelle with Scallops, Saffron, Tomatoes, and Fresh Corn

The scallops and saffron in this dish seem distinctly French, but the cornmeal pasta would feel right at home in Tuscany. The combination is a dish with intense aromas of saffron and scallops that gradually give way to subtler hints of corn and tarragon. Cornmeal pasta is exactly the right choice here; its textured, rustic quality keeps the dish from tipping over into unctuousness.

MAKES 4 ENTRÉE SERVINGS

PAPPARDELLE
1⅓ cups unbleached all-purpose flour, plus more
    for rolling out the dough
2 tablespoons fine cornmeal
2 extra-large eggs

SAUCE
2 ears corn
¼ cup plus 2 tablespoons extra virgin olive oil
1 medium red onion, thinly sliced
1 garlic clove, minced
Kosher salt and freshly ground black pepper
Small pinch of saffron, steeped in ½ cup dry
    white wine
8 plum tomatoes, peeled (see page 55), seeded, and
    chopped into ½-inch dice
1 pound bay or small sea scallops
½ teaspoon chopped fresh tarragon
¼ cup chopped fresh flat-leaf parsley
1 teaspoon freshly squeezed lemon juice

1. Put the flour and cornmeal in a food processor. Beat the eggs in a bowl with a fork. With the food processor running, add the beaten eggs in a steady stream. Process until the dough comes together and is smooth and elastic, about 4 minutes. If the dough seems sticky, add a little more flour. If it's too dry, add a few drops of water. Put the ball of dough in a bowl and cover with plastic. Let rest for 20 minutes.

2. Divide the dough into 6 pieces. Cover 5 of the pieces with plastic. Flatten the remaining piece of dough slightly with your hand, dust it with flour, and crank it through a manual pasta machine with the rollers set at their maximum distance apart, the #1 setting. Fold the dough in thirds as though you were folding a business letter and run it through the machine again, feeding the narrow side into the rollers. Repeat the process of folding and rolling 4 or 5 more times. This process kneads the dough and prepares it for the next step of thinning it. Don't hesitate to sprinkle the dough with flour as necessary as you continue running it through the machine; you don't want it to stick to the rollers.

3. Gradually roll the dough to the correct thinness, narrowing the distance between the rollers with each pass of the dough. After you've rolled the sheet through the #6 setting, it should be thin enough. Transfer the sheet of pasta to a towel dusted with flour and let it dry for 5 to 10 minutes before cutting. While the first sheet is drying, roll out the next piece of dough.

4. To cut the pappardelle, lay the sheet of pasta on a floured surface and use a pastry wheel (to give it a zigzag edge) or a sharp knife to cut into ¾-inch-wide noodles. Arrange the pappardelle in a soft pile on a board or kitchen towel dusted with semolina flour. Repeat the process with the remaining pieces of dough. The pasta can sit out at room temperature for several hours.

5. Bring a medium pot of water to a boil and season with salt. Prepare a bowl of ice water. Add the corn to the boiling water and cook for 2 minutes. Pull out the corn and submerge it in the ice water. After the corn has cooled, cut the kernels off the cobs and set aside. Run the dull edge of a knife down the cobs to extract the remaining corn "milk." Add to the corn kernels.

6. Put a large pot of water on to boil for the pasta. When it starts to simmer, proceed to the next step.

7. Heat ¼ cup of the olive oil in a medium sauté pan over medium-high heat. Add the onion and garlic, season with salt and pepper, and cook until the onion is tender, about 3 minutes. Add the saffron and white wine and simmer for 2 minutes. Add the tomatoes and cook for 3 minutes. Season with salt and pepper and set aside.

8. Heat the remaining 2 tablespoons olive oil in a large sauté pan over high heat. Season the scallops with salt and pepper and add to the pan in a single layer. Sear until golden brown on the first side. Don't move them around until they've gotten a good sear and are ready to be flipped; they tend to release their juices if jostled, and then they steam rather than sear. Flip and sear on the opposite side. The scallops should still have a creamy texture inside when done.

9. Add the tomato mixture, corn, and herbs to the pan with the scallops. Toss until heated through, about 30 seconds. Season with the lemon juice and salt and pepper. Remove from heat and keep warm.

10. Meanwhile, season the boiling water with salt, add the pappardelle, and stir so that the strands don't stick together. Cover the pot if necessary to bring the water back to a boil. Cook for 1 minute, then stir again. Continue to check periodically to make sure the strands aren't sticking together, and cook until the pasta is tender but still offers a little bit of resistance when you bite into it, about 3 minutes. Before draining the pasta, use a measuring cup to scoop out ¼ cup of the pasta water. Set it aside.

11. Pour the pasta into a colander, then transfer it to a large warm bowl. Pour the sauce over the pasta and toss well. If the sauce is too thick to coat the pasta, add a little of the reserved pasta water to thin it, then toss again. Serve immediately.

Tagliatelle with Shad Roe, Pancetta, and Spinach

Don't let another spring pass without tasting fresh tagliatelle sauced with a creamy combination of shad roe, pancetta, and spinach. The distinctively nutty flavor and silky texture of shad roe, available for only a few brief weeks, is not to be missed. Shad roe are usually sold in "pairs," or "sets," attached twin pink lobes or sacs containing a firm mass of eggs. Take care not to overcook the roe during the initial poaching, or the resulting sauce will be grainy rather than creamy. Don't worry if you can't remove all the membranes holding the roe sacs together. When the sacs are mashed with a fork, any remaining membranes will break down.

MAKES 4 ENTRÉE SERVINGS

2 cups water

¼ cup dry white wine

½ small onion, thinly sliced

½ celery stalk, thinly sliced crosswise

1 sprig thyme

1 bay leaf

Kosher salt and freshly ground black pepper

1 pair shad roe (about ½ pound)

¼ cup extra virgin olive oil

3 ounces thinly sliced pancetta, cut into ¼-inch-wide strips

6 shallots, minced

2 small garlic cloves, minced

¾ pound Fresh Pasta (pages 142–43), cut into tagliatelle (see page 144)

3 cups lightly packed flat-leaf spinach, trimmed of thick stems, washed, dried, and cut into ¼-inch-wide strips

½ teaspoon finely chopped fresh tarragon

1 tablespoon freshly squeezed lemon juice

DO AHEAD: Poach the roe and clean the spinach a day in advance.

1. Bring the water, white wine, onion, celery, thyme, and bay leaf to a boil in a medium saucepan. Season with salt and pepper. Lower the heat to a simmer and cook for 15 minutes. Gently slip the roe sacks into the liquid (you don't want the membranes holding everything together to rupture) and simmer for 2 minutes. Turn off the heat and allow the roe to cool in the liquid.

2. Carefully remove the cooled roe sacks from the poaching liquid. Remove the blood vessel and any thick pieces of membrane. Split the membranes holding the roe, and scrape it into a bowl. Use a fork to mash the clumps into individual eggs. Remove any obvious remaining membrane. Season with salt and pepper, cover tightly, and refrigerate.

3. Put a large pot of water on to boil.

4. Meanwhile, heat the olive oil in a medium sauté pan over medium heat. Add the pancetta and cook until the fat starts to render, about a minute. Don't let it get too crispy. Add the shallots and garlic and cook until tender, about 2 minutes. Keep warm.

5. Season the boiling water with salt and add the pasta, stirring so the individual strands remain separate. Cover the pot if necessary to bring the water back to a boil. Cook for 1 minute, then stir again. Continue to check periodically to make sure the strands aren't sticking together, and cook until the tagliatelle is tender but still offers a little resistance when you bite into it, about 3 minutes. Before draining the pasta, use a measuring cup to scoop out ¼ cup of the pasta water. Set it aside.

6. Pour the pasta into a colander. While it's draining, return the pancetta, garlic, and shallots to high heat. Add the spinach and tarragon and toss quickly, just until the spinach has wilted. Season with salt and pepper; remove from heat and keep warm.

7. Transfer the pasta to a large warm bowl. Pour the spinach mixture over it and add the roe. Toss well. If the sauce seems too thick to coat the pasta, add a little of the reserved pasta water to thin it, then toss again. Season with the lemon juice, salt, and pepper, being especially generous with pepper. Serve immediately.

Brandade Lasagna with Broccoli Rabe

This is not the lasagna your mother (or grandmother) used to serve you. Deceptively spare, elegant, with about a third of the cheese of traditional lasagna, it's suffused with the assertive flavor of brandade, the Provençal purée of salt cod, cream, and a little potato. By itself, brandade would be too rich a filler for lasagna—you'd be sated after a bite or two—but the sharp flavor of broccoli rabe and the mild acid of the tomato sauce keep the brandade in line. Just when you think you've had enough, the richness is erased, and you want to go back for more.

MAKES 4 ENTRÉE SERVINGS

SAUCE
¼ cup extra virgin olive oil

1 small onion, chopped into ¼-inch dice

2 garlic cloves, minced

2½ cups diced tomatoes (high-quality canned tomatoes are fine)

Kosher salt and freshly ground black pepper

1 teaspoon sugar

¼ teaspoon hot red pepper flakes

LASAGNA
Kosher salt

1½ pounds broccoli rabe, tough or split stems removed, rinsed

5 tablespoons extra virgin olive oil

3 large leeks, white part only, trimmed of roots and tough outer leaves, thinly sliced crosswise, and swirled vigorously in a bowl of cold water to remove any grit

Freshly ground black pepper

4 garlic cloves, chopped

¼ teaspoon hot red pepper flakes

Eight 6 × 8-inch sheets Fresh Pasta (pages 142–43; use half a recipe [about ½ pound], roll it out to setting #6, and cut into 8-inch lengths)

1 recipe Brandade de Morue (page 22)

½ cup chopped fresh flat-leaf parsley

1¼ cups freshly grated Pecorino Romano

4 teaspoons capers, rinsed, for garnish

DO AHEAD: Make the brandade 2 days ahead. The sauce can also be made ahead and reheated.

1. Heat the olive oil in large saucepan over medium heat. Add the onion and cook until tender, about 4 minutes. Add the garlic and cook until aromatic, about a minute. Add the tomatoes, season with salt and pepper, and add the sugar and red pepper flakes. Lower the heat to a simmer and cook for 20 minutes. If the sauce seems too thick, thin it with a little water as it cooks.

2. Transfer the sauce to a blender and purée. Strain, if desired, and set aside.

3. Bring a large pot of water to a boil and season with salt. Prepare a large bowl of ice water. Add the broccoli rabe to the boiling water and cook at a rolling boil until tender, about 4 minutes. Scoop out the broccoli and plunge it into the ice water. When it's chilled, drain and pat dry. Coarsely chop and set aside.

4. Heat 3 tablespoons of the oil in a large sauté pan over medium-high heat. Add the leeks, season with salt and pepper, and cook until tender, about 4 minutes. Add the garlic and cook until aromatic, about a minute. Add the broccoli rabe and red pepper flakes, season with salt and pepper, and toss well. Remove from the heat and let cool.

5. Bring a fresh pot of water to a boil and season with salt. Prepare another bowl of ice water. Lay out a sheet of plastic wrap on the counter large enough to hold one sheet of pasta. Add the pasta sheets to the boiling water and blanch for 1 minute, stirring constantly. Drain the sheets in a colander, then immediately plunge them into the ice bath. Stir the sheets gently until they've cooled, about 30 seconds. Remove one pasta sheet, drain, and lay it out on the plastic wrap. Cover with a second sheet of plastic, then remove and drain a second pasta sheet, lay it on top of the first, and cover with plastic. (Work quickly; if you leave the pasta sheets in the water too long, they'll stick together.) Repeat the process with the remaining sheets, then cover with a final layer of plastic wrap. Set aside until ready to use.

6. Preheat the oven to 375°F.

7. Rub a 9 × 13-inch lasagna pan with 1 tablespoon of the olive oil. Mix the brandade with the parsley. Lay 2 of the pasta sheets side by side in the pan so the bottom is covered. Spread the sheets evenly with one-third of the brandade. Top with one-third of the leek and broccoli rabe mixture, sprinkle with ¼ cup of the cheese, and cover with 2 more sheets of pasta. Repeat the layering two more times, finishing with a final layer of pasta sheets. Brush the top with the remaining 1 tablespoon olive oil and sprinkle with the remaining ½ cup Pecorino Romano.

8. Bake the lasagna for 25 minutes, or until it is heated through and the top is lightly browned. Let rest for 5 minutes before cutting.

9. While the lasagna is resting, warm the sauce. Cut the lasagna into 4 equal pieces. Make a pool of warm tomato sauce in the center of each plate. Set a serving of lasagna in the center of each pool of sauce. Sprinkle with the capers and serve.

Spaghetti with Maine Crabmeat, Toasted Bread Crumbs, and Garlic

I *was skeptical on first hearing* that in southern Italy bread crumbs sautéed in olive oil were the poor man's substitute for cheese. I didn't doubt that this was a technique that was used, just whether it tasted good. I've since revised my opinion: Sautéed bread crumbs lend a great texture and delicious flavor to pasta, even when there is nothing else to accompany them except a few cloves of garlic and a handful of chopped fresh herbs.

MAKES 4 ENTRÉE SERVINGS

½ cup extra virgin olive oil

1½ cups slightly dry coarse bread crumbs

4 garlic cloves, thinly sliced

1 pint cherry tomatoes, cut in half

¼ teaspoon hot red pepper flakes, or more to taste

Kosher salt

1 pound high-quality dried spaghetti

1 pound Maine (or other high-quality) crabmeat (fresh or thawed frozen), picked through to remove any shells

½ cup chopped fresh flat-leaf parsley

1. Put a large pot of water on to boil.

2. Meanwhile, heat ¼ cup of the olive oil in a medium sauté pan over medium heat. Add the bread crumbs and stir until they're toasted and golden brown. Remove from the pan and set aside.

3. Wipe out the pan with a paper towel and add the remaining oil. Add the garlic and cook over medium heat until golden. Add the tomatoes and red pepper flakes, season with salt, and cook until the tomatoes are tender but not falling apart, about 3 minutes. Set aside.

4. Season the boiling water with salt and add the pasta, stirring so the strands remain separate. (If the pot isn't large enough for the spaghetti to lie flat, either break the strands in half or hold one end of the pasta bundle while the other end softens in the boiling water, then release the pasta into the water.) Cover the pot if necessary to bring the water back to a boil, cook for 1 minute, then stir again. Continue to check periodically to make sure the strands aren't sticking together, and cook until the spaghetti is tender but still offers a little bit of resistance when you bite into it. Begin checking for doneness after 8 minutes. Before draining the pasta, use a measuring cup to scoop out ¼ cup of the pasta water. Set it aside.

5. Pour the pasta into a colander. While it's draining, return the tomatoes to high heat. Add the crabmeat and parsley and heat through.

6. Transfer the spaghetti to a large warm bowl. Pour the sauce over it and toss well. If the sauce is too thick to coat the spaghetti, add enough of the reserved pasta water to thin it, then toss again. Toss with the bread crumbs and serve.

Fregola—Sardinian Pasta with Lemon, Favas, Parmesan, and Lots of Parsley

Fregola *is a granular Sardinian* pasta. The pasta dough is rolled by hand into peppercorn-sized balls and then baked. In the last few years it has been appearing on American menus, either under its own name or billed as "giant couscous," which it does indeed resemble. In Sardinia, fregola is often added to soup or broth, not unlike orzo, or matched with seafood, especially mussels or clams. You can cook it like regular pasta—boiling it in stock or water—but I prefer to treat it like risotto, which results in a much creamier texture.

MAKES 4 APPETIZER OR SIDE-DISH SERVINGS

4 to 5 cups Chicken Stock (page 31) or high-quality canned low-sodium chicken broth

Kosher salt and freshly ground black pepper

2 tablespoons extra virgin olive oil

1 medium onion, cut into ¼-inch dice

½ pound fregola (Sardinian pasta, available in the Mediterranean section of specialty food stores)

Grated zest of 2 lemons

2 tablespoons freshly squeezed lemon juice

¼ cup freshly grated Parmesan, plus extra for serving

2 tablespoons unsalted butter

½ cup shelled fresh fava beans, long-blanched (see Fava Notes, page 88) and peeled (about 1 pound in the pod; if favas are unavailable, you can use blanched fresh lima beans or fresh peas)

½ cup chopped fresh flat-leaf parsley

1. Bring the chicken stock to a boil in a medium saucepan, then lower the heat to a simmer. Season with salt and pepper if it's unseasoned or you're using low-sodium broth. Keep the stock hot.

2. Heat the oil in a large deep saucepan over medium heat. Add the onion and cook until tender, about 5 minutes. Add the fregola and lemon zest and cook, stirring often, for 5 minutes. Ladle 1 cup of the chicken stock over the fregola, stirring constantly, and cook until the stock is almost completely absorbed. Add 3 more cups of the stock, 1½ cups at a time, waiting until the previous addition is almost absorbed before adding more. Lower the heat if the stock seems to disappear as soon as it hits the pan or seems to be boiling. When finished, the pasta should be tender but not mushy. Add more chicken stock if necessary; the dish should be a little soupy. Season with salt and pepper. Stir in the lemon juice and cheese. Keep warm.

3. Melt the butter in a small saucepan over medium heat. Add the favas and toss in the butter until heated through. Season with salt and pepper.

4. Stir the parsley into the fregola. Spoon the pasta into four warm bowls, top with the fava beans, and serve, offering additional cheese.

Penne with Shrimp, Artichokes, and Feta

At a conference of women chefs in Mexico City, I tasted a perfect shrimp dish prepared by Monique Andrée Barbeau, the chef of Fullers in Seattle. The shrimp were saturated with flavor, but still mysteriously tender. The trick, she explained, was to first simmer aromatic ingredients in oil, then to cook the shrimp over low heat, all the while keeping them completely submerged in the flavored oil. In this recipe, fennel, hot red pepper flakes, oregano, garlic, and lemon zest create the first level of flavor, followed by a long simmer of artichoke quarters. Only then do the shrimp enter the pan for their own slow cooking.

MAKES 4 ENTRÉE SERVINGS

2 cups extra virgin olive oil

1 teaspoon coriander seeds

1 teaspoon fennel seeds

1 teaspoon dried oregano

½ teaspoon hot red pepper flakes

4 garlic cloves, chopped

1 medium onion, chopped into ½-inch dice

Grated zest of 1 lemon

Kosher salt

3 large artichokes, trimmed (see page 85), cut into quarters, chokes removed, and rubbed with a lemon half

1 pound medium shrimp (20 to 25), peeled and deveined

2 tablespoons freshly squeezed lemon juice

½ pound penne

3 tablespoons chopped fresh mint, plus 4 sprigs for garnish

3 tablespoons chopped fresh oregano

6 ounces feta, crumbled into large pieces

1. Combine the olive oil, coriander seeds, fennel seeds, oregano, red pepper flakes, garlic, onion, and lemon zest in a large sauté pan. Season generously with salt. Bring to a simmer and cook for 10 minutes, so the seasonings flavor the oil.

2. Add the artichokes, lower the heat if necessary (the oil should be barely bubbling), and cook until tender, 20 to 30 minutes. Use a slotted spoon to transfer the artichokes to a bowl.

3. Add the shrimp to the oil and cook at the same low simmer, turning once, until done, about 10 minutes.

4. Remove the shrimp from the oil and let cool on a plate. Pour off 1 cup of the oil from the pan, strain, and refrigerate for another use. (The oil is delicious and can be used in vinaigrettes or for sautéing another dish.) Leave the pan over low heat.

5. As soon as they're cool enough to handle, remove the leaves from the artichokes and save for another use. Chop the artichoke hearts and stems into 1-inch pieces and return to the bowl. Add the shrimp and toss with the lemon juice.

6. Meanwhile, bring a large pot of water to a boil and season with salt. Add the penne and stir constantly until the water returns to a boil. Cook until the pasta is tender but still offers some resistance when you bite into it, about 10 minutes. Before draining the pasta, use a measuring cup to scoop out ¼ cup of the pasta water; reserve. Drain the pasta in a colander and add to the sauté pan with the oil.

7. Add the artichokes, shrimp, herbs, and feta and toss until heated through. Taste for seasoning. Depending on the saltiness of the feta, it may not be necessary to add additional salt. If the pasta seems too dry, add some of the reserved pasta water as needed.

8. Divide among four warm bowls. Garnish each portion with a sprig of mint and serve.

Big Ravioli Stuffed with Wild Mushrooms, Spinach, and Poached Eggs

T*his is a spectacular brunch* or weekend lunch dish whose first impression is innocently innocuous—a pair of large square ravioli dusted with cheese on each diner's plate. The first cut through the pasta gives the game away—molten egg yolk flows voluptuously over a stuffing of wild mushrooms, tomato, and spinach. It is at once sensual, surprising, and delicious. The raviolis were inspired by *brik,* a North African fried pastry containing an egg.

MAKES 8 LARGE RAVIOLI OR 4 SERVINGS

FILLING

4 tablespoons unsalted butter

½ pound mixed wild mushrooms, cleaned and finely chopped

Kosher salt and freshly ground black pepper

2 garlic cloves, minced

2 shallots, minced

½ pound flat-leaf spinach, trimmed of thick stems, washed, and dried

¼ pound cream cheese, at room temperature

2 plum tomatoes, peeled (see page 55), seeded, and chopped into ½-inch dice

1 tablespoon chopped fresh flat-leaf parsley

1 teaspoon chopped fresh thyme

½ recipe Fresh Pasta (see pages 142–43)

9 extra-large eggs

Kosher salt and freshly ground black pepper

8 thin slices pancetta (3 to 4 ounces)

4 tablespoons unsalted butter

1 sprig thyme

½ cup freshly grated Parmesan

¼ cup chopped fresh flat-leaf parsley

DO AHEAD: The ravioli can be made up to 4 hours ahead and refrigerated until you are ready to cook them.

1. Heat 2 tablespoons of the butter in a large sauté pan over medium-high heat. As soon as the butter stops foaming, add the mushrooms and cook until they have released their juices, and the juices are almost gone. Season with salt and pepper, then transfer to a bowl.

2. Lower the heat to medium and add the remaining 2 tablespoons butter to the pan. As soon as it melts, add the garlic and shallots. Cook until they soften, 2 to 3 minutes, lowering the heat if necessary so they don't burn. Increase the heat to high. Add the spinach and stir until it wilts, about 2 minutes. Season with salt and pepper. Remove the spinach from the pan, draining any excess water if necessary, and allow to cool.

3. Mix the cream cheese with the mushrooms, then add the tomatoes, parsley, thyme, and spinach. Taste and adjust the seasonings if necessary. Refrigerate until ready to use.

4. Preheat the oven to 350°F.

5. Roll out the pasta according to the directions on page 143, until thin enough for ravioli (the #7 or #8 setting, depending on your machine). Lay the pasta sheets out on a floured countertop and use a pastry wheel to cut out sixteen 4-inch squares. Discard the pasta scraps.

6. Beat 1 of the eggs with 1 tablespoon water to form an egg wash. Brush the edges of 1 pasta square with the egg wash. Put 3 to 4 tablespoons of the mushroom mixture in the center of the pasta and make a well in the mixture. Crack an egg into a teacup, taking care not to break the yolk. Pour the yolk and about half the white into the well in the filling. (Discard the remaining egg white or reserve for another purpose.) Season with salt and pepper. Cover with a second sheet of pasta and gently push out as much air as possible. Seal the edges with your fingertips or the tines of a fork. Set the ravioli aside on a lightly floured baking sheet. Repeat the process to make 7 more ravioli.

7. Lay the pancetta slices on a sheet pan and bake until crispy, about 6 minutes. Keep warm.

8. Meanwhile, bring a large pot of water to a boil. Season with salt. Slip the ravioli into the water. Cook, stirring gently several times, until done. To test for doneness, cut a small bit of pasta off the edge of a ravioli and taste to see that the pasta is cooked through; 5 minutes is usually long enough to cook the ravioli and the eggs while leaving the yolks still runny. Cook longer for a firmer yolk.

9. While the ravioli are cooking, melt the 4 tablespoons of butter with the sprig of thyme over medium heat in a small sauté pan. Season with salt and pepper and lower the heat to keep warm.

10. Scoop the ravioli out of the pot with a slotted spoon and place 2 ravioli on each plate. Allowing some of the pasta water to cling to the ravioli will help the cheese to stick as well as keep the pasta moist. Drizzle with the thyme butter (discard the sprig of thyme). Arrange the pancetta slices on top of the ravioli. Sprinkle with the cheese and parsley and serve.

Ravioli Bundles of Roasted Beets with Walnuts, Poppy Seeds, and Garlic Cream

A *Venetian recipe for beets with* nuts gave me the idea for these ravioli "party favors." I assumed that they would taste good, but I was unprepared for how beautiful they are. Some of the juice from the beet filling seeps through the translucent pasta dough and creates a lovely ruby splash against the white poppy seed cream. This dish is truly a jewel. You can easily double the recipe and serve it as a sophisticated main course for a late night supper or special lunch.

MAKES 4 APPETIZER SERVINGS

½ recipe Fresh Pasta (see pages 142–43)

FILLING AND SAUCE

½ pound beets
¼ cup extra virgin olive oil
Kosher salt and freshly ground black pepper
1 shallot, minced
2 tablespoons ricotta
1 tablespoon chopped fresh basil
2½ to 3 tablespoons freshly grated Parmesan
8 garlic cloves, peeled
1 cup heavy cream
1 teaspoon balsamic vinegar
1 teaspoon poppy seeds
4 teaspoons chopped toasted walnuts

4 beautiful basil leaves for garnish

DO AHEAD: Roast the beets.

1. Following the directions on page 143, roll out half the dough to ravioli thinness (the #7 or #8 setting, depending on your machine). Cut into eight 3×4-inch rectangles. Transfer the rectangles to a kitchen towel dusted with flour. Reserve the remaining dough for another use (or roll it into sheets and hand-cut it into irregular shapes. Refrigerate to use in soup or broth the next day.) These ravioli squares don't have to remain moist like classic ravioli because they will be cooked individually, like lasagna noodles. If they dry out a little while you're preparing the rest of the recipe, it's okay.

2. Preheat the oven to 400°F.

3. Toss the beets with 1 tablespoon of the olive oil and season with salt and pepper. Place in a small roasting pan and roast for an hour or so, or until tender all the way through. Allow to cool, then peel (see page 103). Leave the oven on.

4. Heat 1 tablespoon of the olive oil in a small sauté pan over medium heat. Add the shallot and cook until tender, about 3 minutes. Let cool.

5. Purée the beets in a food processor. Add the ricotta and process to mix well. Transfer to a bowl and add half the shallots, all the chopped basil, and 1 tablespoon of the Parmesan. Season with salt and pepper.

6. Put the garlic in a small saucepan and cover with 2 inches of water. Season with salt, bring to a boil, reduce the heat to a simmer, and cook until very soft, about 10 minutes. Drain the garlic, rinse, and drain again.

7. Heat the cream and garlic in a medium saucepan over medium heat until it starts to bubble. Reduce the heat to a simmer and cook, skimming the foam and impurities, until the cream has reduced by one-quarter. Transfer the reduced cream and garlic to a blender and purée. Return the garlic cream to the pan. Add the balsamic vinegar, the remaining shallots, and the poppy seeds. Simmer for 2 minutes. Season with salt and pepper. Reheat before serving.

8. Meanwhile, bring a large pot of water to a boil and season with salt. Prepare a bowl of ice water. Rub a sheet pan with 1 tablespoon of the olive oil. Add the pasta sheets to the boiling water and cook through, about 1 minute. Shock in the ice water, then drain. Lay the pasta sheets on the sheet pan.

9. Put a spoonful of beet filling in the center of each pasta sheet. Roll up starting from a long side and twist the ends to form a bundle. Arrange the bundles side by side on the baking sheet and drizzle with the remaining 1 tablespoon olive oil.

10. Bake the bundles for 8 minutes, or until heated through.

11. Stir 1 tablespoon of the Parmesan into the sauce. Pour a pool of sauce into the center of each of four warm plates. Arrange 2 bundles on each plate. Sprinkle with the walnuts and a little more Parmesan. Garnish each plate with a basil leaf and serve.

Nidimi—"Little Nests" Stuffed with Prosciutto, Fontina, and Spinach

Emilia-Romagna is famed for its stuffed pasta dishes, and it was there I saw my first "little nests." The *nidimi* were chunky pasta bundles, thick as cucumbers, standing upright in a red pool of smooth tomato sauce, with swirls of green herbed ricotta visible in the upright end, spiraling hypnotically between layers of pasta. The dish immediately struck me as a more elegant, sophisticated take on manicotti, those humble pasta tubes stuffed with a meat or cheese filling.

Since then I've applied all kinds of fillings to nidimi; as long as the filling is flat and flexible (like slices of cured meat or grilled eggplant) or easily spread, it will usually work. The trick is to roll the nidimi tightly and reheat them carefully so they don't dry out. One of my favorites is made with grilled eggplant, peppers, spinach, and feta and served with a spicy tomato sauce. This particular version takes the classic tagliatelle accompaniments of prosciutto, spinach, and Fontina and reconfigures them as nidimi with a Parmesan cream sauce.

MAKES 4 APPETIZER SERVINGS

½ recipe Fresh Pasta (see pages 142–43)
Kosher salt

1 tablespoon chopped fresh flat-leaf parsley

FILLING

8 paper-thin slices prosciutto (about ¼ pound)
3 ounces flat-leaf spinach, trimmed of thick stems, washed, and dried
¼ pound semisoft Italian cheese, such as Fontina, fresh Asiago, or Taleggio, thinly sliced

SAUCE

1 cup light cream
¼ cup freshly grated Parmesan
Kosher salt and freshly ground black pepper
Extra virgin olive oil
¼ cup fresh or frozen peas, blanched briefly in boiling salted water
1 teaspoon freshly squeezed lemon juice
2 teaspoons minced fresh chives

DO AHEAD: You can prepare as much or as little of this dish ahead as you like, from simply cooking the pasta sheets to completely filling and rolling the pasta. I like to do everything ahead, leaving only the sauce and the final heating of the nidimi for the day of serving.

1. Following the directions on page 143, roll the dough out in sheets 6 inches wide. Roll the sheets to noodle thickness (the #6 setting). You don't need to let the pasta dry before cutting it. Using a pastry wheel, cut 4 rectangles, each measuring 6 × 8 inches. Discard the rest of the pasta.

2. Bring a large pot of water to a boil and season with salt. Prepare a large bowl of ice water. Add the pasta sheets and cook, stirring occasionally, until the pasta is cooked, but still firm, about 1 minute—it's going to bake, so it should still have a little bite to it. Transfer the sheets to the ice bath to cool, stirring them around in the cold water so they don't stick together.

3. Drain each sheet individually in a colander for a minute, then shake off the excess water and lay it on a piece of plastic wrap on a flat work surface. Lay the sheets out so a narrow end of each is toward you. Work quickly; if you leave the pasta sheets in the water too long they'll stick together. Blot any excess water off the pasta with a paper towel. (If you're going to assemble the nidimi later, stack the sheets on top of each other, with a layer of oiled plastic wrap between each one, and on the top and bottom as well. Refrigerate until ready to use.)

4. Arrange the prosciutto in a single layer over the sheets of pasta, leaving an empty 2-inch border along the short side farthest from you. Follow the prosciutto with a heavy layer of spinach and then a layer of cheese. The cheese won't cover the spinach completely; just make sure you distribute it as evenly as possible. The next step is to roll up the pasta sheets and filling: Starting at the short edge close to you, roll up each sheet as tightly as you can without tearing the pasta. (Take care not to roll up the plastic wrap with the pasta.) The uncovered strip of pasta will stick to the roll, sealing it.

5. Cut each roll into 3 even pieces, making your cuts straight across the rolls—each piece of nidimi needs to be able to stand upright. (The nidimi can be made up to this point and refrigerated overnight.)

6. Preheat the oven to 425°F.

7. Heat the cream in a small saucepan over medium heat. As soon as the cream is warm, whisk in the Parmesan and keep whisking until it has completely melted. Season with salt and pepper and keep warm.

8. Brush a baking dish with extra virgin olive oil. Stand the nidimi on their ends in the baking dish. Sprinkle 2 tablespoons water around the nidimi. Cover the nidimi with a layer of plastic wrap (tuck the edges inside the dish) and a layer of foil (crimped over the edges of the dish). Bake until the rolls are hot and the cheese has started to melt, about 15 minutes.

9. Add the peas, lemon juice, and herbs to the sauce and warm through. Make a small pool of sauce on each of four warmed plates. Arrange 3 nidimi in the center of each plate. Serve immediately.

Fazzoletti—"Handkerchiefs" with Lemon Cream, Pistachios, Spinach, and Slow-Roasted Tomatoes

Fazzoletti, *handkerchiefs* in Italian, is a reference to the similarity between these folded pasta sheets and the dapper two- or three-pointer that used to grace the breast pockets of men's suit coats. A couple of generations from now, will anyone still make the connection? I latched on to this dish because it's a quick and elegant alternative to ravioli. The spinach is put in the center of large pasta squares, then each square is folded in half to make a triangle, then folded again to make a smaller triangle. The "handkerchiefs" are then baked briefly in a lemon cream with the slow-roasted tomatoes and pistachios. It almost makes you wish for the return of snap-brim fedoras.

If you don't have any slow-roasted tomatoes, you can substitute regular cherry tomatoes, but the effect will be milder.

MAKES 4 APPETIZER SERVINGS

2 tablespoons unsalted butter

3 medium shallots, 1 minced, 2 thinly sliced

1 cup heavy cream

Grated zest of 1 lemon

Kosher salt and freshly ground black pepper

½ pound flat-leaf spinach, trimmed of thick stems, washed, and dried

½ recipe Fresh Pasta (see pages 142–43)

½ recipe Slow-Roasted Tomatoes (page 117), using 12 cherry tomatoes or 6 plum tomatoes

2 tablespoons pistachios, toasted (see page 16) and coarsely chopped

¼ cup freshly grated Parmesan

1. Melt 1 tablespoon of the butter in a small saucepan over medium heat. Add the minced shallot and cook until tender, about 3 minutes. Add the cream and lemon zest and simmer until reduced by one-quarter. Skim off the foam that collects on top of the cream. Season with salt and pepper and remove from the heat.

2. Melt the remaining 1 tablespoon butter in a large sauté pan over medium-high heat. Add the sliced shallots and cook until they just begin to brown, 2 to 3 minutes (they'll cook faster than the other shallot because the pan is hotter). Add the spinach, season with salt and pepper, and stir until wilted, about 2 minutes. Transfer to a plate to cool.

3. Roll out the pasta according to the directions on pages 142–43 until thin enough for ravioli (the #7 or #8 setting, depending on your machine). Lay the pasta sheets out on a floured

countertop and use a pastry wheel to cut out 12 squares measuring 5 to 6 inches on a side. Discard the rest of the pasta. These ravioli squares don't have to remain moist like classic ravioli because they're cooked individually, like lasagna noodles. If they dry out a little while you're bringing the water to a boil, it's okay.

4. Bring a large pot of water to a boil. Prepare a bowl of ice water. Season with salt and add the pasta squares to the boiling water, stirring constantly, until cooked, about 1 minute. Scoop the pasta squares out of the pot and plunge them into the ice water, stirring until cool.

5. Preheat the oven to 450°F.

6. If using plum tomatoes, cut each half into 4 pieces. Coat the bottom of a shallow 2-quart gratin dish with ¼ cup of the lemon cream. Distribute 12 cherry tomato halves or 12 pieces of plum tomatoes over the bottom of the dish. Sprinkle with 1 teaspoon of the pistachios.

7. Remove the pasta squares from the cold water, drain, and lay them out on a flat work surface covered with plastic wrap. Put a spoonful of spinach in the center of each square. To make the fazzoletti, fold each square in half to make a triangle, then fold in half again to make a smaller triangle. Arrange the fazzoletti in overlapping rows in the gratin dish. Pour the remaining sauce over the pasta. Scatter the remaining tomatoes over the top, and sprinkle with the remaining pistachios and the Parmesan.

8. Bake for 10 minutes, or until the fazzoletti are brown and crispy. Serve immediately.

Semolina Gnocchi with Red Wine Mushroom Sauce and Roasted Marrowbones

Semolina gnocchi, with their light, puffy texture, cheesy crust, and passage from the stovetop to the oven seem more related to polenta (which is also cooked on top of the stove, allowed to firm up, and then may be baked) than to classic potato gnocchi, which are poached. For sheer versatility, they have few rivals. Accompanied by a red wine and mushroom sauce, as in this recipe, they serve as an elegant first course; without the sauce, they're a side dish for rabbit or veal. At home, my husband likes them as a main course, either with this sauce or a wild mushroom ragout. You can even serve them as an hors d'oeuvre—cut them into canapé-sized diamonds, top with cheese, and bake without layering.

I've simplified the traditional marrow and mushroom sauce by creating a separate easy recipe for Roasted Marrowbones. Most people's experiences with marrow are confined to osso buco, but in this dish you get a beef bone three times the size of an ordinary veal shank, with a triple portion of marrow. The marrowbones require very little effort and the marrow is such a creamy treat when spooned over the gnocchi that you owe it to yourself to try them. If you double the gnocchi recipe (use a shallow oval 2-quart casserole dish instead of a pie plate to bake the gnocchi) and add the marrowbones, you will have a stylish entrée.

MAKES 4 APPETIZER OR, WITHOUT THE SAUCE, SIDE-DISH SERVINGS

GNOCCHI

2 cups milk

Kosher salt and freshly ground black pepper

½ cup semolina flour

½ cup freshly grated Parmesan

1 extra-large egg yolk

1½ tablespoons unsalted butter, at room temperature

SAUCE

2 to 4 tablespoons unsalted butter

4 shallots, minced

¼ pound domestic or wild mushrooms, cleaned and coarsely chopped into ½-inch pieces

Kosher salt and freshly ground black pepper

1 cup dry red wine

2½ cups Chicken Stock (page 31) or 5 cups high-quality canned low-sodium chicken broth, reduced to 2½ cups (see page 32)

½ teaspoon chopped fresh thyme

1 recipe Roasted Marrowbones (recipe follows; optional)

DO AHEAD: Soak the marrowbones a day before roasting in order to draw out the blood. Both the gnocchi and sauce can be made in advance if you want to save yourself some effort on the day of serving. Take the gnocchi through Step 3, then cover with plastic wrap and refrigerate.

Allow the gnocchi to come to room temperature before baking them. If making the sauce ahead, allow it to cool, then cover with plastic wrap and refrigerate. Reheat while the gnocchi are baking.

1. Heat the milk in a heavy saucepan over medium heat. Season with salt and pepper. When the milk is just about to boil, add in the semolina in a slow, steady stream, whisking constantly. Continue whisking until the mixture is very thick, about 5 minutes. Remove from the heat.

2. Stir ⅓ cup of the cheese, the egg yolk, and 1 tablespoon of the butter into the semolina mixture. Season with salt and pepper. Pour the mixture into an 8-inch glass pie plate and allow to cool and firm.

3. Once the semolina mix is firm, use a wet knife to cut gnocchi diamonds with 1-inch sides (15 to 20 gnocchi). Rub a clean glass or glazed ceramic pie plate with the remaining ½ tablespoon butter. Arrange the gnocchi in the dish in overlapping rows. (If not serving immediately, cover with plastic wrap and refrigerate. Allow to come up to room temperature before baking.)

4. Heat 2 tablespoons butter in a sauté pan over medium heat. Add the shallots and cook until tender, about 3 minutes. Add the mushrooms and season with salt and pepper. Cook until tender, about 10 minutes. Transfer to a plate.

5. Add the red wine to the pan and reduce to a glaze, about 15 minutes. Return the mushrooms to the pan, add the chicken stock, and reduce by half, about 30 minutes. Keep warm (or allow to cool, cover with plastic wrap, and refrigerate until you need it; the sauce will keep for a day).

6. Meanwhile, preheat the oven to 450°F.

7. Sprinkle the gnocchi with the remaining cheese and bake until golden brown, about 20 minutes. If the gnocchi aren't a lovely golden brown after 20 minutes, run them under the broiler for a minute or two, until they turn the proper color. Allow to rest for 10 minutes before serving.

8. While the gnocchi are resting, reheat the sauce over low heat. When the sauce is hot, whisk in the remaining 2 tablespoons butter, if desired. Add the thyme and season with salt and pepper.

9. If serving the marrowbones, return them to the oven for 3 minutes so the marrow begins to melt.

10. Scoop the gnocchi onto four serving plates, and, if you have them, stand a marrowbone on its end next to each portion of gnocchi. Spoon the mushroom sauce over the gnocchi and serve immediately, accompanied by small spoons for scooping out the marrow.

❧ Roasted Marrowbones ❧

A s a matter of strategy, bake the marrowbones ahead of the gnocchi, then increase the oven temperature to 450°F. Allow the bones to sit on top of the stove, covered with foil, while the gnocchi finish baking.

4 beef marrowbones, each about 4 inches long,
    soaked 6 hours in several changes of cold water
    in the refrigerator to draw out the blood
Kosher salt and freshly ground black pepper
4 small sprigs thyme

1. Preheat the oven to 350°F.

2. Rinse the marrowbones and pat dry. Season the ends of the bones with salt and pepper. Arrange the bones on their ends on a small baking sheet—the ends with the greatest amount of exposed marrow should be facing up. Insert a spring of thyme into the exposed marrow in each bone.

3. Roast until the marrow of each bone wiggles like custard when the bone is shaken, about 45 minutes. Cover the baking sheet with foil and leave atop the stove to keep warm while you bake the gnocchi.

Potato Gnocchi Gratin

In the pantheon of comfort foods, potato gnocchi yield to no dish, with the possible exception of chicken soup made by your mother. To consume a forkful of potato gnocchi gratin with all the associations it conjures up of cheese and tomatoes and good things baked in an oven, followed by a swallow of red wine, is to breathe new life into the phrase "back to basics." Although they were probably developed as a way of using leftover potatoes, potato gnocchi have become an aim in themselves, a major staple in the cuisine of northern Italy. I've encountered them in literally dozens of preparations, in soups, with meat ragouts, with tomato or cream sauce, or baked in gratins— alone, as in this recipe, or with a Wild Mushroom Fricassee (page 101) or salt cod (page 22). Squash, spinach, ricotta, and different herbs are sometimes introduced into this basic recipe, and there are many other variations, including eggless ones. They are all delicious.

Making gnocchi may seem arcane, but in truth they are not much more than poached bits of mashed potato. If you follow the suggestions in the Gnocchi Notes on page 171, you shouldn't have any problem. They freeze quite well, and a bag of them in your freezer, like a bag of frozen cubes of lobster stock, is a blessed store against a bare larder.

MAKES 4 SIDE-DISH SERVINGS

GNOCCHI

2 pounds baking potatoes, scrubbed

1 cup unbleached all-purpose flour, plus more if needed

1 tablespoon kosher salt

1 extra-large egg, beaten

2 cups light cream

Kosher salt and freshly ground black pepper

4 plum tomatoes, peeled (see page 55), seeded, and chopped into ½-inch dice

1 tablespoon unsalted butter

¾ cup freshly grated Parmesan

2 tablespoons chopped fresh flat-leaf parsley

DO AHEAD: Make the gnocchi the night before serving, arrange them in the gratin or casserole dish, cover, and refrigerate. If you need to prepare as much of this dish as possible several days in advance, follow the box instructions for making gnocchi and freezing them raw.

1. Preheat the oven to 400°F.

2. Roast the potatoes for 40 to 50 minutes— they should be just done. If they cook too long, they won't rice properly.

3. Let the potatoes cool for 5 minutes, no longer. Using a kitchen towel to hold the potatoes, cut each one in half, scoop out the potato flesh, and rice into a large bowl. Add the flour and salt and mix well. Add the egg and quickly knead everything together into a sticky dough; work the dough no longer than 3 minutes. If it's too wet, add a small amount of additional flour. If you add too much flour or knead the dough for too long, the gnocchi will be gluey.

4. Fill a large pot with 4 inches of water; bring to a boil and season with salt. (You need the water deep enough to cook the submerged gnocchi, yet shallow enough that you can maintain a good boil. If you want the process to go faster, put on two large pots.) Fill another large pot with ice water. Dust your hands with flour. Cut off a piece of dough about the size of a gumball to make a trial gnocchi. Roll it between your palms into a ball, then drop it into the boiling water. After it cooks for a minute, it will bob to the surface. Let it cook for a minute longer, then remove it with a slotted spoon. Plunge it into the ice water for a few seconds, then taste it. (Don't worry if the outside looks a little filmy as it comes out of the ice water. The film will disappear as the gnocchi dries and the moisture evaporates.) The gnocchi should be cooked through but still soft. If it falls apart, knead a little more flour into the dough, taste for seasoning, and test again.

5. Using more flour as needed, roll the dough under your palms into ½-inch-thick logs. There should be enough dough to make between 4 and 5 logs about 18 inches long. Cut the logs diagonally into 1-inch lengths. You should get 65 to 70 gnocchi. Gnocchi are gen-erally given a final shaping either by making a depression in the center of each piece with your finger or rolling them off the back of the tines of a fork.

6. Preheat the broiler. Grease a shallow 2-quart baking dish with the butter. (The dish has to be large enough to accommodate the gnocchi in a single layer.)

7. Add the gnocchi to the boiling water in several batches. Again, let them bob to the surface, then cook for an additional minute. Using a slotted spoon, transfer the gnocchi from the boiling water to a sheet pan, shaking off excess water. Let them cool for a couple of minutes, then transfer to the buttered baking dish. (If not baking the gnocchi immediately, see Gnocchi Notes.)

8. Heat the cream in a small saucepan over medium heat. When it starts to simmer, season with salt and pepper. Remove from the heat and add the tomatoes.

9. Arrange the gnocchi in the dish in a single layer. Pour the cream and tomatoes over the gnocchi. Sprinkle with the Parmesan. Place under the broiler until the gnocchi are toasted and golden, about 5 minutes.

10. Sprinkle with the chopped parsley. Serve immediately.

GNOCCHI NOTES

Potato gnocchi aren't hard to make, but there are two things that will result in gummy gnocchi—overcooked potatoes and potatoes that are allowed to cool before being riced. The cooler a potato gets, the more difficult it is to rice, and the gummier the gnocchi will be. Scoop out and rice the roasted potatoes as soon as they're cool enough to handle.

Raw gnocchi should be refrigerated and cooked within 24 hours. Cooked gnocchi will keep for a day if refrigerated. If you want to cook gnocchi ahead, prepare a pot of ice water along with the pot of boiling water. As the gnocchi finish cooking, plunge them into the ice water. Let them cool for a minute, then drain and let dry on plastic wrap or wax paper. Put them in a plastic container large enough to hold them in a single layer and refrigerate.

To freeze raw gnocchi, lay them out on a tray dusted with flour and put them in the freezer. As soon as they've frozen solid, transfer them to a plastic freezer bag. To cook frozen gnocchi, drop them into lots of boiling salted water. Gently stir the water until they bob to the surface, so they don't stick together. Cook for an additional minute after they have come to the surface, just as you would fresh gnocchi. They should be cooked through, but still somewhat soft.

Buckwheat Polenta with Chestnuts, Figs, and Gorgonzola

I've experimented with lots of different additions to polenta—sun-dried tomatoes, chopped mushrooms, and corn kernels, to name a few—but the one I return to most frequently is buckwheat flour. It contributes an earthy element to the corn flavor. Buckwheat flour, polenta, Gorgonzola, chestnuts, and grappa are all staples of the cuisine of Lombardy. The figs here are my innovation, and a fine match with the other ingredients for a hearty dish. Add a salad and a dessert of roasted pears, and you're got a rustic repast just right for an autumn evening.

MAKES 4 ENTRÉE SERVINGS

1 cup dried figs, preferably Turkish, stems removed, cut into quarters

½ cup grappa (or Cognac or brandy)

2 cups cooked and peeled (see page 244) chestnuts (if fresh chestnuts are unavailable, substitute 2 cups frozen or jarred chestnuts, crumbled or coarsely chopped)

4 tablespoons unsalted butter

3 medium onions, thinly sliced

Kosher salt and freshly ground black pepper

2 tablespoons chopped fresh sage

8 cups water

2 cups coarse cornmeal

6 tablespoons buckwheat flour (available at health food stores or whole-foods grocery stores)

½ cup freshly grated Parmesan

¼ pound Gorgonzola

DO AHEAD: Boil and peel the chestnuts.

1. Combine the figs and grappa in a small saucepan over low heat, taking care not to ignite the alcohol. Bring to a simmer, remove from the heat, and let steep for 30 minutes. The figs should be tender and all the grappa should be absorbed. If there is still grappa remaining, remove the figs, put the pan on the stove, and reduce to almost a glaze. Pour over the figs. Set aside.

2. Heat the butter in a large sauté pan over medium heat. When the foam subsides, add the onions and season with salt and pepper. Cook until tender and golden, 10 minutes. Add the chestnuts, season with salt and pepper, and cook until golden and tender, about 4 minutes. (If using frozen or jarred chestnuts, they may not color; just heat them through.) Remove from the heat, add the sage, and set aside.

3. Bring the water to a boil in a large saucepan over high heat. Add 1 tablespoon salt and then add the polenta in a slow, steady stream through your fingers, whisking constantly so it doesn't clump up. Do the same with the buckwheat flour. If you get any lumps, mash them against the side of the pot with a wooden spoon and keep stirring. Lower the heat to a simmer and cook, stirring frequently, until the polenta is thick and shiny and begins to pull away from the sides of the pan, about 30 minutes. Regulate the heat as necessary so the mixture doesn't boil over. Season with salt and pepper.

4. Meanwhile, preheat the oven to 450°F.

5. Rub a glazed 9-inch shallow casserole or deep-dish pie plate with vegetable oil. When the polenta is done, pour one-third of it into the casserole. Cover with the chestnuts. Sprinkle with ¼ cup of the Parmesan. Pour another third of the polenta over the chestnuts. Scatter the figs over it and dot with the Gorgonzola. Cover with the final one-third of polenta. Sprinkle with ½ teaspoon pepper and the remaining Parmesan.

6. Bake the polenta until bubbling and heated through, 12 to 15 minutes. Serve immediately.

Goose or Duck Risotto

Leftover goose or duck is a rare opportunity for an extraordinary risotto. In my family, we have a tradition of using the carcasses of the Christmas geese to make a stock (see Chicken Stock headnote, page 31), which we then use, along with leftover goose meat, to make goose risotto on December 26. I freeze extra stock, saving it for a treat with friends sometime in February.

To make the risotto, follow the recipe below, substituting alternative ingredients for the listed ones as necessary—you don't need all of the first-choice ingredients. If you have goose stock, excellent; if you have leftover goose or duck, or even dark-meat turkey, but no stock, fine. Any of these alternatives will still make an excellent dish. When using rich meats like goose or duck, an acidic ingredient like dried cranberries or balsamic vinegar added just before serving can help balance the flavors.

MAKES 4 ENTRÉE SERVINGS

6 cups goose, duck, or Chicken Stock (page 31) or high-quality canned low-sodium chicken broth

¼ cup goose fat or 3 tablespoons unsalted butter plus 1 tablespoon extra virgin olive oil, or as needed

1 medium onion, chopped into ¼-inch dice

1 large garlic clove, minced

1 ounce dried porcini, reconstituted in warm water (see page 271), soaking liquid saved, and coarsely chopped

Kosher salt and freshly ground black pepper

1½ cups Arborio rice

½ cup dry white wine

½ cup crispy goose or duck skin cut into matchsticks (optional)

½ pound duck or goose meat, trimmed of skin and fat and coarsely chopped into 1- to 2-inch pieces

½ cup dried cranberries (optional)

½ cup pine nuts, toasted

1 cup freshly grated Parmesan, plus extra for serving

2 teaspoons chopped fresh thyme

2 tablespoons chopped fresh flat-leaf parsley

1 to 2 tablespoons balsamic vinegar, if needed

1. Heat the stock to a simmer. Keep warm.

2. Heat 1½ tablespoons of the goose fat (or butter) in a risotto pan or a large deep saucepan over medium heat. It's important to use a pan with a heavy bottom that conducts heat evenly or the rice could burn when you cook the risotto. As soon as the fat melts, add the onion and garlic and cook until tender, about 3 minutes. Add another 1½ tablespoons goose fat (or butter) to the pan. As soon as it melts, add the chopped porcini mushrooms, season with salt and pepper, and cook for 2 minutes. Add the rice and cook for 5 minutes, stirring so the fat coats all the rice. Season with salt and pepper.

3. Add the wine and cook, stirring frequently, until most of it has been absorbed. Add ½ cup of the stock and cook, stirring frequently, making sure that nothing sticks to the bottom of the pan, until most of the stock has been absorbed, then add another ½ cup. If you find that the stock is absorbed instantly, or you have to stir violently to prevent the rice from sticking and burning, then lower the heat. Continue adding the stock ½ cup at a time, waiting until most of it has been absorbed before adding more each time. Stop adding stock when the rice is creamy and tender but there's still a slight amount of resistance when you bite into it. Don't worry if there's still stock left—you may not have to use it all. The total cooking time for the rice will be about 30 minutes.

4. While the risotto is cooking, heat the remaining 1 tablespoon goose fat (or the olive oil) in a small sauté pan. Add the skin and sauté until crisp, 1 to 2 minutes. Drain on a paper towel.

5. As soon as the rice is finished, stir in the goose meat, cranberries, if using, pine nuts, cheese, and thyme. Season with salt and pepper. Taste and add a splash of balsamic vinegar if necessary. (Depending on whether you've used goose stock, and the amount specified of goose or duck meat, and whether you added the cranberries, the risotto may or may not taste quite rich. If it tastes too rich, a splash of acid will balance the flavor.) The texture should be creamy and slightly runny. Add ¼ cup more stock (or hot water if you've run out of stock) just before serving.

6. Spoon into warmed large shallow bowls or onto warmed plates and sprinkle with the cracklings, if you have them, and parsley. Serve immediately, offering additional cheese on the side.

Panisse with Tomatoes and Black Olives

Tomatoes and olives and basil and anchovies—close your eyes, and the aroma of this dish could fool you into thinking you're in Provence or Liguria, if only you could identify that toasty, cozy part of the smell. The mystery ingredient is chickpea flour, used to make a polenta called *panisse*. Like the familiar cornmeal polenta, panisse recipes often call for letting the cooked mixture firm up, then frying or baking it, perhaps with a topping of mushrooms or tomatoes.

MAKES 4 ENTRÉE SERVINGS

1½ cups chickpea flour

2 cups water

5 tablespoons extra virgin olive oil

Kosher salt and freshly ground black pepper

2 extra-large eggs, separated, yolks lightly beaten

1 medium onion, thinly sliced

4 garlic cloves, finely chopped

1 pint cherry tomatoes

3 anchovy fillets, rinsed and coarsely chopped

½ teaspoon dried oregano

¼ cup chopped fresh basil

½ cup coarsely chopped pitted Niçoise olives

2 tablespoons capers, rinsed

¼ cup freshly grated Parmesan

1. Mix the chickpea flour with the water, 2 tablespoons of the olive oil, 2 teaspoons salt, and 1 teaspoon pepper. Let sit for 1 hour.

2. Preheat the oven to 425°F. Rub an 8 × 12-inch baking dish with 1 tablespoon of the olive oil.

3. Beat the egg yolks into the batter. Whip the egg whites until they hold soft peaks and then fold into the batter. Pour the batter into the prepared pan. Bake until it sets, 12 to 15 minutes. Let cool for 15 minutes.

4. Meanwhile, heat the remaining 2 tablespoons olive oil in a large sauté pan over high heat. Add the onions and cook until they start to brown, about 5 minutes. Be careful not to let them burn. Add the garlic and tomatoes and cook for 3 minutes. Add the anchovies, oregano, basil, olives, and capers, season with pepper, and cook for 2 minutes. Remove from the heat.

5. Preheat the broiler. Spread the onion mixture over the cooled panisse "crust," sprinkle with the cheese, and place under the broiler until the top is brown, about 5 minutes. Serve hot or at room temperature. Let cool for 3 minutes if you want to serve it right away.

Seafood

ॐ

According to the National Fisheries Institute, Americans consume a paltry 15 pounds of seafood a year (compared to 220 pounds of meat and poultry) and the whale's share of that—about two-thirds—is prepared in restaurants. Subtract the 3½ pounds of canned tuna from the approximately 5 pounds of seafood each of us consumes at home, and there's hardly enough left over for a decent Friday night dinner of fish and chips.

I suspect that these statistics conceal a far different story, a reality in which there is a vast majority of people who cook no seafood at all, and a small minority who do, and know they're on to a good thing. These are the people lining up at seafood counters in grocery stores and fishmongers to buy salmon fillets, or tuna steaks, even when those fillets cost roughly double the price of flank steak and fresh tuna's in the same league as filet mignon. These are the people who get excited when August rolls around, because they know the bluefish will be running. A very few of them actually buy squid and octopus, to the amazement of their friends, while again, the others only wonder, "What do you do with that?" None of these people is eating only 15 pounds of fish a year—they're eating a lot more. If you recognize yourself in these portraits, this chapter is for you.

Fish (I'm using the term interchangeably with "*seafood*") is often expensive and tolerates the smallest margin of error of any animal protein in how it's cooked. The first thing to understand about seafood is that the texture of any individual type of fish has a lot to say about the method and length of cooking time. Fish with sturdy flesh that holds together can be grilled, pan-seared, fried, or even braised. Thin-filleted white fish like sole demand to be fried. The more delicate the flesh, the lighter the flavor, and the greater the need for your attention. A few minutes of overcooking can turn that fifteen dollars worth of salmon into cat food.

Unlike meat and poultry, whose flavors can often be successfully enhanced (as with marinades) or blended with other ingredients (in long braising), seafood works best when its natural flavors are allowed to shine with minimal interference. I rarely use acidic marinades with fish, and when I do resort to a marinade, it's usually nothing more than a little oil flavored with fresh herbs. That's not to say that some fish can't stand up to spicy flavors, but the seasonings should always work in counterpoint with the flavor and texture, not overwhelm it. Even when I cook fish with other ingredients, as in the braised dishes or any of the fish stews, the flavors don't blend so much as complement each other.

Always buy bright, fresh seafood and try to cook it within a day of purchase, sooner if possible. When selecting seafood, it should appear moist, and freshly cut or filleted; cut seafood looks dull and blurry after a couple of days. When in doubt, ask to smell it; most fresh seafood has little aroma, except perhaps a slight brininess. Any other odor is a signal to pass.

Seared Tuna with Green Caper Sauce

*I*s there a cuisine that doesn't have its own brilliant green sauce? There must be some deep-rooted universal appeal in the idea of puréeing fresh herbs or spring greens to make a condiment with a color as vivid as its taste. I always come back to this recipe because the anchovies, lemon, and tarragon steer the cart off the expected track of spinach flavor—and because it creates a vibrant green streak against the rosy center of a tuna steak. Serve this dish with Panisse with Tomatoes and Black Olives (page 176) on the side.

MAKES 4 ENTRÉE SERVINGS

SAUCE

¼ cup extra virgin olive oil

3 garlic cloves, minced

Kosher salt

3 cups packed spinach leaves trimmed of stems, washed

1 cup flat-leaf parsley leaves

4 scallions, trimmed and sliced paper-thin

1 tablespoon chopped fresh tarragon

1½ tablespoons capers, rinsed

6 anchovy fillets, rinsed and finely chopped

Freshly ground black pepper

2 teaspoons freshly squeezed lemon juice

TUNA

Four 5-ounce tuna steaks, approximately 1½ inches thick

Kosher salt and freshly ground black pepper

2 tablespoons extra virgin olive oil

2 teaspoons capers, rinsed

4 sprigs flat-leaf parsley

1. Heat 2 tablespoons of the olive oil with the garlic in a small sauté pan over medium heat until aromatic, about 2 minutes. Set aside.

2. Bring a medium pot of salted water to a boil. Add the spinach, parsley leaves, and scallions and blanch for 2 minutes. Drain, reserving ¼ cup of the blanching water.

3. Put the warm spinach mixture in a blender with the garlic, tarragon, capers, anchovies, and the reserved blanching water. Purée until smooth and with a sauce consistency; add more water if necessary. Season with salt and pepper. Transfer to a small saucepan and keep warm.

4. Season the tuna with salt and pepper. Heat the olive oil in a large sauté pan over medium-high heat. Add the tuna and cook for 3 to 4 minutes on each side, or until a crisp brown crust forms, for rare. If you like your tuna cooked further, reduce the heat to medium and cook for a minute or so longer on each side. Remove from the pan and let rest for 3 minutes before serving.

5. To serve, slice the tuna pieces in half across the grain, exposing the beautiful center, and arrange on four plates. Add the lemon juice to the sauce and pour next to the fish. (If you add the lemon juice earlier than just before serving, the sauce will turn olive green.) Sprinkle the tuna with the capers and garnish each plate with a sprig of parsley.

Chilled Lobster with Potato–Blood Orange Salad and Lime

In the summer, I run with the crowd when it comes to lobster—steamed or grilled, with lots of butter and lemon—but during the rest of the year I'm open to alternatives. A *salade composée*, the French term for a cold salad plate in which several distinct elements are prepared separately then assembled for the finished dish, is a perfect technique for lobster. Lime vinaigrette lightly dresses the lobster without overwhelming it. The other ingredients maintain a complementary yet respectful distance.

MAKES 4 ENTRÉE SERVINGS

Kosher salt

Two 1- to 1½-pound lobsters (see page 181)

1 teaspoon minced shallots

¼ cup freshly squeezed lime juice

½ teaspoon Dijon mustard

¼ cup plus 2 tablespoons extra virgin olive oil

½ cup crème fraîche

1 teaspoon grated lime zest

Freshly ground black pepper

2 tablespoons Pernod

2 tablespoons honey

2 blood oranges, skin and membrane removed, cut into segments over a bowl and stored in their own juice (use other sweet oranges if blood oranges are unavailable)

½ pound fingerling or small Red Bliss potatoes, scrubbed

2 tablespoons chopped fresh tarragon

3 tablespoons chopped fresh chervil

2 tablespoons minced fresh chives

12 cherry tomatoes or other small sweet tomatoes, cut in half

4 small bunches small greens such as watercress or mâche, washed and dried

1 lime, sliced into 4 wedges

DO AHEAD: The recipe can be prepared a day ahead up through Step 4. If you're making this salad with the intention of having leftovers, don't dress what you won't serve.

1. Pour 1 inch of salted water into a large pot, invert a colander in the pot, and bring to a boil. Put the lobsters in the pot and cover tightly. Steam for 5 minutes, then open the pot carefully (steam is *hot*) and, using a pair of tongs, change the lobsters' position so they will cook evenly. Quickly replace the lid and steam for 5 more minutes. Remove the lobsters from the pot and allow to cool.

2. Separate the tail, claws, and knuckles from the body of each lobster. Save the bodies for lobster stock or discard. Remove the lobster meat from the shells, trying to keep it in as large pieces as possible. (Shells don't provide as much flavor for stock as lobster bodies, so I discard them.) Cut the shelled tails in half lengthwise and remove the digestive tract, the dark vein-like structure. Cover and refrigerate the meat.

3. To make the vinaigrette, whisk the shallots, 1 tablespoon of the lime juice, and the Dijon mustard together in a small bowl. Slowly add ¼ cup of the olive oil in a steady stream. Season with salt.

4. Mix the crème fraîche with the lime zest, 1 tablespoon of the lime juice, and the remaining 2 tablespoons olive oil in a bowl. Season with salt and pepper. Cover and refrigerate.

5. Mix the Pernod with the honey and pour over the blood orange sections. Let sit for 30 minutes.

6. While the blood oranges are soaking, cut the potatoes into ½-inch-thick slices. Put the slices in a small saucepan and cover with cold water. Add 1½ teaspoons salt per quart of water. Bring to a boil and simmer until the potatoes are just done, 4 to 5 minutes. Drain. Toss with 2 tablespoons of the lime vinaigrette and set aside to cool at room temperature.

7. Mix the chopped tarragon, chervil, and chives together.

8. Right before serving, toss the lobster meat in a bowl with the remaining vinaigrette and 5 tablespoons of the herbs. Mix the potatoes with the remaining chopped herbs. Put 2 tablespoons of the crème fraîche in the center of each of four plates. Overlap the potato slices in a ring on the crème fraîche. Arrange the meat from half a lobster on top of each portion of potatoes—start with the knuckles, then the tail and then the claw (reserve the remaining vinaigrette in the bowl). Form a crescent of 6 tomato halves on one side of the lobster on each plate.

9. Toss the watercress with the lime vinaigrette left in the lobster bowl. Place a bunch of dressed greens on each plate on the side of the lobster opposite the tomatoes. Distribute the orange segments around the edges of the plates and drizzle with any remaining syrup. Garnish each plate with a wedge of lime, and serve.

LOBSTER—HARD-SHELL OR SOFT-SHELL?

I've suggested variability in the size of the lobsters in order to accommodate different pocketbooks and different times of the year when you might prepare this dish. If you're shopping in the late spring or fall, you'll find hard-shell lobsters are what's primarily available. In July, August, and September, molting season, soft-shell lobsters will dominate. January, February, and March see only hard-shells. The meat of a recently molted lobster is particularly sweet to some people, but by comparison to a hard-shell lobster of the same weight, there seems to be quite a bit less of it. In order to accomplish the Houdini-like feat of shedding their shells, lobsters shrink their bodies, especially their claws, through dehydration. A 1-pound hard-shell lobster will yield between 3 and 3¼ ounces of meat from the claws, knuckles, and tail; a soft-shell lobster of the same size will produce 2½ to 2¾ ounces. During months when soft-shells are primarily available, you will need to buy larger lobsters to get the same amount of meat you would from smaller hard-shells. If you want to be sure you're getting a hard-shell lobster, ask to squeeze it. Soft-shells have some give; they're flexible. Hard-shells are rigid, and the lobster will feel heavier than other lobsters of similar appearance.

Spicy Mussel Salad with Saffron Mayonnaise, Black Olives, and Roasted Peppers

T his is a composed salad of classic Spanish ingredients—mussels, saffron, and peppers handled in a slightly offbeat way. While all shellfish release juices into the cooking liquid as they steam, mussels are in a league of their own. The French reverently refer to their juice as mussel liquor. Cooking the steaming broth down to a glaze for the basis of a warm sauce is a standard technique, but this recipe is a little unusual in that the mussel glaze flavors a cold mayonnaise. With its intense flavor of mussels, the mayonnaise makes a nice olfactory bridge between the mussels and the roasted peppers. All of the major components of this dish—the roasted peppers, steamed mussels, and saffron mayonnaise can be prepared as much as 24 hours ahead of time and refrigerated. Prepare the chopped garnishes just before serving.

MAKES 4 ENTRÉE SERVINGS

2 tablespoons extra virgin olive oil

2 shallots, thinly sliced

2 garlic cloves, finely chopped

2 serrano peppers, stemmed and thinly sliced (to make this a milder dish, remove the seeds from the peppers)

Kosher salt

48 mussels, scrubbed and debearded

Pinch of saffron

¼ cup dry white wine

1 extra-large egg yolk

1 teaspoon freshly squeezed lemon juice

¼ cup vegetable oil

Freshly ground black pepper

3 large bell peppers—1 red, 1 yellow, and 1 green, roasted (see page 99), peeled, stemmed, seeded, and cut into quarters

½ cup peeled, seeded, and diced (¼-inch) cucumber

¼ cup diced (¼-inch) red onion

¼ cup chopped oil-cured black olives

¼ cup flat-leaf parsley leaves

1 tablespoon chili oil or extra virgin olive oil

1 lemon, halved

1. Heat the olive oil in a large sauté pan over medium heat. Add the shallots, garlic, and serrano peppers, season with salt, and cook until tender, about 5 minutes. Add the mussels, saffron, and white wine. Cover and steam just until the mussels have opened, about 5 minutes. Don't overcook, or the mussels will be tough. Remove from the heat.

2. Scoop the mussels out of the pan and spread them on a tray in a single layer to cool. (Do not discard the cooking juices.) When they are completely cooled, remove and discard the top shells. Cover the mussels with plastic wrap and refrigerate until ready to serve.

3. While the mussels are cooling, simmer the cooking juices (with the shallots, garlic, and serrano peppers) over medium-high heat until reduced to about 1 tablespoon of liquid. Transfer the reduction (with the shallots, etc.) to a bowl. Use a rubber spatula to get all the juices if necessary.

4. To make the saffron mayonnaise, add the egg yolk and lemon juice to the mussel reduction and whisk until foamy. Whisk in the salad oil one drop at a time until an emulsion forms. Carefully whisk in the rest of the oil in a thin, steady stream. Season with salt and pepper. Cover and refrigerate until ready to serve.

5. To serve, arrange one of each of the pepper quarters on each of four plates and season with salt and pepper. Distribute the mussels, in their half-shells, in and around the peppers. Set a spoonful of mayonnaise next to the peppers. Sprinkle the plates with the cucumber, red onion, olives, and parsley leaves. Drizzle with the chili oil and a squeeze of lemon juice.

Grilled Bluefish with Pomegranate Glaze and Cucumber-Yogurt Sauce

So much to grill, so little time. Every August, just when I think it might be the summer when I might squeeze in everything I love to grill before Labor Day, the bluefish arrive and throw my backyard repertoire into chaos. Salmon and tuna may be available, but if someone offers me a fresh-caught bluefish, it's hard to resist. Slathered with pomegranate molasses, the bluefish tastes barbecued, if you can imagine barbecued fish with zither music playing in the background. As far as condiments go, a simple, cooling cucumber-yogurt sauce is absolutely essential, but if I have the time, I also make Skordalia (page 106) for the garlic lovers in the crowd.

MAKES 4 ENTRÉE SERVINGS

MARINADE

⅓ cup pomegranate molasses (available in specialty stores and groceries that stock Middle Eastern ingredients)

3 garlic cloves, chopped

1 small red onion, sliced as thin as possible

1 tablespoon chopped fresh mint

1 teaspoon crushed toasted coriander seeds

1 tablespoon grated orange zest

Four 6-ounce bluefish fillets, skin on, 1 to 1½ inches thick

SAUCE

¼ cup peeled, seeded, and diced (¼-inch) cucumbers

Kosher salt

½ cup thick Greek yogurt (substitute whole-milk yogurt if Greek yogurt is unavailable)

2 tablespoons finely diced red onion

1 tablespoon chopped fresh mint

1 tablespoon chopped fresh cilantro

2 teaspoons freshly squeezed lemon juice

Kosher salt and freshly ground black pepper

¼ cup vegetable oil

2 tablespoons pomegranate molasses for garnish

¼ cup pomegranate seeds for garnish

1. Mix all the marinade ingredients together in a bowl. Toss the bluefish in the marinade until evenly coated. Put the fish and any remaining marinade in a nonreactive container, cover, and refrigerate for 1 hour, turning once or twice.

2. Toss the cucumbers with salt and drain in a colander for 30 minutes.

3. Pat the cucumbers dry to remove moisture and excess salt. Mix the cucumbers with the yogurt, red onion, herbs, and lemon juice. Season with salt and pepper.

4. Prepare a grill with both hot and medium zones (see page 265). A grill is hot when you can hold your hand near the grilling surface for no longer than a count of 2 before having to pull it away; it is medium when you can keep your hand near it for no longer than 4 seconds. The cooking times given are for a gas grill, with the lid closed; if using a wood or charcoal-burning grill, cook with the lid off. Make sure the grill grate is clean in order to minimize sticking.

5. Season the bluefish with salt and pepper. Brush generously with the vegetable oil. Put the fish skin side down on the hottest part of the grill. Do not disturb the fillets until the surface is charred and a corner of a fillet releases from the grill when you carefully lift it with a spatula, after about 5 minutes. Flip the fillets and cook until opaque, another 4 to 5 minutes.

Because the marinade has sugar in it, you need to keep a close eye out for burning. If it looks as though the surface is turning too dark too quickly, or burning, slide a spatula carefully under the fillets and finish cooking them on the medium section of the grill.

6. To serve, put a fillet in the center of each of four plates. Put a spoonful of yogurt sauce next to each fillet. Drizzle the fish with the pomegranate molasses and sprinkle with the pomegranate seeds. Serve immediately.

Grilled Tuna with Romesco Sauce

Romesco is a Catalan sauce traditionally served with grilled fish, poultry, or vegetables. The basic recipe calls for roasted red peppers, garlic, almonds, vinegar, and olive oil, although I've seen variations that include tomatoes, bread, and hot peppers. I like the nuance that hazelnuts contribute. As a condiment for grilled food, especially tuna or shrimp, it is without equal. It's worth firing up your grill 15 or 20 minutes ahead of time to char the peppers for romesco. While the peppers cook, you can prepare the rest of the ingredients. Making the sauce itself is a snap—everything is just pulsed together in a food processor.

When grilling tuna, make the fire as hot as possible. If using a gas grill, turn all the burners to high and allow it to heat with the lid down for 15 minutes. If you like your tuna rare (red in the center), be sure to buy fillets at least 1½ inches thick to minimize the chance of overcooking. The cooking times given are for a gas grill, with the lid closed. If using a wood or charcoal grill, which will be hotter, cook with the lid off and subtract a minute from each of the times.

MAKES 4 ENTRÉE SERVINGS

SAUCE

2 red peppers, roasted (see page 99), peeled, stemmed, and seeded

1 ancho pepper, soaked in warm water to cover until tender (about 30 minutes), drained, stemmed, and seeded

2 garlic cloves, finely chopped

¼ cup almonds, toasted (see page 16)

2 tablespoons hazelnuts, toasted (see page 16)

¼ cup pine nuts, toasted (see page 16)

¼ cup chopped fresh flat-leaf parsley

2 tablespoons red wine vinegar

2 tablespoons chopped fresh mint

½ cup extra virgin olive oil

Kosher salt

Pinch of hot red pepper flakes (optional)

TUNA

Four 5-ounce tuna steaks, approximately 1½ inches thick

Kosher salt and freshly ground black pepper

1 tablespoon paprika, preferably Spanish

¼ cup extra virgin olive oil

1. Combine all the romesco sauce ingredients except the salt and hot pepper flakes in a food processor and process to a coarse purée. Season with salt to taste. Add the red pepper flakes, if desired.

2. Prepare a hot fire in a grill. A grill is hot when you can hold your hand near the grilling surface for no longer than a count of 2 before having to pull it away.

3. Season the tuna with salt, pepper, and the paprika. Brush with the oil. Grill on each side for 3 to 3½ minutes for rare (red in the center), about a minute longer for medium-rare (a trace of red, but mostly pink), or until cooked to desired doneness. Check for doneness by cut-

ting into the center with the tip of a sharp knife and judging the color. Tuna's transition from red to pink-with-some-red occurs quite quickly; also keep in mind that the tuna will continue cooking once it's off the grill, and that cooking time will also vary according to the thickness of the tuna steaks. Err on the side of underdoneness. It's a small matter to return a piece of tuna to the grill if it's too rare. However, the only thing to do with overcooked fish is to throw it away.

4. Serve immediately, accompanied by the romesco sauce.

Grilled Striped Bass with Reine's Potato-Basil Purée

Reine Samut is the chef-owner of the Auberge la Fernière, an extraordinary restaurant in Lourmarin, in Provence. She generously allowed me to work in her kitchen for a day, and several years later I was delighted to host her at Rialto when she came to this country as part of a French cultural exchange. For three nights, we offered a special tasting menu featuring her Provençal specialties. The fish course was *rouget* (a European mullet flown in from France) served atop a potato-basil purée. I usually think of mashed potatoes as cold-weather food, but this dish, with its basil and olive oil, seems saturated with the tastes of summer. Don't attempt it with anything except a first-class extra virgin olive oil.

The closest thing to rouget in this country is probably perch, but striped bass (which is easily grilled, unlike perch) seems a better alternative.

MAKES 4 ENTRÉE SERVINGS

1 pound baking potatoes
3 garlic cloves, coarsely chopped
Kosher salt
½ cup finely chopped fresh basil
Freshly ground black pepper
About 1 cup extra virgin olive oil
Four 6-ounce striped bass fillets, skin on,
   1 to 1½ inches thick
6 ripe plum tomatoes, cut in half lengthwise
2 ounces Niçoise olives, ⅓ cup unpitted, remainder
   halved and pitted
2 lemons, 1 halved, the other cut in quarters
4 basil leaves for garnish

1. Peel the potatoes and chop into 1-inch dice. Put the potatoes and garlic in a pot and just cover with cold salted water. Bring to a boil, then lower the heat to a simmer and cook until the potatoes are falling apart and the water has reduced by a third, 20 to 30 minutes. Remove from the heat; do not drain.

2. Add the chopped basil and 6 tablespoons of the olive oil to the potatoes and purée with an immersion blender or transfer to a food processor if necessary. The purée should be the consistency of a smooth applesauce. Season with salt and pepper. Keep warm.

3. Meanwhile, prepare a hot fire in a grill. (If using a gas grill, turn all the burners to high and allow it to heat with the lid down for 15 minutes.) A grill is hot when you can hold your hand near the grilling surface for no longer than a count of 2 before having to pull it away. The cooking times given are for a gas grill, with the lid closed; if using a wood or charcoal grill, cook with the lid off and reduce the cooking time. Make sure the grill grate is clean in order to minimize sticking.

4. Season the bass fillets on both sides with salt and pepper and brush with olive oil. When the grill is hot, lay the fish skin side down on the grate. Do not disturb until you're ready to turn the fish over—you need to allow the skin to char, or it will stick to the grill. After 5 minutes, gently peel up a corner of a fillet with a spatula to loosen it from the grill, then slowly pry the fish loose and flip it over. Flip the remaining fillets, and cook for 5 minutes, or until done: a sharp knife should slide easily into the fish and the flesh should be opaque.

5. While the fish is cooking, season the tomato halves with salt and pepper and toss with 3 table-spoons of the olive oil. Grill cut side down until charred, 4 minutes or less, depending on the heat of the grill—the idea is to char, not incinerate, them. Don't disturb them until they've gotten a good sear, then carefully peel them off the grill and cook on the second side for another 2 minutes. They should be cooked, but not mushy. If they appear to be cooking too fast (hint: the skin is turning black), either shift them to a cooler part of the grill or remove them and cover. If covered, they'll continue cooking off the grill.

6. Put a healthy dollop of the potato-basil purée on each plate. Arrange the fish on top and sprinkle with the olives. Put 3 tomato halves on each plate. Squeeze fresh lemon juice over the fish, drizzle with 2 tablespoons olive oil, and garnish with the basil leaves and lemon quarters. Serve immediately.

Grilled Mackerel with Eggplant, Tomatoes, and Capers

I'm always surprised when I encounter people who love bluefish but won't give mackerel a chance. I'm convinced its color and price scare people away (it's often the cheapest fish at the fishmonger's—ergo, it *can't* be good). For others it's memories of canned mackerel, which bears no comparison to the fresh whole fish. Mackerel is a firm, dark-fleshed fish with a moist meaty texture and sweet flavor that takes well to relishes. The eggplant dish included here is similar to Sicilian caponata, a sweet-and-sour eggplant salad.

Mackerel is often displayed whole, all the better to judge its freshness. As with bluefish, its fat content makes it more perishable than leaner fish. It should appear glistening and fresh, with clear eyes and no smell. If you've never grilled whole fish, mackerel is a good place to start. A ¾-pound fish is a healthy portion for a single person. The skin crisps deliciously, and its high fat content both keeps the fish moist and cuts down on the likelihood of sticking. With just a little care, you can produce grilled whole fish that looks spectacular and tastes great. For this recipe, though, ask the fishmonger to fillet it for you. Explain that you want to end up with 1½ to 2 pounds of fillets (two fillets for each person) with the skin on.

This is definitely a dish whose leftovers are worth saving. Cold grilled mackerel is a tasty fish, especially with a spicy mayonnaise like aïoli or rouille (page 13). The eggplant salad is actually intended to be served at room temperature, and it even improves with a day of sitting in the refrigerator.

MAKES 4 ENTRÉE SERVINGS

EGGPLANT RELISH

½ cup plus 2 tablespoons extra virgin olive oil, plus additional (optional) for drizzling

1 medium eggplant (about 1 pound), chopped into ½-inch dice

1 small white onion, chopped into ¼-inch dice

2 celery stalks, peeled and chopped into ¼-inch dice

1 garlic clove, minced

1 teaspoon crushed toasted coriander seeds

½ teaspoon hot red pepper flakes

1 teaspoon tomato paste

2 medium tomatoes, peeled (see page 55), seeded, and chopped into ½-inch dice

3 tablespoons red wine vinegar

2 teaspoons sugar

3 tablespoons chopped and pitted Sicilian green olives

2 tablespoons capers, rinsed

1 cup canned tomatoes, coarsely chopped, with their juices

Kosher salt and freshly ground black pepper

3 tablespoons chopped fresh flat-leaf parsley

1½ to 2 pounds mackerel fillets, skin on (8 fillets)

¼ cup vegetable oil, or as needed

1 lemon, quartered

DO AHEAD: The eggplant relish can be prepared a day ahead and refrigerated. Allow it to come up to room temperature before serving.

1. Heat ¼ cup of the oil in a large sauté pan over high heat. Add the eggplant and sear until golden on all sides (it won't be cooked through). Season with salt and pepper. Transfer to a plate. Add 2 tablespoons more oil to the pan. Add the onion and celery and cook until they start to brown, about 4 minutes. Add the garlic and cook until aromatic, less than a minute. Add the coriander seeds, red pepper flakes, and tomato paste and cook for 1 minute.

2. Add the remaining ¼ cup olive oil to the pan, along with the fresh tomatoes, vinegar, sugar, olives, and capers. Reduce the heat to medium and cook for 4 minutes. Add the canned tomatoes with their juices, and the eggplant. Lower the heat to a simmer and cook until the eggplant is tender. Season with salt and pepper and stir in 2 tablespoons of chopped parsley. Let cool to room temperature.

3. Prepare a hot fire in a grill. A grill is hot when you can hold your hand near the grilling sur- face for no longer than a count of 2 before having to pull it away. The cooking times are given for a gas grill, with the lid closed; if using a wood or charcoal grill, cook with the lid off and reduce the cooking times. Make sure the grill grate is clean to minimize sticking.

4. Season the mackerel fillets with salt and pepper on both sides, and brush both sides with the vegetable oil. Grill skin side down until the fish is three-quarters cooked, about 4 minutes, depending on the thickness of the fillets. The skin should be charred, and the fish should come off the grill easily.

5. Flip the fish and cook on the second side until done, probably only a minute or two. The fillets should be opaque all the way through.

6. Spoon a quarter of the eggplant mixture into the middle of each plate. Place 2 mackerel fillets (or a fillet, depending on the size) on top of the eggplant mixture. Sprinkle with the remaining chopped parsley. Drizzle with additional olive oil, if desired. Garnish with the lemon quarters and serve immediately.

Seared Shad Roe with Smoky Lentils

S*had roe was one of* the strange foods like kippered herring that my father occasionally made for breakfast—and I avoided. Now I think it's a treat, a genuine seasonal delicacy. It's available only a few short weeks in mid-March and April, and its appearance always reminds me that despite the snow on the ground, warm weather is indeed on the way.

Shad roe are usually sold in "pairs," or "sets," attached pink lobes or sacs containing a firm mass of eggs. Cooked, the roe has a rich, distinctively nutty flavor and silky texture. Bacon, capers, and lentils are all traditional French accompaniments. In this recipe the pairs are briefly poached, then sautéed and served accompanied by lentils and wilted greens. You could easily double the recipe for an entrée, but the roe is so rich that an appetizer portion really is more than enough.

MAKES 4 ENTRÉE SERVINGS

LENTILS

2 ounces thinly sliced smoked bacon, cut crosswise into ½-inch thick pieces

½ small carrot, peeled and chopped into ½-inch dice

½ celery stalk, peeled and chopped into ½-inch dice

3 shallots, chopped into ½-inch dice

1 garlic clove, minced

½ cup French green lentils (le Puy), rinsed and picked over for stones

2 bay leaves

Kosher salt and freshly ground black pepper

½ teaspoon chopped fresh thyme

2 tablespoons chopped fresh flat-leaf parsley

SHAD ROE

4 cups water

½ cup dry white wine

1 small onion, sliced ¼ inch thick

1 celery stalk, peeled and sliced ¼ inch thick

2 sprigs thyme

10 peppercorns

2 bay leaves

Kosher salt and freshly ground black pepper

2 pairs shad roe (about ½ pound each)

About ½ cup unbleached all-purpose flour

7 tablespoons unsalted butter

1 shallot, thinly sliced

3 tablespoons freshly squeezed lemon juice

1 tablespoon capers, rinsed

2 tablespoons chopped fresh flat-leaf parsley

¼ pound bitter greens, such as arugula or chicory

1. In a heavy saucepan, cook the bacon over medium heat until it has rendered its fat but is not yet crispy. Add the carrot, celery, shallots, and garlic and cook until they just begin to brown around the edges but are still crisp, about 3 minutes. Transfer the vegetables and bacon to a bowl, leaving the fat in the pan.

2. Add the lentils and bay leaves to the saucepan. Add enough water to cover the lentils by an inch. Bring to a boil, then immediately lower the heat to a simmer and cook for

20 minutes; add additional water if necessary while the lentils are cooking.

3. Return the vegetables and bacon to the pan and continue cooking until the lentils and vegetables are tender, 15 to 20 more minutes. The liquid should be almost completely absorbed, with a hint of soupiness. Season with salt and pepper and stir in the thyme and chopped parsley; discard the bay leaves. Keep warm.

4. To poach the roe, put the water, white wine, onion, celery, thyme sprigs, peppercorns, and bay leaves in a medium saucepan. Season with salt and pepper. Bring to a boil, then simmer for 15 minutes. Gently slip the pairs of roe into the liquid and poach for 1 minute. Turn off the heat and allow the pairs to cool in the poaching liquid.

5. When the shad roe is cool, remove from the liquid. Trim off any dangling membranes, tak-ing care not to rip the membrane that holds the eggs together. Separate each pair into 2 lobes. Season with salt and pepper. Dredge in flour.

6. Distribute the lentils among four warm plates. Keep warm.

7. Heat 6 tablespoons of the butter in a large sauté pan over medium heat. As soon as the foam subsides, add the lobes and sear on each side until golden, about 3 minutes per side. Transfer the roe to the plates with the lentils.

8. Add the shallot to the pan and cook until tender, about 2 minutes. Add the lemon juice and capers and bring to a boil. Season with salt and pepper, add the parsley, and pour over the roe.

9. Add the remaining 1 tablespoon butter to the pan, increase the heat to high, and add the greens. Season with salt and pepper and toss until they're slightly wilted. Divide the greens among the plates and serve immediately.

Salmon Marinated in Mint and Basil with Summer Vegetable Gratin

For the most part, I try to keep things as simple as possible when combining seafood and summer vegetables. But not so the French—and on some occasions, jumping through their hoops makes sense. This is a lovely decadent dish whose major effort goes into a rich gratin of summer vegetables with cream. The salmon is very lightly flavored with basil and mint. After the gratin is baked, the salmon is given a quick sear and served atop the vegetables.

MAKES 4 ENTRÉE SERVINGS

Grated zest of ½ lemon

3 tablespoons chopped fresh mint, plus 4 sprigs for garnish

3 tablespoons chopped fresh basil

3 tablespoons extra virgin olive oil

Four 6-ounce salmon fillets, skin removed

Kosher salt

¼ pound sugar snap peas, strings removed

¼ pound thin string beans, trimmed

¼ pound zucchini, scrubbed and cut into ½-inch dice

¼ pound flat-leaf spinach, trimmed of thick stems, washed, dried, and coarsely chopped

1 ear corn, husked

¼ pound leeks, white part only, trimmed of roots and tough outer leaves, thinly sliced crosswise and swirled vigorously in a bowl of cold water to remove any grit

1 baking potato (about 8 ounces), peeled and cut into ½-inch dice

1 cup heavy cream

1 lemon, halved

Freshly ground black pepper

1 garlic clove, finely chopped

1 tablespoon finely chopped shallots

½ cup toasted bread crumbs

DO AHEAD: Marinate the salmon with the herbs an hour before cooking. You can shave some preparation time from the final assembly by blanching the vegetables ahead.

1. In a shallow dish, toss the lemon zest with 2 tablespoons of the mint, 2 tablespoons of the basil, and 1 tablespoon of the olive oil. Rub the mixture on the salmon. Marinate for 1 hour in the refrigerator.

2. Bring a large pot of salted water to a boil. Fill a large bowl with ice water—it should be large enough to hold all of the vegetables. One at a time, briefly blanch the snap peas, string beans, zucchini, spinach, and the ear of corn in the boiling water, then plunge them into the ice water to stop the cooking. The goal is to cook everything just to the point where an element of crispness still remains. The snap peas and string beans will take 1 to 2 minutes, the zucchini about a minute; the spinach only 15 to 30 seconds, and the corn 2 minutes. Remove the corn from the water and use a sharp knife to strip the corn kernels from the cob. Discard the cob.

3. Fill a small pot with salted water. Add the leeks and potato, bring to a boil, then lower the heat to a simmer and cook until tender, about 15 minutes. Plunge into the ice water with the other vegetables. Drain and dry all the vegetables.

4. Toss the blanched vegetables (including the corn) in a bowl with 1 tablespoon each of the remaining mint and basil, the cream, and the juice of half the lemon. Season with salt and pepper and toss well. Spread the vegetables in a 1-inch layer in a gratin dish.

5. Preheat the oven to 350°F.

6. Heat 1 tablespoon of the olive oil in a small sauté pan over medium heat. Add the garlic and shallots and cook until tender, about 2 minutes. Toss with the bread crumbs and season with salt and pepper. Spread over the vegetables. Bake the gratin until the vegetables are tender and the cream is bubbling, about 10 minutes.

7. While the gratin is baking, heat the remaining 1 tablespoon olive oil in a large sauté pan over medium-high heat. Sprinkle the salmon liberally with salt and pepper. When the oil is hot, almost smoking, add the salmon fillets (the side that used to have the skin on it should be up) and sear until golden brown, about 3 minutes. Do not try to move the fillets until they've gotten a good sear, or they'll stick to the pan. Cook them on one side only. Remove from the heat.

8. As soon as the gratin finishes baking, set the salmon fillets, seared side up, on top of the gratin. Return to the oven until the fish is cooked to medium, another 10 minutes or so. Squeeze the remaining lemon half over the fish and garnish with the mint sprigs. Serve immediately.

Striped Bass with Fried Green Tomatoes and Figs

I grew up with "stipers" as a summer staple, but overfishing took it off the table for many years. The inviting pale rose-white color of the fillets seems to predict a delicate flavor, but the fish actually has a strong, meaty taste and a firm texture. In this recipe, the bass is seared in one pan and then finishes cooking in a second pan atop an aromatic bed of fried green tomatoes sweetened with a few fresh figs. If you have a presentable skillet or sauté pan, the fish can brought directly to the table and served as a gorgeous one-pot dish.

MAKES 4 ENTRÉE SERVINGS

3 green tomatoes (4 to 5 ounces each), sliced
   ½ inch thick
Kosher salt and freshly ground black pepper
¼ cup unbleached all-purpose flour
6 tablespoons extra virgin olive oil
4 ripe figs, cut in half lengthwise
1 large fennel bulb (about 6 ounces), trimmed of
   tough outer layers, cored, and chopped into
   ¼-inch dice
2 garlic cloves, finely chopped
1 teaspoon grated orange zest
16 basil leaves
4 striped bass fillets, about 1 inch thick, skin on
⅓ cup white wine vinegar
½ cup water
2 tablespoons chopped fresh flat-leaf parsley

1. Season the tomato slices on both sides with salt and pepper. Dust with the flour. Heat 2 tablespoons of the olive oil in a large sauté pan over medium heat. Add the tomato slices and sear on both sides until golden brown, about 5 minutes per side. Transfer to a plate. Add the figs, cut side down, to the pan and sear, until golden brown, about 3 minutes. Transfer to the platter with the tomatoes and wipe out the pan.

2. Add 2 more tablespoons of the olive oil to the pan. Add the fennel, season with salt and pepper, and sauté until tender, about 5 minutes. Add the garlic and cook until aromatic, just a minute or two. Stir in the orange zest and basil leaves and remove the pan from the heat. Return the tomatoes and figs to the pan, laying them atop the fennel.

3. Heat the remaining 2 tablespoons olive oil in a second large sauté pan over medium-high heat. Season the bass with salt and pepper. When the oil is hot but not quite smoking, add the bass, skin side down, and sear until golden brown, about 5 minutes. Flip the fish and cook

for 1 minute on the second side. Transfer the bass to the first sauté pan, laying the fillets skin side up atop the tomatoes and figs.

4. Pour the vinegar and water into the pan used for cooking the fish. As the liquid starts to boil, scrape the bottom of the pan with a wooden spoon to dissolve the crispy bits. Pour this pan juice over the fish and vegetables.

5. Cover and cook over low heat until the fish is cooked through, about 8 minutes. Transfer the dish to a warm platter or serve directly from the pan. Sprinkle with the chopped parsley just before serving.

Pan-Roasted Salmon with Warm Cucumber Salad

*I*sn't it funny how ingredients come in and out of fashion? After receiving some smoked salt from Norway, I wanted to develop a dish that was consistent with the salt's Scandinavian origins. My instincts led me straight to salmon and then to dill. From there it was an easy to step to cucumbers, fennel, mustard, and then crème fraîche. The effect reminds me of an old-fashioned Sunday dinner platter—seared salmon fillets accompanied by toast points and a creamy sauce.

MAKES 4 ENTRÉE SERVINGS

3 tablespoons chopped fresh dill, plus 4 sprigs for garnish

2 tablespoons chopped fresh tarragon

1 tablespoon grated lemon zest

Four 6-ounce salmon fillets, skin on

2 tablespoons extra virgin olive oil

Smoked sea salt (available in specialty stores; or substitute regular sea salt)

1 small celery root, peeled and cut into ¼-inch dice

1 small red onion, sliced ¼ inch thick

Kosher salt and freshly ground black pepper

1 cucumber, peeled, halved, seeded, and cut into ½-inch slices on the diagonal

2 slices dense pumpernickel bread

1 tablespoon unsalted butter

¼ firm red apple, skin on, cut into ¼-inch dice

¾ cup crème fraîche

3 tablespoons spicy grainy mustard

1 tablespoon freshly squeezed lemon juice

1. Mix the chopped dill, tarragon, and lemon zest together. Transfer half the herbs to a small bowl for use in the sauce, cover, and refrigerate. Toss the salmon fillets in the other half. Cover and marinate in the refrigerator for at least an hour and up to 24 hours.

2. Preheat the oven to 400°F.

3. Heat the olive oil in an ovenproof sauté pan over medium heat. Season the fillets with the sea salt and pepper. When the oil is hot, add the salmon skin side down to the pan and cook, on the one side only, until the skin is crispy, about 5 minutes. Remove the fish from the pan.

4. Add the celery root and onions to the pan, season with salt and pepper, and cook for 5 minutes, or until just tender. Add the cucumber and toss well.

5. Place the fish skin side up on top of the vegetables and roast in the oven for 7 minutes, or until the fish is cooked to medium.

6. Meanwhile, toast and butter the pumpernickel slices. Trim the crusts, then cut each slice into 4 triangles.

7. Transfer the fish to a platter, skin side up. Off the heat, add the apple, crème fraîche, mustard, and the reserved herb mixture to the pan and mix in. Season with salt, pepper, and the lemon juice.

8. Spoon the salad and sauce next to—not over—the fish. Garnish with the toast points and dill sprigs, and serve.

Salmon with Walnuts and Dried Cranberries

Dried cranberries and walnuts are a pair of obvious New England ingredients for an easy variation on seared salmon, and both go well with spinach. Red cranberries, orange salmon, green spinach, and a golden sauce make a seafood entrée that looks festive, tastes great, and is easy and quick to prepare.

The dish is easily doubled, especially if you grill the salmon instead of sautéing it. Any leftovers translate into an instant lunch. The spinach is delicious cold, and the salmon can be sliced thin and drizzled with fresh lemon juice or given a completely different spin with a flavored mayonnaise (pages 13–14).

MAKES 4 ENTRÉE SERVINGS

8 tablespoons (1 stick) unsalted butter

1 shallot, minced

½ cup dry white wine

2 tablespoons dried cranberries, soaked in ½ cup freshly squeezed orange juice

2 tablespoons grated fresh horseradish, or 2 tablespoons bottled horseradish, drained

1½ teaspoons freshly squeezed lemon juice

Kosher salt and freshly ground black pepper

2 tablespoons extra virgin olive oil

Four 6-ounce salmon fillets, skin on

1 pound flat-leaf spinach, trimmed of thick stems, washed, and dried

2 tablespoons chopped toasted walnuts

1. Heat 1 tablespoon of the butter with the shallots in a saucepan over medium heat and cook until the shallots are tender, 3 to 4 minutes. Add the white wine and reduce to 2 tablespoons. Pour the orange juice from the cranberries into the saucepan (set the cranberries aside). Reduce the orange juice to just ¼ cup. Off the heat, whisk in the remaining 7 tablespoons butter, a tablespoon at a time. Add the horseradish and lemon juice, then season with salt and pepper. Cover and keep in a warm spot, away from the direct heat—or the sauce will break.

2. Heat 1 tablespoon of the olive oil in a large sauté pan (nonstick if possible) over high heat. (Use two pans if all the fish won't fit comfortably in a single pan.) Sprinkle the salmon liberally with salt and pepper. When the oil is hot, almost smoking, add the salmon fillets, skin side up, and sear until golden brown, about 3 minutes. Do not try to move the fillets until they've gotten a good sear, or they'll stick to the

pan. Flip and cook on the other side. A 2-inch-thick fillet will take 3 to 4 minutes per side for medium.

3. While the salmon is cooking, heat the remaining 1 tablespoon oil in a large sauté pan over high heat. Add the spinach, season with salt and pepper, and cook, tossing, until the spinach has just wilted, a minute or so. Add the walnuts and cranberries and cook for another 30 seconds to heat everything through.

4. Place a quarter of the spinach and cranberries in the center of each of four warm plates. Set the salmon skin side up over the spinach. Spoon the sauce around the plates. Serve immediately.

Sea Scallops with Cider Cream

S imple ingredients exploited to maximum effect—that's the story behind this recipe. Hard cider combines with crème fraîche to pick up the sweetness of fresh scallops. The scallops rest on a bed of spinach and shiitake mushrooms, flavors from the opposite end of the taste spectrum, so that everyone's palate isn't exhausted from all of that creamy richness. The most challenging aspect of this recipe is to cook the scallops correctly. The key is to brown them quickly over high heat for just a couple of minutes without disturbing them, then turn them once to finish cooking on the other side. They should still be slightly translucent in the center. Don't shake them around while they're cooking, or they'll release their juices, a double whammy—they dry out and the juice in the pan prevents them from browning correctly.

MAKES 4 ENTRÉE SERVINGS

1½ cups hard cider
½ cup crème fraîche
Kosher salt and freshly ground black pepper
¼ cup vegetable oil
1¼ pounds large fresh sea scallops, 1 to 1½ inches across, tough muscles removed
¼ pound shiitake mushrooms, stems removed and thinly sliced
2 shallots, thinly sliced
1 pound flat-leaf spinach, trimmed of thick stems, washed, and dried
½ cup chopped toasted hazelnuts
2 tablespoons minced fresh chives

1. Bring the cider to a boil in a small saucepan. Reduce the heat to medium and cook until the cider has reduced to a glaze, 15 to 20 minutes. Let cool.

2. Mix the cider with the crème fraîche. Season with salt and pepper. Cover and refrigerate until ready to serve.

3. Heat 2 tablespoons of the vegetable oil in a large sauté pan over high heat. Season the scallops with salt and pepper. When the oil is very hot, almost at the smoking point, add the scallops in a single layer, with at least ½ inch of space between them, and allow them to cook, undisturbed, until golden brown on the first side, 2 to 3 minutes. Flip and cook the second side. They should still be slightly translucent in the center. Transfer to a plate and keep warm.

4. Add the remaining 1 tablespoon oil to the pan, if necessary. Add the shiitakes and shallots, season with salt and pepper, and cook until tender, about 2 minutes. Add the spinach, season with salt and pepper, and toss several times, until wilted.

5. Make a bed of spinach and mushrooms on each of four warm plates. Arrange the scallops on top. Put a spoonful of the crème fraîche and cider sauce over the scallops, sprinkle with the hazelnuts and chives, and serve immediately.

Venetian-Style Sweet-and-Sour Sole

This dish seems antique to me. It's not at all something that a modern Western sensibility would devise. The exotic combination of pine nuts, raisins, vinegar, and orange juice seems to call from some ancient time and place, half-European, half-Middle Eastern, strange and appealing at the same time. One of the easiest ways of preserving fish in a hot climate is to store it in vinegar. A sweet sauce or condiment helped create a balanced flavor when the fish was served. I've modified *sfogli i saor*, a traditional Venetian sweet-and-sour fish, by adapting it to fresh sole and serving the dish warm, instead of at the traditional room temperature.

MAKES 4 ENTRÉE SERVINGS

1½ pounds fresh sole fillets

Kosher salt and freshly ground black pepper

About ½ cup unbleached all-purpose flour for dredging

About ¾ cup extra virgin olive oil

4 shallots, thinly sliced

1 garlic clove, finely chopped

¼ teaspoon hot red pepper flakes

2 tablespoons raisins, soaked in 6 tablespoons dry Marsala or dry sherry

2 tablespoons pine nuts, toasted

¾ cup freshly squeezed orange juice

1 teaspoon champagne vinegar

2 ounces flat-leaf spinach, trimmed of thick stems, washed, and dried

1. Preheat the oven to 200°F. Place a platter in the oven while it warms.

2. Season the sole fillets with salt and pepper and dredge in the flour. Shake off any excess flour. Heat 2 tablespoons of the olive oil in each of two large sauté pans over high heat. You'll have to cook the fish in two batches, adding additional olive oil with the second batch. Sauté the sole on the first side for 3 minutes, then flip and cook on the other side until just done, 1 to 2 minutes; it should be golden brown and just cooked through. Transfer the fillets to the platter in the oven as they finish cooking.

3. Add the shallots to one of the pans (set the other pan aside). Lower the heat to medium, and cook until tender, about 4 minutes. Add the garlic and cook until aromatic, about a minute. Add the red pepper flakes, the raisins, with the Marsala, and the pine nuts and bring to a boil. Add the orange juice and bring to a boil, then remove from the heat. Whisk the remaining ¼ cup olive oil into the orange juice to create an emulsion. Whisk in the vinegar and season with salt and pepper to taste.

4. Add the spinach to the second pan and cook over high heat, tossing, until it wilts, a minute or two. Season with salt and pepper.

5. To serve, spoon the sauce over the sole. Garnish the platter with the wilted spinach and serve immediately.

Bay Scallops with Celery Root and Tangerines

Small exquisitely sweet scallops are caught off the coast of Massachusetts and available only during the late fall and winter. The fact that I can get them for only part of the year helps preserve their special status for me. Their sugary sweet flavor makes them a dynamite partner to root vegetables or citrus fruit. This recipe sauces the scallops with pan juices flavored with tangerine and cooked celery, then pairs the seafood with a celery root salad.

Be sure to peel the muscle—the white strip that runs down the side—off the scallops before sautéing (it's easy). Don't add the scallops to the pan until it's really hot, and then leave them alone. If you disturb them while they're searing, they'll release their moisture, and they'll steam instead of searing.

MAKES 4 ENTRÉE SERVINGS

½ cup Mayonnaise (page 13)
1 tablespoon Dijon mustard
1 teaspoon minced shallots
¼ cup freshly squeezed lemon juice
Kosher salt and freshly ground white pepper (if you only have pre-ground white pepper, use freshly ground black pepper)
1 small celery root, peeled, sliced very thin, and cut into matchsticks
¼ cup plus 2 tablespoons extra virgin olive oil
1 bunch scallions, white part and the first inch of the green part only, cut into ½-inch pieces on the diagonal
3 stalks celery, peeled and chopped into ½-inch dice
2 garlic cloves, thinly sliced
⅛ teaspoon anise seeds
2 tangerines, skin and membrane removed, cut into segments over a bowl to save the juices
1¼ pounds bay scallops, tough muscles removed
¼ cup chopped fresh flat-leaf parsley

1. Mix the mayonnaise, mustard, shallots, and 2 tablespoons of the lemon juice together in a small bowl. Season with salt and pepper. The mayonnaise should be assertively seasoned. Add the celery root and toss well. Taste and adjust the seasoning if necessary. Cover and refrigerate for at least 1 hour, or until ready to use. (You can make up to 12 hours ahead.)

2. Heat ¼ cup of the olive oil in a small sauté pan over medium heat. Add the scallions, celery, garlic, and anise seeds, season with salt and pepper, and cook until just tender, about 3 minutes. Remove from the heat and set aside.

3. Heat the remaining 2 tablespoons olive oil in a large sauté pan over high heat. Season the scallops with salt and pepper. When the oil is hot but not quite smoking, add the scallops in a single layer, leaving a ½-inch space between them so they don't steam (you may have to use two pans or cook them in two batches). Cook,

without moving the scallops, on one side only, until they are golden brown, about 2 minutes. Toss the scallops once, then transfer to a large plate.

4. Add the tangerine juice from the segments to the pan and reduce to a glaze. (This will happen very quickly.) Add the cooked celery mixture, the remaining 2 tablespoons lemon juice, the parsley, and the tangerine sections to the pan. Toss until heated through, about 30 seconds, then remove from the heat.

5. Put a spoonful of the celery root salad in the middle of each warmed plate. Distribute the scallops evenly around the celery root. Spoon the vegetables and the pan juices over the scallops and serve.

Skate Wings with Brown Butter, Capers, and Anchovies

Skate has a satisfyingly firm texture without being chewy, a delicious sweet taste, and it's affordable. In this country, it's considered a trash fish, with a small amount diverted to devotees and upscale restaurants. Europe, especially France, happily snaps up the rest. Skate's lowly status is just fine with me. With seafood regularly commanding prices that make rib-eye steaks seem a bargain, it's a special pleasure to find great taste at a modest price.

The skin of skate is inedible, like sharkskin, but I've never seen it sold with the skin still on. Because skate have no kidneys, they require careful handling after being caught, or the urea secreted through their skin can contaminate the flesh of the "wings," the edible part of the fish, with ammonia. Always ask to smell skate before buying it. It should smell absolutely clean, or of nothing at all. Soaking skate in a solution of water and lemon juice will purge it of any ammonia, but why bother? I'd rather wait for the next batch.

A delicate cartilage frame fans through a skate wing, with edible fillets both above and below it. The flesh should be translucently pinkish white to rose. Once cooked, the flesh is fork-tender and slides off the cartilage. This classic French preparation of sautéed skate with brown butter and capers, the first way I ever tasted it, remains my favorite. Before you make the sauce, line up your ingredients in little bowls where you can easily reach them. Read through the instructions several times *before* you start cooking. The sauce isn't difficult, just speedy, with little time between each of the steps, and you won't want to waste time wondering where you put each of your ingredients.

MAKES 4 ENTRÉE SERVINGS

Four 8-ounce pieces skate wing (cartilage left in)
Kosher salt and freshly ground black pepper
3 tablespoons clarified butter (see page 111)
8 tablespoons (1 stick) unsalted butter
1 large shallot, minced
½ to 1 teaspoon finely chopped rinsed anchovy
   fillets, according to taste
4 teaspoons capers, rinsed
2 tablespoons freshly squeezed lemon juice
2 tablespoons finely chopped fresh flat-leaf parsley,
   plus 4 sprigs for garnish
1 lemon, cut into 4 wedges

DO AHEAD: Clarify the butter (see page 111). Clarified butter enables you to cook the skate at a higher temperature than you would if you used whole butter.

1. Season the skate pieces on each side with salt and pepper—skate is naturally salty, so go lightly. Heat the clarified butter in two large sauté pans over high heat until quite hot. (If you have a sauté pan large enough to hold all of the skate pieces with at least 2 inches of space between them then, you can use it.) Add the skate and sear on the first side until golden

brown and cooked a little more than halfway through, about 5 minutes. Do not move the fish before the first side is well seared, as it will stick to the pan. Flip and cook on the other side until done, about another 4 minutes. If the fish browns too much before it's cooked through, lower the heat to medium-high. Set aside in a warm spot while you make the sauce.

2. Add the whole butter to one of the pans and cook over high heat until it starts to foam. Immediately add the shallot and cook until it is golden and the butter is a pale hazelnut brown, only a minute. Add the anchovy, capers, and lemon juice. The butter should foam again. Remove from the heat, season with salt and pepper, and add the parsley.

3. Quickly put a piece of skate on each plate. Pour the brown butter over the fish. Add a lemon wedge and parsley sprig to each plate, and serve immediately.

IS THE SKATE DONE YET?

The flesh of skate wings is almost translucent, as is the cartilage frame inside each wing. As skate cooks, its flesh changes color, giving you a guide to doneness. While the skate sizzles on the first side, the color of the up side will gradually fade from a deep rose color to a paler pink. The flesh will turn opaque, beginning at the thin tapered outer edges, gradually reducing the area of pinkness in the thicker part of the piece. The flesh along the thicker edges will also change, turning opaque first in the bottom surface, then climbing up toward the midpoint, where the cartilage is. When the opaque rim has grown to 1 inch wide, it's time to flip the pieces. After you flip the pieces you can tell how you're doing by watching the thick edge. Is it opaque all the way through? Use 5 minutes per side as a rough guide. If the fish changes color more quickly, flip it sooner.

Hot-and-Spicy Seared Squid Stuffed with Sorrel

This is a jazzy little recipe that is both simple to prepare and equally good served warm or at room temperature, like certain Spanish tapas or Greek meze. The hot-and-spicy part of the recipe comes from an old Spanish technique for preparing eels. Stuffing a little sorrel inside the squid was my idea. I can't cook squid without peering down the mantles (the "tubes" or bodies, minus the heads and tentacles) and thinking, *Hmmm . . . something ought to be cooked in there.* Sorrel is a lovely green herb with a decidedly citrus accent, a good partner for hot and spicy flavors. The bread crumbs add texture. Don't be apprehensive about cleaning squid—most squid is already cleaned soon after it's caught, leaving minimal work for the consumer. Just make sure you buy squid large enough to contain a teaspoon or so of sorrel—the mantles need to be at least 2 and preferably 4 inches long—or you'll be stuffing them with tweezers. This recipe can easily feed six or even eight if you serve it over pasta.

MAKES 4 ENTRÉE SERVINGS

2 pounds (cleaned) small squid (see Squid Notes)

2 tablespoons chopped fresh sorrel (remove tough stems before chopping)

1 cup extra virgin olive oil

8 garlic cloves, sliced paper-thin

8 small dried hot red peppers or ½ teaspoon hot red pepper flakes

Kosher salt

½ cup slightly dry coarse bread crumbs

2 tablespoons chopped fresh flat-leaf parsley

1. Make sure no cartilage, viscera, sand, or ink remains inside the squid mantles. If the translucent skin is still on the mantles, scrape it off with a sharp knife. Rinse out the mantles. If it is still attached, remove the beak—the ball-like thing—from the center of the tentacles.

2. Stuff a teaspoon of the chopped sorrel into each mantle.

3. Heat the oil in a large sauté pan over high heat. When it's almost smoking, add the squid, garlic, and hot peppers. Cook, tossing constantly, for 1 minute, or until the squid turns white. Scoop the squid, garlic, and peppers onto a platter and toss with salt.

4. Add the bread crumbs to the oil and cook until toasted. Season with salt and sprinkle over the squid. Sprinkle with the parsley and serve.

SQUID NOTES

Frozen squid is quite common in supermarkets, and fresh squid is available at fishmongers, especially ones that cater to a Mediterranean clientele. Fresh squid should smell clean and perhaps slightly sweet. If the smell gives you any reservation, don't buy it. It is extremely perishable; buy it and use it the same day.

Defrost frozen squid in the refrigerator or in a bowl of cold water. Most squid is cleaned right after it's caught so it can be frozen at sea; you'll probably have to do minimal cleaning. Check to see that the mantle—the long tube-like body—is completely empty. There should be no trace of remaining viscera. If there is, remove it gently with your finger, so you don't tear the mantle, and rinse under cold running water. You may also have to peel the skin from the mantle (don't bother with the tentacles unless you're cleaning a monster). The skin is a clear tinted membrane that loosely adheres to the flesh. Use a knife if you like, but you can usually peel it away with your fingernails.

If you ever find you need to clean fresh squid (if you're on an island in the Mediterranean, waiting for help to arrive), here's what to do:

As when working with any raw fish, make sure your hands are impeccably clean. Grasp the mantle in one hand and the tentacles and head in the other. Gently pull on the tentacles until the head begins to come away from the mantle. As you keep pulling, the narrow cartilaginous "quill" and attached viscera should emerge from the mantle. Set the mantle aside for the moment.

Separate the quill and viscera from the head and discard them. Slice the head off the tentacles just below the eyes. The tentacles should still be attached together. If you get lucky, the squid beak will still be attached to the head. If so, discard the head and the bony beak inside. More likely, the beak will still be attached to the tentacles. The top of the beak is round, like a marble; the business end, which points down between the tentacles, is shaped like a beak. Pinch the tentacles where they all join together. The beak should pop out from the tentacle cluster. Remove it and discard.

Peel the skin off the mantle. Some people also trim the "wings" (the fins) off the body, especially if they intend to cut the body crosswise to make squid rings. If the wings are tough, I cut them off; if not, I leave them alone. Refrigerate until ready to cook.

Roast Cod in Terra-Cotta, with Bacon and Horseradish

*H*ere's *a delicious puzzle: How* do you roast cod, potatoes, leeks, and spinach in a single terra-cotta dish without turning everything to mush by the time the potatoes are done? The solution is to partly bake the layer of potatoes first, then add the remaining ingredients. The layer of bacon and leeks flavors the potatoes below and the cod above so the mixture tastes as though everything were cooked at the same time. A terra-cotta casserole has a rustic charm, can travel directly to the table, and holds heat so the food stays warm throughout the meal.

MAKES 4 ENTRÉE SERVINGS

8 Red Bliss potatoes, scrubbed and cut into
  ¼-inch-thick slices
¼ cup extra virgin olive oil
Kosher salt and freshly ground black pepper
4 ounces smoked bacon, chopped into ½-inch dice
2 large leeks, white part only, trimmed of roots and
  tough outer leaves, sliced ½ inch thick, and
  swirled vigorously in a bowl of cold water to
  remove any grit
2 celery stalks, peeled and chopped into ½-inch
  dice
3 garlic cloves, finely chopped
1 cup dry vermouth
1 tablespoon chopped fresh tarragon
2 teaspoons chopped fresh thyme, plus 4 sprigs for
  garnish
6 ounces flat-leaf spinach, trimmed of thick stems,
  washed, and dried
Four 6-ounce cod fillets, skin removed
1 cup heavy cream
¼ cup prepared horseradish, drained if necessary
¼ cup dry bread crumbs

1. Preheat the oven to 375°F.

2. Toss the potatoes with 2 tablespoons of the oil and season with salt and pepper. Layer evenly in a 3-quart terra-cotta or ceramic casserole and bake for 30 minutes.

3. While the potatoes are roasting, cook the bacon in a large sauté pan over medium heat until it renders its fat, about 5 minutes—stop before it gets too crispy. Remove the bacon from the pan and set aside.

4. Add the leeks and celery to the pan and season with salt and pepper. Cook until tender, about 10 minutes. Add the garlic and cook until aromatic, about a minute. Add ½ cup of the vermouth and, as it heats, scrape the bottom of the pan with a wooden spoon to dissolve the crispy bits. Stir in the tarragon and thyme and take the pan off the heat.

5. Lay the spinach over the potatoes, season with salt and pepper, and then cover with the leek and bacon mixture. Season the cod fillets with salt and pepper and set on top of the vegetables. Pour the remaining ½ cup vermouth over the fish and drizzle with 1 tablespoon of the olive oil. Cover with foil, pressing the foil down so it touches the fish, and bake for 15 minutes.

6. While the cod is cooking, whip the cream and horseradish together until the mixture holds soft peaks. Season with salt and pepper. Refrigerate until ready to serve.

7. After the fish has baked for 15 minutes, remove the foil, sprinkle with the bread crumbs, and drizzle with the remaining tablespoon of olive oil. Roast for 5 minutes more, or until the crumbs are golden brown and the cod is opaque. Garnish with the thyme sprigs and serve, offering the horseradish cream on the side.

Halibut Braised in Ginger-Lemongrass Broth with Cilantro, Basil, and Mint

*T*his dish is as close a foray into fusion cuisine as you'll ever see me make. Lemongrass isn't a Mediterranean herb, although I think it would feel right at home in Provence, paired with basil. I tried to develop this dish as an alternative to my usual Mediterranean treatment of halibut, but my technique kept steering me in the direction of the *bourride,* a fish soup from southern France. The result is a piece of lightly cooked fish sitting in an extraordinary aromatic mixture of broth and Asian vegetables. If I were to strictly adhere to an Asian (or nonfat) approach, the herbs, halibut, mushrooms, and other vegetables would simply be poached in the broth. But it was too hard for me to resist sautéing them, in extra virgin olive oil or butter, before adding them to the broth. Then the entire dish simmers together just before serving.

MAKES 4 ENTRÉE SERVINGS

BROTH

2 tablespoons vegetable oil

1 large onion, sliced ¼ inch thick

4 garlic cloves, coarsely chopped

1 ounce fresh ginger, thinly sliced

Kosher salt and freshly ground black pepper

6 stalks lemongrass, finely chopped (remove any tough ends or hard outer husks before chopping)

¼ teaspoon hot red pepper flakes

1 tablespoon fennel seeds

1 tablespoon coriander seeds

4 bay leaves

1 cup dry white wine

4 cups Fish Stock (page 33) or 2 cups high-quality low-sodium canned chicken broth combined with 2 cups bottled clam juice

HALIBUT

2 tablespoons vegetable oil

Four 6-ounce halibut fillets, skin removed

Kosher salt and freshly ground black pepper

12 shiitake mushrooms, stems removed

¼ pound celery root, peeled and cut into ⅛-inch-thick matchsticks

1 ounce fresh ginger, peeled and cut into ¹⁄₁₆-inch-thick matchsticks

4 large scallions, trimmed and cut into 2-inch lengths

28 sugar snap peas, strings removed (about 1 cup)

20 fresh cilantro leaves

20 fresh mint leaves

20 fresh basil leaves

Four ¼-inch-thick lemon slices cut in half

2 tablespoons unsalted butter

1. To make the broth, heat 2 tablespoons of vegetable oil in a large pot over medium-high heat. Add the onion, garlic, and ginger and season with salt and pepper. Sauté the vegetables until they begin to brown, about 4 minutes. Add the lemongrass, hot pepper flakes, fennel seeds, coriander seeds, bay leaves, white wine, and fish stock. Lower the heat and simmer for 40 minutes. Strain and set aside.

2. To sear the halibut, heat 1 tablespoon of the oil in a large nonstick sauté pan over medium heat. Season the fish with salt and pepper on both sides. Sear the fillets for about 3 minutes on each side—they should be a light golden color, but not even close to cooked through. Transfer to a plate.

3. Add the remaining 1 tablespoon vegetable oil to the pan. When the oil is hot, add the shi-itake mushrooms and sear on one side. Flip and add the celery root, ginger, and scallions. Cook for 5 minutes, until the celery root is just tender. Season with salt and pepper. Add the broth and sugar snap peas and return the fish to the pan. Bring to a simmer, then lower the heat, cover, and simmer for 5 minutes, or until the halibut is medium-rare. The texture of cooked halibut resembles that of salmon: When medium-rare, the center of the fillet will still be moist and slightly translucent, unlike the opaque outer flesh. Also like salmon, if cooked all the way through, it dries out.

4. Add the herbs and lemon slices and swirl in the butter. Divide the fish among four warmed bowls, then pour the broth and other ingredients evenly over each portion. Serve immediately.

OCTOPUS NOTES

Like squid, octopus is quite perishable, so it is almost always cleaned and frozen at sea. Freezing has no ill effect on texture or flavor, so don't be concerned about buying it frozen. In the unlikely event that you do stumble across a fresh octopus (or even a thawed, previously frozen one), be sure to sniff it. It should smell of nothing but the sea, if it has any aroma at all. Your fishmonger will clean it if necessary. Use octopus within a day of purchasing or thawing. Octopus shrinks by about half during cooking, so figure on ¾ pound raw octopus per person for an entrée portion, half of that for an appetizer.

Grilled octopus is one of our summer favorites—especially the tentacles. A few years ago during a trip to Greece, my husband ordered octopus, typically grilled over a very hot fire of olive wood, in every restaurant we tried for two weeks. After a while, our meals seemed incomplete unless they included at least one oval platter with its familiar g-cleft of tentacle in olive oil with rosemary and lemon.

To tenderize octopus for grilling or sautéing, put it in a pot, cover with cold water, and season with salt, the juice of 1 lemon, and several bay leaves. Bring to a boil. Depending on the size, octopi vary considerably in the length of time they require to become tender. For one of less than 2 pounds (or several smaller octopi totaling the same weight), start checking after 15 minutes of boiling. For an octopus of 2 pounds or larger, start checking after 30 minutes. Octopus is done when the point of a thin sharp knife easily penetrates the mantle, the area where the head joins the tentacles.

What you do next depends on the size of your octopus. If it's a large one, leave the tentacles whole and cut the head into strips several inches wide. If the tentacles are much smaller (say, narrower than your fingers), cut the octopus into pieces that can be threaded onto skewers. If you're using small octopi, ones the size of a large man's hand, leave them whole. Rub the boiled octopus with finely chopped fresh rosemary, sprinkle with salt and pepper, and brush with extra virgin olive oil.

When the grill is hot, lay the octopus crosswise across the grill bars. Watch closely. Since the octopus is already cooked, you really only need to grill it long enough to give it a good sear and heat it through, a few minutes at the longest, for large ones, on each side. If you cook it any longer, the meat dries out. Serve with lemon wedges.

Goat Cheese Terrine with Dried Figs and Hazelnuts (page 15) and Parchment Bread (page 21)

Fresh Tomato Soup with Seared Eggplant Sandwiches (page 42)

Warm Spring Vegetable Salad with Favas, Green Beans, Peas, and Radicchio (page 90) and Walnut Breadsticks (page 19)

Tarte Flambée with Caramelized Onions, Smoked Bacon, and Creamy Cheese (page 132)

Penne with Shrimp, Artichokes, and Feta (page 156)

Nidimi—"Little Nests" Stuffed with Prosciutto, Fontina, and Spinach (page 162)

Chilled Lobster with Potato–Blood Orange Salad and Lime (page 180)

Monkfish and Clam Bourride with Aïoli and Green Olive Tapenade (page 218)

Roast Rack of Lamb with Romaine Salad and Anchovy Dressing (page 284)

Fried Rabbit in Hazelnut Crumbs with Peaches (page 289)

Squash Blossoms Stuffed with Herbed Cheese in Fritter Batter (page 308)

Fresh and Salt Cod Wrapped in Pancetta with Wilted Greens (page 314)

Roasted Marinated Long Island Duck with Green Olive and Balsamic Vinegar Sauce (page 316)

Lemon-Almond Butter Cake (page 350)

Braised Octopus with Paprika and Linguine

If you've ever wondered whether octopus is as mouthwateringly good as its fans claim, here's your chance to find out. This is a straightforward recipe that takes advantage of the delicious affinity between octopus's sweet flavor and equally sweet or smoky pepper. Octopus and Spanish paprika (sweet) or Aleppo pepper (smoky) were made for each other. Don't concern yourself with octopus's reputation for rubberiness. Braising automatically makes it tender. The texture recalls that of other mildly resistant seafood like lobster tails or monkfish, although it really is its own creature.

If you want to grill or sauté octopus, you need to boil it first (see Octopus Notes). It's definitely worth the effort. Nothing—absolutely nothing—beats it when it comes time to present the dish to the table.

MAKES 4 ENTRÉE SERVINGS

½ cup extra virgin olive oil

3 medium onions, 2 chopped into ½-inch dice,
   1 thinly sliced

3 celery stalks, chopped into ¼-inch dice

9 garlic cloves, chopped

Kosher salt and freshly ground black pepper

2 cups dry red wine

½ cup ouzo (substitute Pernod if ouzo is
   unavailable)

1 cup canned plum tomatoes, with their juice

3 bay leaves

1 tablespoon dried oregano

1 tablespoon plus 1 teaspoon Turkish pepper, such
   as Aleppo

3 pounds fresh or frozen (thawed) whole small
   octopus, rinsed

1 teaspoon grated lemon zest

¼ teaspoon anise seeds

½ cup paprika, preferably Spanish

½ pound dried linguine

¼ cup flat-leaf parsley leaves

1 lemon, cut into 4 wedges

1. Heat ¼ cup of the olive oil in a large Dutch oven or braising pan over medium-high heat. Add the chopped onions, celery, and two-thirds of the chopped garlic and season with salt and pepper. Cook until the vegetables start to brown, about 7 minutes.

2. Add the wine, ouzo, plum tomatoes and their juice, bay leaves, 2 teaspoons of the oregano, and 1 tablespoon of the Turkish pepper. Add the octopus, season with salt and pepper, and enough water to come halfway up the octopus. Bring the liquid to a boil, then reduce the heat to a simmer. Cover with foil, pressing it down so it just touches the octopus, then cover with a lid. Braise until tender but not mushy, about 1 hour. The point of a knife should easily penetrate the mantle, the area where the head joins the body. The skin will also start breaking apart and sliding off the body. Remove the octopus from the pot and set aside.

3. Strain the braising liquid, discarding the solids. Return the strained liquid to the pot and boil until it is reduced to 1 cup. Remove from the heat.

4. Meanwhile, cut the head off the octopus, then cut the head in half. Peel away the gelatinous lining inside the head and discard. Divide the individual tentacles. Toss the octopus pieces in a bowl with the lemon zest, anise seeds, 1 tablespoon of the paprika, and the remaining 1 teaspoon oregano. Cover and set aside.

5. Heat the remaining ¼ cup olive oil in a large sauté pan over medium-high heat. Add the sliced onion and the remaining garlic, season with salt and pepper, and cook until they start to brown, about 7 minutes. Add the octopus and cook for 5 minutes. Reduce the heat to low,

add the remaining 1 teaspoon Turkish pepper and 7 tablespoons paprika, and cook until aromatic, about 3 minutes.

6. Add the reduced braising liquid and heat through. If the liquid seems too thin to serve as a sauce for pasta, continue cooking until it thickens slightly. Keep warm.

7. Meanwhile, bring a large pot of water to a boil and season with salt. Add the linguine and cook until al dente, about 10 minutes.

8. Drain the pasta, add to the sauce, and toss with the parsley. Divide into warm bowls. Garnish each serving with a lemon wedge.

Clam and Mussel Stew with Italian Ham, Walnuts, and Leeks

H*aving grown up in Providence's* heavily Portuguese neighborhood of Fox Point, I've always loved the combination of clams and pork. This hearty stew of potatoes, leeks, and shellfish takes advantage of the way clams and mussels flavor their steaming liquid. The Italian alternative is to add cured pork, in the form of pancetta or one of the dried cured specialty meats. The addition of capocollo, similar to prosciutto but with a stronger, more rustic flavor, at the end of the cooking adds an unexpected depth. This recipe is quite simple once you assemble the ingredients; the entire dish takes less than half an hour to cook. As a luxurious alternative to the garlic toast in the bottom of the bowl, try serving it over Lemon Mashed Potatoes (page 107).

MAKES 4 ENTRÉE SERVINGS

2 tablespoons extra virgin olive oil

4 large leeks, white part only, trimmed of roots and tough outer leaves, thinly sliced on the diagonal and swirled vigorously in a bowl of cold water to remove any grit

2 garlic cloves, chopped

Kosher salt and freshly ground black pepper

16 sun-dried tomatoes (dry, not in oil), cut in half lengthwise and softened in fish stock (preferably) or water

24 littleneck clams, scrubbed

⅔ cup dry white wine

3 cups Fish Stock (page 33) or 1½ cups clam juice plus 1½ cups high-quality canned low-sodium chicken broth

32 mussels, scrubbed and debearded

¼ pound capocollo, cut into ¼-inch-wide 2-inch-long strips

¼ cup chopped fresh flat-leaf parsley

4 thick slices French bread, toasted and rubbed with a garlic clove

2 tablespoons chopped walnuts

1 teaspoon grated lemon zest

1. Heat the olive oil in a large sauté pan over medium heat. Add the leeks and garlic and season with salt and pepper. Cook, stirring occasionally, until tender and translucent, 5 to 7 minutes. Add the tomatoes, clams, and wine. Cover and cook until the clams just start to open, about 4 minutes.

2. Add the fish stock and mussels. Season with salt and pepper, cover, and cook until the mussels open, about 3 minutes. Add the capocollo and parsley and stir.

3. Put a slice of toast in each of four warmed bowls. Ladle the shellfish stew over the toast, sprinkle with the walnuts and lemon zest, and serve.

Monkfish and Clam Bourride with Aïoli and Green Olive Tapenade

Some dishes so excite your senses that even reading about them seems to set off an avalanche of gustatory anticipation. The sense of shock and delight upon first encountering a bourride as a young cook reading about Provençal cuisine was one of those experiences for me. A garlicky fish soup thickened with garlic *mayonnaise*—Is that allowed? I almost swooned. At the time I hadn't yet been to Provence and didn't know just how rich a true bourride could be. Some recipes called for thickening the broth with egg yolks (just in case it's already not rich enough) then adding the mayonnaise. In any event, this has remained one of my all-time favorite seafood dishes, right up there with *soupe de poisson,* although more rustic—and less work.

MAKES 4 ENTRÉE SERVINGS

6 small Red Bliss potatoes, scrubbed and quartered
Kosher salt
3 tablespoons extra virgin olive oil (plus 2 table-spoons if using cherry tomatoes)
Eight 2-ounce pieces monkfish fillet, trimmed of membrane
Freshly ground black pepper
½ recipe Slow-Braised Tomatoes (page 118), in their oil, or 16 cherry tomatoes, halved
1 fennel bulb, stalks and tough outer layers removed, cut lengthwise in half, cored, and thinly sliced
4 shallots, thinly sliced
2 large leeks, white part only, trimmed of roots and tough outer leaves, sliced ¼ inch thick, and swirled vigorously in a bowl of cold water to remove any grit
4 garlic cloves, 3 thinly sliced, 1 only peeled
1 teaspoon hot red pepper flakes
1 teaspoon grated lemon zest
½ cup dry white wine

24 littleneck clams (I prefer Wellfleet because I live nearby, but you can use any high-quality fresh littlenecks)
4 thick slices rustic bread, toasted
16 basil leaves, 8 sliced into thin strips, 8 left whole for garnish
2 tablespoons chopped fresh flat-leaf parsley
1 cup Aïoli (page 13)
1 recipe Green Olive Tapenade (page 25)

DO AHEAD: Make the tapenade and the braised tomatoes, if using. (Both items have myriad uses and last for some time, so I often double the quantities.) Make the aïoli several hours in advance and keep refrigerated until needed.

1. Put the potatoes in a pot large enough to hold them comfortably, cover with cold water, and season with salt. Bring to a boil, then reduce the heat and cook until tender, about 7 minutes. Drain and let cool.

2. In a large deep pan, heat 2 tablespoons of the olive oil over medium-high heat. Season the monkfish with salt and pepper and sear lightly on each side, until lightly golden. Do not cook through. Remove the monkfish from the pan and set aside.

3. Add 2 tablespoons of the oil from the slow-braised tomatoes (or 2 tablespoons olive oil if using cherry tomatoes) to the pan. Add the fennel, shallots, and leeks and season with salt and pepper. Cook over medium-high heat until the vegetables are tender and the edges begin to brown, about 4 minutes. Add the garlic and cook just until it releases its perfume, 2 to 3 minutes. Be careful not to let the garlic burn. Add the pepper flakes, lemon zest, the tomatoes, white wine, and clams. Cover and let the clams steam open.

4. Meanwhile, rub the toast slices with the garlic clove and brush with the remaining 1 tablespoon olive oil.

5. Check the clams after 5 minutes. If they haven't opened, cover and continue to steam. All of them should have opened after 8 to 10 minutes; discard any that haven't opened by then. Transfer the clams to a bowl large enough to hold the bourride when finished. Cover and keep warm.

6. Add the monkfish and potatoes to the pan and cook for about 2 to 3 minutes. The monkfish will finish cooking while the potatoes warm. Give everything a stir and taste for seasoning. Add the basil strips and parsley, then pour over the clams.

7. Divide the stew evenly among four warmed pasta bowls. Add a garlic toast to each, top with a spoonful each of aïoli and tapenade, and garnish with the basil leaves. Serve immediately, offering extra aïoli and tapenade on the side.

WHY ISN'T THAT CLAM OPENING?

I've been served cooked seafood dishes with unopened clams or mussels more times than I care to remember. Clams and mussels, like lobsters, are usually cooked alive. But, unlike with lobsters, there's no convenient way of telling if a clam has given up the ghost before it hits the pan. After cooking, however, a closed shell is a dead giveaway. Shellfish deteriorates incredibly rapidly after death. Never open—let alone eat—any clams or mussels that don't open during cooking. Discard them immediately.

Lobster, Littleneck Clam, and Andouille Sausage Stew

*T*he Iberian tradition of thickening seafood soups with toasted noodles inspired this dish. Catalan variations call for *fideus*, a dried thin short noodle, to be toasted in oil in a deep pan on top of the stove. The cook adds stock, various fish, shellfish, and sausage; the noodles soak up the stock, transforming the dish into something closer to stew than soup. If you have 3 cups of homemade Lobster Stock (page 34) sitting around, you can use it here, but the recipe includes instructions for a quick lobster stock (30 minutes), a technique worth learning and taking almost no time at all.

Reheated seafood stew loses much of its original texture. The noodles overcook and become soft; the clams and lobster can turn rubbery. If you won't be serving all the stew the first night, prepare the recipe as indicated, but stop just short of adding the capellini. Figure out how much stew you want to eat today, and how much tomorrow. Divide the mixture of onions, peppers, and tomatoes in the casserole and set tomorrow's aside. Only assemble as much of the dish as you intend to serve, reducing the proportion of the other ingredients accordingly. Refrigerate tomorrow's onion, tomato, and pepper mixture, stock, lobster, clams, and basil and parsley. Reheat the stock the next day, and finish the stew by repeating the final steps of the recipe.

MAKES 4 ENTRÉE SERVINGS

LOBSTER AND STOCK
Kosher salt
Two 1-pound lobsters
2 tablespoons extra virgin olive oil
½ small white onion, thinly sliced
¼ celery stalk, thinly sliced
1 cup dry white wine
¼ teaspoon fennel seeds
1 strip orange zest (½ inch wide and 3 inches long)
2 bay leaves
Pinch of saffron (optional)

¼ pound capellini, broken in half
5 tablespoons extra virgin olive oil
1 medium onion, thinly sliced

1 red pepper, stemmed, seeded, and sliced into ½-inch-wide strips
Freshly ground black pepper
4 garlic cloves, chopped
6 ripe plum tomatoes, each cut into 8 chunks
12 littleneck clams, scrubbed
Juice of 1 orange
1 cup cooked chickpeas (see page 230), or rinsed canned chickpeas
½ pound andouille sausage, cut into ¼-inch-thick slices
½ cup coarsely chopped fresh flat-leaf parsley
½ cup coarsely chopped fresh basil
1 tablespoon hot red pepper flakes (optional)

DO AHEAD: All of the major features of the stew—cooking the lobster, making the lobster stock, toasting the pasta—can be done a day ahead, leaving only the cooking of the pasta and assembling the stew.

1. Bring a large pot of water to a boil. Add 1 tablespoon salt per quart of water. Add the lobsters, bring the water back to a boil, and cook for 7 minutes. Drain and cool the lobsters.

2. Separate the tails, claws, and knuckles from the bodies of the lobsters. Set the bodies aside for making the stock. Remove the lobster tails from the shells, cut the tails in half lengthwise, and remove the vein-like digestive tracts. Cover and refrigerate the lobster meat.

3. To make the stock, heat 2 tablespoons olive oil in a large saucepan over high heat. Break each lobster body into 3 or 4 pieces, add to the oil, and sear all over, turning frequently. Add the sliced half onion and celery and sear as well. Add the white wine and enough water to just cover the shells. Add the fennel seeds, orange zest, and bay leaves and simmer for 30 minutes. Strain the stock and discard the solids. (You should end up with 3 cups of liquid.) Add the optional pinch of saffron.

4. Meanwhile, preheat the oven to 350°F.

5. Toss the capellini with 2 tablespoons of the olive oil, then spread it evenly over a sheet pan. Bake until the pasta is golden and toasted, about 20 minutes. Toss the pasta several times during baking to ensure it toasts evenly. Set aside.

6. Heat the remaining 3 tablespoons olive oil in a large Dutch oven or braising pan over medium heat. Add the onion and red pepper, season with salt and pepper, and cook until tender, about 15 minutes. Add the garlic and tomatoes and cook an additional 2 minutes. Add the lobster broth, littlenecks, and orange juice and cook until the clams just begin to open, about 10 minutes.

7. Add the chickpeas, andouille, and pasta. After 5 minutes, the pasta should be cooked and all the clams should have opened. Remove and discard any unopened clams. Add the lobster, parsley, and basil, and just heat through.

8. Fill four warm bowls with the stew, making sure that each portion contains lobster, clams, and sausage. Serve immediately, accompanied by the optional red pepper flakes.

Poultry

☙

Poultry *is like a huge* family with two different branches. The members of one branch—chicken—are respectable, reliable . . . and boring. The members of the second branch are like a band of crazy interlopers whom no one invited to the reunion—duck, quail, and geese. They're wild, they're messy, and they never clean up after themselves. The first group is bland, and the challenge is to figure out how to put some pizzazz back into their character. The quail-duck-and-geese branch has the opposite problem: they come packed with flavor, but how do you cook them, especially without having to hire a cleaning crew to come in after you're finished?

This chapter tells you how to deal with both branches of the family.

You don't have to be a culinary romantic to deduce that chickens used to be better. A simple comparison of a roasted organic, free-range chicken with its factory-bred counterpart demonstrates the depth of decline. The meaty flavor of the former tastes as distinctly and immediately of itself as duck or goose; the latter tastes . . . , no, *feels* pleasant enough, but without much flavor.

The simplest way to improve the taste of the poultry you cook then is to buy organic, free-range chickens. Their flavor more than compensates for their premium price, especially in dishes that call for chicken breasts. Finding organic chicken pieces can be a trial, however, and I often resort to ordinary legs and thighs; everything else being equal, dark meat always offers deeper flavor than light.

The second strategy is to bring strong flavors to bear on chicken, by seasoning it with spicy rubs or marinades, or by braising, grilling, or smoking the meat. With chicken, you want as many of the external flavors as possible to penetrate the meat. All of these strategies, alone or in combination, are put to good use in the following pages.

Duck, quail, and geese are the tastiest participants in any discussion about poultry, and the most neglected by home cooks. There's really no excuse for this with quail; it's the bird I recommend for red-meat lovers. Easily grilled or sautéed, quail involves none of the mess people associate with other dark-meat fowl and has great flavor. Duck and geese, on the other hand, require strategic know-how. The problem with traditional recipes is that they tend to smoke up your kitchen with burning fat. This chapter offers you a foolproof method for producing a duck with crisp skin and moist, tender meat cooked completely on top of the stove. (Fans of duck and goose will find additional recipes for these birds in "A Mile in a Chef's Shoes," page 297.) If you've prepared duck in the past and decided it was too much of a hassle, then you may find this recipe a relief.

As always, an instant-read digital thermometer takes some of the guesswork out of telling whether a bird is properly cooked; also, nonstick cooking racks and roasting pans are indispensable when it comes to roasting poultry. Their very minor extra cost will seem trivial during cleanup after roasting a chicken or turkey, let alone a goose.

Sautéed Boneless Chicken Breasts with Brown Bay Butter

For years, I automatically added bay leaves to soups and stocks without much consideration of their effect on flavor. Laura Brennan, my sous-chef at Michela's, and I began experimenting with steeping bay leaves in a variety of liquids—melted butter, white wine for poaching fish, extra virgin olive oil for grilling lamb and dressing salads, even the sweet wine Muscat de Beaumes-de-Venise used to poach pears. We made a simple discovery: when used in large quantities, bay leaves produce an extraordinary combination of butterscotch and eucalyptus that you'd never suspect from their subtler application. Chicken breasts, the culinary equivalent of a blank sheet of paper, take well to a bay-infused butter sauce. This is an extremely easy dish to prepare, with a flavor far out of proportion to the effort involved.

MAKES 4 ENTRÉE SERVINGS

CHICKEN

4 boned chicken breasts (approximately ½ pound each), skin on, split in half to make 8 half-breast cutlets

2 shallots, thinly sliced

2 tablespoons chopped fresh savory

2 tablespoons chopped fresh thyme

2 tablespoons grated lemon zest

6 tablespoons vegetable oil

Kosher salt and freshly ground black pepper

SAUCE

2 cups Chicken Stock (page 31) or 4 cups high-quality canned low-sodium chicken broth, reduced to 2 cups (see page 32)

4 tablespoons unsalted butter

4 bay leaves

1 tablespoon high-quality sherry vinegar

2 tablespoons capers, rinsed (optional)

Kosher salt and freshly ground black pepper

DO AHEAD: Marinate the chicken for at least 4 hours; longer won't hurt.

1. Toss the chicken breasts in a large bowl with the shallots, savory, thyme, lemon zest, and 4 tablespoons vegetable oil. Cover with plastic wrap and refrigerate. Marinate for at least 4 hours and up to 24 hours.

2. Since the cutlets will cook so quickly, it's a good idea to make the sauce first. Bring the stock to a boil in a medium saucepan and let it cook until there's only ½ cup left.

3. While the stock is reducing, melt the butter with the bay leaves in a small saucepan over medium-high heat. Cook until the butter just turns brown, 4 to 5 minutes; take care that it doesn't burn. Remove from the heat and let steep for 20 minutes. Remove the bay leaves.

4. Combine the bay butter and reduced stock in a blender and blend until they're completely mixed. Transfer to a small saucepan and add

the vinegar and capers and season with salt and pepper. Keep the sauce warm.

5. Preheat the oven to 200°F.

6. Remove the chicken cutlets from the marinade; do not scrape off the marinade. Set the bowl aside. Sprinkle the chicken on both sides with salt and pepper. Heat 1 tablespoon of the vegetable oil in a large sauté pan (preferably nonstick) over medium-high heat. If you have the good fortune to have two large sauté pans, heat a second one with 1 tablespoon of vegetable oil. If you're using only one pan, you'll have to cook the cutlets in two batches. When the oil is hot, add 4 cutlets to each pan, skin side down, and cook for 3 to 4 minutes. Flip the cutlets and cook for an additional 3 minutes, or until cooked through. If some of the cutlets are smaller or thinner and cook faster, remove them from the pan and put them on a platter in the oven. If you're relying on a digital thermometer, it should read 160°F when inserted into the center of the meat when it's done. Remove the chicken, scrape any leftover shallots out of the marinade bowl into the pan, and cook until caramelized. Sprinkle over the chicken breasts.

7. Serve immediately, with the warm bay butter.

Roasted Chicken Breasts
Stuffed with Herbed Ricotta

I'm always searching for ways to jazz up chicken breasts. One summer, after I'd finished making a batch of chicken and ricotta ravioli, it occurred to me that there had to be an easier way of bringing chicken and herbed ricotta together. Why not just stuff chicken breasts with a ricotta filling and dispense with the pasta altogether? Roasting split breasts on the bone proved to be the simplest way of preparing this dish. The stuffing goes under the skin. Leaving the bones in helps keep the skin anchored in place, and the meat stays juicier.

If you have access to different brands of fresh ricotta, use the firmest you can find; the less moisture in the filling, the better it will stay in the chicken. Because the cheese stuffing comes into contact with the raw chicken, this dish should never be prepared ahead. Stuff the breasts, coat them with the marinade, and roast them right away.

Cooked breasts will keep for a couple of days in the refrigerator. Cut the cold chicken off the bone and slice crosswise into medallions. Sprinkle the medallions with any leftover crumbled ricotta stuffing and drizzle with a squeeze of fresh lemon and extra virgin olive oil.

MAKES 4 ENTRÉE SERVINGS

STUFFING
1 cup ricotta
¼ cup freshly grated Parmesan
2 teaspoons chopped fresh chives
2 teaspoons chopped fresh thyme
2 tablespoons chopped fresh basil
1 teaspoon freshly squeezed lemon juice
Kosher salt and freshly ground black pepper to taste

4 large bone-in chicken half-breasts (approximately 10 ounces each)

MARINADE
2 shallots, thinly sliced
2 tablespoons chopped fresh tarragon
2 tablespoons chopped fresh thyme
2 tablespoons minced lemon zest
¼ cup vegetable oil

Kosher salt and freshly ground black pepper
1 lemon, cut into 4 wedges

1. Preheat the oven to 375°F.

2. Combine all of the stuffing ingredients, mixing well.

3. Gently insert your fingers into the end of one of the chicken breasts to make an opening between the skin and the breast meat, keeping as much of the edges of the skin attached to the meat as possible. Spoon one-quarter of the herbed ricotta into the opening. Gently squeeze and knead the mixture evenly over the breast between the meat and skin. Repeat with the remaining breasts.

4. Mix all of the marinade ingredients together in a large bowl. Carefully toss the stuffed breasts in the marinade to coat on all sides. Sprinkle each coated breast with salt and pepper and set skin side up on a rack in a roasting pan.

5. Roast the chicken for 25 to 35 minutes, depending on the size and thickness of the breasts. The internal temperature of the breast should read 155°F. It's all right if some of the cheese mixture leaks out from under the skin as the chicken roasts. Let rest for 5 minutes before serving. The temperature will come up another 5 degrees or so as the breasts repose.

6. If you prefer crispier skin, run the chicken under the broiler for a minute or two before serving. Serve with the lemon wedges.

Roasted Rock Cornish Game Hens with North African Flavors

If I don't have access to free-range chickens, my second choice is Rock Cornish game hens. One-pound birds, if you can find them, make ideal generous single portions, but sometimes the selection runs between 1½ and 2 pounds. Instead of serving each person an individual bird, I simply carve the larger birds into breasts and leg-thigh pieces and serve them family-style on a platter.

We roast and grill game hens year-round at my house, but by December we begin looking for alternatives to the usual lemon-garlic-thyme-rosemary-extra-virgin-olive-oil we've been rubbing into them. The saffron, cinnamon, cumin, and ginger in this recipe shift the flavor into a Moroccan key, a welcome change in the cold-weather months. Onions, chickpeas, and tomatoes roast beneath the hens, catch their drippings, and turn into a wonderfully rich mash. Be careful not to use more than a pinch of saffron, or it will overpower all the other spices (and the hens and anything else you're eating).

MAKES 4 ENTRÉE SERVINGS

4 garlic cloves, finely chopped

2 tablespoons paprika

2 teaspoons ground cinnamon

2 teaspoons ground ginger

2 teaspoons freshly ground black pepper

2 teaspoons ground cumin

2 teaspoons ground coriander

Pinch of saffron, soaked in ¼ cup freshly squeezed lemon juice

¼ cup plus 2 tablespoons vegetable oil

4 Rock Cornish game hens (about 1 pound each)

Kosher salt

2 lemons, washed well and cut into quarters

2 tablespoons dark raisins

2 large white onions (about 1½ pounds total), sliced 1 inch thick

1 pound ripe plum tomatoes, each cut into 4 wedges, then halved crosswise

2 cups cooked chickpeas (see page 230), if using canned chickpeas, rinse well

¼ cup chopped fresh flat-leaf parsley

DO AHEAD: Make the spice paste and rub it into the hens 4 hours ahead of time; cover the hens loosely with plastic wrap and refrigerate until ready to cook. Cook the chickpeas.

1. Preheat the oven to 375°F.

2. Mix the garlic, paprika, cinnamon, ginger, pepper, cumin, coriander, saffron with its lemon juice, and ¼ cup of the vegetable oil in a large bowl to make a spice paste. Toss the hens in the bowl with the spice paste and rub them until they're evenly coated. Cover the bowl with plastic wrap and refrigerate. Marinate for at least 4 hours and up to 24 hours.

3. Remove the hens from the refrigerator; do not scrape off the marinade. Sprinkle the hens liberally inside and out with salt. Put a lemon quarter and one-quarter of the raisins in the cavity of each bird. Put the onions in the bottom of a roasting pan, season with salt and pepper, and toss with the remaining 2 tablespoons vegetable oil. Put two V-racks (or arrange two regular racks into a V) over the onions, and place 2 hens breast side down on each rack.

4. Roast for 30 minutes, then turn the birds breast side up, give the onions a stir, and roast for an additional 15 minutes. Add the tomatoes and chickpeas to the pan and roast for an additional 15 minutes, or until the skin has browned and the hens are cooked through.

The juices should run clear from the thickest part of the thigh when poked with a skewer; an instant-read digital thermometer inserted at the same spot should read 165°F. Transfer the hens to a platter.

5. Add the chopped parsley to the vegetable mixture in the roasting pan, stir, and taste for seasonings. Spoon the mixture around the platter. Garnish with the remaining lemon quarters. Serve immediately.

❧ How to Cook Chickpeas ❧

O*ne cup of dried chickpeas* will make about 2½ cups cooked. Dried chickpeas are so hard they need to be treated more like beans than peas, which means they need to soak before cooking. You can soak them using either the overnight or the quick-soak method. Whichever method you use, pick through them first to remove any stones or debris.

MAKES 2½ TO 3 CUPS

OVERNIGHT METHOD: Soak the chickpeas in 4 times their volume of cold water (e.g., cover 1 cup chickpeas with 4 cups water). Here "overnight" actually means "for at least 4 hours," which could mean all morning or all afternoon, or whatever your schedule dictates. The point is, they need to soak for at least 4 hours, and a few hours longer won't hurt them. Skim off any chickpeas that float to the surface. Drain and rinse the soaked chickpeas thoroughly and examine them again to be sure no small stones have escaped your notice.

QUICK-SOAK METHOD: Place the chickpeas in a large pot with 4 times their volume in water. Bring to a boil for a full minute, then turn off the heat, cover, and let soak for an hour. Drain and rinse thoroughly, and examine again for any remaining stones.

1 cup dried chickpeas, soaked, drained, and rinsed
1 tablespoon extra virgin olive oil
½ small onion, cut into quarters
½ small celery stalk
2 bay leaves
Kosher salt

1. Put the soaked chickpeas in a medium saucepan with 8 cups cold water. Boil for 10 minutes, then lower the heat to a simmer. Skim off any scum.

2. Add the olive oil, onion, celery, and bay leaves. Simmer, partly covered, until the chickpeas are tender, 1½ hours or more. Depending on their quality and age, chickpeas vary considerably in cooking time.

3. After the chickpeas are tender, add the salt. (If you add the salt before they're tender their skins will toughen.) Simmer for 10 minutes more so they can absorb the salt. Drain. Refrigerate, covered, until ready to use.

Peppered Chicken Cooked Under a Brick with Hot-and-Spicy Ginger Sauce

When I get a craving for chicken with crispy skin, I go straight to this variation on the classic *pollo ala diavolo*. Crackling skin and copious amounts of red pepper—that's enough for me. Weighting butterflied chickens with bricks or other heavy objects as they cook keeps the birds flat, pressing their skin against the cooking surface so they crisp evenly. I rely on bricks wrapped in foil, but you can use just about anything as long as it's clean and heatproof (antique pressing irons would be ideal). Leftovers are perfect picnic fare; the skin doesn't become soggy after it cools, as cold fried chicken skin does.

Look no further than this recipe for a reason to purchase a few extra inexpensive cast-iron skillets (each flattened bird cooks in its own frying pan). I've tried playing with the technique, searing the birds briefly and then letting them finish cooking in the oven, but they just don't taste the same and the skin isn't as crisp.

MAKES 4 ENTRÉE SERVINGS

CHICKEN

4 free-range baby (poussin) chickens or Rock
  Cornish game hens (about 1 pound each)

1 tablespoon hot red pepper flakes

2 tablespoons finely chopped fresh ginger

3 garlic cloves, finely chopped

1 tablespoon fennel seeds

½ cup plus 2 tablespoons vegetable oil, plus more
  if needed

Kosher salt

SAUCE

1½ teaspoons finely chopped fresh ginger

1½ garlic cloves, finely chopped

2 shallots, thinly sliced

½ cup dry sherry

2 cups Chicken Stock (page 31) or 4 cups high-
  quality canned low-sodium chicken broth,
  reduced to 2 cups (see page 32)

3 tablespoons unsalted butter

1 teaspoon sherry vinegar

Kosher salt

DO AHEAD: Prepare the chickens and marinate overnight (see Step 1).

1. Butterfly the chicken (see page 234), removing the backbone and wing tips, but leaving the breastbone. Sprinkle the chickens with the red pepper flakes, ginger, chopped garlic, and fennel seeds. Rub with the oil, cover, and marinate overnight in the refrigerator.

2. Season the chicken with salt. Heat four large frying pans each with 2 tablespoons vegetable oil over medium heat. Place the chickens skin side up in the pans, flatten each one with a weight, and cook halfway through, about 20 minutes. Flip the chickens, replace the weights, and cook until done, about another 20 minutes. The skin should be crispy and golden brown. Transfer the chickens to a cutting board (set one of the pans aside) and remove the breastbones. Transfer the chickens to a plate, skin side up.

3. Sauté the ginger, garlic, and sliced shallots in the reserved pan over medium heat, adding an additional tablespoon of oil if necessary, until tender, about 5 minutes. Deglaze the pan with the sherry and cook at a simmer until it has reduced by three-quarters, 5 to 8 minutes. Add the stock and cook until it has reduced by two-thirds, about 30 minutes. Whisk in the butter and season with the vinegar and salt.

4. Make a pool of sauce on one side of each of four warm plates. Set the chicken atop the sauce so it rests half on, half off the sauce (you've worked hard for the crispy skin, so don't drown it in sauce). Serve immediately.

Grilled Smoked Chicken with Poppy Seeds and Pancetta

P*oppy seeds may seem like* an unusual ingredient in roast chicken, but their nuttiness and affinity for lemon are what started this recipe. It began life as an oven-roasted chicken, but I just couldn't figure out a way to get the smoky flavor as intense as I wanted it without setting off my fire alarm. Time for the outdoor grill. The result is an exquisitely flavored bird the color of pale mahogany, crusted with poppy seeds and a mixture of lemon, rosemary, fennel, and parsley bound together with honey. Slices of pancetta inserted beneath the skin prevent the breast from drying out before the legs are done. The lemon quarters inside the cavity become saturated with the chicken's juices as the bird roasts; squeeze them over the chicken just before serving.

The times given for roasting the chicken are somewhat imprecise. My 3¾-pound bird took 2 hours in a covered gas grill, using medium indirect heat. (A medium heat is one where you can hold your hand near the cooking surface for a count of 4 before having to remove it.) Adjust your time according to the size of your bird and your ability to manage the heat in your grill. Judge the chicken's doneness by using an instant-read digital thermometer and the color of the thigh juices, not by time. Do not omit the wood chips—the smoke is an essential component of the bird's flavor.

MAKES 4 ENTRÉE SERVINGS

2 cups of wood chips, soaked in water for
   30 minutes

One 3½- to 4-pound chicken
4 thin slices pancetta
Grated zest of 3 lemons (reserve the lemons)
¼ cup poppy seeds
4 garlic cloves, finely chopped
2 teaspoons fennel seeds, crushed
2 tablespoons honey
½ cup chopped fresh flat-leaf parsley
2 tablespoons chopped fresh rosemary
3 tablespoons vegetable oil
Kosher salt and freshly ground black pepper

1. Using a sturdy knife or cleaver, chop the wing tips off the chicken. Using your fingers, separate the skin from the breasts, forming a pocket over each breast. Slip 2 slices of pancetta into each pocket, then press the skin back down to hold the pancetta in place.

2. Drain the wood chips and put them into a small foil pan. Prepare a medium fire in a grill; allow the grill to heat with the top closed and the pan of chips directly over the flames or coals until the entire grate is hot and the chips are smoking well, at least 15 minutes. Then adjust the heat source so there is a space in the center of the grate that is not directly above the coals or flames, large enough to hold the chicken with plenty of room to spare. Turn off the middle burner if using a gas grill, or push the coals to the sides of a charcoal grill. The chicken should cook by indirect heat—it should not grill. Only the pan of wood chips should be over direct heat.

3. Meanwhile, mix the lemon zest with the poppy seeds, garlic, fennel seeds, honey, parsley, rosemary, and oil to form a paste. Season the chicken inside and out with salt and pepper. Smear the paste evenly over the exterior of the chicken. Cut 2 of the zested lemons into quarters (save the remaining lemon for another use). Place as many of the lemon quarters inside the cavity as will fit comfortably (don't squish them). Tie the legs together with butcher's twine and truss the chicken so the cavity is closed.

4. Place the chicken breast side up on the grill. Close the grill and roast for 1½ to 2 hours. An instant-read digital thermometer should read 165°F when inserted into the thickest part of the thigh. This will give you a moist juicy chicken. If you prefer chicken a little more well done, wait until the thermometer reads 170°F. When the thigh is pricked near where it joins the body, the juices should run clear. Remove and let the chicken rest for 10 minutes before carving.

5. Remove the lemon quarters from the cavity (I know—they're a mess) and set aside. Carve the chicken and arrange on a platter. Squeeze the lemon quarters over the chicken, or offer them on the side. Serve immediately.

HOW TO BUTTERFLY A CHICKEN

Butterflying a chicken opens the bird out of its natural football shape into a single flat layer (presumably resembling a butterfly), making it easier to grill or sauté the entire bird evenly. Theoretically you can butterfly any poultry, but the technique is most conveniently applied to small fowl—chickens under 1½ pounds, game hens, and quail. Larger birds become unwieldy when butterflied and the increased time you have to spend cooking them on top of the stove can make the preparation a chore.

Set the chicken breast side down. Using a sturdy knife, cleaver, or kitchen scissors, split the chicken lengthwise down one side of the backbone. (Do not split the breast.) Cut down the other side of the backbone. Remove the backbone and discard, or save it for stock. Clip off the wing tips (the last joint) and discard. Lay the flat side of a chef's knife or cleaver across the breastbone and apply pressure until you feel the breastbone break. If the chicken doesn't lie perfectly flat after the first break, advance the knife along the ridge of the breastbone and break it again. Keep doing this along the bone until the chicken lies flat. (Do not remove the breastbone.)

Braised Chicken in Mustard with Garlic and Mascarpone

Once in a while I taste a classic treatment for meat or fish and immediately imagine applying the same approach to a completely different animal. A French recipe for rabbit in a luscious mustard cream was the springboard for this dish. Instead of the crème fraîche called for in the version with rabbit, I've used mascarpone. American crème fraîche is more acidic than the French product, and I wanted a softer, sweeter flavor for the chicken. This dish definitely falls into the category of braises that improve with a day of sitting, so make it a day ahead if you can.

MAKES 4 ENTRÉE SERVINGS

MARINADE
1 tablespoon vegetable oil

2 shallots, thinly sliced

2 garlic cloves, crushed

½ cup Dijon mustard

1 tablespoon chopped fresh thyme

½ teaspoon cracked black pepper

2 bay leaves

4 chicken leg-thigh quarters

2 tablespoons vegetable oil

Kosher salt and freshly ground black pepper

2 ounces sliced pancetta, cut into ¼-inch pieces

12 garlic cloves, peeled

12 shallots, peeled

¼ cup white wine vinegar

1 teaspoon tomato paste

2 cups Chicken Stock (page 31) or 4 cups high-quality canned low-sodium chicken broth, reduced to 2 cups (see page 32)

1 tablespoon chopped fresh thyme

½ teaspoon hot red pepper flakes

¼ pound mascarpone

DO AHEAD: Prepare everything through Step 5 (i.e., don't make the sauce or add the mascarpone) and refrigerate the chicken in the braising juices. Reheat everything on top of the stove the next day and make the sauce just before serving.

1. To make the marinade, heat the vegetable oil in a small sauté pan over medium heat. Add the shallots and garlic and cook until tender, about 5 minutes. Let cool. Transfer the shallots and garlic to a larger bowl.

2. Whisk the cooked shallots and garlic, Dijon mustard, thyme, cracked pepper, and bay leaves together in a large bowl. Add the chicken and toss it about so all of the surfaces come in contact with the marinade. Cover with plastic wrap and marinate in the refrigerator for at least 2 hours (it can be left overnight, if that's more convenient), turning the chicken once or twice.

3. Heat 2 tablespoons vegetable oil in a large sauté pan over medium heat. Remove the chicken from the bowl, reserving the marinade, and season all over with salt and pepper. Sear the chicken on both sides until brown. Transfer to a plate. Add the pancetta to the pan and cook just until the fat starts to melt but the pancetta is not yet crispy, about a minute. Remove from the pan and set aside.

4. Add the whole garlic cloves and shallots to the pan and season with salt and pepper. Sauté until lightly browned. Pour off the fat. Add the vinegar to the pan. The vinegar will foam up and reduce almost instantly; scrape the bottom of the pan with a wooden spoon to dissolve any crispy bits. Continue stirring as the vinegar quickly reduces to a glaze, about 30 seconds. Add the tomato paste and cook 1 minute, then add the reserved marinade and the chicken stock. Bring to a boil.

5. Return the chicken pieces to the pan. Stir in the pancetta, thyme, and red pepper flakes. Cover, reduce the heat to low, and simmer until the chicken is tender, but not falling off the bone, 40 to 45 minutes. Turn the chicken every 10 minutes so the exposed side doesn't dry out.

6. Remove the chicken from the pan and keep warm. Cook the sauce, uncovered, until it thickens slightly, about 10 minutes. To finish the sauce, remove the pan from the heat and add the mascarpone, whisking until smooth.

7. Place a chicken quarter on each of four warmed plates, top with the sauce, and serve immediately.

Braised Chicken Thighs with Ancho Peppers and Andouille Sausage

This recipe came about when I needed seasoned chicken to go into the paella at our second restaurant, Red Clay. Then the chicken thighs began showing up at the staff family meal more frequently, and in larger portions, than would suggest they were simply leftovers from the paella. When a dish becomes a staff favorite, it's worth trying to figure out the appeal. The paprika, sausages, and ancho peppers give the chicken a smoky peppery quality usually found with "hotter" dishes. Using skinless thighs allows the flavor of the spices to penetrate the chicken meat instead of remaining on the surface. With a little rice, this makes a comforting supper for cold nights. I can serve it to my four-year-old without fear of rejection.

This dish improves with a day of sitting, so prepare it ahead if possible. Also, if fat is a concern, a day of refrigeration makes it easy to scrape off the layer of fat that rises to the top of the dish. If you're in a hurry, pour the sauce into a Pyrex measuring cup, put it in the freezer for an hour, and then scrape off the fat.

MAKES 4 ENTRÉE SERVINGS

⅓ cup paprika

¼ teaspoon cayenne pepper

Kosher salt

1½ pounds skinless chicken thighs

¼ cup vegetable oil

2 large white onions (about 1 pound total), cut into
   1-inch dice

6 garlic cloves, smashed

2 ancho peppers, stemmed, seeded, and cut into
   ½-inch-wide strips

1 tablespoon tomato paste

1 cup canned crushed tomatoes

1 cup Chicken Stock (page 31) or high-quality
   canned low-sodium chicken broth

½ pound andouille sausage, cut into ½-inch slices

Freshly ground black pepper

2 tablespoons chopped fresh cilantro, plus 6 sprigs
   for garnish

1. Mix the paprika and cayenne pepper in a large bowl. Sprinkle the thighs all over with salt. Add the thighs to the bowl and toss until evenly coated with the pepper mixture.

2. Heat the oil in a large sauté pan over medium-high heat. When the oil is hot, add the thighs and sear for 5 to 7 minutes. Your aim is to get a good sear on the outside of the thighs, not cook them through. Turn the thighs over and sear the other side for 2 minutes. Remove the chicken from the pan and keep warm.

3. Add the onions, garlic, and ancho peppers to the pan and cook until they begin to brown, about 8 minutes. Add the tomato paste and cook for 1 minute. Add the tomatoes and chicken stock and reduce the liquid by a third, about 7 minutes.

4. Return the chicken to the pan, add the sausage, cover, reduce the heat to low, and cook until the chicken is almost falling off the bone, about 1 hour. Adjust the heat if the braising juices are boiling. If the dish cooks too fast, the chicken will dry out.

5. When the chicken is done, the pan juices should be thick enough to serve as a sauce. If they're too thin, transfer the chicken to a platter, increase the heat to medium-high, and reduce the juices to the desired consistency. Taste the sauce and add salt and pepper if necessary. Stir in the chopped cilantro.

6. Place the thighs on a warm platter. Spoon the sauce over them, garnish with the sprigs of cilantro and serve.

Roasted Brined Turkey with Fennel-Herb Stuffing

Brining poultry before roasting produces an amazingly succulent bird, but brining a 15-pound turkey can present some problems, such as, "What kind of container can hold it for brining?" "Where do I store it?" A nonreactive 16-quart stockpot will work, but since I don't have one, I simply purchased an inexpensive extra-large plastic bucket from Home Depot, identical in size to a large bucket of joint compound. (Never use a container that ever held any kind of building materials, no matter how seemingly benign—the plastic may contain chemical residues.) Whatever your container, wash it thoroughly beforehand.

When we recently purchased a new refrigerator, we moved the old one into our basement to call into service for recipes like this. Before I had two refrigerators, I simply made this recipe during cool weather. The bucket fit neatly on the stairs inside the bulkhead leading to my basement, where it was cold, but certainly not freezing. If you don't live in a part of the country that gets cool, you'll have to engage in a draconian refrigerator purge, for at least a day, to make this work. The final alternative is simply to try the recipe with a smaller bird, the size of a container that will fit in your refrigerator.

I try to match the size of the turkey to the size of the gathering so I don't have to worry about too many leftovers. I like to save enough for a few days of sandwiches and maybe a risotto or pasta dish. The rest goes into soup—stuffing and all—and I then freeze the soup. A month or two later, people are actually happy to have some turkey soup.

MAKES 10 ENTRÉE SERVINGS

1 fresh (or defrosted frozen) 15-pound turkey

BRINE
2 gallons water
2 cups kosher salt
½ cup packed brown sugar
10 bay leaves
4 sprigs fresh rosemary, roughly chopped
1 cup chopped fresh sage

STUFFING
8 tablespoons (1 stick) unsalted butter
2 large white onions (about 1½ pounds total), chopped into ½-inch dice

4 celery stalks, peeled and chopped into ½-inch dice
2 fennel bulbs, trimmed of stalks and tough outer layers, cut lengthwise in half, cored, and chopped into ½-inch dice
6 garlic cloves, finely chopped
Kosher salt and freshly ground black pepper
8 cups ½-inch cubes rustic white bread, lightly toasted
¼ cup chopped fresh sage
2 tablespoons chopped fresh thyme
2 tablespoons chopped fresh rosemary
1 cup chopped fresh flat-leaf parsley
About 1½ cups apple cider

8 tablespoons (1 stick) unsalted butter

6 bay leaves

1 teaspoon fennel seeds

Freshly ground black pepper (optional)

GRAVY

¼ cup unbleached all-purpose flour

⅔ cup dry Madeira or dry sherry

3 cups Chicken (or turkey) Stock (page 31) or
    6 cups high-quality canned low-sodium chicken
    broth, reduced to 3 cups (see page 32)

Kosher salt and freshly ground black pepper

DO AHEAD: Brine the turkey for 10 to 12 hours. Before you unwrap the turkey, make sure your brining container is large enough and that 2 gallons of brining solution (the amount in this recipe) will actually cover your bird. To check, place the wrapped turkey in the container and pour 2 gallons of water over it. As long as the turkey is completely submerged, it doesn't matter if you don't use all the brining solution. If the turkey fits in the container but isn't completely covered, adjust the quantities to make 3 (or more) gallons of brine, as necessary.

1. To prepare the turkey, remove the bag of organs from its cavity. Set aside for another use. Rinse the turkey thoroughly and pat dry.

2. To make the brine, mix 8 cups of the water with the remaining brine ingredients in a large pot. Bring to a boil over high heat, reduce the heat to medium-low, and simmer for 10 minutes. Transfer to your clean brining bucket, add the remaining 1½ gallons water, and let cool completely.

3. Immerse the turkey in the brining solution. Cover. Put the bucket into the refrigerator or a cool place for 10 to 12 hours.

4. To make the suffing, melt the butter in a large sauté pan over medium-high heat. When the foam subsides, add the onions, celery, and fennel and cook for 5 minutes. Add the garlic and cook until it just releases its aroma, about a minute. Season with salt and pepper. Combine the cooked vegetables with the remaining stuffing ingredients except the cider in a large bowl. Toss well. Then add only enough cider so the stuffing is moist, but not soggy. Taste and season if necessary. Remember the turkey will be brined, so be careful not to oversalt the stuffing.

5. To make the basting butter, melt a stick of butter in a small saucepan with the bay leaves and fennel seeds. Remove from the heat and let sit for 30 minutes. Remove the bay leaves, pour into a small container, and chill until firm. (You can do this up to 48 hours ahead and reheat.)

6. To roast the turkey, preheat the oven to 350°F. Remove the turkey from the brine and rinse well. Dry well inside and out. Do not salt, but season with pepper if desired.

7. Fill the turkey cavity loosely with the stuffing, then sew up the cavity. Do not truss the legs together—although a turkey with its legs tied looks neater, the meat of the inner legs and thighs tends to cook more slowly than the breast if it is trussed. Brush the bird all over with the bay butter. Set breast side down on a buttered rack in a roasting pan.

8. Roast for 2 hours. After 2 hours, flip the bird so the breast is up. Roast for an additional

hour. Baste with bay butter every 30 minutes throughout the roasting time.

9. Increase the heat to 400°F and roast until the skin is crisp and brown and the bird is done: the juices should run clear when the thigh is pierced at the thickest point, and an instant-read digital thermometer inserted at that point should register 165°F. Transfer to a platter for 30 minutes before carving.

10. Meanwhile, make the gravy: Pour off all but ¼ cup of fat from the roasting pan. Be careful not to pour off the caramelized drippings. Put the pan on top of the stove over medium heat. Sprinkle the flour into the pan. Using the back of a slotted spoon, stir the flour about the pan, scraping the crispy bits of drippings loose. Cook until the flour starts to brown, about 5 minutes. Add the Madeira and continue stirring until it thickens. Add the stock and simmer for 10 minutes. Strain. Season with salt and pepper. Keep warm.

11. Scoop the stuffing out of the turkey into a serving bowl. Present the turkey at the table, along with the stuffing and gravy, then carve. I like to return to the kitchen for the business of carving, especially since I prefer removing the breast whole, then cutting it into cross-wise slices. I also slice the meat off the drumsticks. Arrange the meat on the platter and serve.

Seared Quail Stuffed with Mascarpone and Green Peppercorns

Quail deserve to be more popular with home cooks in this country. They're relatively inexpensive; they're readily available already boned (except for the legs); they make a dramatic presentation; *and* our children love them. Quail are a great bird for grilling or sautéing, and their succulent dark meat is a rich alternative to the bland white-meat chicken that fills the poultry sections of most supermarkets. It's always amusing to me to see how long dinner guests can resist using their fingers after they've consumed as much of the quail as possible using their knives and forks. They just have to gnaw those remaining morsels off the legs.

MAKES 4 ENTRÉE SERVINGS

2 cups apple cider

1 tablespoon grainy mustard

8 semi-boneless quail

1 tablespoon extra virgin olive oil

½ celery stalk, peeled and cut into ¼-inch dice

1 shallot, minced

4 ounces (½ cup) mascarpone

2 teaspoons chopped fresh thyme

2 teaspoons green peppercorns in brine, rinsed and drained

2 teaspoons prepared horseradish, drained

Kosher salt and freshly ground black pepper

2 tablespoons vegetable oil

DO AHEAD: Marinate the quail for at least 2 hours; they can marinate overnight without the taste suffering if it's more convenient.

1. Bring the cider to a boil in a medium saucepan. Lower the heat to medium and reduce the cider to ½ cup, about 20 minutes. Remove from the heat.

2. When the cider is cool, stir in the mustard. Toss the quail with the cider reduction in a nonreactive container and refrigerate for at least 2 hours.

3. Heat the olive oil in a small sauté pan over medium heat. Add the celery and shallots. Cook until tender, 3 to 4 minutes. Remove from the heat and let cool.

4. Mix the vegetables with the mascarpone, thyme, peppercorns, and horseradish. Season with salt and pepper. The mixture will be quite stiff. Divide it equally into 8 portions and form them into ovals. Place them on a baking sheet lined with wax paper. Freeze until semi-solid, about 2 hours. (They have to be at least semi-solid before you use them, or they'll melt too fast during cooking; if you want to freeze them for longer, that's fine.)

5. When ready to cook, place a frozen cheese oval in the cavity of each quail. Thread a toothpick through the skin on either side of the cavity opening to hold the opening shut, or tie the legs together with butcher's twine to close the cavity. Sprinkle the quail liberally with salt and pepper.

6. Heat the vegetable oil in a large sauté pan over medium heat. Add the quail breast side down (you may have to cook them in two batches, or use two pans; put the finished birds on a platter in a warm 200°F oven) and cook until golden brown, about 10 minutes. Pay close attention to the pan: The cider reduction has a high sugar content, and if it gets too hot, it will start to burn; lower the heat as necessary. Turn the birds over and cook for an additional 10 minutes. At 10 minutes per side, the birds should be cooked medium. An instant-read digital thermometer inserted into the thickest part of the leg should read 165°F for medium. Cook longer if desired. Don't worry if some of the melted mascarpone starts to leak out after 15 minutes or so—just drizzle it over the quail before serving. Present the platter of quail at the table.

HOW TO GRILL QUAIL

This dish adapts easily to the grill, and if you can use wood chips to smoke the quail while they're cooking, all the better. The quail are first seared on a hot portion of the grill, then finish cooking in disposable aluminum pie plates on a cooler part of the grate, with the grill cover closed. If you want to omit the mascarpone filling, simply cook the marinated quail on a hot grill for 4 to 6 minutes per side.

1. Prepare a grill with hot and medium cooking areas (see page 265 if you're unfamiliar with how to do this). A grill is hot when you can't hold your hand near the grill surface for longer than 2 seconds; it's medium when you can't hold your hand there for longer than 4 seconds.

2. Brush the hot part of the grate with oil and set the quail breast side down on it. Leave them just long enough to get a good grill mark, only a minute or two. Transfer the quail to two disposable aluminum pie plates. Close the cover of the grill, reduce the heat (on a gas grill lower the heat to medium; on a charcoal grill, close the vents halfway), and cook for 15 minutes, then check for doneness. (Don't be concerned if some of the mascarpone runs into the pie plates. Just pour it over the quail before serving.) An instant-read digital thermometer inserted into the thickest part of the leg should register 165°F for medium. If you poke the leg with a skewer and the juices run clear, it's well-done—of course, the puddle of molten cheese in the pie plate will also be a clue. If the quail need to cook longer, close the top and try again in a few minutes. After you've grilled quail a few times, you'll find you're able to tell how done it is just by pinching the breast.

WHAT IS FARRO?

Farro is a Mediterranean cereal grain similar to spelt (if that doesn't mean anything to you, think barley). From prehistoric times through the sixth and seventh centuries it was a staple of both European and Near Eastern Mediterranean peoples, but the appearance of higher-yielding strains of wheat after the fall of the Roman Empire eventually displaced it except as a local specialty in a few isolated areas. It has experienced something of a revival and is now exported to the United States, where chefs find its complex nuttiness and slightly resistant texture a worthwhile addition to their palate of grains. In Italy, it is customary to soak farro overnight before cooking it, but I've found the difference between the soaked and unsoaked grain to be so minor it's not worth the effort.

HOW TO PEEL CHESTNUTS

Use a sharp knife to cut an X in the flat side of each chestnut. Put the chestnuts in a saucepan, cover with salted water, cover, and bring to a boil. Cook for 4 minutes, then turn off the heat. After the pan has cooled for a few minutes, remove a chestnut. Leave the remaining chestnuts in the water; if you remove them all, they'll become difficult to peel. (This is a good time to use disposable latex gloves—they insulate your fingers against the heat.) Peel away the shell and inner skin of the chestnut, using a paring knife. The chestnuts should be tender. If they are not, don't try cooking them longer; simply chop coarsely and proceed. They'll finish cooking in the pan or in the stuffing. A pound of fresh chestnuts yields about 1 cup peeled cooked chestnuts.

Quail, Farro, and Chestnut Stew

Save this hearty winter stew for a weekend getaway with friends. Farro is a Mediterranean grain whose mildly chewy texture and rustic flavor make it a perfect match for the gamy flavor of quail. Don't let the ingredients list overwhelm you—give everybody a job chopping herbs or vegetables, and soon all the ingredients will be ready. The actual cooking is quite simple and the results are more than worth it. After all, how often do you get to eat anything stuffed with cherries soaked in grappa? When the stunning finished dish of quail sitting atop a steaming mound of aromatic farro and chestnuts arrives, everybody will feel they had a hand in its creation.

MAKES 4 ENTRÉE SERVINGS

MARINADE

2 tablespoons extra virgin olive oil

2 shallots, minced

¼ cup pure maple syrup

1 tablespoons chopped fresh thyme

1 teaspoon chopped fresh rosemary

1 tablespoon chopped juniper berries

1 tablespoon cider vinegar

4 semi-boneless quail

4 teaspoons dried cherries, soaked in
   2 tablespoons grappa for 30 minutes (optional)

Kosher salt and freshly ground black pepper

5 tablespoons extra virgin olive oil

1 medium onion, chopped into ¼-inch dice

1 celery stalk, peeled and chopped into ¼-inch dice

1 small carrot, peeled and chopped into ¼-inch
   dice

2 garlic cloves, finely chopped

1 cup farro (available in specialty food stores,
   Italian markets, and some health food stores)

4 cups Chicken Stock (page 31) or high-quality
   canned low-sodium chicken broth

1 tablespoon chopped fresh thyme

1 teaspoon chopped fresh rosemary

4 bay leaves

1 teaspoon grated lemon zest

2 tablespoons unsalted butter

1 cup cooked and peeled chestnuts (page 244),
   sliced ¼ inch thick

1 tablespoon pure maple syrup

¼ pound arugula or other tender, quick-cooking
   green, such as spinach

2 teaspoons balsamic vinegar

DO AHEAD: Marinate the quail 4 to 6 hours in the refrigerator.

1. To make the marinade, heat 2 tablespoons of olive oil with the shallots in a small sauté pan over low heat and cook until the shallots are tender, about 5 minutes. Remove from the heat and let cool.

2. Combine the shallots with the remaining marinade ingredients in a large bowl. Add the quail and rub inside and out with the marinade. If using the cherries, put a teaspoon of cherries in the cavity of each bird. Cover and marinate for 4 to 6 hours in the refrigerator.

3. Sprinkle the quail inside and out with salt and pepper. Heat 2 tablespoons of the olive oil in a large sauté pan over medium-high heat. Sear the quail breast side down until golden brown, about 4 minutes. Turn the birds over and cook for an additional 4 minutes. They should still be rare. Remove the quail to a plate and let cool, then cover and refrigerate.

4. Meanwhile, wipe any burned bits out of the pan with a paper towel. Add the remaining 3 tablespoons olive oil, the onion, celery, and carrot. Season with salt and pepper. Cook, stirring occasionally, until the vegetables are tender and lightly browned, about 8 minutes. Add the garlic and cook until aromatic, only a minute or two.

5. Add the farro, chicken stock, thyme, rosemary, bay leaves, and lemon zest. Season with salt and pepper. Lower the heat to a simmer, cover, and cook until the farro is tender, about 35 minutes. It should be quite creamy, like a loose risotto.

6. While the farro is cooking, heat the butter in a small sauté pan over medium-low heat. Add the chestnuts, season with salt and pepper, and cook until golden brown. Add the maple syrup and stir well. Remove from the heat.

7. Add the glazed chestnuts and arugula to the farro and toss well. Set the quail on top of the farro, cover, and cook until the quail are done, about 10 minutes. An instant-read digital thermometer inserted into the thick part of the thigh should read 160°F for medium-rare. Cook more or less, according to amount of doneness desired.

8. Transfer the quail to a plate. Spoon the farro onto a platter; remove the bay leaves. Arrange the quail atop the farro, drizzle with balsamic vinegar, and serve.

Steamed and Pan-Roasted Duck with Honeyed Quince Compote

Home cooks who wouldn't think twice about roasting chickens, turkeys, and game hens come down with an extreme case of the willies when presented with duck. Their reasoning goes something like this: Duck is swathed in fat; to get the skin to crisp properly, you need to roast the duck at a high temperature; roasting duck at a high temperature causes the fat to smoke. Result: a trashed kitchen, duck with insufficiently crisp skin, and an unpleasant layer of fat that still remains between the skin and the meat. You give up.

This recipe offers a foolproof alternative. The duck is steamed in a roasting pan on top of the stove, which renders much of the fat (without the mess), then pan-roasted in pieces on top of the stove at a relatively low temperature. The skin is crisp, the fat is either removed or rendered, and the meat is juicy and rich. In addition, the recipe offers you several different ways of serving the duck, depending on the number of diners and the amount of time and energy you wish to invest. The simplest approach is just to serve the duck unadorned. Believe me, the taste of the meat and the skin will carry the day. With very little more effort, you can make a spicy duck glaze or a honeyed quince compote. A really fancy occasion will call for both. The directions on page 319 explain how to double this recipe; you can even stretch a single duck to serve 4.

A nonstick or disposable deep roasting pan will significantly reduce or eliminate cleanup after the steaming; a nonstick V-rack is also a cleanup timesaver. You will also need a large cast-iron frying pan or heavy sauté pan (nonstick, if you prefer, but not absolutely necessary), along with a lid.

If you have leftovers, pan-roasted duck will keep for several days. Instead of reheating it, I prefer to treat it like the rare ingredient it is and use it to enhance other dishes. Chopped duck (without the skin) can be added to mushroom risotto during the last addition of broth. While the risotto is cooking, slice the skin into matchsticks and crisp it in a small sauté pan. When the risotto is finished, garnish each portion with a sprinkling of duck cracklings. A little chopped duck meat also adds incredible depth to a simple tomato sauce for pasta. Sauté ¼ cup diced pancetta until the fat begins to render, add the chopped duck, and cook for another minute. Add this mixture to a plain tomato sauce and simmer for 20 minutes. Serve over fresh pappardelle.

MAKES 2 ENTRÉE SERVINGS (SEE DUCK FOR MORE THAN TWO, PAGE 319, IF YOU WANT TO STRETCH IT

One 5-pound Long Island duck

STEAMING MIXTURE
2 tablespoons finely chopped fresh ginger
2 tablespoons 5-spice powder
¼ cup honey
¼ cup dry sherry
Kosher salt and freshly ground black pepper

¼ cup vegetable oil, or as needed
Kosher salt and freshly ground black pepper
Honeyed Quince Compote (recipe follows; optional)
Spicy Duck Glaze (recipe follows; optional)

DO AHEAD: The duck can be rubbed with spices, steamed, and cut apart a day before pan-roasting if you're facing a time crunch on the day of serving, but don't pan-roast it until you're ready to serve it. In an ideal world, the best thing to do would be to rub the duck with the mixture of steaming spices and then let it sit uncovered in the refrigerator for a day before finishing the recipe. The Honeyed Quince Compote can also be made a day ahead, then warmed before serving.

STEAMING

1. Remove the paper sack containing the gizzard, heart, and liver from the cavity of the duck and discard or reserve for another use. The neck may be in the sack or in the cavity of the duck; in either event, discard it too or reserve for another use. Rinse the duck inside and out. Pat dry. Cut off the last two segments of the wings and discard. Cut off the fatty flaps around the neck opening and trim the fat from around the opening of the body cavity. Discard the trimmings. Carefully poke the skin of the bird all over with a fork or skewer. Try not to penetrate beyond the fat layer into the meat—if you go too far, the meat juices will run out during cooking as well as the fat. Approaching the skin from a sharp angle instead of straight in will help.

2. Mix the ginger, 5-spice powder, honey, and sherry together. Rub the mixture all over the duck, inside and out. Sprinkle the duck liberally with salt and pepper, inside and out.

3. Set the duck breast side down on a rack, preferable a V-rack, in a roasting pan. Add 1 inch of water. Bring to a boil on top of the stove. Lower the heat to a simmer. Cover (use foil if your roasting pan doesn't have a lid) and steam for 30 minutes. Flip the duck and steam for another 30 minutes. Remove the duck from the pan and allow to cool.

PAN-ROASTING

4. Cut the duck into 4 pieces (see How to Break Down a Duck, page 250).

5. Heat an ⅛-inch layer of vegetable oil in a large sauté pan over high heat. The pan must have a thick heavy bottom so it conducts the heat evenly; hot spots will cause the duck skin to burn. A nonstick pan will help alleviate the chance of sticking, but it's not necessary if the pan is heavy and you wait to add the duck until the oil is quite hot. If the oil is not hot when you add the duck pieces, the skin will stick and burn. Sprinkle the duck pieces liberally with salt and pepper. When the oil is hot, almost smoking, add the duck pieces skin side down—do not disturb them once you have set them in the pan—allow them to sear

for 1 minute, then adjust the heat to low, cover the pan, and cook until the meat is tender and the skin is crisp, 50 to 60 minutes. Check every 15 minutes to be sure the skin isn't burning. Pour off excess fat as it accumulates. An instant-read thermometer should read 180°F when inserted into one of the thighs when the duck is finished.

6. Meanwhile, make the Honeyed Quince Compote and the duck glaze if using, and keep warm.

7. Place a duck breast and leg/thigh piece on each plate. Place 2 honeyed quince quarters on each plate, if using. Sauce the duck with the glaze, if using. Serve immediately.

HOW TO BREAK DOWN A DUCK

This is a great method for cutting a whole duck into pieces, especially if you intend to sauté the duck in order to crisp the skin. The old-fashioned tableside technique was to carve or pry the meat off the breast, then cut the legs off by slicing through the joint where the thigh meets the body. The technique described below is the one used by restaurant cooks. It's a little messier, but it's faster and easier, results in very neat duck pieces, and has the added advantage of allowing you to remove left-over pockets of fat. Wait until the duck has cooled if possible—it's more comfortable to handle. Wearing a pair of disposable latex gloves provides a layer of insulation if the duck is still warm and makes cleanup easier.

1. Begin by cutting the duck in half lengthwise, using a sharp chef's knife or poultry shears. First slice through the breastbone, then carefully slice down along both sides of the backbone. Discard the backbone or save for stock.

2. Lay a duck half in front of you, skin side up. Make a single diagonal slice to separate the leg-thigh piece from the breast. Be generous—you want to leave as much thigh meat attached to the leg as possible. If you're uncertain where to cut, flip the breast over and locate the joint where the thigh joins the body. You want to cut a few inches forward of that joint to get all the meat. Repeat with the remaining duck half.

3. Flip over the duck breast. Snap the joint where the wing joins the breastbone, but leave the wing attached. Peel off the breastbone and any other surface bones. If you see any pocket of fat remaining under the breast, use your finger to scoop it out. Repeat with the remaining breast.

4. Examine each leg/thigh. Your goal is to peel away all the exposed bone on the underside. This will probably include a small portion of hip that joins the thigh. Snap the joint where the thigh bone joins the drumstick. Pull out the thigh bone. When you finish, there shouldn't be any bones left in the piece except the drumstick. If you can see a pocket of fat next to the thigh, remove it with your finger.

5. You now have 4 pieces of almost boneless duck with skin intact—2 breast pieces, with wings attached, and 2 legs/thighs.

❧ Honeyed Quince Compote ❧

The quinces take on a lovely rose color in this sweet syrup. Although I've suggested that the fruit accompany duck, it goes well with just about any strong, dark meat, including dark-meat turkey, goose, quail, and venison.

MAKES 4 SERVINGS

¾ cup water

¼ teaspoon kosher salt

¼ cup freshly squeezed lemon juice, plus
   additional to make acidulated water

⅔ cup honey

½ teaspoon 5-spice powder

1 cinnamon stick

1 star anise

2 ripe quinces, peeled, cored, and quartered
   (if preparing ahead, store in water acidulated
   with lemon juice)

1. Combine everything except the quinces in a small nonreactive saucepan. Bring to a boil, then reduce the heat to medium-low and add the quince quarters. Poach until tender (a knife should slide through the fruit easily), about 30 minutes. The fruit will have a lovely pink-orange hue.

2. Remove the quince pieces. Reduce the poaching liquid to a syrup, then return the quince pieces to the pan. Serve the quinces warm in their syrup.

❧ Spicy Duck Glaze ❧

MAKES ½ CUP

¼ cup honey

¼ cup dry sherry

1 teaspoon 5-spice powder

1 teaspoon grated fresh ginger

Kosher salt and freshly ground black pepper to
   taste

1 tablespoon freshly squeezed lemon juice

Combine everything except the lemon juice in a small nonreactive saucepan and bring to a boil, then lower the heat to a simmer. Cook for 3 minutes. Remove from the heat and add the lemon juice. Pour over the duck just before serving.

Beef, Veal, Pork, Lamb, and Game

❧

ny cook can blunder her way through a few bad roast chickens until she manages to produce an edible one; with a shoulder of veal, though, there are too many variables that need to be right, or relatively right, to create a glorious finale. The process is comparable to the difference between riding a bicycle and driving a car with a standard transmission: you can learn to do the first on your own; for the second, you need an instructor. This chapter is a short course in traditional meat know-how.

A selection of grilling and pan-searing recipes, the simplest approaches to meat, will appeal to straight-ahead carnivores. But the heart of the chapter is in the methods for cooking meat slowly—braising and roasting. Braising, or long, slow cooking in a moist environment flavored with wine and aromatics, reduces even the most recalcitrant cut of meat to spoon-tender succulence. Roasting, by contrast, caramelizes the exterior of the meat, and the recipes in this chapter demonstrate the variety of effects possible with marinades, rubs, and crusts.

I hope a few of these dishes will lure you into unfamiliar territory. Thin-Sliced Calves' Liver with Greens, Dijon Mustard Sauce, and Vinegared Grapes should make it clear why liver on the French side of the Atlantic is a bistro staple—it's simple to prepare and tastes great. If you've ever hesitated about taking the plunge and trying to cook venison at home, Peppered Venison with Sherry Sauce and Dried Fruit Chutney will get you started.

Before you launch into these recipes, you may want to consider investing in a few kitchen essentials. An instant-read digital thermometer is indispensable for determining doneness, especially with roasts. If you combine the use of a thermometer with testing grilled or sautéed meat by poking it with your finger, you will soon be able to tell the doneness of a steak or other thinly cut piece of meat by feel alone. Two pieces of cookware are necessary for successful sautéing and braising: a heavy-bottomed skillet or sauté pan (two would be ideal), and a large Dutch oven or cast-iron casserole. Heavy-bottomed cookware conducts heat evenly; by preventing "hot spots," it ensures that the pot's contents cook evenly, which is necessary for pan-searing or sautéing. The Dutch oven, as large and heavy as you can afford (6 quarts is good; 8 is better), must be both capacious enough to contain several pounds of meat, vegetables, and braising liquids and, again, heavy enough to conduct heat evenly for slow, even cooking over several hours. Finally, a seemingly common item that all of us have—except when we need it—is butcher's twine, essential for holding stuffed pieces of meat together or helping thick medallions to maintain their shape in a sauté pan.

Seared Sirloin Tips with Red Wine Pan Juices and Anchovy Butter

S irloin tip steaks are cut, as their name suggests, from the bottom tip of the sirloin. They're a moderately priced cut of meat with a great sink-your-teeth-into-this texture and beefy flavor that takes well to marinating and pan-searing or grilling. Supermarkets tend to package them cut into either cubes (for skewers) or strips 4 to 6 inches long, about an inch thick, and a couple of inches wide. If you have an agreeable butcher, ask him to cut 1½ to 2 pounds of sirloin tip into just four pieces, which will make them about double the ordinary width; otherwise, just buy them in their usual strip shape. By the way, some stores sell sirloin tips as "steak tips," while others see "steak tips" as a more attractive way to market stewing beef. If you're at all uncertain, you can't go wrong by simply substituting the slightly more expensive flank steak for sirloin tips and cutting it into four pieces yourself at home.

Treating meat to an anchovy marinade, pan-searing it, and then serving it with a flavored butter is a classic French bistro formula for handling an inexpensive cut of beef. It's also my husband's favorite recipe for sirloin tips or flank or skirt steaks on the grill during the summer. Cold leftovers make excellent sandwiches on crusty bread; or add cut-up pieces to tomato sauce and serve over pasta.

MAKES 4 ENTRÉE SERVINGS

MARINADE
2 tablespoons vegetable oil
2 shallots, minced
4 garlic cloves, minced
2 anchovies, rinsed and chopped
1 cup dry red wine
4 bay leaves
2 tablespoons freshly cracked black pepper
1 tablespoon chopped fresh thyme

1½ to 2 pounds sirloin tips (depending on appetite)
Kosher salt
2 to 4 tablespoons vegetable oil
2 tablespoons water
½ teaspoon red wine vinegar
2 tablespoons unsalted butter

Freshly ground black pepper (optional)
1 recipe Anchovy Butter (page 256; optional)

DO AHEAD: Marinate the meat for at least 3 hours (12 is optimal).

1. To make the marinade, heat 2 tablespoons vegetable oil with the shallots and garlic in a sauté pan over medium heat and cook until they are tender and aromatic, 2 to 3 minutes. Add the anchovies and red wine. Bring to a boil, then lower the heat and simmer for 2 minutes. Remove from the heat and allow to cool.

2. Place the meat in a nonreactive container or a couple of large resealable plastic freezer bags.

Add the bay leaves, cracked black pepper, and thyme to the marinade. Pour the marinade over the meat. Make sure the meat is completely covered. Cover (or seal the bags) and marinate in the refrigerator for at least 3 hours and up to 12 hours, turning occasionally.

3. Remove the sirloin tips from the marinade and pat dry. Do not discard the marinade. Sprinkle the meat on both sides with salt.

4. Heat 2 tablespoons of the vegetable oil in a large sauté pan over high heat. If the tips won't fit comfortably in the pan without touching, use a second pan and another 2 tablespoons oil. Add the tips and sear on each side, turning once. The tips will get a nice brown crust as they cook. After they've had a chance to sear for 2 to 3 minutes on each side (less, if you want them rare), check them for doneness with an instant-read digital thermometer. Remove them at 126°F for medium-rare. Transfer the tips to a platter and cover loosely with aluminum foil while you make the sauce.

5. Add the reserved marinade and the water to the pan. (If you cooked the meat in two pans, just use one of them to make the sauce.) Bring to a boil, then lower the heat and let simmer for 4 minutes. Remove the pan from the heat, add the vinegar, and whisk in the butter. Taste and adjust the seasoning as necessary.

6. Pour the sauce over the tips. Dot the meat in three or four places with a tablespoon of the anchovy butter, if using. Serve immediately, offering additional anchovy butter on the side.

❧ Anchovy Butter ❧

I learned to make anchovy butter from Lydia Shire, one of Boston's pioneer female chefs, who served it with lobster. The experience was a revelation. I was amazed at how the anchovies metamorphosed from their salty incarnation as a topping for pizza into something almost sweet. People who instinctively shy away from unadulterated anchovies can find themselves quite taken by anchovy butter, especially with seafood.

The butter needs to be at room temperature (65° to 70°F, no warmer) before you can prepare the recipe. In a pinch, you can use the anchovy butter as soon as everything is blended together, but it tastes and looks better if you allow it to chill for 45 minutes before serving. I usually double this recipe and put half of it in my freezer; we inevitably find a use for it within a month. After a day or two in the refrigerator, the flavors of fresh thyme and parsley in the anchovy butter fade and the anchovy becomes more pronounced. Frozen anchovy butter keeps its flavor for about a month.

MAKES ABOUT ¼ POUND

8 tablespoons (1 stick) unsalted butter, at room temperature
1 large shallot, minced
2 garlic cloves, minced
½ teaspoon chopped fresh thyme
1 tablespoon chopped fresh flat-leaf parsley
6 anchovy fillets, rinsed and finely chopped
Kosher salt and freshly ground black pepper
½ teaspoon freshly squeezed lemon juice

1. Melt 1 tablespoon of the butter in a small pan over low heat. Add the shallot and garlic and cook until the shallot becomes translucent and you can smell the garlic's aroma, 3 to 4 minutes. Remove the pan from the heat and allow to cool.

2. Mix the shallot and garlic with the remaining butter, the herbs, and anchovies in a bowl. Season with salt and pepper. Add the lemon juice. Taste and adjust the seasoning if necessary.

3. Place on a sheet of plastic wrap, form into a roll, and chill until firm, at least 45 minutes.

4. Once the butter is firm, you can open the plastic wrap and slice off tablespoon-sized pieces as needed. Place 1 piece on top of each portion of meat or seafood just before serving. If the butter was molded in a ramekin, offer the anchovy butter in the ramekin on the side, along with a small serving knife or spoon.

Braised Short Ribs of Beef with Red Wine, Apricots, and Black Olives

S *hort ribs are one of* my favorite meats for braising, a fail-safe illustration of the transformative powers of slow cooking with a little liquid. The ribs start out unappealingly tough and covered with fat, but 2½ to 3 hours of braising softens them into a dish of otherworldly tenderness. The fat melts off the meat and, in this recipe, the apricots and olives blend into something with a distinctive eastern Mediterranean flavor. Although you can certainly enjoy this dish on the same day you make it, like all braised meats, these ribs taste better made a day or two before serving. The ribs and sauce should be refrigerated in the same container so that the meat absorbs the flavors of the braising juices. After scraping any congealed fat from the surface of the sauce, reheat, covered, in a 350°F oven for 20 to 30 minutes.

MAKES 4 ENTRÉE SERVINGS

8 beef short ribs (6 ounces each)
Kosher salt and freshly ground black pepper
2 tablespoons unbleached all-purpose flour for dusting
2 tablespoons vegetable oil
3 ounces smoked bacon, cut into 1 × ¼-inch lardons
2 medium carrots, peeled and chopped into ½-inch dice
1 medium onion, chopped into ½-inch dice
16 garlic cloves, smashed
1 tablespoon tomato paste
2 cups dry red wine
½ cup brandy
2 bay leaves
1 tablespoon fresh thyme leaves
1 teaspoon celery seeds
2 cinnamon sticks
5 whole cloves
2 cups Chicken Stock (page 31) or high-quality canned low-sodium chicken broth
⅓ cup Kalamata olives, pitted
18 dried apricot halves
2 tablespoons chopped fresh flat-leaf parsley

1. Preheat the oven to 325°F.

2. Season the ribs with salt and pepper. Dust with the flour. Heat the oil in a large braising pan or ovenproof casserole over medium-high heat. Add the bacon and cook until most of the fat is rendered, then remove and set aside.

3. Add as many ribs as can fit in a single layer to the pan. You will need to cook them in batches. Sear the ribs on both sides until well browned, then remove from the pan and set aside. Repeat with the remaining ribs. Discard all but 2 tablespoons of the fat from the pan.

4. Lower the heat to medium, add the carrots and onions, season with salt and pepper, and

sauté until the vegetables begin to brown, about 10 minutes. Add the garlic and tomato paste and cook for 4 more minutes. Add the red wine and brandy and reduce by half, about 6 minutes.

5. Return the ribs and bacon to the pot. Add the remaining ingredients except the apricots and parsley and bring to a boil. The liquid should come one-third of the way up the ribs— if not, add some water. As soon as the liquid comes to a boil, turn off the heat and cover the ribs tightly with foil, pressing the foil down into the pan, then place a lid on the pan.

6. Braise the ribs in the oven for 2 hours, turning them every 30 minutes so they cook evenly. Add water as necessary to keep the braising juice one-third of the way up the ribs.

7. After 2 hours, add the apricots and cook for an additional 30 minutes. The meat should be almost falling off the bones. Transfer the short ribs to a large platter. Spoon the vegetables, olives, and apricots over them. Keep warm.

8. Strain the braising juices into a clear glass container and siphon or skim off the fat. The braising juices may already be the consistency of a sauce. If not, return them to the pan and boil for a few minutes to thicken. If you prefer an absolutely smooth sauce, strain out any remaining pieces of vegetable. Taste, season with salt and pepper, and add the parsley. Pour the sauce over the ribs and serve immediately.

Pot Roast of Beef with Green Peppers and Pancetta

Pot roast ought to be one of the great glories of anyone's home repertoire—once you know the rules, it's actually quite easy to produce a fork-tender masterpiece. Unfortunately, if you don't know the rules, it's easy to go wrong with either the texture or flavor. Pot roasts cook by braising. Long, slow cooking breaks down muscle fibers, helping to tenderize the meat, but if there isn't enough fat in the muscle fibers to keep the meat moist during the cooking, then the end result will be dry. The greater the marbling of fat in the meat, the more tender and juicy the pot roast will be. Use chuck or rump cuts, not the bottom round (a boneless muscle from the back leg) that is often promoted as an ideal pot roast cut. To my taste, there just isn't enough fat to make bottom round work. Chuck and rump cuts, by contrast, are richly marbled and produce beefy, juicy pot roasts.

The second issue is flavor. Slow cooking gives the meat the opportunity to absorb the flavors of other ingredients. The more intense the flavors, the stronger their influence. If the ingredients are too mild, the final taste will be bland. This recipe includes red wine vinegar, a potent enhancement to the powerful influence of pancetta, anchovies, and green peppers. When I first made this dish, the flavor reminded me so much of the American South that I served it with grits instead of potatoes, but polenta would be just as good.

MAKES 6 TO 8 ENTRÉE SERVINGS

1 boneless beef chuck or rump roast (about 4 pounds)
Kosher salt and freshly ground black pepper
3 tablespoons vegetable oil
¼ pound pancetta, cut into ¼-inch dice
2 medium onions, chopped into ½-inch dice
8 garlic cloves, minced
2 tablespoons tomato paste
8 anchovies, rinsed and coarsely chopped
½ cup red wine vinegar
4 bay leaves
4 cups Chicken Stock (page 31) or high-quality canned low-sodium chicken broth, or as needed
2 tablespoons chopped fresh sage
4 green peppers, roasted (see page 99), peeled, stemmed, seeded, and cut into ½-inch-wide strips

2 cups canned tomatoes, drained and coarsely chopped

1. Season the meat all over with salt and pepper. Heat the oil in a large braising pan or a Dutch oven over medium-high heat. Add the pancetta and cook until the fat is partially rendered, then remove with a slotted spoon and set aside.

2. Sear the meat all over in the fat until well browned, then remove from the pan and set aside.

3. Lower the heat to medium. Add the onions, season with salt and pepper, and sauté until they begin to brown, about 10 minutes. Add the garlic and tomato paste and cook, stirring occasionally, for 4 more minutes. Add the anchovies and vinegar.

4. Return the meat and pancetta to the pan, then add the bay leaves and enough chicken stock to come one-quarter of the way up the roast. As soon as the liquid comes to a boil, lower the heat to a simmer and cover the roast with foil, pressing the foil down into the pan, then place a lid on the pan.

5. Braise the meat for 3 hours, turning the meat every 30 minutes or so, and adding more stock as needed to keep the juices one-quarter of the

way up the meat. Adjust the heat if the liquids are at more than a simmer. The meat should be very tender, offering little resistance when pierced with a fork.

6. Add the sage, peppers, and tomatoes and cook for an additional 30 minutes. Transfer the meat to a large platter.

7. Skim any fat off the juices. Remove the bay leaves. If the braising liquid seems too thin, increase the heat to medium and cook until the liquid thickens.

8. Thinly slice the roast and arrange overlapping slices on the platter. Spoon the braising liquid and vegetables over the slices and serve.

Braised Oxtails with White Beans

*I*magine a pot roast so juicy and tender it falls apart as soon as you wave your fork over it—you're really thinking about oxtails, you just don't know it. If there were a Braising Hall of Fame, the oxtails display would be front and center. Their secret advantage is a huge reservoir of collagen that melts during braising. The collagen thickens the braising liquid into a sensuously velvety sauce and the meat, which has its own helpfully high fat content, takes on the remarkably tender richness that only happens in braising.

You can certainly enjoy this the day you make it, but to my palate, braises taste better if made a day or two before serving, allowing their flavors to blend. Refrigerate everything in the same container, then reheat after scraping any congealed fat off the surface of the sauce.

MAKES 4 ENTRÉE SERVINGS

1 cup navy beans, picked over for stones and broken beans and rinsed

4 pounds oxtails (from the thick end of the tail), cut into 3-inch sections, trimmed of excess fat

Kosher salt and freshly ground black pepper

¼ cup unbleached all-purpose flour for dusting

2 tablespoons vegetable oil

3 medium carrots, peeled and cut into 1-inch lengths

3 medium onions, sliced 1 inch thick

1 celery stalk, peeled and cut into ½-inch pieces

3 red peppers, stemmed, seeded, and chopped into 1½-inch pieces

1 garlic clove, chopped

1½ cups dry red wine

½ cup red wine vinegar

2 cups canned tomatoes, drained

Grated zest of 1 lemon

2 bay leaves

1 teaspoon hot red pepper flakes

2 teaspoons coriander seeds

2 cups Chicken Stock (page 31) or high-quality canned low-sodium chicken broth

2 tablespoons chopped fresh flat-leaf parsley

1. Either soak the beans overnight or put them in a pot, cover with 1 inch of water, and bring to a boil. Boil for 1 minute. Turn off the heat and let sit for 1 hour. Drain.

2. Preheat the oven to 325°F.

3. Season the oxtails with salt and pepper. Dust with the flour. Heat the oil in a large braising pan or ovenproof casserole over medium-high heat. Sear the oxtails in batches, cooking no more than will fit in a single layer in the pan at a time, until browned all over. Remove from the pan and set them aside.

4. Lower the heat to medium. Add the carrots, onions, celery, and peppers to the pan and sauté until they begin to brown, about 10 minutes. Add the garlic and continue cooking until it becomes aromatic, a couple of minutes. Add the red wine and vinegar and cook until reduced by half, 8 to 10 minutes.

5. Return the oxtails to the pan and add the remaining ingredients, except the parsley; add the drained beans. Cover the oxtails tightly

with a piece of aluminum foil, pressing it down into the pan, then cover with a lid. Put the pan in the oven to braise.

6. After 45 minutes, remove the pan from the oven and give everything a quick stir, so the beans will cook evenly. Check to make sure the liquid hasn't dropped below halfway up the bones; if necessary, add more liquid. Replace the foil and lid and return the pan to the oven. Braise the oxtails for approximately 3½ more hours, stirring and checking the level of the liquid every 30 minutes. The dish is done when the meat is beginning to fall off the bone and the beans are tender. Taste and adjust the seasonings. (If giving the dish a day or two of rest before serving, remove the oxtails from the heat and allow them to cool, then transfer the entire dish to a fresh container for refrigerating. The next day, after skimming off the fat, reheat on top of the stove; if you prefer the dish without bones, remove them as described below before reheating. Proceed as directed.)

7. Skim the fat off the surface of the braising liquid. If you prefer to serve the dish without bones (I leave the bones on board), remove the oxtails from the pan, trim off the meat, and return it to the pan. Stir everything together, sprinkle with the parsley, and serve from the pan at the table.

Tuscan-Style Sirloin with Parmesan, Lemon, and Truffle Oil

Bistecca alla fiorentina is a staggeringly simply preparation: top-quality steak dressed with a little olive oil, salt, and pepper, grilled quite rare, and garnished with lemon. Traditionally prepared with a T-bone steak, weighing in at a little over a pound, this is a dish for devoted carnivores. I put my version of this dish on the menu when we opened Rialto, using sirloin instead of T-bone and serving it atop a salad of endive, arugula, mushrooms, shavings of Parmesan, and a drizzle of truffle oil. Eight years later, I can't take it off the menu—it is by far our biggest seller. All you need is a sangiovese wine from Tuscany.

MAKES 4 ENTRÉE SERVINGS

4 sirloin steaks (10 to 12 ounces each), preferably prime

Kosher salt and freshly ground black pepper

Vegetable oil for brushing the steaks

1 head endive, separated into leaves (about 12 leaves)

4 cups lightly packed arugula leaves, washed and dried

1 large portabella mushroom cap (about 5 inches across), cleaned and sliced paper-thin

1 lemon, halved

6 tablespoons extra virgin olive oil

2 ounces Parmesan shavings

4 teaspoons truffle oil (optional)

1. Prepare a grill with hot and medium cooking areas (see page 265 if you're unfamiliar with how to do this).

2. Sprinkle the steaks liberally on both sides with salt and pepper. Brush on each side with vegetable oil.

3. Set the steaks on the hottest part of the grill. Sear the steaks for 2 minutes, then flip and sear on the other side for 2 minutes. After the initial searing, move the steaks to the medium part of the grill and continue cooking until done, flipping them regularly so they cook evenly. When their temperature registers between 5 and 10 degrees below the desired state of doneness pull them off the grill: Figure on 120°F for rare; 126°F for medium-rare; or 134°F for medium. If you like your steaks rare, begin checking their internal temperature as soon as the initial searing finishes. It's unlikely they'll be done, but it's always better to be safe than sorry. Steaks and grills are variable, so judge when a steak is done by its look and feel, or internal temperature as indicated by an instant-read digital thermometer, not by the number of minutes it has cooked. (As a *very general* guideline, for 1½-inch-thick steaks cooked on a charcoal grill, rare steaks should be pulled 2 to 4 minutes after the initial searing; medium-rare steaks will need another 5 to 7 minutes, medium steaks, 8 to 9 minutes. Steaks cooked on a gas grill will take slightly longer.)

4. Put the steaks on a warm platter, cover loosely with foil, and let them rest for 5 minutes.

5. Meanwhile, put the endive, arugula, and mushroom slices into a large bowl. Squeeze the juice of one lemon half over the salad. Add the olive oil, season with salt and pepper, and toss well. Taste, then adjust the seasonings if necessary.

6. Cut the second lemon half into 4 wedges. Distribute the salad among four plates. Set a steak on top of each salad, sprinkle with the shaved Parmesan, drizzle with the truffle oil, if using, and garnish each with a lemon wedge. Serve immediately.

GRILL NOTES

Thin cuts of meat, poultry, or fish can cook on a hot grill, but the outside of thicker pieces tends to incinerate before the interior is properly cooked. The easiest method of dealing with the problem is to use a grill with two temperature regions—one hot and one medium. A grill is hot when you can hold your hand near the grill surface for no longer than a count of 2 before having to pull it away; it is medium when you can keep your hand near the grilling surface for 4 seconds before you have to move it. After searing a thick steak or piece of chicken over the hot region of the grill, shift it to the cooler area, where it can finish cooking without burning on the outside.

For a gas grill, preheat the grill on high with the cover closed for 15 minutes so everything is nice and hot when you start to cook. After the grill has had time to heat, leave the burners on one part of the grill on high, and lower the heat on the others until you can hold your hand near the grilling surface for 4 seconds.

For a charcoal grill, arrange the hot coals in two zones. The area below what will be the hot part of the grill should be several times as thick as the layer below the medium part of the grill. After arranging the coals but before putting the grate in place, hold your hand over the two regions to make sure you've distributed the coals properly. Replace the grate and allow it to heat for 10 minutes before beginning to cook.

Also bear in mind:

◦ A clean grill grate minimizes sticking.

◦ Most home gas grills do not get as hot on "high" as grills using charcoal. Adjust cooking times accordingly. Learn to judge doneness by look and feel or by using an instant-read digital thermometer, not by relying on cooking times.

◦ Grilling with the cover in place shortens cooking time. Refer to your grill's instructions regarding the vents in your grill's cover.

◦ Use charwood, if possible, not charcoal, for covered grilling. Most popular brands of charcoal briquettes are compressed sawdust impregnated with flammable chemicals and molded into briquettes. For open grilling, briquettes can be acceptable, but I often detect a chemical element in the flavor of food cooked with briquettes in a covered grill. Charwood, by contrast, is composed of solid chunks of genuine charcoal, that is, whole pieces of wood heated in a low-oxygen environment until they carbonize. Charwood burns hotter (but shorter) than commercial briquettes, without any chemical aroma.

◦ Keep a small spray bottle handy when grilling meats to extinguish fat fires. Alternatively, lower the heat or use the grill cover to help minimize flaming.

Braised Veal Shanks with Flageolets and Preserved Lemon

February is the absolute nadir of the culinary year in New England. Spring has yet to arrive, and root vegetables have grown too familiar. These veal shanks are my personal antidote to the late-winter blahs. As a genre, braised veal shanks can be fairly heavy going—rich beyond enduring. This is a lighter treatment. None of the ingredients is actually from spring, but the bright fresh flavors of vermouth, pale green flageolets, tarragon, and tangy preserved lemon seem to suggest that lighter days are just around the corner. And there's always the buttery marrow for the die-hard lover of rich culinary treasures.

MAKES 4 ENTRÉE SERVINGS

½ pound dried flageolet beans (if flageolets are unavailable, use Great Northern white beans), picked over for stones or broken beans and rinsed

¾ pound pearl onions

2 tablespoons unsalted butter

Kosher salt and freshly ground black pepper

1 teaspoon sugar

3½ cups Chicken Stock (page 31) or high-quality canned low-sodium chicken broth

4 large meaty veal shanks, about 2 inches thick (about 3½ pounds total)

3 tablespoons vegetable oil

1 large carrot, peeled and chopped into ½-inch dice

1 celery stalk, peeled and chopped into ½-inch dice

1 medium onion, chopped into ½-inch dice

6 garlic cloves, minced

3 bay leaves

1 tablespoon chopped fresh thyme

1 cup dry vermouth

5 tablespoons chopped fresh tarragon

1 cup water

4 plum tomatoes, seeded (see page 55) and coarsely chopped

¼ cup chopped fresh curly parsley

½ Preserved Lemon (page 268; also available in stores that sell Middle Eastern food), pulp and pith removed, the skin cut into thin strips (if preserved lemon is unavailable, substitute the zest of 1 lemon removed with peeler and cut into thin strips)

1. Soak the flageolets overnight, or put them in a pot, add water to cover by 1 inch, and bring to a boil. Turn off the heat and let sit for 1 hour. Drain.

2. While the flageolets are soaking, bring a large pot of salted water to a boil. Prepare a large bowl of ice water. Blanch the pearl onions in the boiling water for 10 seconds, then plunge them into the ice water. Drain, then remove their skins with a sharp paring knife.

3. Heat the butter in a large sauté pan over medium heat. Add the pearl onions and season with salt and pepper. Cook until they start to brown, about 5 minutes. Sprinkle them with the sugar. As soon as the sugar melts (watch closely so it doesn't burn), add ½ cup of the chicken stock and reduce the heat to low. Cook for 10 minutes, then add another ½ cup chicken stock and continue cooking until the onions are tender and golden and the stock has reduced to a glaze, 10 to 15 minutes. Set aside.

4. Preheat the oven to 325°F.

5. Season the veal shanks all over with salt and pepper. Heat 2 tablespoons of the vegetable oil in a large braising pan or Dutch oven over medium-high heat. Sear the shanks on both sides until browned, about 5 to 7 minutes per side. Transfer the shanks to a platter.

6. Lower the heat to medium and add the remaining tablespoon of oil. Give the oil a minute to heat, then add the carrot, celery, and diced onion, season with salt and pepper, and sauté, stirring occasionally, until the vegetables begin to brown, about 10 minutes. Add the garlic and cook until it becomes aromatic, just a minute or two.

7. Add the bay leaves and thyme, return the shanks to the pan, and add the vermouth. Bring to a boil, then lower the heat to a simmer.

Cover the shanks with a piece of aluminum foil, pressing it down into the pan, then cover with a lid, and braise for 1 hour.

8. Remove the veal from the pan. Add the flageolets, 3 tablespoons of the tarragon, the water, and 1 cup chicken stock to the pan. Return the shanks (opposite sides down) to the pan, setting them on top of the beans, cover again with foil and the lid, and braise for another hour. The meat should be meltingly tender.

9. Remove the veal shanks from the pan; set aside. Add 1½ cups chicken stock, the pearl onions, tomatoes, and 1 tablespoon of the tarragon to the pan. Cook, uncovered, for 30 minutes, or until the flageolets are tender and creamy. If there seems to be too much liquid, reduce the juices over medium heat until they thicken. Return the shanks to the pan and heat through.

10. Right before serving, add the parsley and the remaining 1 tablespoon tarragon to the beans, and season with salt and pepper. Place a veal shank and generous helping of flageolets on each of four plates. Sprinkle strips of the preserved lemon (or fresh lemon zest) over each shank and serve.

❧ Preserved Lemons ❧

The skin of preserved lemon has a distinctive tangy quality that's both exotic and refreshing and is ideal for cutting through other strong flavors. The skin of half a lemon, sliced into thin strips, with all traces of pith or pulp removed, is more than enough to serve four people as a condiment for a rich braised-meat dish. You can also add preserved lemon to salads, but be discreet with them until you've become familiar with their effect. It's easy to inadvertently transform a dish into a "preserved lemon salad," as their flavor overwhelms subtler ingredients.

MAKES 4 PRESERVED LEMONS

4 lemons
¾ cup kosher salt
About 1½ cups freshly squeezed lemon juice
(from about 8 lemons)
Extra virgin olive oil

1. Sterilize a glass jar large enough to hold 4 lemons (washing it in a dishwasher is fine). A 1-quart mayonnaise jar works well.

2. Scrub the lemons well, then slice them lengthwise almost in half, leaving a 1½-inch section uncut at one end so the halves remain attached. Hold a lemon over a bowl and pour 3 tablespoons salt into the lemon cut, letting the excess salt fall into the bowl. Squeeze the lemon, rubbing the salted cut surfaces back and forth and releasing the juice into the bowl. Put the lemon in the jar. Repeat with the remaining lemons. Pour the salt and lemon juice from the bowl into the jar. Add enough of the 1½ cups lemon juice to completely cover the lemons. Cover with plastic wrap.

3. Allow the lemons to sit in a cool dark place or the refrigerator for 3 days, giving the jar a stir with a sterile spoon once a day to distribute undissolved salt.

4. After 3 days, carefully pour a thin (¼ inch) layer of olive oil on top of the lemon juice and replace the plastic wrap. Let the lemons cure for 6 weeks before using. Preserved lemons will keep for 6 months in the refrigerator.

Braised Stuffed Veal Breast with Porcini Mushrooms

Judging by the appearance of a raw veal breast—tough, fatty, and weirdly flat—you'd never know what a melt-in-your-mouth treat lies in store after it's braised. Lengthy slow-cooking breaks down the muscle fibers, inviting the flavors of porcini mushrooms and Marsala to penetrate the meat; the fat provides a kind of natural larding, so the end product is tender and succulent. The conveniently flat shape of a veal breast fairly begs for stuffing and rolling. I selected mushrooms and kale for the stuffing because both have earthy flavors and neither will break down during the long braising time. If you make this dish on a cold day when everyone's trapped inside, the aroma from the braising juices will drive everyone crazy as they keep asking, "When is it going to be ready?"

MAKES 4 ENTRÉE SERVINGS

STUFFING

Kosher salt

¼ pound kale, hard center ribs removed

1 small carrot, peeled and chopped into ¼-inch dice

3 tablespoons extra virgin olive oil

1 medium onion, chopped into ¼-inch dice

Freshly ground black pepper

½ pound assorted mushrooms, such as shiitake, portabella, and/or chanterelle, cleaned and chopped into ½-inch dice

2 garlic cloves, minced

¼ teaspoon ground allspice

¼ cup dry bread crumbs

¼ cup freshly grated Parmesan

1 teaspoon chopped fresh thyme

2 teaspoons chopped fresh oregano

BRAISING LIQUID

½ large boneless veal breast, trimmed of excess fat (about 3 pounds after trimming; have your butcher point out which side of the breast was attached to the bone)

Kosher salt and freshly ground black pepper

3 tablespoons vegetable oil

1 small onion, chopped into ¼-inch dice

1 small carrot, peeled and chopped into ¼-inch dice

1 celery stalk, peeled and chopped into ¼-inch dice

1 ounce dried porcini, reconstituted in warm water (see page 271), and coarsely chopped (soaking liquid saved)

2 garlic cloves, minced

1 tablespoon tomato paste

1½ cups dry Marsala

1 cup drained high-quality canned tomatoes, coarsely chopped

4 cups Chicken Stock (page 31) or high-quality canned low-sodium chicken broth, or as needed

4 bay leaves

2 teaspoons chopped fresh thyme

2 tablespoons chopped fresh oregano

1. To make the stuffing, bring a large pot of salted water to a boil. Have a large bowl of ice water ready. Add the kale to the boiling water and blanch for 2 minutes. Add the carrots and blanch for an additional 2 minutes. Drain the vegetables and plunge into the ice water. Drain again and squeeze gently in paper towels to remove excess moisture.

2. Heat 3 tablespoons of olive oil in a large sauté pan over medium heat. Add the onion, season with salt and pepper, and cook until tender, about 5 minutes. Add the mushrooms, season with salt and pepper, and cook until mushrooms have released their moisture and it has been cooked off. Add the garlic and allspice and cook until aromatic, only a minute or two. Add the kale and carrots and toss well. Remove from the heat and allow to cool.

3. Add the remaining stuffing ingredients to the mushroom mixture. Taste for seasoning and add salt and pepper if necessary.

4. Trim any excess fat from both sides of the veal breast and lay it on a flat surface in front of you, with the side that had the bones facing up. Sprinkle with salt and pepper. Spread the stuffing evenly over the breast, leaving a 1-inch border. Make sure the kale is distributed evenly. Roll the breast up like a jelly roll, beginning with whichever side will produce the stoutest roll. Tie the roll together with butcher's twine, and season the exterior of the roll with salt and pepper.

5. To make the braise, heat 2 tablespoons of the vegetable oil over medium-high heat in a braising pan or Dutch oven that will hold the veal snugly. Put the veal in the pan and sear on all sides. Remove to a platter.

6. Add the remaining 1 tablespoon oil to the pan, with the onion, carrot, and celery; season with salt and pepper, and cook, stirring occasionally, until the vegetables start to brown, about 7 minutes. Add the porcini, garlic, and tomato paste and cook for 2 minutes. Add the reserved porcini soaking liquid (strained to remove the grit), the Marsala, and tomatoes. Scrape the bottom of the pan with a wooden spoon to dissolve any crispy bits.

7. Return the veal to the pan and add enough chicken stock to come a third of the way up the side of the roll (about 2 cups) and the bay leaves. Bring to a boil, then lower the heat to a simmer. Cover the veal tightly with a piece of aluminum foil, pressing it down into the pan, then cover with a lid. Reduce the heat to low and braise for 3 hours, turning the roll several times during the braising so it cooks evenly. Add chicken stock as necessary to keep the braising juice one-third of the way up the veal. The veal is done when a cake tester slides in and out of the roll with no resistance. Remove the veal to a platter and cover loosely with foil.

8. There should be about 3 cups of juices left in the pan with the vegetables. If the juices seem too thin for a sauce, increase the heat and reduce until they thicken. Remove the bay leaves, add the thyme and oregano, and season with salt and pepper.

9. Remove the string from the veal and cut into 8 slices, each about 1 inch thick. Pour the sauce onto a warm platter, arrange overlapping slices of the veal on top of the sauce, and serve.

HOW TO RESTORE DRIED PORCINI MUSHROOMS

Dried porcini return more flavor bang per dollar than just about any ingredient I can imagine. The deeply resonant flavor of wildness gained from an ounce or two more than compensates for their expense. To reconstitute dried mushrooms, place them in a small bowl and cover them with warm water. Use about 1 cup per ounce of dried mushrooms. Allow them to soak, covered, for 20 minutes. Some cooks like to use red wine, sherry, or Marsala for part or all of the reconstituting liquid, but I prefer to use only water if alcohol is included elsewhere in the recipe.

After the mushrooms have soaked, lift them out of the liquid and gently squeeze them to remove the excess. Reserve the liquid. Carefully inspect the stems for any remaining dirt or grit. If the stems are still tough after soaking (or embedded with grit), slice them off. Chop the mushrooms or leave whole, as the recipe requires. Allow sand or grit to settle to the bottom of the bowl, then carefully pour off the liquid—through a coffee filter if you don't have a steady hand. The mushroom liquor is quite flavorful. If you are not using it in the recipe, it can be refrigerated for several days for use in a stock, soup, or sauce.

Grilled Maple-Brined Pork Chops with Roasted Pear Chutney

One hundred fifty years ago, home cooks and commercial food processors relied on brining (along with salting and smoking) to prevent meats, fish, and vegetables from spoiling. Today, brining is making a comeback. Brined chicken and pork dishes appear on upscale restaurant menus. Cooks are rediscovering that brining is a simple way of improving texture and flavor. Since brining causes meat to absorb liquid, a seasoned brining solution makes meat juicier and tastier than it would be otherwise, a godsend for ultra-lean American pork and even for turkey.

My friend Nancy Oakes, chef-owner of the San Francisco restaurant Boulevard, gave me her recipe for brining, which I've adapted for this easy dish. I like to serve these pork chops with Versatile Buttermilk Mashed Potatoes (page 107) and Fiery Garlicky Greens (page 91).

If there are leftovers, cooked chops will keep for several days in the refrigerator. Their low fat content makes it too easy to dry them out during reheating, so I prefer to use them cold. Trim the meat off the bone, remove any of the fat remaining along the outer edge, and then slice the meat as thin as possible. Use in a sandwich or a salad, or as part of a cold meat plate, with Roasted Pear Chutney (page 274) or Herbal Mayonnaise (page 14).

Twelve hours is the optimal time for brining the chops, so plan on making the brine and marinating the chops the night before you intend to grill them. Brining them for slightly less time is fine, but longer than 12 hours, and the chops will start to take on the texture and flavor of ham. Once brined, however, they can be refrigerated for several days before cooking.

MAKES 4 ENTRÉE SERVINGS

BRINE
1 cup kosher salt
¾ cup sugar
1 cup Grade B maple syrup
3 tablespoons Dijon mustard
2 teaspoons hot red pepper flakes
2 tablespoons juniper berries
½ teaspoon whole cloves
¼ cup fresh rosemary, chopped
2 tablespoons chopped fresh thyme
12 garlic cloves, smashed
2 tablespoons chopped fresh ginger
8 cups water

4 center-cut loin pork chops, 1½ inches thick
Freshly ground black pepper
¼ cup vegetable oil for grilling
Roasted Pear Chutney (recipe follows; optional)

1. Mix all of the brine ingredients together in a nonreactive pot and bring to a boil. Turn off the heat and stir the brine to ensure that the salt, sugar, and maple syrup have dissolved. Let the brine cool, then put it in a large nonreactive container and add the pork chops. Cover and refrigerate for no more than 12 hours.

2. Remove the pork from the brine and pat dry (without rinsing).

3. Prepare a grill with hot and medium cooking areas (see page 265). A grill is hot when you can't hold your hand near the grill surface for longer than 2 seconds without pulling it away; it's medium when you can't hold your hand there for longer than 4 seconds.

4. Season the chops with pepper (not salt—remember, the brining solution is salty) and brush with the oil. Sear the chops directly over the hottest part of the open grill for about 1½ minutes on each side. Then move the chops to the medium area of the grill, cover the grill, and cook to the desired doneness. Use an instant-read digital thermometer to check the internal temperature of the center of the chops. A reading of 145° to 150°F will give you a pink, moist chop, 160°F is well-done. Serve immediately, accompanied by the chutney, if using.

WHERE'S THE FAT?

The American pig began slimming down in the 1950s, but the lean pork we know today really only emerged over the last twenty years. Since the 1970s, a growing public awareness of the link between saturated fat and heart disease has pumped up the demand for leaner meat products. Pork producers have been happy to comply. The result: "the other white meat." A 3-ounce portion of pork loin today contains just under 7 grams of fat. If you'd sat down to a dinner with the same serving back in 1963, you would have been consuming almost 30 grams of fat. This is why cooking a pork loin or pork loin chops today requires a slightly different approach than it did several decades ago. Less fat means the meat dries out more quickly during cooking.

There are several measures you can take to avoid overcooking pork. First, never cook pork beyond an internal temperature reading of 150°F, at which point the pork is still pink and juicy. I prefer to cook pork only to 140°F, assuming there's going to be a rest period when the temperature will continue to rise to around 150°F. The trichina parasite, considered a low risk these days because of improvements in sanitation and production methods, is killed at 137°F. Cooking pork to 150°F won't kill salmonella, if that's a concern to you, but it wouldn't kill salmonella in veal or beef at that temperature either. The USDA recommends that the internal temperature of pork be 160°F for medium, but at that temperature, pork tenderloin begins to taste like shoe leather. Try cooking it to the lower temperature range first; then, if it's not done to your satisfaction, put it back in the oven.

Second, cook thick, cook fast. Buy thick center-cut loin chops, at least 1½ to 2 inches thick. Cook them no more than 6 minutes per side on a grill, less if you're sautéing them. Their thickness will help keep the center of the meat moist. If you have time to brine them beforehand, all the better; their increased moisture content will further decrease the risk of drying the meat out (and add a minute or two to the cooking time). Finally, keep in mind that the leanest cuts of pork are the tenderloin and the other loin cuts. Other cuts, like the Boston butt used in Red Clay's Roasted Spice-Rubbed Pork (page 328), have more fat in them. You can cook them longer with less chance of drying them out.

❧ Roasted Pear Chutney ❧

*T*he most difficult part of this recipe, other than assembling the ingredients, is marshaling the patience to wait while the chutney rests in the refrigerator. The chutney will keep for 2 weeks, as long as it's covered and refrigerated.

MAKES 2 TO 3 CUPS

2 ripe Bosc pears, peeled and cut in half
2 tablespoons freshly squeezed lemon juice
¼ cup plus 1 tablespoon sugar
¾ teaspoon ground cinnamon
¼ teaspoon ground cloves
2 tablespoons vegetable oil
¼ cup pure maple syrup
1 small red onion, cut into ½-inch slices
1 garlic clove, chopped
1 teaspoon grated fresh ginger
3 tablespoons currants
3 tablespoons golden raisins
½ cup white wine vinegar
1 teaspoon hot red pepper flakes
1 teaspoon chopped fresh thyme
1 cup diced mango (optional)

1. Preheat the oven to 350°F.

2. Toss the pears with the lemon juice, 1 tablespoon of the sugar, the cinnamon, and cloves. Coat a sheet pan with half the vegetable oil. Set the pears cut side down on the pan. Brush the pears with the remaining oil. Roast until caramelized and tender, 40 to 50 minutes, depending on the degree of ripeness. Remove from the oven and allow to cool.

3. While the pears are roasting, bring the remaining ingredients to a boil in a nonreactive saucepan. Reduce the heat and simmer for 5 minutes. Remove from the heat and allow to cool.

4. Using a small spoon or a melon baller, scoop out the cores of the cooked pears. Cut the pears into ½-inch slices.

5. Combine the pears and the onion mixture. Cover and refrigerate for at least 1 day before serving.

Grilled and Roasted Pork Tenderloin with Toasted Pumpkin Seed Sauce

This recipe matches the intensely nutty flavor of pumpkin seeds with the flavors of hot pepper, anise, and paprika in the marinade. The pork is seared in a grill pan, then finished in the oven. Given the willingness of various European regional cuisines to crush and mash seeds and nuts into sauces or condiments (pesto comes to mind, as do various Catalan condiments), it seems downright strange that no one hit on the idea of doing the same with pumpkin seeds, especially since pumpkin seed sauce is quite popular in Mexican cooking. Judge for yourself—the seeds make a great sauce.

Supermarkets sometimes put whole pork loins on sale, a good time to consider using this recipe for a much larger group of people. Double, triple, or even quadruple the ingredients and cook the pork in a covered grill.

MAKES 4 ENTRÉE SERVINGS

MARINADE
2 tablespoons coriander seeds
1 teaspoon cumin seeds
1 teaspoon anise seeds
1 tablespoon paprika
½ teaspoon cayenne pepper
1 tablespoon chopped garlic
2 tablespoons vegetable oil
1 teaspoon brown sugar

1½ pounds pork tenderloin, trimmed of all fat and silver skin

SAUCE
2 tablespoons vegetable oil
½ small white onion, chopped into ¼-inch dice
1 tablespoon chopped garlic
1 teaspoon chopped serrano pepper
½ cup pumpkin seeds, toasted and coarsely chopped

1¼ cups Chicken Stock (page 31) or 2½ cups high-quality canned low-sodium chicken broth reduced to 1¼ cups (see page 32)
2 tablespoons freshly squeezed lime juice
Kosher salt and freshly ground black pepper

Kosher salt
2 tablespoons vegetable oil

GARNISH
½ lime, cut into 4 wedges
4 sprigs cilantro

DO AHEAD: Marinate the pork in the garlic and spice mixture for at least 12 hours; longer is fine.

1. To make the marinade, toast the coriander, cumin, and anise seeds in a dry pan over medium heat until aromatic, about 2 minutes. Remove from the heat. Grind the seeds in a coffee grinder or mortar and pestle.

2. In a small bowl, mix the ground spices with the paprika and cayenne pepper. Set aside 1 teaspoon of the mixture for the sauce.

3. Stir the garlic, vegetable oil, and brown sugar into the remaining spice mix. Rub the pork all over with the spice marinade, cover, and allow to marinate for 12 hours in the refrigerator.

4. Preheat the oven to 400°F.

5. Heat the vegetable oil in a small saucepan over medium heat. Add the onion and garlic and sauté, stirring periodically, until tender, about 3 minutes. Add the serrano pepper and cook for 3 more minutes. Add the pumpkin seeds, chicken stock, and the 1 teaspoon of reserved spice mixture from the marinade. Cook for 20 more minutes, or until thickened, then remove from the heat. Purée the mixture in a blender or with an immersion blender, then set aside while you cook the pork.

6. Season the pork with salt. Rub a large oven-proof grill pan with the vegetable oil and heat over medium-high heat. (Or heat the oil in a large overproof skillet or sauté pan.) Put the pork tenderloin in the pan when the oil starts to smoke. Sear the pork, turning occasionally, until it has a nice crust on all sides, about 5 minutes.

7. Transfer to the oven and roast until done, about 5 more minutes. The internal temperature of the pork should read no more than 140°F (see page 273). Allow the pork to repose for 10 minutes before slicing. During this time, the temperature will come up to about 150°F.

8. Reheat the sauce in a small saucepan while the pork reposes. Add the lime juice and cilantro and season with salt and pepper. Slice the meat across the grain on a diagonal. Arrange the slices on a warm platter. Drizzle with the sauce and garnish with the lime wedges and cilantro sprigs. Serve immediately.

Seared Loin Lamb Chops with Saffron and Roasted Garlic Pan Sauce

During a trip to Spain, I kept encountering a combination of saffron and garlic used to flavor various lamb dishes. In this country, saffron is more often associated with seafood than with meat and my Spanish experience was like discovering a new color in the crayon box. I've played with the formula by introducing basil, another herb not often associated with lamb, and using roasted garlic rather than fresh. Roasting the garlic changes the flavor from sharp to mellow, and using the whole cloves helps to thicken the sauce, so less butter is needed.

MAKES 4 ENTRÉE SERVINGS

MARINADE

¼ cup Roasted Garlic (page 119)

½ teaspoon hot red pepper flakes

1 teaspoon fennel seeds

2 tablespoons chopped fresh Thai basil (substitute Italian basil if Thai basil is unavailable)

1 teaspoon grated lemon zest

2 tablespoons vegetable oil

Eight 5-ounce loin lamb chops

¼ cup vegetable oil

Kosher salt

SAUCE

½ cup dry white wine

Pinch of saffron

2 cups Chicken Stock (page 31) or 4 cups high-quality canned low-sodium chicken broth, reduced to 2 cups (see page 32)

2 tablespoons Roasted Garlic (page 119)

1 tablespoon unsalted butter

1 teaspoon freshly squeezed lemon juice

1 tablespoon chopped fresh flat-leaf parsley

Kosher salt

DO AHEAD: Marinate the chops for at least 12 hours; longer won't hurt.

1. Mix all of the marinade ingredients together in a bowl. Add the chops and turn to coat with the marinade. Cover and refrigerate overnight.

2. Heat 2 tablespoons of the vegetable oil in each of two large sauté pans over medium-high heat. Season the lamb chops evenly with salt. (Don't scrape off the marinade.) When the oil is hot, put 4 chops in each pan. Sear on both sides, about 5 minutes per side for medium-rare. Transfer the chops to a plate.

3. Set aside one of the pans. To make the sauce, deglaze the remaining pan with the wine, using a wooden spoon to make sure the crispy bits dissolve completely, and add the saffron. Reduce the wine to a glaze, about 5 minutes. Add the chicken stock and continue cooking until the liquid in the pan has reduced to ¾ cup, about 15 minutes. Do not overreduce.

4. Off the heat, whisk in the roasted garlic and butter. Add the lemon juice and parsley; season with salt.

5. Put 2 chops on each of four plates, sauce each portion at once, and serve immediately.

Seared Lamb Steaks with Balsamic Vinegar and Red Pepper Marinade

Lamb steaks are cut from the sirloin end of the leg. Meaty, chewier than sirloin chops, they're an ideal cut for searing or grilling, especially if you marinate them first. Just be sure to buy them at least ¾ inch thick, or they'll dry out during cooking. After marinating in a highly seasoned purée of roasted red peppers, the steaks are seared for a few minutes on each side. Then the marinade is briefly reduced over high heat to thicken it into a sauce and poured over the meat just before serving. Primal ingredients, primal flavors.

Leftovers will keep for 2 to 3 days in the refrigerator. Rather than trying to reheat the steaks whole, slice them into thin strips, simmer briefly in tomato sauce, and toss with pasta.

MAKES 4 ENTRÉE SERVINGS

MARINADE

4 large red peppers, roasted (see page 99), peeled, stemmed, and seeded

3 garlic cloves, coarsely chopped

½ teaspoon anise seeds

1 celery stalk, peeled and chopped into ¼-inch dice

1 teaspoon dried oregano

¼ teaspoon hot red pepper flakes

2 tablespoons chopped fresh flat-leaf parsley

2 tablespoons balsamic vinegar

2 tablespoons vegetable oil

4 lamb blade steaks, 1 inch thick (10 to 12 ounces each)

Kosher salt and freshly ground black pepper

2 tablespoons vegetable oil

DO AHEAD: The lamb needs to marinate for at least 3 hours; 12 would be ideal.

1. Purée the red peppers in a blender or food processor. You should end up with about a cup of purée. Combine the purée with the remaining marinade ingredients in a large bowl and mix well. Put the steaks in the bowl and turn to coat evenly on both sides with the marinade. Cover with plastic wrap and refrigerate for at least 3 hours, ideally, 12 hours.

2. Remove the steaks from the marinade. Scrape the marinade off the lamb back into the bowl; reserve.

3. Season the steaks with salt and pepper. Heat the vegetable oil in a large sauté pan over medium-high heat. Add the steaks and cook, turning once, until done, about 5 minutes per side for medium-rare. Transfer the lamb steaks to a platter.

4. Lower the heat to medium. Wipe out the pan if there are any burned bits. Add the marinade to the pan and cook for 4 minutes, stirring constantly, until thick and bubbling. Spoon over the lamb and serve at once.

Braised Rosemary-Stuffed Lamb Shanks with Roasted Fennel and Red Onions

U *sually you cut a pocket* into a piece of meat and stuff it with herbs when you're going to roast the meat, but I've adapted the technique for this dish of braised lamb shanks. This recipe is also unusual in that its accompanying ingredients are cooked separately. Ordinarily a braised meat recipe would include all the vegetables in the braising pot, rather than cooking them individually, but roasted fennel is so appealing in its own right that it seems a shame to lose its distinct flavor in the braise. Why not let it stand as a complement to the rosemary-infused lamb?

Braised lamb shanks are exquisite right out of the pot, but letting them rest in their braising juices for a day or two allows the other flavors to penetrate the meat more deeply. Reheat them, covered, in a 375°F oven for 40 minutes. If you have leftovers, cut the meat off the bone (discard the bones) before refrigerating the meat in the sauce. Reheating is quicker that way, making it a simple step to serve the meat and sauce over fresh pappardelle noodles (see page 144) or rice.

MAKES 4 ENTRÉE SERVINGS

LAMB
Four 1-pound lamb shanks (from the back leg—
   it's meatier)
2 tablespoons plus 1 teaspoon fresh rosemary
   (use any left over in the braise)
Kosher salt and freshly ground black pepper
2 tablespoons vegetable oil
1 medium carrot, peeled and chopped into ½-inch
   pieces
1 medium onion, sliced ½ inch thick
1 celery stalk, peeled and chopped into ½-inch
   pieces
6 garlic cloves, coarsely chopped
2 cups dry white wine
1 cup chopped drained canned tomatoes
2 cups Chicken Stock (page 31) or high-quality
   canned low-sodium chicken broth
2 bay leaves
6 anchovies, rinsed and chopped
1 teaspoon fennel seeds

8 allspice berries
1 cup chopped fresh basil

ROASTED VEGETABLES
1 fennel bulb, trimmed of stalks and tough outer
   layers, cut lengthwise into quarters, and cored
1 large red onion, cut into quarters
2 tablespoons extra virgin olive oil
2 tablespoons Pernod
Kosher salt and freshly ground black pepper

DO AHEAD: Stuff the lamb shanks with the rosemary at least 6 hours, and preferably 12, before braising. The lamb can be braised up to 3 days ahead of time as long as it's kept tightly covered and refrigerated. This has the added advantage of making it easy to remove the fat, which, when chilled, forms a layer at the top of the dish. Roast the fennel and red onion on the day of serving.

1. Using the tip of a sharp paring knife, make 12 small incisions, ¾ inch deep, in each shank. Push a couple of rosemary leaves into each incision. (Save any remaining rosemary.) Wrap the shanks tightly in plastic wrap and refrigerate for at least 6 hours or, preferably, overnight.

2. Unwrap the shanks and sprinkle liberally with salt and pepper. Heat the vegetable oil in a deep braising pan or Dutch oven over medium-high heat. When the oil starts to smoke, sear the shanks until browned on all sides, about 10 minutes. Set the shanks aside.

3. Pour off all but 1 tablespoon of fat from the pan. Lower the heat to medium, add the carrot, onion, celery, and garlic, season with salt and pepper, and sauté until the vegetables begin to brown, about 10 minutes; set aside the vegetables. Deglaze the pan with the white wine and continue cooking until it reduces by half, 6 to 8 minutes.

4. Preheat the oven to 325°F.

5. Add all the remaining braising ingredients except the basil (including any remaining rosemary) to the pan. Take note of how high the liquid reaches up the sides of the pan, and cook until it has reduced by half, about 15 minutes. Return the shanks to the pan, along with half the basil. The liquid should reach one-third of the way up the shanks. If not, add enough water to make up the difference. Cover the shanks tightly with a piece of aluminum foil, pressing it down into the pan, then place a lid on the pan.

6. Put the pan in the oven. Braise until the meat is very tender, about 2½ to 3 hours, checking the level of liquid every 30 minutes and adding water as necessary to keep the braising juice

one-third of the way up the shanks. After 1½ hours, flip the shanks.

7. Meanwhile, after the lamb has braised for 30 minutes, toss the fennel and onion quarters with the olive oil and Pernod in a small roasting pan. Season with salt and pepper. Put the vegetables in the oven. Roast until tender and golden, about 2 hours. If by some chance the lamb finishes cooking before the vegetables, remove the shanks from the oven, increase the oven temperature to 400°F and continue roasting until done.

8. After the lamb has finished cooking, remove the shanks from the pan and keep warm. Strain the braising vegetables out of the juices. Purée them in a blender or food processor with the remaining basil and return them to the juices to make a sauce.

9. Place a lamb shank, a piece of fennel, and a piece of onion on each plate. Ladle some sauce over all, including the fennel and onion, and serve immediately. Offer the extra sauce on the side.

Grilled Rosemary-Stuffed Lamb Shanks

A spectacular variation on this recipe is to braise the shanks and refrigerate them, then grill them a day or two later. The shanks acquire all the rich flavor of braising, with the wonderful addition of a smoky, crusty exterior. The technique can be applied to just about any braised meat that is either still on the bone or in large chunks.

1. Braise the shanks exactly as in the recipe, but save the basil for later. Don't roast the fennel or onion—they'll be grilled too.

2. Prepare a medium fire in a grill (see page 265 if you're unfamiliar with how to do this). You should be able to hold your hand near the grilling surface for 4 seconds before you have to pull it away.

3. While the grill is heating, remove the shanks from their braising juices and pat dry. Reheat the juices, adding the basil. If the braising juice is too thin for a sauce, boil it for a few minutes until it reaches the desired consistency. Set aside. Reheat before serving.

4. Sprinkle the shanks liberally with salt and pepper and brush with oil. Grill on all sides until heated through and lightly charred. Push the shanks to the edge of the grill to keep warm while you grill the vegetables.

5. Toss the fennel and onions with 3 to 4 tablespoons olive oil and season with salt and pepper (no Pernod in this variation). Grill until lightly charred and tender. It may be necessary to move the vegetables off to the side (off the direct heat of the coals) to cook them through without burning.

6. To serve, arrange the grilled shanks, fennel, and onions on a large platter. Pour the sauce over the meat and vegetables. Serve immediately.

Roast Leg of Lamb with Mustard Crumbs

Every family has at least one mistaken culinary tradition that becomes enshrined in memory. I know people who only enjoy turkey dry or macaroni and cheese out of a box because that's what they ate at the table of their childhood. I was well into my college years before I discovered that leg of lamb—a favorite holiday preparation of my grandmother—didn't automatically turn gray when roasted. This recipe, which takes its inspiration from a French family classic, is a much juicier preparation. A marinade of olives, rosemary, sage, and thyme flavors the meat, while a crumb and Dijon mustard crust helps the leg stay moist.

Leg of lamb makes great cold leftovers. Accompany it with horseradish, Dijon mustard, hot mango chutney, or Vinegared Grapes (page 288).

MAKES 6 TO 8 ENTRÉE SERVINGS

One 6- to 8-pound bone-in leg of lamb

MARINADE
4 garlic cloves, finely chopped
2 shallots, finely chopped
¼ cup chopped fresh rosemary
½ cup chopped fresh thyme
2 tablespoons chopped fresh sage
¼ cup finely chopped pitted Gaeta olives
¼ cup extra virgin olive oil

Kosher salt and freshly ground black pepper
2 tablespoons extra virgin olive oil

CRUMB MIXTURE
¼ cup Dijon mustard, plus more as necessary
2 cups dry bread crumbs
2 tablespoons extra virgin olive oil
Kosher salt and freshly ground black pepper

DO AHEAD: Marinate the lamb for 4 hours; longer won't hurt.

1. Trim the lamb leg of excess fat and membrane. Mix the marinade ingredients together in a small bowl. Set the lamb in a large nonreactive container and smear it with the marinade. Refrigerate for 4 hours.

2. Preheat the oven to 450°F.

3. Remove the lamb from the refrigerator and season generously all over with salt and pepper (do not scrape off the marinade). Set the leg on a rack in a roasting pan.

4. Roast for 10 minutes at 450°F, then reduce the heat to 350°F. Roast for 30 minutes, then drizzle with 2 tablespoons of olive oil. Let the lamb roast for another 30 minutes.

5. Remove the lamb from the oven. Brush the surface with the mustard. Press the bread crumbs onto the mustard. Drizzle with the olive oil and season with salt and pepper. Return the lamb to the oven and roast until the bread crumbs are toasty and the meat has reached the desired degree of doneness, about

30 minutes for medium-rate. Bear in mind this is only an approximation: the actual time depends on your oven and the size of the lamb leg. To check, insert an instant-read digital thermometer into the thickest part of the lamb leg, taking care not to let the tip touch the bone. For rare meat, remove the leg from the oven when it reaches 115° to 120°F; for medium-rare, 125° to 130°F; for medium, 130° to 140°F. Although temperatures may seem a little bit low, the lamb will continue to cook after you've removed it from the oven, and the internal temperature will rise another 5 to 10 degrees during the resting period.

6. Remove the lamb from the oven and let rest for 15 minutes.

7. Transfer the lamb to a platter and carve at the table.

Roast Rack of Lamb with Romaine Salad and Anchovy Dressing

*T**he expense of rack of* lamb usually elevates it to special-dinner status, with all the attendant anxiety about breaking away from anything but tried-and-true approaches. This recipe offers a great alternative to the classic Dijon mustard sauce and fancy baby vegetable garnishes so often seen with lamb racks. When my son was young, he referred to rack chops as "steak on a stick," which jogged me into thinking about how I would handle rack of lamb if I had the same freedom to play around with seasonings that I did with kebabs. An old-fashioned Italian anchovy marinade for grilled lamb seemed particularly appealing. Why not go even one step further and serve the lamb with a Romaine salad dressed with anchovy vinaigrette and Parmesan croutons? The dish is filled with big appealing flavors and is a lot easier than the usual way of handling racks.

MAKES 4 ENTRÉE SERVINGS

MARINADE
4 garlic cloves, finely chopped
6 anchovies, rinsed and finely chopped
2 tablespoons grated lemon zest
2 tablespoons dried mint
¼ cup vegetable oil

Two 7- or 8-bone racks of lamb, trimmed to leave a
    thin layer of fat, chine bone removed so you can
    cut between the chops
1 medium red onion, sliced into ½-inch-thick
    rounds
¾ cup extra virgin olive oil
Kosher salt and freshly ground black pepper
Eight ¼-inch-thick slices rustic bread
2 tablespoons plus 2 teaspoons freshly grated
    Parmesan
2 tablespoons vegetable oil
1 garlic clove, minced and then mashed with a
    pinch of salt to a paste
1 teaspoon minced shallots
6 anchovies, rinsed and finely chopped

½ teaspoon Dijon mustard
2 tablespoons red wine vinegar
1 head Romaine lettuce, washed, dried, and cut
    crosswise into strips 3 inches wide
2 ounces Parmesan cheese shavings
1 lemon, cut into 4 wedges

DO AHEAD: Marinate the lamb.

1. Mix the marinade ingredients together in a small bowl. Set the lamb racks in a nonreactive container and smear the meat with the marinade. Cover with plastic wrap and marinate in the refrigerator for at least 4 hours, or up to a day.

2. Preheat the oven to 450°F.

3. Toss the onions with 2 tablespoons of the olive oil in a small bowl and season with salt and pepper. Arrange in a single layer in a small roasting pan and roast until brown around the edges and tender, about 30 minutes. Remove from the oven and set aside.

4. To make the croutons, lay the bread slices in a single layer on a sheet pan. Brush each slice with ¾ teaspoon of the olive oil and sprinkle with 1 teaspoon of the Parmesan cheese. When the onions are done, bake the croutons for 5 to 7 minutes, or until the cheese has melted and the bread is toasted. Set aside. Leave the oven on.

5. To sear the lamb racks, heat 1 tablespoon of the vegetable oil in each of two large ovenproof sauté pans over medium-high heat. (If you don't have two large ovenproof pans, sear the racks individually, then transfer to a large roasting pan that has been heating in the oven.) Season the lamb all over with salt and pepper. (Don't scrape off the marinade.) Add the racks to the pans, meat side down, and sear until brown, about 4 minutes.

6. Turn the meat, then transfer the pans to the oven. Roast until an instant-read digital ther-mometer inserted in the center of the rack reads 125°F for medium-rare (120°F for rare). Start checking after 15 minutes. Remove from the oven and let rest. Return the onions to the oven to warm while you make the salad.

7. To make the dressing, combine the garlic, shallots, anchovies, and mustard in a small bowl. Whisk in the red wine vinegar. Whisk in the remaining ½ cup olive oil in a thin, steady stream until the vinaigrette is smooth and emulsified. Season with salt and pepper. Toss the lettuce in a large bowl with the vinaigrette. Taste, then season with salt and pepper if necessary.

8. Arrange the salad on a platter or individual plates. Sprinkle with the Parmesan shavings. Slice the lamb into individual chops and arrange in front of the salad. Drape the salad with the roasted onions and garnish with the croutons. Add a lemon wedge to each plate and serve immediately.

Thin-Sliced Calves' Liver with Greens, Dijon Mustard Sauce, and Vinegared Grapes

*C*alves' *liver has a mild,* delicate taste overlaying a rich texture, a true connoisseur's treat. Sharp or acidic elements, like the sweet-and-sour mustard sauce and vinegared grapes of this recipe, balance the richness. Beef liver, on the other hand, is quite strong, with a taste that's well . . . *livery.* You shouldn't have any problem distinguishing the latter from the former—calves' liver (sometimes called "veal liver") is quite pale; beef liver is a deep purple. Don't be fooled by "baby beef liver," which is just another name for liver from a mature steer.

This preparation calls for first soaking the liver in milk. The milk sweetens the meat by purging it of any remaining blood

MAKES 4 ENTRÉE SERVINGS

1½ pounds very fresh calves' liver, outer membrane removed and sliced ½ inch thick

2 cups milk

Kosher salt and freshly ground black pepper

About ½ cup unbleached all-purpose flour for dredging

¼ cup vegetable oil, as needed

4 to 5 tablespoons unsalted butter, as needed

8 cups lightly packed greens, such as arugula, watercress, or spinach, washed, dried, and stems removed as necessary

2 shallots, thinly sliced

1 tablespoon honey

4 to 5 tablespoons high-quality red wine vinegar

2 cups Chicken Stock (page 31) or 4 cups high-quality canned low-sodium chicken broth, reduced to 2 cups (see page 32)

2 tablespoons Dijon mustard

Vinegared Grapes (optional; recipe follows)

DO AHEAD: Make the Vinegared Grapes.

1. Soak the liver slices in the milk in the refrigerator for 1 hour to remove any remaining blood.

2. Preheat the oven to 200°F.

3. Drain the liver and pat dry. Season on both sides with salt and pepper, then dredge in the flour. Tap off any excess. Heat 2 tablespoons of the vegetable oil in a large nonstick sauté pan over medium-high heat. As soon as the oil is hot, add as many slices of liver as will fit in the pan without crowding. Unless you have an exceptionally large sauté pan, you'll need to cook the liver in two batches. Brown the slices on one side, about 2 minutes, then flip, add 1 tablespoon of the butter, and brown the other side, also for 2 minutes. The liver will be between medium and medium-rare. Transfer the cooked slices to a platter and put the platter in the warm oven. Wipe out the pan, or leftover bits of flour will burn as the new arrivals start to brown. Add more oil before beginning the second batch, and then more butter after flipping the slices.

4. Wipe the pan clean after all the liver is cooked, then add 2 tablespoons butter to the pan. Add the greens, season with salt and pepper, and stir them about the pan until they wilt, about 2 minutes. Arrange the greens on the platter with the liver, and return the platter to the oven.

5. To make the sauce, lower the heat to medium and add 1 tablespoon butter to the pan. As soon as it melts, add the shallots and cook until soft, about 4 minutes. Add the honey and 4 tablespoons of the red wine vinegar and con-

tinue cooking until the liquid reduces to a glaze, less than a minute. Add the chicken stock and cook until it reduces to ¾ cup, 15 to 20 minutes.

6. Whisk in the mustard and season with salt and pepper. Pour the sauce over the liver and greens and serve immediately.

Variations
Instead of the sweet-and-sour mustard sauce, try serving the liver with Brown Bay Butter sauce (page 224). This recipe also works well with veal scaloppine. Don't bother soaking the veal in milk before sautéing it.

❧ Vinegared Grapes ❧

These grapes make a great cold complement to rich meats such as liver or venison, and are an unusual foil for a rich cheese like Stilton or Gorgonzola. They can easily fill the gap when you don't want to make a sauce or need a cold condiment for a picnic. Leftovers will keep for a week if refrigerated.

MAKES 2½ CUPS

½ cup high-quality white wine vinegar

⅓ cup sugar

½ teaspoon mustard seeds

1 bay leaf

¼ teaspoon crushed coriander seeds

⅛ teaspoon hot red pepper flakes

1 shallot, minced

2 cups red grapes, cut in half and seeds removed

1. Combine all the ingredients except the grapes in a nonreactive saucepan. Bring to a boil and simmer for 2 minutes.

2. Add the grapes and simmer for 3 minutes. Remove from the heat. Chill, then serve as a relish.

Fried Rabbit in Hazelnut Crumbs with Peaches

Serve this special-occasion dish to guests who've never tried rabbit. The aroma of its spectacular flavors from the Italian Riviera—lemon zest, basil, peaches, and ginger—and golden hazelnut crust is almost impossible to resist. Despite the usual comparison, rabbit has a stronger, more complex taste than chicken, although it's still quite mild. The flesh is leaner than that of chicken, which makes it easy to overcook when sautéed, but the hazelnut crust in this preparation keeps the meat moist.

This dish works perfectly well without a sauce, but I had to include one. A sauce made with rabbit parts is such a rare treat that I always take the extra step, making it a day ahead if necessary. Fresh rabbit is almost always sold packed in Cryovac in this country. If there's a butcher on hand, he may be willing to cut the rabbit in pieces for you as described in Step 1, but if not I've included instructions for cutting it up.

MAKES 4 ENTRÉE SERVINGS

2 rabbits (about 3 pounds each)

1 tablespoon grated lemon zest

¼ cup chopped fresh basil

2 teaspoons finely chopped fresh ginger

6 tablespoons vegetable oil

About ¼ cup unbleached all-purpose flour for dredging

1 extra-large egg

⅓ cup dry bread crumbs

⅓ cup finely chopped lightly toasted hazelnuts

Kosher salt and freshly ground black pepper

4 small ripe peaches

2 tablespoons extra virgin olive oil

¼ cup balsamic vinegar

2 teaspoons sugar

Riesling Sauce (recipe follows; optional)

DO AHEAD: Marinate the rabbit for 12 hours. The peaches can be prepared a day ahead and reheated before serving (as can the sauce, if you decide to make it). The legs can be breaded 3 hours in advance.

1. Have your butcher cut each rabbit into the following pieces: 2 forelegs, 2 back legs, 2 loins trimmed of all silver skin, and the carcass. If you have to do it yourself, think of the process as similar to removing the leg/thigh pieces and wings from a chicken. In addition, you need to remove and trim the loins. The loins are the two thick strips of meat that run along the backbone. A sharp boning knife with its thin blade makes the task easier than using the wide blade of a chef's knife. Be sure to remove all the silver skin from the loins. Set the forelegs and carcasses aside if you're going to make the sauce.

2. Combine the lemon zest, basil, ginger, and 2 tablespoons of vegetable oil in a bowl large enough to comfortably accommodate the rabbit pieces. Toss the rabbit loins and back legs in the marinade, cover, and refrigerate for 12 hours.

3. Remove the rabbit from the refrigerator. Put the flour in a medium bowl. Beat the egg with 1 teaspoon water in another medium bowl. Combine the bread crumbs and chopped hazelnuts in a large bowl. Season the back legs with salt and pepper and toss them in flour. Dip the legs in the egg and coat completely. Roll in the nut and crumb mixture.

4. Heat 4 tablespoons of vegetable oil in a large sauté pan over medium-low heat. Add the back legs and cook on both sides until done, 10 to 15 minutes per side. The trick here is to cook the legs slowly so the crumb crust and rabbit meat finish more or less at the same time. At a higher temperature, you risk finishing the crust when the rabbit meat is still quite rare. The crust should be a deep golden brown. Transfer the legs to a plate. Season the loins with salt and pepper (the loins do not have a crumb coating), sear on both sides, 5 to 8 minutes, and then cook to desired doneness.

5. Meanwhile, as soon as you get the rabbit legs into the pan, start the peaches. Split the peaches and remove the pits. Heat the olive oil in a medium sauté pan over medium-high heat. Add the peaches, skin side down, and cook until they begin to brown, about 5 minutes. Add ½ teaspoon pepper, the balsamic vinegar, and sugar. Flip and cook on the second side until browned, about another 4 minutes, then remove from the heat. If you're not going to use them immediately, keep them warm in a low oven (200°F) until ready to serve.

6. To serve, slice the loins against the grain into diagonal pieces ½ inch thick. Arrange 2 peach halves, a leg, and a sliced loin on each plate. Drizzle with the sauce, if using, and serve immediately.

❧ Riesling Sauce ❧

A*lthough the rabbit can be served* without a sauce, I'm the sort of obsessive cook who can't bear to discard perfectly good rabbit parts—not when I know they can be turned into a great sauce. Put the main pieces of the rabbit in the marinade, reserving the forelegs and carcasses for the sauce. Either make the sauce then and refrigerate it, or wait to make it the next day.

MAKES ABOUT ¾ CUP

2 rabbit forelegs

2 rabbit carcasses

Kosher salt and freshly ground black pepper

2 tablespoons vegetable oil

4 shallots, thinly sliced

½ celery stalk, chopped

½ medium carrot, peeled and chopped

1 cup Riesling (or 1 cup dry white wine in which you've dissolved 1 tablespoon honey)

4 cups Chicken Stock (page 31) or 8 cups high-quality canned low-sodium chicken broth, reduced to 4 cups (see page 32)

1. Season the forelegs and carcasses with salt and pepper. Heat the vegetable oil in a medium sauté pan over medium heat. Sear the carcasses and forelegs. Transfer to a plate.

2. Add the shallots, celery, and carrots to the pan and cook until they just begin to brown, about 10 minutes. Return the rabbit pieces to the pan. Add the wine and continue cooking until it reduces to a glaze, about 20 minutes.

3. Add the chicken stock and reduce it until the sauce is thick enough to coat the back of a spoon, to about ¼ cup, about 45 minutes. Remove the sauce from the heat and strain it. Season with salt and pepper to taste. Refrigerate if using it the next day, then reheat before serving; or keep it warm if serving soon.

Sweet-and-Sour Braised Rabbit with Chocolate

The use of chocolate in savory cooking almost always calls to mind Mexican *mole*, but southern Italians have also used chocolate and spicy chiles to flavor meat dishes. Chocolate thickens and enriches the sauce without sweetening it. My recipe combines the best of the New World—chocolate and chile pepper flakes—with the Old—juniper berries and pancetta. Serve with wide noodles, spaetzle, or rice.

When purchasing the rabbits, ask your butcher to cut each of them into 6 pieces, as described in Step 1. The rabbit is wonderful the day it's made, but if you refrigerate the rabbit pieces in the braising liquid for a day before serving, the meat will absorb more of the flavor of the chocolate and chile. Reheat, covered, on top of the stove over low heat.

MAKES 4 ENTRÉE SERVINGS

2 rabbits (about 3 pounds each)
¼ teaspoon hot red pepper flakes
¼ teaspoon ground cinnamon
¼ teaspoon ground allspice
⅛ teaspoon mace
About ½ cup unbleached all-purpose flour for dredging
Kosher salt and freshly ground black pepper
½ cup vegetable oil, plus more if needed
¼ pound thickly sliced pancetta, chopped into ¼-inch dice
1 small onion, cut into ½-inch dice
12 shallots, peeled
3 garlic cloves, finely chopped
1 teaspoon tomato paste
2½ cups Chicken Stock (page 31) or 5 cups high-quality canned low-sodium chicken broth, reduced to 2½ cups (see page 32)
2 tablespoons sugar
1 cup Marsala
¼ cup red wine vinegar, or more to taste
¼ tablespoon crushed fennel seeds

¼ tablespoon crushed juniper berries
¼ teaspoon cayenne pepper
1 bay leaf
1½ ounces semisweet chocolate, finely chopped

1. You can ask the butcher to cut up the rabbits for you when you purchase them; otherwise, it's no more difficult than cutting up a chicken. Remove the front and rear legs of one of the rabbits where the joints meet the body. A thin-bladed boning knife is the ideal tool for this task, but you can use just about any sharp knife. Remove the neck and discard, or use for stock. Using a cleaver or heavy chef's knife, cut the body in half crosswise. You will now have 6 pieces—2 hind legs, 2 forelegs, and 2 halves of the body. Repeat with the remaining rabbit.

2. Combine the red pepper flakes, cinnamon, allspice, mace, and flour in a large bowl. Sprinkle the rabbit pieces liberally with salt and pepper, then toss them in the seasoned flour. Heat 3 tablespoons of vegetable oil in a large sauté pan over medium heat and brown the rabbit pieces on all sides. You will have to do this in a couple of batches—don't crowd the pan. Place the browned rabbit in a large Dutch oven or cast-iron casserole. If the sauté pan is covered with blackened bits of flour, wipe it out and add another few tablespoons of vegetable oil.

3. Add the pancetta to the sauté pan and cook over medium heat until the fat turns translucent and starts to render, about 1½ minutes. Add the onion, shallots, and garlic and stir them about until they start to brown, 5 to 7 minutes. Add the tomato paste and cook for 1 more minute. Transfer the vegetables to the pot with the rabbit.

4. Deglaze the sauté pan with the chicken stock: bring the stock to a boil, scraping the bottom of the pan with a spoon to dissolve any crispy bits in the hot liquid. Pour over the rabbit.

5. Melt the sugar in a nonreactive small saucepan over medium heat. Watch the sugar closely, and remove it from the heat as soon as it caramelizes.

Stir in the Marsala and 2 tablespoons of the red wine vinegar in a slow stream (if you add the wine too fast, it will splatter). As soon as the liquid is blended with the caramelized sugar, pour the mixture into the pot with the rabbit.

6. Add the fennel seeds, juniper berries, cayenne pepper, and bay leaf to the pot and bring to a boil, then lower the heat to a simmer. Cover and cook until the rabbit is tender but not falling off the bone, about 30 minutes.

7. Meanwhile, preheat the oven to 200°F.

8. Transfer the rabbit to a heatproof platter and place in the oven. Reduce the braising liquid over high heat until it's thick enough to coat the back of a spoon. Lower the heat to medium, add the chocolate and the remaining 2 tablespoons vinegar, and stir until the chocolate melts completely. Taste—the flavor should be a balance of sweet and sour. Add more vinegar if necessary. Discard the bay leaf, and season with salt and pepper.

9. Ladle a light coating of sauce over the rabbit. Present the platter at the table and offer the remaining sauce on the side.

Peppered Venison with Sherry Sauce and Dried Fruit Chutney

Venison is a great argument for keeping things simple. Few cooked meats are as capable of making as striking a visual impression as three or four slices of unadorned venison on a plate. Venison's low fat content almost guarantees that it is prepared only rare or medium-rare, which preserves its deep port-like color. Even without its rich, meatier-than-meat flavor, venison's color would earn it a billing on many menus. This recipe involves a simple oil-based marinade that helps to form a peppery crust when the venison is cooked. Pedro Jiménez, a fine, slightly sweet sherry, long a European tradition in sauces for game meats, adds a fruity note to the sauce. The Dried Fruit Chutney elaborates on this theme and adds a lovely visual component to the dish.

Cooked venison will keep for several days, but it's so lean that a quick sear in a sauté pan is as much as I dare reheat it for fear of overcooking it. I'm quite content to eat leftover venison cold, accompanied by Herbal Mayonnaise (page 14) or some of the cold chutney.

MAKES 4 ENTRÉE SERVINGS

VENISON
Four 6-ounce venison steaks from the leg or loin
2 tablespoons cracked black pepper
1 shallot, thinly sliced
1 tablespoon chopped fresh thyme
1 tablespoon chopped fresh sage
¼ cup vegetable oil

SHERRY SAUCE
2 tablespoons vegetable oil
2 shallots, finely chopped
½ teaspoon chopped fresh thyme
2 juniper berries, crushed
1 teaspoon chopped fresh sage
½ cup Pedro Jiménez or other high-quality sweet
  sherry
4 cups Chicken Stock (page 31) or 8 cups high-
  quality low-sodium canned chicken broth,
  reduced to 4 cups (see page 32)

¼ teaspoon sherry vinegar
2 tablespoons unsalted butter
Kosher salt and freshly ground black pepper

2 tablespoons vegetable oil

Dried Fruit Chutney (recipe follows; optional)

DO AHEAD: Marinate the venison for 12 hours. The Dried Fruit Chutney can be prepared up to 10 days in advance.

1. Trim the sinew and silver skin from the venison steaks. Refrigerate the trimmings for use in the sauce. To make the marinade, mix the pepper, shallots, thyme, and sage with ¼ cup of vegetable oil in a bowl or plastic container. Add the venison steaks and marinate, covered, for 12 hours in the refrigerator, turning occasionally.

2. To make the sauce, heat 2 tablespoons of vegetable oil in a large sauté pan over high heat. Add the reserved venison trimmings and brown them all over. Lower the heat to medium-high, add the shallots, and cook, tossing occasionally, until golden brown and tender, about 3 minutes. Do not let them burn; lower the heat further if necessary.

3. Add the thyme, juniper berries, sage, and sherry. Bring to a boil and cook until the liquid reduces by half, about 5 minutes. Add the chicken stock and reduce to ¾ cup, about 30 minutes. Strain and return to the sauté pan.

4. Add the sherry vinegar to the sauce and heat over medium heat until hot. Remove from the heat and whisk in the butter. Season with salt and pepper. Keep warm.

5. Warm the chutney in a small saucepan. While it heats, remove the venison from the marinade. Do not pat the venison dry—you want to leave as much of the marinade on it as possible. Season the meat on both sides with salt.

6. Heat 2 tablespoons of vegetable oil in a large sauté pan over high heat. Sear the venison for 5 minutes on both sides for rare. With its low fat content, venison tends to dry out and become tough if cooked to more than medium-rare. To cook the meat more than that, lower the heat to medium and cook to the desired doneness.

7. To serve, slice the venison steaks ½ inch thick across the grain. Arrange the slices on warm plates. Drizzle with sauce. Place a spoonful of the chutney, if serving, on one side of each plate. Offer the remaining sauce and chutney on the side.

❧ Dried Fruit Chutney ❧

Chutney was a staple in my childhood. We lived in England during my father's sabbaticals, and during our first extended trip, when I was in elementary school, I discovered that we had left the land of ketchup for the kingdom of chutney. I smeared chutney on everything, including Cornish pasties. This particular recipe results in a rich, heavy condiment with concentrated sweet-sour flavors of dried fruit, sherry, and vinegar. It's a good match for venison, duck, and other dark meats, or strong cheeses like traditional farmhouse Cheddar.

MAKES 2 CUPS

1 small onion (about 4 ounces), cut into ¼-inch dice
½ cup white wine vinegar
½ cup sugar
2 bay leaves
1 cinnamon stick
2 star anise
¼ teaspoon hot red pepper flakes
¼ cup dried cranberries
¼ cup golden raisins
½ cup dried apricots
½ cup dried figs, preferably Turkish, cut in half
½ cup prunes
1 cup sweet sherry

Combine the onion, vinegar, sugar, bay leaves, cinnamon stick, star anise, and red pepper flakes in a nonreactive medium saucepan. Bring to a boil, then reduce the heat to a simmer and cook for 1 minute. Add the fruit and sherry. Bring to a boil, then reduce the heat to a simmer and cook for 5 minutes. Remove from the heat and let cool. The chutney will keep for 2 weeks if refrigerated. Keep tightly covered so it doesn't absorb odors from other food in the refrigerator.

A Mile in a Chef's Shoes

This is the near-and-dear-to-my-heart chapter. It returns to the question that opens this book—what am I about as a cook? If I had to boil down all of my cooking philosophy and experience to a handful of recipes, they would be the ones that appear in the following pages. They are, not surprisingly, also my most-requested recipes, whether from guests at Rialto or friends at our home.

Some items, like Soupe de Poisson or Roasted Marinated Long Island Duck with Green Olive and Balsamic Vinegar Sauce, fall into the category of signature dishes. For a young chef, a signature dish can seem like a curse. Just at the time in your career when you're bursting to demonstrate to the world that you're the sharpest knife in town, here comes the roast duck with green olives that everyone demands you put back on the menu, again and again and. . . . *Do they love me only for my duck?* Later in your career, your perspective changes. Signature dishes are like familiar furniture; you learn to build a menu around them, and if somebody comes to your restaurant specifically because they depend on finding a dish that they've come to think of as "the duck we eat on our anniversary," you feel grateful, not hemmed in. The other type of recipe found here might be called home-front favorites, food that I associate with family traditions (Roast Christmas Goose) or that continues to provoke enthusiasm among our guests at home (Squash Blossoms Stuffed with Herbed Cheese in Fritter Batter).

All of this food is doable in a home kitchen—I know, because these are the recipes that I've given to friends most often. What these dishes demand of you is generally a little extra time, for a lot of extra satisfaction. But I also hope this chapter gives you the experience of walking in the shoes of the chef that life has made me. What is it about duck, about salt cod, about squash blossoms that makes them so satisfying to me? To be honest, I'm not really sure I know the answer, but I can give you a taste of my experience, my perspective. Cook this food.

Salt Cod, Artichoke, and Celery Root Fritters

Deep-frying was considered distasteful in my house while I was growing up. Not only was it unhealthy, but worse—it smelled. That the lingering aroma might be of something delicious was of no account. The silver lining to this experience is a thrilling sense of breaking a taboo every time I take out the vegetable oil and deep-fry thermometer. As a technique, it's something I apply in moderation, but I resort to it often when preparing hors d'oeuvres or garnishes, anything that comes in small bites or portions.

Salt cod fritters are one of my favorite munchies. In this recipe, I've paired the cod with artichokes (another traditional combination) and added celery root for crunch and an almost apple-like flavor. These are fabulous with a really spicy bottled hot sauce—Inner Beauty is a good choice—on the side.

MAKES 20 TO 25 FRITTERS

½ pound center-cut salt cod (the thickest part of the fillet)

1 cup unbleached all-purpose flour

½ cup cornstarch

2 extra-large egg whites

1 cup cold beer

6 baby artichokes, trimmed (see page 85) and rubbed with lemon juice, or 6 frozen artichoke hearts (frozen artichoke hearts are often already cut in half—if so, use 12 halves), thawed

Kosher salt

2 tablespoons freshly squeezed lemon juice

4 cups vegetable oil for deep-frying

1 small celery root (about 1 pound), peeled, sliced paper-thin, and cut into fine julienne

¼ cup fresh flat-leaf parsley leaves

Freshly ground black pepper

2 lemons, cut crosswise in half, then each half cut into quarters

DO AHEAD: Soak the salt cod for 12 hours in a large bowl of cold water, changing the water 3 or 4 times. When finished, the cod should be moist and should *not* be *completely* salt-free, or it will have lost its distinctive flavor. It should taste about as salty as fish that you've seasoned and cooked with salt.

1. Drain and rinse the cod, then put it into a medium pot and cover with cold water. Bring to a boil. Reduce the heat and simmer until the fish is cooked through, about 10 minutes. Allow to cool in the liquid.

2. After it is cool, drain the cod and pat dry with paper towels, then remove any skin, bones, or cartilage. Break the fish into 1-inch pieces.

3. Meanwhile, to make the batter, mix the flour with the cornstarch in a medium bowl. Beat the egg whites with the beer in a separate bowl, then stir this into the dry ingredients until just mixed. If you overbeat the batter, the fritter coating will be tough. Cover and refrigerate for 20 minutes (it can rest, chilled, up to 2 hours).

4. If using fresh artichokes, put them in a non-reactive pot large enough to hold them in a single layer. Add cold water to cover by 1 inch. Season with salt, and place a small plate over the artichokes to keep them submerged. Bring to a boil, then reduce the heat and simmer until the artichokes are tender, about 20 minutes. Drain, cut lengthwise into quarters, and toss with the lemon juice. If using frozen artichoke hearts, cut lengthwise into quarters and toss with the lemon juice.

5. Preheat the oven to 200°F. Line a sheet pan with paper towels and put it in the oven.

6. Heat the oil in a deep pot to 350°F. Use a deep-fry thermometer to check the temperature.

7. Toss the salt cod with the artichokes, celery root, and parsley leaves; season with salt and pepper, and stir everything into the batter. Scoop out a couple of tablespoons of batter in a single dollop and carefully lower it into the oil. Add 2 more dollops of the mixture to the oil. The fritters will bob to the surface. Don't worry if the mixture spreads out a little bit, but try to keep the fritters separate. When they are golden brown on one side, 1 to 3 minutes, depending on how thick they are, flip the fritters and cook on the second side, another 1 to 3 minutes. As they finish cooking, transfer them to the sheet pan in the oven. Repeat until all the mixture is used. Transfer to a warm platter, sprinkle with salt, garnish with the lemon wedges, and serve.

Roasted Potatoes Stuffed with Wild Mushrooms and Truffled Eggs

The idea for this dish arrived in a dream, hokey as that sounds. I awoke one morning and there it was, a gift, fully formed and assembled in my head out of fragments of other things I love, like a poem cobbled out of phrases whose connection had eluded you until a moment of insight. The common denominator in this dish is things-that-go-well-with-truffles-in-the-Piedmont: mushrooms, eggs, potatoes, and cheese. But I'd never seen all of them brought together, and certainly not in the form of a hollowed-out roasted potato filled with the other ingredients. Since it's the only recipe, before or since, to come to me via whatever culinary inspiration clanks away in dreams, I don't mind admitting its origins. It's now one of my few signature dishes, and one of the most popular items we've ever served at Rialto.

If you're fortunate enough to have a fresh white truffle, this dish is the perfect medium for a few aromatic shavings on top, either just before serving or at the table. It's actually quite easy to double the recipe and serve everyone two potatoes as an entrée, especially if you accompany it with Fiery Garlicky Greens (page 91). If anyone politely protests that he can only eat one, there will surely be a volunteer ready to step into the breach and eat three.

MAKES 4 APPETIZER SERVINGS

4 medium baking potatoes (preferably short and fat, about ½ pound each), scrubbed
2 tablespoons extra virgin olive oil
Kosher salt and freshly ground black pepper
1 tablespoon white wine vinegar
1 teaspoon vegetable oil
4 extra-large eggs
½ ounce dried porcini, reconstituted in warm water (see page 271) and coarsely chopped (soaking liquid saved)
½ cup warm water
1 teaspoon unsalted butter
½ recipe Wild Mushroom Fricassee (page 101), made without the chicken stock
6 tablespoons crème fraîche
4 teaspoons minced chives

¼ cup freshly grated Parmesan
2 tablespoons truffle oil (optional)

1. Preheat the oven to 400°F.

2. Trim both ends of the potatoes so they will stand upright. Rub the potatoes with 2 tablespoons of the olive oil. Season with salt and pepper. Stand the potatoes upright on a sheet pan. Roast until tender—a thin-bladed knife should easily penetrate the flesh—about 1 hour. Remove from the oven and let cool briefly. Leave the oven on.

3. Meanwhile, bring a deep skillet or medium pot of water to a boil. Add the vinegar and season with salt. Lower the heat to a simmer. Rub a small baking dish or deep plate with the vegetable oil. Crack an egg into a teacup. Tilt the cup and slowly lower it into the simmering water. When the egg is covered with water, tip the cup and release the egg. Repeat with the other 3 eggs. Poach the eggs until the whites are set, 2½ to 3 minutes. Scoop out with a slotted spoon and transfer to the oiled dish. Set aside.

4. Heat the butter in a small sauté pan. As soon as it stops foaming, add the porcini, season with salt and pepper, and cook for 2 minutes. Add the porcini soaking liquid to the pan and cook until it reduces by half. Transfer the porcini, with their reduced juices, to a bowl with the mushroom fricassee and mix well.

5. Mix the crème fraîche and chives together. Season with salt and pepper.

6. When the potatoes are cool enough to handle, use a grapefruit spoon or melon baller to scoop out the centers, leaving ¼ inch at the sides and ½ inch at the bottom. Return them to the sheet pan. Season the insides with salt and pepper. Sprinkle 1½ teaspoons of the Parmesan into the bottom of each potato, followed by 2 tablespoons of the warm mushroom mixture, and then the remaining Parmesan. Top each with an egg and season with salt and pepper.

7. Return to the oven until the potatoes, mushroom filling, and eggs are warm, about 5 minutes. Transfer to warm plates, and top with the chive crème fraîche. Drizzle with the truffle oil, if using, and serve immediately.

Soupe de Poisson

For first-time diners, the experience of soupe de poisson can be a little tough to grasp. The feel of the soup in your mouth is slightly grainy, with a light body and no visible pieces of fish. The flavor is unexpectedly intense, concentrated, almost smoky—and then it's served with a spicy mayonnaise and grated Gruyère. How to make sense of all this?

Soupe de Poisson is a rustic dish, created by fishermen from the tiny unwanted fish left at the bottom of the net. Too small to be easily gutted and boned, they were traditionally cooked whole in the soup, pounded in a mortar and pestle—bones, guts, and all—then strained. After straining, all that remained was the flavorful liquid, with a fine residue of ground fish, the mark of properly made soup. It is also one of a handful of recipes friends and clients asked me to put in this book, threatening to boycott me if I didn't.

This isn't a daunting recipe, but it does take time and involves a couple of steps that don't often take place in most American kitchens, like roasting and puréeing fish bones. This is also not a recipe that tolerates shortcuts in technique or ingredients. A few things to bear in mind:

- Saffron, Pernod, and orange are essential flavorings. Omitting any of them will dramatically change the final product.

- Similarly, the deep base flavor of the soup comes from caramelizing the vegetables and bones. Make sure the bones and vegetables are cooked until browned.

- The traditional French method of making this soup uses a food mill, but unless you're working on developing your shoulder and arm muscles, I suggest a food processor. A punched metal strainer, known as a China cap—like an applesauce strainer, not a lightweight mesh one—is also necessary.

- You need an implement with which to pound the cooked fish bones and lobster bodies in the China cap. We use a rolling pin with blunt ends, but the wooden kitchen tool used for mashing apples into applesauce works as well.

MAKES 6 TO 8 SERVINGS

SOUP

2 pounds fish bones, including the heads, from white-fleshed fish, such as cod, halibut, haddock, or flounder

1 pound inexpensive white fish pieces, such as cod bellies, perch, or pollack

2 pounds lobster bodies (the body—where the legs attach—should be rinsed clean of tomalley and any loose viscera; discard the carapace, the outer shell)

¼ cup extra virgin olive oil

1 medium onion, skin on (for color), coarsely chopped

1 leek, white part only, trimmed of roots and tough
    outer leaves, thinly sliced crosswise, and swirled
    vigorously in a bowl of cold water to remove
    any grit
1 celery stalk, thinly sliced
1 small fennel bulb, trimmed of stalks and tough
    outer layers, cut in half lengthwise, cored, and
    thinly sliced crosswise
1 small carrot, thinly sliced
4 garlic cloves, cut in half
Kosher salt and freshly ground black pepper
1 cup dry white wine
2 cups chopped fresh tomatoes or high-quality
    canned tomatoes
2 oranges, peel and pith removed, cut into chunks,
    plus juice from an additional orange if necessary
⅓ cup Pernod, or more to taste
1 teaspoon fennel seeds
6 sprigs flat-leaf parsley
3 bay leaves
2 teaspoons paprika, preferably Spanish
2 large pinches of saffron

GARNISH
½ cup extra virgin olive oil
1 baguette French bread, sliced into 18 to 24 slices
    ½ inch thick, toasted
1 cup Rouille (page 13)
1 cup grated Gruyère

DO AHEAD: The soup will keep for 4 to 5 days refrigerated, so there's no problem if you want to make it a day or two ahead. Make the rouille, the spicy garlic mayonnaise garnish, the day of serving.

1. Using kitchen shears, remove the eyeballs and gills from the fish heads. Put the bones and heads (not the fish or lobster bodies) in a large pot and rinse under cold running water for at least 30 minutes. Drain.

2. Preheat the oven to 450°F.

3. Spread the fish bones and heads in a large roasting pan and pat dry with paper towels. Add the fish and lobster bodies. Drizzle with 2 tablespoons of the olive oil and toss well. Spread everything in an even layer. Roast for 30 minutes, or until everything is golden brown. When cool, chop or break the bones and lobster bodies into 2-inch pieces.

4. Heat the remaining 2 tablespoons olive oil in a large stockpot over high heat. Add the onion, leek, celery, fennel, carrot, and garlic; season with salt and pepper. Cook, stirring frequently, until the vegetables are golden brown, about 10 minutes.

5. Add the roasted fish bones and heads, and fish and lobster bodies, along with the white wine. Continue cooking until the liquid has reduced by one-third. You will have to use your best judgment, since the pot will be full of seafood and vegetables; in any event, cook no longer than 2 to 3 minutes.

6. Add the remaining soup ingredients to the stockpot and add enough water to just barely cover the bones. Bring to a boil, reduce to a simmer, and cook for 40 minutes.

7. Purée everything—bones and all—in the food processor, as finely as possible. You will have to do this in batches, pouring the purée into a bowl or other container as you finish each batch. Then pound the purée firmly

through a coarse China cap (metal strainer) to strain out the large pieces. The resulting soup will be slightly grainy. If the soup seems too thin, return it to the stove and reduce. Taste for seasoning and add more orange juice, Pernod, salt, and pepper if necessary.

8. To serve, pour the olive oil into warmed soup bowls, then ladle in the soup. Serve immediately, offering the croutons, rouille, and Gruyère. It's accepted practice to place a dollop of rouille on a crouton, sprinkle it with grated cheese, and then set it afloat in your soup.

Acquacotta—Porcini Broth with Soft Polenta, Taleggio, and a Poached Egg

*A*quacotta, *literally, "cooked water," is* a dish eaten by shepherds and herdsmen of the Maremma region of Tuscany roughing it in the hills with their sheep or cattle. The dish begins with a pot in which foraged ingredients are cooked with a little oil—often no more than a little garlic and wild greens. Hot water is poured into the pot, and the flavored broth is then ladled into bowls containing a piece of bread and a beaten egg. Numerous variations testify to the resourcefulness of cooks who rely on whatever is at hand: garlic, onions, greens, mushrooms, tomatoes, and perhaps some sheep's milk cheese.

This is an unabashedly luxurious reworking of the hot-water-goes-over-the-starch-and-egg technique. Chicken broth, unavailable to herdsmen on the move, is flavored with dried porcini mushrooms and poured over polenta with melted Taleggio. This is one case where I always use a homemade stock. A poached egg slips into the broth at the last moment. The touch of a soup spoon breaks the yolk, releasing a rich vein of gold into the mushroom broth. A drizzle of truffle oil doesn't hurt either.

MAKES 4 SERVINGS

BROTH

1 ounce dried porcini mushrooms, reconstituted in 1 cup warm water (see page 271), coarsely chopped (soaking liquid reserved)

4½ cups Chicken Stock (page 31)

¾ cup dry Marsala

Kosher salt and freshly ground black pepper

POLENTA

2½ cups water

Kosher salt and freshly ground black pepper

½ cup coarsely ground cornmeal

2 tablespoons freshly grated Parmesan

1 tablespoon distilled white vinegar

4 extra-large eggs

1 teaspoon vegetable oil

¼ pound Taleggio, trimmed of rind and cut into 12 pieces

Freshly ground black pepper

4 teaspoons truffle oil (optional)

1. Combine the chopped porcini, soaking liquid, chicken stock, and Marsala in a medium saucepan over medium heat. Bring to a boil, reduce heat to a simmer, and cook for 45 minutes. Season with salt and pepper. If you like a clear soup, strain out the mushrooms; if not, leave as is. Keep warm.

2. Meanwhile, bring 2½ cups of water to a boil in a medium saucepan. Add ¾ teaspoon salt and then add the polenta in a slow, steady stream through your fingers, whisking constantly with the other hand so it doesn't clump up. If you get any lumps, mash them against the side of the pot with a wooden spoon and keep stirring. Lower the heat to a simmer and cook, stirring frequently, until the polenta is thick and shiny and begins to pull away from the sides of the pan, about 30 minutes. Regulate the heat as necessary so the mixture doesn't boil over or cook too quickly. Stir in the Parmesan. Season with salt and pepper. Cover and keep warm.

3. Bring a small pot or skillet of water to a boil. Add the vinegar and season with salt. Lower the heat to a simmer. Crack an egg into a teacup. Tilt the cup and slowly lower it into the simmering water. When the egg is covered with water, tip the cup and release the egg. Repeat with the other 3 eggs. Poach the eggs until the whites are set, 3 to 4 minutes. While the eggs are poaching, rub a small baking dish or deep plate with the vegetable oil. Scoop the eggs out with a slotted spoon and transfer to the dish. Set aside.

4. Meanwhile, preheat the oven to 350°F.

5. Divide the polenta among four large warm ovenproof soup bowls. Set 3 pieces of Taleggio on the polenta in each bowl and put a poached egg on top. Sprinkle the eggs with salt and pepper. Put the bowls in the oven until the eggs are heated through, about 4 minutes.

6. While the eggs are heating, bring the porcini broth back to a simmer. Remove the bowls from the oven.

7. Pour the hot broth into the bowls around the polenta. Drizzle with the truffle oil, if using. Serve immediately.

Squash Blossoms Stuffed with Herbed Cheese in Fritter Batter

*E*very August, zucchini seem to multiply on their vines like the vegetable equivalent of the animated brooms in "The Sorcerer's Apprentice," an explosion of late-summer fecundity that exhausts the cravings of even the most ardent zucchini lover. I say, throttle them in their infancy—pick the zucchini flowers ("squash blossoms," as they're also known) before they can grow up.

This dish naturally evolved out of ingredients purchased one afternoon in an open-air market—beautiful fresh goat cheeses and several different tapenades. I've since lightened the goat cheese mixture with ricotta. The tapenade should be served as a small garnish on the side, a complementary taste rather than a big spoonful.

MAKES 4 SERVINGS

½ cup unbleached all-purpose flour

¼ cup cornstarch

1 extra-large egg, separated (the white should be chilled)

½ cup very cold beer

6 tablespoons high-quality ricotta

6 tablespoons soft goat cheese

1 teaspoon minced shallot

3 tablespoons minced fresh chives

3 tablespoons finely chopped fresh flat-leaf parsley

3 tablespoons finely chopped fresh chervil

Kosher salt and freshly ground black pepper

1 tablespoon freshly squeezed lemon juice

20 large squash blossoms

4 cups vegetable oil for deep-frying

¼ cup Green Olive Tapenade (page 25; optional)

1. To make the batter, mix the flour and cornstarch in a bowl. In another bowl, beat the egg white and beer together. Stir this into the flour mixture. Do not overbeat, or the batter will be tough; there should still be some lumps. Cover and refrigerate (it can rest, chilled, up to 2 hours) while you make the stuffing.

2. Mix the cheeses in a bowl with the egg yolk, shallot, and herbs. Season with salt and pepper and 1 teaspoon of the lemon juice.

3. Carefully pry apart the petals of each blossom. Remove the stamen. Place a small spoonful of the cheese mixture inside each blossom and gently twist the tips of the blossoms shut.

4. Heat the vegetable oil in a large deep pot over medium heat to 350°F. Use a deep-fry thermometer to check the temperature.

5. Remove the batter from the refrigerator and stir it once. Dip the blossoms into the batter, then carefully lower them into the hot oil. Fry them in batches until they are golden brown and crisp, 3 to 5 minutes.

6. Divide the blossoms among four warm plates. Drizzle with the remaining 2 teaspoons lemon juice. Garnish each plate with spoonful of tapenade, if using, and serve.

SQUASH BLOSSOMS OR ZUCCHINI FLOWERS

Squash blossoms rarely appear in specialty produce stores; the most reliable place to find them is your own backyard or a farmers' market. If you ask around, you will almost certainly find a zucchini vendor willing to bring you a bag of the flowers the following week. Of course, if you're growing zucchini in your backyard garden, you have a ready source. When shopping for blossoms, look for crisp, fresh petals with no trace of wilting. As the flowers age, the petals, beginning at the tips, start to wilt, then turn slimy. Refrigerate them in a single layer in a lightly covered container and, if possible, use them within a day of purchase. If you refrigerate them in a plastic bag or wrapped in plastic, they'll spoil faster.

Celery Root Ravioli with Sage Butter or Crispy Pork Confit

ike the Robert Frost poem, this is a two-roads-diverged-in-a-wood recipe. At the end of one road awaits a luscious dish of ravioli with the brown butter and sage sauce traditionally served with squash ravioli. The other road will take you—after many a twist and turn—to one of the most flavorful dishes in this entire book, a fabled taste combination from France, confit plus a slightly sweet root vegetable.

At first glance, Crispy Pork Confit sauce seems like a daunting effort: first you make confit, and that takes *hours and hours,* and then you make celery root purée, and *then* you make ravioli from scratch. *Puh-lease!* Actually, the dish requires more advanced planning than actual labor, and if you buy high-quality pasta sheets to make the ravioli, then even that is reduced. The advanced planning comes in with the confit. True, it does take several hours to make, but it also keeps for several weeks, so all you have to do is find a time when you know you're going to be home for several hours while it cooks. You can even make the ravioli several hours ahead, leaving you with the simple dinner tasks of boiling the ravioli and sautéing the ingredients that accompany the confit. This ought to be reserved for people whom you really care about—and who'll bring lots of expensive red wine when you tell them what you're planning for dinner.

MAKES 4 SERVINGS (40 RAVIOLI)

CELERY ROOT

1 celery root (about 1¼ pounds)
1 tablespoon plus 1 teaspoon freshly squeezed
    lemon juice, or more to taste
4 tablespoons unsalted butter
1 medium white onion, thinly sliced
2 garlic cloves, minced
Kosher salt and freshly ground black pepper
1½ cups Chicken Stock (page 31) or high-quality
    canned low-sodium chicken broth
½ teaspoon grated lemon zest
1 teaspoon finely chopped fresh sage
¼ teaspoon finely chopped fresh rosemary

1 recipe Fresh Pasta (page 142)

IF USING SAGE SAUCE

6 tablespoons unsalted butter
1½ tablespoons chopped fresh sage
Kosher salt and freshly ground black pepper

IF USING PORK CONFIT SAUCE

2 tablespoons strained duck fat, goose fat, or olive
    oil from cooking the confit (see below)
2 garlic cloves, thinly sliced
½ pound spicy greens (e.g., turnip greens, mustard
    greens, or arugula), washed and coarsely
    chopped
Kosher salt and freshly ground black pepper
1 recipe Crispy Pork Confit (page 313), drained of
    any excess fat

1 apple, peeled, cored, and chopped into ½-inch dice

2 cups Chicken Stock (page 31) or 4 cups high-quality low-sodium canned chicken broth, reduced to 2 cups (see page 32)

¼ cup freshly grated Pecorino Romano (for either version)

1. Peel the celery root. Its knobby exterior is more easily tackled with a paring knife than a conventional vegetable peeler. Dice the root into 1-inch cubes. (You should end up with about 1 pound peeled, cubed celery root.) Toss with 1 tablespoon of the lemon juice so it doesn't discolor and set aside.

2. Melt 2 tablespoons of the butter in a heavy saucepan over medium heat. Sauté the onions until lightly browned, 10 to 15 minutes. Take care not to burn them. Transfer to a bowl.

3. Add the remaining 2 tablespoons butter to the saucepan. Increase the heat to medium-high and sear the celery root on all sides. Add the garlic, return the onions to the pan and season with salt and pepper. Add the chicken stock, bring to a boil, cover, and lower the heat to a simmer. Cook until the celery root is tender enough to purée and the stock has reduced to a glaze, about an hour.

4. Purée the celery root in a food processor. The texture should resemble that of mashed potatoes. Stir in the lemon zest, sage, rosemary, and the remaining 1 teaspoon lemon juice. Taste for seasoning and add more salt and pepper and lemon juice, if necessary. Transfer to a bowl and let cool.

5. Following the instructions beginning on page 142, roll out the pasta dough to ravioli thickness (the #7 or #8 setting, depending on your machine). Follow the instructions for making ravioli on page 144, using a small spoonful of celery root purée for each ravioli. Transfer the completed ravioli to a lightly floured baking sheet.

IF YOU'RE GOING TO SERVE THE RAVIOLI WITH THE BROWN BUTTER AND SAGE

1. Bring a large pot of water to a boil and season it with salt.

2. While the water heats, melt the butter in a small saucepan over medium heat. Add the sage and cook until the butter turns a deep gold, about 5 minutes. Season with salt and pepper and remove from the heat; cover to keep warm.

3. Add the ravioli to the boiling water and cook, stirring constantly but very carefully until the water returns to a boil. Continue to cook until the ravioli have all floated to the surface and their edges are al dente, 3 to 4 minutes. Drain.

4. Place the ravioli in a large nonstick sauté pan over very low heat. Pour the brown butter and sage over the ravioli and swirl the ravioli to coat them with the sauce. Transfer to four warmed plates, sprinkle with the cheese, and serve.

IF YOU'RE GOING TO SERVE THE RAVIOLI WITH THE CONFIT

1. Bring a large pot of water to a boil and season it with salt.

2. While the water is heating, heat 1 tablespoon of the strained fat in a large sauté pan over medium heat. Add the garlic and cook for 30 seconds. Add the greens, season with salt and pepper, and toss until the greens are tender and wilted. Transfer to a plate.

3. Add the remaining 1 tablespoon fat to the pan and increase the heat to medium-high. Add the pork and sear on the first side until crispy, about 4 minutes, then flip and sear on the other side. Transfer to a plate. Add the apple to the pan and sear until golden. Transfer to the plate with the pork. Add the chicken stock to the pan and reduce by half.

4. Meanwhile, when the chicken stock has almost finished reducing, add the ravioli to the boiling water and cook, stirring constantly but very carefully, until the water returns to a boil. Continue to cook until the ravioli have all floated to the surface and their edges are al dente, 3 to 4 minutes. Drain.

5. Add the ravioli to the pan with the sauce. Add the greens, pork, and apples and gently stir everything together to heat through. Transfer to four warmed plates, sprinkle with the pecorino, and serve.

✺ Crispy Pork Confit ✺

*C*onfit *started out as a* technique for cooking and preserving game and other types of meat, especially duck, goose, and pork. Pieces of meat were salted and braised slowly in fat, usually goose or duck fat, then stored in crocks, with a layer of rendered fat covering the cooked meat. Throughout the winter, a dish of root vegetables or cabbage could be considerably enlivened with the addition of a scoop or two of confit. Confit can also be served by itself as a luxurious appetizer (this recipe makes more than enough for 4), accompanied with sautéed apples and wilted greens.

MAKES 1 POUND

SPICE MIX
¼ **teaspoon ground cinnamon**
¼ **teaspoon ground ginger**
¼ **teaspoon ground allspice**
⅛ **teaspoon ground cloves**
½ **teaspoon dried sage**
½ **teaspoon dried thyme**
½ **teaspoon celery seeds**
½ **teaspoon fennel seeds**
2 **bay leaves, crushed**
½ **cup kosher salt**

1 **pound pork butt, cut into 8 pieces**
6 **cups duck or goose fat (substitute extra virgin olive oil if you cannot get the fat)**
4 **garlic cloves, chopped**
1 **medium onion, thinly sliced**

DO AHEAD: Marinate the pork.

1. Combine the spice mixture ingredients in a medium bowl. Toss the pork pieces with the spice mix, cover, and marinate in the refrigerator for at least 12 to 18 hours.

2. Heat the duck fat in a large heavy Dutch oven over medium heat. (It's important to use a pot with a heavy bottom so that it conducts the heat evenly.) Add the garlic cloves and onion and cook for 5 minutes. Reduce the heat to low. Check the temperature with a deep-fry thermometer—it should read 185°F. Lower the heat if necessary.

3. Remove the pork from the refrigerator, rinse well, and pat dry with paper towels. Carefully lower the pork into the fat. It should be submerged. Cook, uncovered, until the meat is falling apart, 2½ to 3 hours. Let cool in the fat.

4. Remove the pork from the pot and shred into ½-inch pieces. Strain the fat. Transfer the pork to a glass or ceramic container and add enough fat to just cover it. Cover tightly with plastic wrap and refrigerate. Strain the remaining fat into a container, cover with plastic wrap, and refrigerate for another use. The confit and fat will keep for several weeks refrigerated.

Fresh and Salt Cod Wrapped in Pancetta with Wilted Greens

Both fresh cod and salt cod are often paired with greens or pancetta in classic Italian recipes, but you rarely see the two served on the same plate. Early in my career, I came up with the idea of creating a pocket of salt cod inside a piece of fresh cod and then giving each portion a "belt" of crisp pancetta to hold it together. I come back to it again and again because of the contrasting textures and flavors, and because it makes me feel good. Serve it with polenta for a fabulous comfort meal.

This recipe asks you to slice partway through a fresh cod fillet, leaving it attached on one side. This creates a pocket for the salt cod. Obviously, the thicker the fillet, the easier it is to slice through it. But really hefty cod fillets—¾ inch thick or more—are difficult to come by in these days of diminishing cod stocks, especially since seafood wholesalers often reserve the thickest cuts for the restaurant trade. If you can't find thick fillets, simply buy thin ones flexible enough to wrap around a piece of salt cod. Skip the instructions in Step 3 that call for you to slice the fresh fillets. Instead, season one side of the fillets with salt and pepper and thyme, as per the recipe, then wrap the fresh fillets around the salt cod. Continue with Step 4. When placing the bundles in the sauté pan, cook the side with the overlapping layers of pancetta first. The pancetta slices will bind together as they cook, holding the fillets in place.

MAKES 4 ENTRÉE SERVINGS

¼ pound skinless, boneless salt cod of even
  thickness, center cut
Kosher salt and freshly ground black pepper
Four 6-ounce cod fillets, approximately ¾ inch thick
  (see headnote)
2 teaspoons fresh thyme leaves
12 thin slices pancetta (5 to 6 ounces) (see box)
¼ cup extra virgin olive oil
1 small red onion, thinly sliced
1 garlic clove, minced
6 to 8 cups mixed greens (such as watercress,
  radicchio, mustard greens, and Belgian endive)
¼ cup water
3 tablespoons freshly squeezed lemon juice
8 tablespoons (1 stick) unsalted butter, chilled

2 tablespoons capers, rinsed
4 lemon wedges

DO AHEAD: Soak the salt cod for 12 hours.

1. Soak the salt cod for 12 hours in a large bowl of cold water, changing the water 3 or 4 times. When finished, the cod should *not* be completely salt-free, or it will have lost its distinctive flavor. It should taste about as salty as a fish that you've seasoned and cooked with salt. Drain the cod.

2. Place the salt cod in a small saucepan, cover with cold water, and bring just to a boil over moderate heat. Remove from the heat and let stand until the cod is barely cooked through, about 5 minutes. Drain and trim away any bones and membranes. Cut into quarters, cover. (Refrigerate if doing ahead.)

3. Using a chef's knife, slice horizontally through each fresh cod fillet to within an inch of the opposite side, so that the two halves of the fillet can be opened (see headnote if you're using thin fillets of cod). Season the inside of the fillets with salt and pepper and sprinkle the inside of each with ½ teaspoon of the thyme. Put a piece of poached salt cod inside each fillet and close the two halves. Spread 3 overlapping slices of the pancetta side by side on a work surface and place a cod fillet in the center. Bring the pancetta up and over the cod, wrapping it snugly to form a neat package. Repeat with the remaining cod and pancetta to form 4 packages. (Before you proceed to the next step, read About Pancetta.)

4. Heat 2 tablespoons of the olive oil in a large sauté pan over high heat. As soon as the oil is hot, sear the cod bundles on one side until the pancetta is pink and slightly crispy, about 5 minutes. Carefully turn the cod over and cook until the fish is opaque, 3 to 4 more minutes. Transfer the cod to a platter and keep warm.

5. Heat the remaining 2 tablespoons olive oil in the sauté pan over medium heat. When the oil is hot, add the onion and cook, stirring, until soft, about 2 minutes. Stir in the garlic and then add the greens. Season with salt and pepper. Cook, stirring, until just wilted, about 1 minute. Transfer the greens to four warm plates.

6. Add the water and lemon juice to the sauté pan and bring to a boil. Remove from the heat and whisk in the butter, 1 tablespoon at a time. Whisk in the capers and any juices that have accumulated on the fish platter, and season to taste with salt and pepper.

7. Transfer the fish to the plates with the greens. Spoon the sauce over the fish, garnish with the lemon wedges, and serve immediately.

ABOUT PANCETTA

Although pancetta is often called "Italian bacon," that description is misleading. Pancetta is hung and cured in a process similar to that of prosciutto, and it can be eaten in its uncooked state, an adventure most cooks would forgo when it comes to bacon. One of the most delicious samples of street food I've ever eaten was a grilled cheese, potato, and pancetta sandwich in Aix. A line of eager customers was snapping up the sandwiches as fast as the streetcorner vendor could pump them out with his old-fashioned hinged waffle iron. The potatoes were sliced thin and precooked. The pancetta was only heated long enough for the cheese to melt and the bread to crisp. It was still pink and soft, though warm, and incredibly good. Keep this in mind when sautéing the cod bundles—the pancetta wrapping should only be partially crisp, and still fairly pink, when finished. Don't treat it like bacon— you'll only sacrifice the pancetta's rich texture, as well as overcook the fish.

Roasted Marinated Long Island Duck with Green Olive and Balsamic Vinegar Sauce

I created this duck dish more than eleven years ago for my first menu at Michela's, based on a Sicilian tradition of pairing duck with green olives. It was an immediate hit. When my partners and I opened Rialto, the first thing customers familiar with my food asked was, "Where's the duck?" It's been on the menu almost continuously ever since.

In Steamed and Pan-Roasted Duck (page 247), I instruct you to steam the bird and then to slowly pan-roast it on top of the stove. This recipe uses a different strategy for rendering the fat and crisping the skin. It calls for roasting the duck in the oven at a low temperature (so the fat renders without smoking), then crisping the duck pieces in a covered heavy sauté pan on top of the stove.

Much of this recipe can be prepared in advance. You can make the optional sauce the day before and reheat it later. You can also roast the duck ahead and cut it into pieces, leaving yourself only the step of crisping it on top of the stove before serving.

Unless your idea of a good time is scraping roasting pans, use a nonstick or disposable deep roasting pan and a nonstick V-rack.

MAKES 2 ENTRÉE SERVINGS (SEE DUCK FOR MORE THAN TWO, PAGE 319, IF YOU WANT TO STRETCH IT)

One 5-pound Long Island duck, with neck and
   gizzard

MARINADE
½ cup balsamic vinegar
¼ cup soy sauce
¼ cup Dijon mustard
1½ teaspoons mustard seeds
1½ teaspoons dried rosemary
1½ teaspoons freshly ground black pepper
½ small white onion, chopped into ¼-inch dice
2 garlic cloves, finely chopped

Kosher salt and freshly ground black pepper
About ¼ cup vegetable oil
4 teaspoons balsamic vinegar

Green Olive and Balsamic Vinegar Sauce
   (recipe follows; optional)
4 sprigs rosemary for garnish

DO AHEAD: Marinate the duck the night before roasting.

1. Remove the paper sack containing the gizzard, heart, and liver from the cavity of the duck. If you're going to make the sauce, rinse the gizzard, then wrap with plastic wrap and refrigerate until you're ready to make the sauce. Set the heart and liver aside for another use or discard (the liver would only make the sauce muddy). The sack may contain the neck of the

duck, or the neck may simply have been placed inside the cavity. In either event, retrieve the neck and rinse, wrap, and refrigerate it until ready to use in the sauce.

2. Cut off the wing tips (the last two segments of the wings) and refrigerate with the neck for use in the sauce. Cut off the fatty flaps around the neck opening and trim the fat from around the opening to the cavity. Discard the fatty trimmings. Rinse the duck inside and out and pat dry. Carefully poke the skin of the bird all over with a fork or skewer. Try not to penetrate beyond the fat layer into the meat—if you poke too far, the juices will run out during cooking along with the fat. Poking the skin from a sharp angle instead of straight in will help.

3. Mix all of the marinade ingredients together in a large bowl. Roll the duck all around in the marinade, making sure that plenty of marinade flows inside the cavity. Cover and marinate overnight in the refrigerator.

4. When ready to begin roasting, preheat the oven to 325°F.

5. Remove the duck from the marinade (don't scrape off the marinade); set the marinade aside. Season the bird inside and out with salt and pepper. Set the marinated duck breast side down on a nonstick V-rack in a roasting pan. The duck must be at least 2 inches above the bottom of the pan. Pour the remaining marinade over it. Add ¼ inch of water to the roasting pan to keep any drippings from burning. Place the pan in the oven and roast for 1 hour.

6. Flip the duck breast side up. Carefully prick the thighs with a fork again (remember not to penetrate the meat). Rotate the pan so the opposite side of the duck is now toward the back of the oven. Continue roasting until the skin is dark brown and just about all of the fat has melted off the body of the duck, another 2 to 2½ hours. (If you're going to make the sauce, now is a good time to do it.) The duck is done when the leg bones have a little play in the socket when you try to wiggle them. If you prick the thickest part of the thigh, the juices should run clear; an instant-read digital thermometer inserted into the thickest part of the thigh should read 180°F. Let the duck rest for 20 minutes before breaking it down.

7. When the duck is cool enough to handle, cut it into 4 pieces, according to the directions on page 250.

8. Heat a ⅛-inch layer of vegetable oil in a large heavy-bottomed sauté pan over high heat until very hot. A nonstick pan will help alleviate the chance of sticking, but it's not necessary if the pan is heavy and you don't add the duck until the oil is quite hot. Sprinkle the duck pieces liberally with salt and pepper. When the oil is almost smoking, add the duck pieces skin side down. Do not disturb the duck pieces once you have set them in the pan. Allow them to sear for 1 minute, then adjust the heat to low, cover the pan, and cook until the meat is warm and the skin is crisp, about 15 minutes. Pour off any excess fat that accumulates. Sprinkle the meat side with the balsamic vinegar.

9. Arrange the duck on a warm platter. If you've made the sauce, drizzle it around the meat, making sure to distribute the olives evenly about the platter. Garnish with the rosemary sprigs and serve.

⚜ Green Olive and Balsamic Vinegar Sauce ⚜

I *usually prepare this sauce* while the duck is roasting, but if it's easier for you, you can make it a day ahead and reheat before serving. Omit the final addition of butter and olives until you're ready to serve it.

MAKES ABOUT ½ CUP

Wing tips, neck, and gizzard from 1 duck
2 tablespoons vegetable oil
2 shallots, coarsely chopped
½ small carrot, peeled and coarsely chopped
½ celery stalk, coarsely chopped
½ teaspoon chopped fresh thyme
½ teaspoon chopped fresh rosemary
2 bay leaves
½ cup dry red wine
2 cups Chicken Stock (page 31) or 4 cups high-quality canned low-sodium chicken broth, reduced to 2 cups (see page 32)
Kosher salt and freshly ground black pepper
1 to 2 tablespoons balsamic vinegar
2 tablespoons unsalted butter (optional)
10 large Sicilian green olives, pitted

1. Using a cleaver or sturdy knife (don't use your favorite knife—chopping bones can ruin the edge), chop the wing tips and neck into 3-inch pieces. Coarsely chop the gizzard. Heat the vegetable oil in a large sauté pan over high heat. Add the chopped wing and neck pieces. Cook until well browned, 8 to 10 minutes. Pour off any excess fat. Add the gizzard, shallots, carrots, and celery. Cook until well browned, about 5 minutes.

2. Lower the heat to medium. Add the herbs and wine and reduce to a glaze, 5 to 7 minutes. Add the chicken stock and reduce until the sauce coats the back of a spoon, about 25 minutes. Strain. (There should be about ½ cup.) Season the sauce with salt, pepper, and 1 tablespoon vinegar, or more, to taste. Keep warm, or reheat when ready to serve. Just before serving whisk in the butter, if using, and add the olives.

DUCK FOR MORE THAN TWO

Almost every duck recipe you'll ever see in a cookbook is for one duck. I didn't know this (or was too obtuse to notice) until the time came to write my own recipes. At our house, we frequently cook two ducks at a time. We have two children, and if we want to have company and duck the same night we have no choice but to cook two ducks. Both of the duck recipes in this book will easily double. Marinade, sauce, etc.—double them all.

A large roasting pan, especially one of the extra-large disposable ones, will usually hold two ducks side by side on V-racks. If you use a disposable roasting pan (and I always use either nonstick or disposable), use two, one inside the other, so there won't be any question of the pan holding the weight of two ducks. You also need two large heavy-bottomed sauté pans for crisping or pan-roasting, depending on the recipe. For the Roasted Marinated Long Island Duck, you could crisp the duck in batches, keeping the first batch warm for 15 minutes in the oven while you crisp the second, but for the Steamed and Pan-Roasted Duck (page 247), which cooks entirely on top of the stove, you definitely need a second pan. I have an inexpensive cast-iron frying pan for just such situations. I improvise the lid, resorting to an old circular platter (the heat is on low, so I'm not worried about breaking it) or even aluminum foil.

Can you stretch one duck to serve four eaters? Yes, if there are plenty of other things to eat, and you make a few adjustments in your carving technique. Begin by following the instructions for How to Break Down a Duck on page 250. Continue the process by cutting each breast piece crosswise in two. Cut the legs off the thighs. You will end up with 4 breast pieces, 2 legs and 2 thighs. Believe it or not, there's usually a leg or thigh piece left over at the end of the meal.

Roast Christmas Goose Stuffed with Brandied Figs, Chestnuts, and Rye Bread

Believe me, if there's a way to go wrong with geese, I've probably done it, including filling my house with a black cloud of acrid smoke when I once tried to "jumpstart" the goose at 500°F. But I love the rich flavor of goose meat so much that I persevered through my mistakes until arriving at the method outlined in this recipe. I've also picked up a few tricks for accurately determining when the goose is not just cooked, but *done*.

Goose meat has an undeserved reputation for tasting greasy—it doesn't, or at least no more than a well-marbled steak does. In this recipe much of the fat is rendered before the goose even begins to roast. Then the goose is roasted at a low temperature, to prevent smoking.

For those willing to try it, roast goose comes with two golden eggs: goose fat, worth its weight in gold in the opinion of anyone who has ever eaten a French fry cooked in it or made Crispy Pork Confit (page 313), and a carcass that is easily transformed into goose stock, an invaluable ingredient for Goose Risotto (page 174).

MAKES 8 TO 10 ENTRÉE SERVINGS

One 10- to 12-pound goose

STUFFING
½ cup Cognac

1 cup dried figs, preferably Turkish, cut into
　quarters

6 ounces smoked bacon, chopped into ½-inch dice

1½ cups cooked and peeled chestnuts (see page
　244), broken into large pieces

2 medium onions, chopped into ½-inch dice

8 celery stalks, chopped into ½-inch dice

Kosher salt and freshly ground black pepper

2 garlic cloves, finely chopped

3 cups ½-inch cubes dry rye bread
　(trimmed of crusts)

2 cups ½-inch cubes dry white bread,
　(trimmed of crusts)

1 cup diced cranberries

1 tablespoon chopped fresh sage

1 tablespoon chopped fresh thyme

½ cup chopped fresh sage

GRAVY
Wing tips, neck, and gizzard from the goose

2 tablespoons vegetable oil

½ carrot, chopped

1 celery stalk, chopped

4 shallots, chopped

1 cup dry vermouth

½ cup Cognac

4 cups Chicken Stock (page 31) or 8 cups high-
　quality canned low-sodium chicken broth,
　reduced to 4 cups (see page 32)

2 tablespoons unbleached all-purpose flour

Kosher salt and freshly ground black pepper

1 bunch of sage, for garnish

DO AHEAD: Blanch the goose and refrigerate for 24 hours.

TO PREP THE GOOSE

1. Bring a large pot of water to a boil. The pot should be large enough so that you can submerge at least half of the goose in the boiling water.

2. Meanwhile, cut the neck flap and any excess fat off the goose. Remove the sack containing the neck and giblets and refrigerate until ready to make the sauce. Using a sturdy knife or poultry shears, clip off the wing tips and reserve for the sauce. Carefully pierce the skin all over with a sharp fork or skewer, to allow the fat to render more efficiently. Jab the skin at a sharp angle so that you poke through the skin into the layer of fat without penetrating into the meat. If you pierce the meat, it will dry out during cooking.

3. Using rubber gloves, carefully lower one end of the goose into the boiling water. At least half of the goose should be submerged in the water. After 1 minute, carefully withdraw the goose and submerge the other end. Take care not to spill any hot water from the goose cavities on yourself. After 1 minute, remove the goose from the pot. Drain any water from the cavities, pat dry, and refrigerate, uncovered, for 24 hours.

TO STUFF AND ROAST THE GOOSE

4. Pour the Cognac over the figs and let them steep for 20 minutes.

5. In a large frying pan, cook the bacon over medium heat until most of the fat is rendered.

Remove the bacon and set aside. Leave the fat in the pan. Add the chestnuts and cook over medium heat until they start to brown, 3 to 4 minutes. Transfer them to a large bowl.

6. Add the onions and celery to the pan, season with salt and pepper, and cook over medium heat until tender, 5 to 7 minutes. Add the garlic and cook until fragrant, another minute or two. Add the figs, with the Cognac, and cook until most of the liquid is gone, about 4 minutes. Let cool.

7. Add the sautéed vegetables, bread cubes, cranberries, bacon, 1 tablespoon of the sage, and thyme to the bowl with the chestnuts; toss to combine. Season with salt and pepper.

8. Preheat the oven to 325°F.

9. Season the goose inside and out with salt and pepper. Poke the bird all over once again, taking care not to penetrate the meat. Fill the cavity of the goose loosely with stuffing. Secure the legs with string. Rub the outside with ½ cup of chopped sage. Set the bird breast side down on a V-rack in a roasting pan, preferably both non-stick. Add ½ inch of water to the pan. Roast for 1½ hours.

10. Turn the goose breast side up and roast for an additional 2½ to 3 hours. Telling when a goose is done can be a little tricky. Using an instant-read digital thermometer at the thickest part of the thigh, as you would for a turkey, is misleading. Theoretically, a reading of 170°F would indicate that the goose is cooked, but in my experience, if you pull the goose out of the oven at this point, the meat is cooked but still very tough. You need to let the goose roast for at least another 45 minutes beyond this point. When the skin starts to pull away from the

breastbone, there's a good chance the goose is done; the skin on both the breast and legs should also be puffed out. If you squeeze the legs, the meat should feel soft, almost as though it were braised and falling apart, not intact. As a final test, prick the skin at the base of the thigh—if the juices are clear (or there are no juices at all), the goose is probably done. If the juices are pink, continue roasting. Begin making the gravy during the final roasting phase.

TO MAKE THE GRAVY

11. Using a cleaver or sturdy knife (don't use your favorite knife—chopping bones can ruin the edge), chop the wing tips, gizzard, and neck into 3-inch pieces. Heat the vegetable oil in a large sauté pan over high heat. Add the wings, neck, and gizzard to the pan and cook until well browned, about 15 minutes. Remove from the pan and discard. Pour off any excess fat. Add the carrot, celery, and shallots. Cook until well browned, 5 to 6 minutes.

12. Off the heat, add the vermouth and Cognac. Return the pan to medium heat and cook until the liquids reduce to a glaze, 10 to 12 minutes. As the liquids reduce, use a wooden spoon to scrape the bottom of the pan so the crispy bits dissolve in the liquid. Add the chicken stock and reduce until the sauce coats the back of a spoon, about 35 minutes. Strain. (There should be about 2 cups reduced stock.) Set aside until the goose finishes roasting.

13. I'm quite picky about crispy goose skin and I've found that the skin acquires an appealing crackly texture in the normal coarse of roast-

ing. If you want the skin even crisper, when the goose is done, increase the oven temperature to 400°F. Transfer the goose, still on its rack, to another roasting pan, and return it to the oven for 15 minutes. (If you don't use a new pan, the goose fat in the old one will start to smoke.) Set the first pan aside for gravy. Whether you go through this last step or not, allow the goose to rest for 30 minutes before carving.

14. To finish the gravy, pour off all but 2 tablespoons of fat from the roasting pan. Save the goose fat for another day when you need a treat (see box). Be careful not to pour off the caramelized drippings. Put the roasting pan on top of the stove over low heat. Sprinkle the flour into the pan. Using the back of a slotted spoon, stir the flour about the pan, scraping the crispy bits of drippings loose. Cook until the flour starts to brown, about 5 minutes. Add 1 cup of the reduced stock and stir until the flour and crispy bits are as mixed with the sauce as possible (some might not dissolve— that's okay). Add the remaining stock and simmer for 10 minutes. Strain. Season with salt and pepper and keep warm.

15. Scoop the stuffing out of the goose. Present the goose at the table, along with the stuffing and gravy. If you're brave, you can carve at the table, but I like to carve goose or turkey in the kitchen. Removing the drumsticks is an untidy task made easier if you flip the bird onto its side. I also prefer to remove each side of the breast whole, then slice each half crosswise. Arrange the meat on the platter, garnish with sage, and serve.

GOOSE FAT

Goose fat is heaven. My own experience suggests it appeals to a little-understood area of the limbic system activated only by duck confit, high-rise doughnuts, and white truffles. Unless you're from a culinary tradition that celebrates frying, it's difficult to imagine the qualitative difference in flavor between foods fried in goose fat and those cooked in ordinary vegetable oil, or even high-quality olive oil. At Rialto, whenever goose fat makes a seasonal appearance, the kitchen staff indulges in what one of my cooks has dubbed "Just Say No Fries," French fries cooked twice in goose fat. First we fry them, then we let them cool, then we fry them again. The second frying gives them an unearthly crispiness. "Addictive" doesn't do them justice.

Whenever I roast a goose, I save the fat. As soon as it's cool enough to handle, I pour it into ½-cup plastic containers with snug lids. Refrigerated, it seems to last for months. Potatoes, turnips, and beets, sliced thin, are all delicious sautéed in goose fat, and Swiss chard and spinach take on an otherworldly flavor when wilted in a tablespoon of goose fat.

Roast Shoulder of Veal with Parmesan Crust

Stuffing a shoulder or other cut of beef or veal with herbs, cheese, vegetables, and other ingredients and then slowly braising or roasting it is an economically prudent way of infusing an inexpensive cut of meat with complex, satisfying flavors. This recipe evolved out of my reading about the food of Abruzzo. The region's mountainous interior is one of the least populated and most agriculturally challenging areas in Italy. This dish includes a traditional Abruzzese combination of spices and peppers, as well as scamorza, a chewier, slightly drier regional variation of mozzarella. Accompany with roast potatoes, soft polenta, or a simple pasta like penne tossed with extra virgin olive oil and cheese.

Leftover roast shoulder of veal is delicious served cold. If you want to serve the leftovers hot, carefully arrange the sliced veal in a lightly oiled roasting pan. Cover tightly with foil and reheat in a 350°F oven for 20 minutes, keeping a close watch so it doesn't overcook and dry out.

MAKES 4 ENTRÉE SERVINGS

1 boneless veal shoulder (about 3 pounds)

MARINADE
2 tablespoons chopped fresh sage
2 tablespoons chopped fresh thyme
1 teaspoon hot red pepper flakes
1 tablespoon fennel seeds, toasted
2 tablespoons grated lemon zest
½ cup extra virgin olive oil

STUFFING
Kosher salt and freshly ground black pepper
2 red peppers, roasted (see page 99), peeled, stemmed, and seeded
¼ cup Roasted Garlic (1 head garlic; page 119) coarsely mashed with a fork
3 anchovies, rinsed and chopped
5 ounces scamorza (use fresh mozzarella if scamorza is unavailable), diced into ½-inch cubes

2 cups spicy greens (arugula, mustard greens, watercress, or any combination), washed and trimmed of tough stems

Kosher salt and freshly ground black pepper
½ pound freshly grated Parmesan

DO AHEAD: Marinate the veal shoulder for at least 12 hours; longer is fine.

1. Unfold the veal shoulder and remove any sinew or cartilage overlooked by the butcher. Mix the marinade ingredients together in a bowl large enough to contain the veal. Add the veal shoulder and turn in the marinade until thoroughly and evenly coated. Cover and refrigerate for 12 hours.

2. Preheat the oven to 450°F.

3. Unfold the shoulder on a work surface and season the exposed surface with salt and pepper. Lay the roasted red peppers evenly over the meat. Season with salt and pepper. Spread the garlic and anchovies over the peppers. Sprinkle with the scamorza and top with the spicy greens. Roll the shoulder up and tie with butcher's twine.

4. Season the outside of the veal with salt and pepper. Set the shoulder on a V-rack in a roasting pan and roast until browned, about 30 minutes. Lower the heat to 350°F and roast for another 30 minutes.

5. Sprinkle the shoulder with the grated Parmesan and press the cheese firmly against the surface of the meat. Roast for an additional 15 to 20 minutes, or until the desired degree of doneness (figure on 20 minutes per pound). The shoulder is done to medium when an instant-read digital thermometer inserted into the center registers an internal temperature of 130°F. Allow the veal to repose for 20 minutes on top of the stove. (During this resting period, the internal temperature will rise to between 145° and 150°F.)

6. To serve, carefully (in order to disturb the cheese crust as little as possible) cut away the twine and place the shoulder on a platter. Slice the shoulder crosswise at the table, one serving at a time, and serve two slices, each about 1 inch thick, per person. Do not attempt to slice the portions and arrange for serving on a large platter—veal shoulder doesn't hold together well, and you could end up with a frustrating jumble of meat and stuffing. If you cut and serve a portion at a time, however, you can make sure each slice arrives at its intended recipient's place as a neat medallion, with the brilliantly colored stuffing intact in the center of each slice.

Glazed Sweetbreads with Capers, Smoked Ham, and Pecans

S weetbreads are easy to love. With a texture like silken dumplings and a mild flavor reminiscent of nuts or mushrooms, what's not to like? Sweetbreads are the thymus glands of young animals. In this country, they almost always come from calves, but in Europe it's not unusual to find lamb and even pork sweetbreads. They take to the same rich sauces that the French and Italians typically reserve for their finest cuts of veal—wine, cream, Cognac, wild mushrooms, and truffles. In this recipe, the sweetbreads' own flavor contrasts with the tastes of balsamic vinegar and pecans, instead of drowning in a pool of luxury.

Preparing sweetbreads seems complicated because several different steps over several days are involved, but the process is simple: soaking the sweetbreads to remove any residual blood, poaching, weighting (see box), marinating, and then searing them in a sauté pan. Poach the sweetbreads a day ahead of serving. On the day of serving, marinate the sweetbreads for 2 to 3 hours before the final sauté.

MAKES 4 ENTRÉE SERVINGS

2 pounds fresh veal sweetbreads

POACHING LIQUID
1 celery stalk, chopped into ½-inch pieces
1 small white onion, chopped into ½-inch dice
2½ cups water
1 cup dry white wine
2 bay leaves
½ teaspoon dried thyme
10 black peppercorns
1 teaspoon mustard seeds
Kosher salt

MARINADE
½ cup balsamic vinegar
¼ cup honey
¼ cup soy sauce
2 tablespoons Dijon mustard

2 tablespoons chopped white onion
2 teaspoons cracked black pepper

¼ cup olive oil
Kosher salt and freshly ground black pepper

SAUCE
1 medium red onion, sliced ¼ inch thick
2 garlic cloves, finely chopped
2 cups dry sherry
½ teaspoon chopped fresh rosemary
4 cups Chicken Stock (page 31) or 8 cups high-quality canned low-sodium chicken broth, reduced to 4 cups (see page 32)
2 tablespoons capers, rinsed
4 thin slices Black Forest ham (or good-quality smoked ham), sliced into 1½-inch-wide strips
¼ cup pecans, toasted and chopped in half crosswise

2 to 4 teaspoons unsalted butter

Kosher salt and freshly ground black pepper

1. A couple of days before you intend to serve them, soak the sweetbreads in cold water for 8 hours to remove any residual blood, changing the water 5 times. With each change, the water should become less cloudy, until the water in the final soaking remains clear. They are now ready to poach.

2. To make the poaching liquid, combine the celery, onion, water, white wine, bay leaves, thyme, peppercorns, and mustard seeds in a large saucepan and bring to a boil, then lower the heat and simmer for 5 minutes. Season with salt. Taste the liquid—the salt should be evident. Add the sweetbreads and poach until semifirm, 15 to 20 minutes, depending on the size of the lobe. Drain. Discard the poaching liquid.

3. After the sweetbreads have cooled, use a paring knife to remove the exterior membrane. Don't try to remove every speck of membrane—if you're too meticulous, the lobes of the sweetbreads will fall apart. Cut the peeled sweetbreads into 8 pieces and refrigerate until ready to marinate.

4. Two to 3 hours before serving, marinate the trimmed pieces: Mix all the marinade ingredients in a nonreactive container large enough to hold the sweetbreads. Add the sweetbreads, turning to coat. Marinate in the refrigerator.

5. Heat 2 tablespoons olive oil in a large sauté pan over medium-high heat. Add the red onion and cook until translucent. Add the garlic and cook just until the garlic releases its aroma, just a minute. Add the sherry and cook until it reduces to a glaze, about 20 minutes. Add the rosemary and chicken stock. Continue cooking until it reduces to ¾ cup, about 30 minutes.

6. Add the capers, ham, and pecans to the sauce and cook for 1 minute. Whisk in the butter. Taste and adjust the seasoning. Keep warm.

7. Heat the remaining 2 tablespoons of the olive oil in a large sauté pan over high heat. Dry the sweetbreads and season with salt and pepper. Brown the sweetbreads on all sides until crispy.

8. Transfer the sweetbreads to the pan with the sauce to heat through. Serve immediately.

TO WEIGHT OR NOT TO WEIGHT

Traditional recipes often call for sweetbreads to be flattened under a weighted dish after poaching. Otherwise, so the reasoning goes, their texture will be spongy. I've never found this to be the case. The only advantage to flattening sweetbreads is that they're slightly easier to sauté, and this seems hardly worth the trouble. To decide for yourself, poach the sweetbreads and then arrange them in a single layer in a shallow pan or dish. Place a second pan on top of the sweetbreads, pressing down directly on the sweetbreads. Weight the pan with 3 pounds of cans. Allow the sweetbreads to rest, weighted, for at least 8 hours in the refrigerator while they flatten, then marinate them and proceed with the recipe.

Roasted Spice-Rubbed Pork with Greens, Rice, Black Beans, and Lime

A t *Red Clay, our second* restaurant, we wanted to offer a menu of classic comfort food from around the world baked in glazed clay pots. In this recipe, four simple preparations—roast pork, black beans, bitter greens, and plain white rice—are cooked separately, then assembled and heated together. Latin cultures bring beans, rice, and pork together in dozens of different ways. For me, nothing beats the combination of black beans, lime, and rum, and I adore pork butt. Although much has been made of the health benefits of lean pork, pork butt is one of the few parts of today's lean pig that tastes the way pork should taste—rich, flavorful, and tender.

The most challenging aspect of the recipe is simply remembering you've got to get started on this dish a day or two before serving it. If I'm planning a midday Sunday dinner, I marinate the pork on Friday night. Sometime on Saturday, I roast the pork. While the pork is roasting, I make the beans, greens, and rice, all simple preparations. On Sunday, all I have to do is assemble the dish and heat it.

Just remember that you'll need a 3-quart glazed clay pot or ceramic casserole. The recipe is easily doubled, but use two 3-quart casseroles for the final assembly instead of trying to heat everything in a single large pot. This is a joy for leftovers. Everything will keep for a couple of days if refrigerated. Cover tightly and reheat in a 375°F oven for 20 minutes.

MAKES 4 ENTRÉE SERVINGS

SPICE RUB
2 tablespoons coriander seeds
2 teaspoons cumin seeds
2 tablespoons fennel seeds
2 tablespoons mustard seeds
1 tablespoon ground ginger
1 tablespoon paprika
1 teaspoon cayenne pepper
2 tablespoons brown sugar
2 teaspoons freshly ground black pepper
1 tablespoon grated orange zest

PORK
One 2½-pound pork butt (Boston butt) roast
Kosher salt

¼ cup freshly squeezed lime juice
1 lime, scrubbed and cut into quarters
½ cup Chicken Stock (page 31), or high-quality,
    low-sodium canned broth, as needed

BLACK BEANS
1 cup dried black beans, picked over for stones and
    broken beans and rinsed
1 teaspoon cumin seeds
1 teaspoon coriander seeds
2 tablespoons vegetable oil
1 medium white onion, chopped into ¼-inch dice
6 garlic cloves, coarsely chopped
½ cup crushed tomatoes, canned or fresh
3 jalapeño peppers, stemmed, seeded, and minced

1 tablespoon dried oregano

¼ cup dark rum

Kosher salt and freshly ground black pepper

3 tablespoons freshly squeezed lime juice

½ cup chopped fresh cilantro

GREENS

2 pounds mustard greens or broccoli rabe, washed and trimmed of tough stems

1 tablespoon vegetable oil

6 garlic cloves, finely chopped

Kosher salt and freshly ground black pepper

4 cups cooked white rice

GARNISH

1 cup Fresh Tomato Salsa (page 331)

1 lime, cut into quarters

4 sprigs cilantro

DO AHEAD: Marinate the pork for at least 12 hours; longer is fine.

FOR THE PORK

1. Toast the coriander, cumin, fennel, and mustard seeds in a dry pan over low heat until they start to pop and are aromatic. Remove from the heat. When they are cool, grind them in a spice mill or with a mortar and pestle.

2. Combine the ground toasted spices with the remaining spice rub ingredients. Rub the spice mixture over the entire pork butt. You will have a good deal of leftover spice rub; set it aside until needed. Cover the pork and allow to marinate for 12 hours in the refrigerator.

3. Preheat the oven to 325°F.

4. Sprinkle the pork all over with salt and rub with the lime juice. Place the butt in a small baking pan (about 9 × 9 inches). There should only be 1 to 2 inches of space between the pork and the sides of the pan. (A small pan will help prevent the water and accumulated pork juices from simply boiling away. You want the pork to braise, not dry-roast.) Add ⅛ inch of water and the quartered lime to the pan. Cover with foil, crimping the edges over the sides of the pan to form a tight seal. Cook for 2 hours.

5. Remove the pan from the oven. Carefully peel back the foil and flip the pork. Set aside 1 tablespoon of the extra spice rub, and sprinkle the remainder over the pork. Sprinkle with salt. Replace the foil, return the pork to the oven, and braise for 2 more hours, or until the meat is very tender and falls apart when prodded with a fork. Remove from the oven and increase the oven temperature to 450°F.

6. Remove the pork from the pan. Discard the limes. Pour the braising juices into a nonreactive container and skim off the fat. You should have about 1 cup braising juices; if you have less, make up the difference with chicken stock. Refrigerate the juices until needed.

7. Return the pork to the pan and roast, uncovered, until the exterior is a crispy brown, another 15 to 20 minutes. Let cool, then cut into 1-inch slices.

FOR THE BEANS

8. Put the beans in a large pot, cover with cold water by 1 inch, and bring to a boil. Remove from the heat, cover, and allow to sit for 1 hour. Drain.

9. While the beans are soaking, toast the cumin and coriander seeds in a dry pan over low heat until they start to pop and are aromatic. Remove from the heat and set aside.

10. Heat the vegetable oil in a large saucepan over medium heat. Add the onion and cook until it begins to brown. Add the garlic and cook for 3 minutes. Add the beans, tomatoes, jalapeños, cumin and coriander seeds, and oregano. Add enough water to cover the beans by 2 inches. Bring to a boil, reduce the heat to medium-low, and cook until the beans are tender, about 1½ hours. Make sure the water level stays ½ inch above the beans until the end of the cooking time nears. Stir regularly.

11. By the time the beans have finished cooking, the water should be almost all absorbed. Add the rum and cook for 10 minutes. Season with salt and allow the beans to cool in their cooking liquid. When cool, drain (there won't be much liquid), taste, and add more salt if necessary. Season with black pepper, then add the lime juice and cilantro.

FOR THE GREENS

12. Bring a large pot of salted water to a boil. Prepare a large bowl of ice water. Drop the greens into the boiling water. If using mustard greens, cook for 3 minutes; if using broccoli rabe, cook for 4 minutes. Drain, plunge the greens into the ice water to stop the cooking, and drain again.

13. Combine the oil and garlic in a small sauté pan over medium heat and cook until the garlic becomes aromatic, about a minute. Add the greens and toss to coat with the garlic and oil. Season with salt and pepper. Remove from the heat.

TO ASSEMBLE THE DISH

14. Preheat the oven to 450°F.

15. Spread the rice in the bottom of a 3-quart clay pot or casserole. Spoon the beans over the rice, then top with the greens. Make a final layer of the sliced pork. Pour ½ to 1 cup of the reserved braising juices over everything. The object is to use enough liquid to moisten everything and provide a firmer-than-soupy consistency without everything literally swimming in braising juices. Sprinkle the pork with salt and the reserved tablespoon of spice rub.

16. Cover with foil and bake for 15 minutes, then uncover and continue baking until heated through and bubbling, another 20 to 30 minutes.

17. To serve, top with the salsa, lime wedges, and cilantro sprigs.

Fresh Tomato Salsa

MAKES 1 CUP

½ pound ripe plum tomatoes, peeled (see page 55), seeded, and chopped into ½-inch dice

¼ cup finely diced red onion

1 garlic clove, minced

1 serrano or jalapeño pepper, stemmed, seeded, and finely chopped

1 to 2 tablespoons chopped fresh cilantro

Kosher salt and freshly ground black pepper

2 to 3 teaspoons freshly squeezed lime juice

Combine the tomato, onion, garlic, and chopped pepper. Add the cilantro to taste. Season with salt, pepper, and 1 teaspoon of lime juice. Taste, adding more lime juice if you like. Cover and refrigerate at least 3 hours. Refrigerated fresh salsa will keep for 24 hours.

Desserts

❧

This is a savory cook's—not a pastry cook's—collection of desserts. Savory cooking is flexible; you can often compensate for mistakes without having to jettison all of your previous efforts. Sauces are recouped, soups redeemed, life sails on. Fine pastry, on the other hand, is a pitiless art, akin to high-altitude mountaineering, where a single misstep can end the project. Understandably, the most ardent pastry chefs are control freaks. Impressive and satisfying as handmade mille-feuille with a spun sugar garnish may be in a restaurant, when I'm cooking at home, I'm looking for ease of preparation as much as great flavor.

I've sifted through menus from Michela's and Rialto, as well as family favorites, for desserts in the spirit of my own savory cooking—that is, they're all a little bit forgiving. Nevertheless, the recipes encompass a broad range of circumstances, with some appropriate for formal dinner parties, and others making happy conclusions to family meals and even tagging along on picnics.

The chapter opens with a trio of sweet fruit endings: Grilled Pineapple with Rum, Lime-Ginger Syrup, and Ice Cream; Fresh Fruit with Balsamic Pepper Syrup; and Roasted Pears with 5-Spice Zabaglione. All three are easy, and once you've tasted grilled pineapple, it becomes hard not to have a summer backyard dinner without considering it as the dessert of choice.

The elegant, formal appearance of Chocolate Espresso Torta and Hot Chocolate Creams from

Provence belie their straightforward preparation. Both are rich, intensely chocolate treats with distinctly different characters. The torta offers a dense, silken response to lovers of unadulterated dark chocolate; the hot chocolate creams hover somewhere between cake and soufflé, served comfortingly warm.

Individual Peppered Peach Tarts with Ginger-Caramel Sauce introduce a section of simple pastries requiring only the most basic skills. Given my druthers, I generally choose tarts over any other dessert. I love the textural contrast of crust, custard, and caramelized fruit. If you can make a basic pastry crust and simple custard, you're capable of dozens of different desserts. In addition to several tarts (my favorite is the Mascarpone Fig), the pastry section includes fruit and nut butter cakes and a couple of desserts that make fine accompaniments to picnics—Ginger Shortbread and Sweet Grape Focaccia.

The desserts conclude with my own family's comfort food favorites, Crema Spessa, the Italian version of baked custard, and Super-Creamy Rice Pudding with Passion Fruit Sauce. I'm a peasant at heart, and these are about as simple and rustic as you can get.

Grilled Pineapple with Rum, Lime-Ginger Syrup, and Ice Cream

Pineapple's firm texture and high sugar content make it an ideal candidate for the grill. Be sure to buy a pineapple that is already ripe—the fruit does a poor job of ripening on the kitchen counter. The spiced syrup involves little more challenge than assembling the ingredients and heating them together. The result is an elegant dessert with almost no effort.

MAKES 4 SERVINGS

SYRUP
1 cup water
⅔ cup sugar
Grated zest and juice of 1 lime
Grated zest of 1 orange
2 bay leaves
¼ teaspoon freshly ground black pepper
2 teaspoons minced fresh ginger
½ vanilla bean, split lengthwise
2 star anise

1 ripe pineapple
2 tablespoons grapeseed oil or other mild-tasting
    vegetable oil
¼ cup dark rum
4 scoops rum, vanilla, or coconut ice cream
2 tablespoons fresh mint leaves cut into very thin
    strips, for garnish

1. Combine all the syrup ingredients in a non-reactive saucepan over medium heat. Bring to a boil, then lower the heat to a simmer and cook for 20 minutes. Remove from the heat. Remove the vanilla bean and allow it to cool. When cool enough to handle, scrape the seeds into the syrup. Discard the pod or save for another use.

2. Prepare a medium fire in a grill. (A grill is medium when you can hold your hand close to the cooking surface for a count of 4 before having to pull it away.)

3. Chop off the pineapple flower (the sprout of spiky leaves) and the top inch or so of the fruit. Cut a slice off the bottom of the pineapple so it will stand upright. Slice off the skin in long vertical strips. If there are any "eyes" remaining, cut them out with a paring knife or potato peeler. If you have a pineapple corer, use it to remove the core, then lay the fruit on its side and cut eight ½-inch-thick slices. If you don't have a corer, just turn the pineapple on its side and cut the 8 slices, then use a paring knife or cookie cutter to remove the woody core at the center of each slice. (Reserve any remaining pineapple for another use.)

4. Brush the pineapple rings with the oil and grill on both sides until lightly charred, about 5 minutes per side.

5. Arrange 2 pineapple rings on each plate. Pour a tablespoon of rum over each set of rings, then drizzle with the spiced syrup. Add a scoop of ice cream to each plate. Sprinkle with the strips of mint and serve.

Fresh Fruit with Balsamic Pepper Syrup

Where would we be without balsamic vinegar? I can still remember my teenage incredulity when a cooking teacher prefaced my first taste with the explanation that it was often served over strawberries. All it took was one taste of a fine ten-year-old sample to erase my skepticism. This dish should really be prepared only a couple of hours before serving. Raspberries and strawberries are particularly fragile and they will turn mushy if cut and allowed to sit in the syrup too far ahead.

Ordinarily people jettison macerated fruit after a night in the refrigerator because its texture deteriorates, but we love smoothies for breakfast, especially with whole-milk Greek yogurt. So I always save these leftovers—somebody will purée them into breakfast the next day.

MAKES 4 SERVINGS

3 tablespoons balsamic vinegar

¼ cup packed brown sugar

2 teaspoons freshly ground black pepper (use a little less if you prefer a milder dish)

2 bananas

1 pint fresh strawberries, washed, hulled, and halved lengthwise

1 pint fresh raspberries

1. Mix the vinegar, brown sugar, and pepper together in a medium bowl.

2. Peel the bananas and cut into ½-inch-thick slices. Add all the fruit to the bowl with the syrup and toss gently to coat. Let sit for 15 minutes, then serve.

Roasted Pears with 5-Spice Zabaglione

Zabaglione, a delightful whipped froth of egg yolks, sugar, and Marsala, can be served as a sauce or a dessert in its own right. Traditional recipes call for it to be served warm, right after it's made, but I sometimes like to thicken it a bit by adding some cream and chilling it.

This particular dessert evolved out of my experience writing Sunday night menus with Gordon Hammersley at his restaurant, Hammersley's Bistro. On Sunday nights, we served a special abbreviated menu, so desserts had to be quick, easy, and flavorful; roasted fruit with zabaglione was ideal. Gordon is a big fan of Chinese 5-spice powder—cinnamon, cloves, fennel seed, star anise, and Szechwan peppercorns—and I happen to like incorporating savory ingredients into sweet desserts. The result is both sensuous and exotic.

MAKES 4 SERVINGS

ZABAGLIONE
4 extra-large egg yolks, at room temperature
¼ cup sugar
½ cup Marsala
1 teaspoon 5-spice powder
Pinch of kosher salt
½ cup heavy cream

PEARS
4 ripe Bosc pears
2 teaspoons freshly squeezed lemon juice
½ cup sugar
4 tablespoons unsalted butter

DO AHEAD: Roast the pears a day or two in advance and reheat in a 400° oven for 5 to 7 minutes before serving; the zabaglione is also fine if made a day ahead.

1. Beat the egg yolks, sugar, Marsala, 5-spice powder, and salt together in a medium metal bowl until smooth. Set the bowl over low heat and whisk vigorously until the mixture is thick, foamy, and pale yellow in color, about 10 minutes. If there is the slightest hint that the eggs are cooking rather than just foaming, remove from the heat and keep beating. If you're uncomfortable setting the bowl directly over the heat source, place it over a pot of simmering water (don't let the bottom of the bowl touch the water). Remove from the heat and refrigerate until thoroughly chilled, at least an hour. Then stir in the cream and chill again at least 15 minutes. While the zabaglione is chilling, you can roast the pears.

2. Preheat the oven to 450°F.

3. Peel the pears and cut them in half. Toss with the lemon juice and sugar.

4. Cut the butter into 8 pieces and place in the smallest baking pan you have that will hold the pears comfortably, but without touching. (Don't put the pears in it yet.) Place the roasting pan in the oven until the butter melts, about 3 minutes; don't let it burn. Remove the pan from the oven. Roll the pears around in the pan until they're evenly coated with butter (reserve any leftover lemon-sugar mixture). Arrange them cut side down in the pan in a single layer without touching and sprinkle with any remaining lemon-sugar.

5. Set the pan on the lowest rack in the oven. Roast for 20 minutes. Flip the pears and continue cooking until caramelized to a deep golden color, about another 20 minutes. Remove from the pan. Remove the cores as soon as the pears are cool enough to handle, but keep the cored pears warm.

6. Place 2 pear halves on each plate. Spoon the zabaglione liberally over the pears and serve.

Chocolate Espresso Torta

Every chef has three or four recipes that haunt her, following her wherever she goes, refusing to change. Ironically, one of my culinary ghosts is a recipe I inherited when I became a chef at Michela's, a dense flourless chocolate torta that had been developed by one of the restaurant's previous pastry chefs. When Michela's closed, loyal clientele followed Michela Larson and me to our new restaurant, Rialto, demanding their old favorites, including the espresso torta. One customer, who eats at Rialto every Wednesday night, wrote me so many adamant notes that I finally threw in the towel and we now keep one or two tortas on hand just for diehards like him, even though the torta is no longer on our dessert menu. Don't fiddle with the recipe—believe me, we've tried—it really can't be improved on. Just be sure to use premium chocolate and espresso.

The torta keeps for 3 to 4 days in the refrigerator, although it should be brought up to room temperature before serving. It will keep for up to a month in the freezer.

MAKES 12 TO 16 SERVINGS

¾ pound (3 sticks) plus 1 tablespoon unsalted butter, or as needed

1 cup sugar

1 cup plus 2 tablespoons espresso or very strong brewed coffee

¾ pound semisweet chocolate, chopped into 1-inch pieces

¼ pound unsweetened chocolate, chopped into 1-inch pieces

6 extra-large eggs, at room temperature

6 extra-large yolks, at room temperature

2 tablespoons cocoa powder for garnish

Vanilla or coffee ice cream (optional)

DO AHEAD: Make the torta batter (minus the eggs, which are added the next day) and allow it to sit covered and refrigerated for 12 hours. (It can sit overnight.) Since the cake is actually better if allowed to rest for a day before serving, start the torta 2 days ahead.

1. Melt ¾ pound of the butter with the sugar and espresso in a nonreactive saucepan over low heat. Add the chocolate and stir until completely melted. Do not let the mixture boil, or the chocolate will separate and seize up. Whisk off the heat until the mixture is smooth and shiny. Let stand, covered, for at least 12 hours, or overnight, at room temperature. After standing, it should have the consistency of peanut butter.

2. Preheat the oven to 350°F. Cut a circle of parchment paper to fit the bottom of a 9-inch cake pan. Grease the pan with as much of the remaining butter as needed, and line it with the

circle of parchment paper, pressing the paper firmly onto the bottom of the pan.

3. Beat the eggs and egg yolks together in a large bowl until just mixed—not until foamy. Stir in the chocolate mixture. Pour the batter into the lined pan.

4. Put the cake pan in the middle of a roasting pan. Pour enough warm water into the pan to come halfway up the sides of the cake pan. Bake in the middle of the oven until the batter is almost set—it should still be slightly wiggly in the center—about 1 hour. Cool on a rack. If possible, allow the torta to rest overnight in the refrigerator.

5. When cool or chilled, remove the torta from the pan, invert it onto a serving platter, and carefully peel away the parchment paper. Invert it onto a serving platter. Sift a thin even layer of cocoa over the torta just before serving. Accompany with ice cream, if you like.

Hot Chocolate Creams from Provence

I *first encountered this unctuous Provençal* indulgence on a trip to France. I was instantly seduced by its wonderful gamut of textures, the crusty outside yielding to a warm creamy interior, as though chocolate had been given the texture of a soft-ripening cheese. Soon after my return, I tried a recipe in a cookbook of traditional Provençal cooking by Jean-André Charial-Thuilier. Ultimately I came up with a version that calls for about as much chocolate as the recipe can handle and still produce the spectrum of textures. It is far and away the most popular dessert I've ever served at Rialto—and it's a breeze to make.

MAKES 4 SERVINGS

9 tablespoons unsalted butter

2 teaspoons unbleached all-purpose flour

½ pound semisweet chocolate, chopped into 1-inch
   pieces

4 extra-large eggs, at room temperature

6 tablespoons sugar

DO AHEAD: You can make the chocolate mixture a day ahead; prepare the mixture as instructed, then refrigerate. Let come up to room temperature before continuing with the recipe.

1. Preheat the oven to 400°F. Grease four 4-ounce ramekins with 1 tablespoon of the butter and then dust each one with ½ teaspoon flour.

2. Melt the chocolate with the remaining 8 tablespoons butter in a small saucepan over low heat. As soon as the chocolate starts to melt, remove from the heat and beat until the mixture is smooth. (If making ahead, cover and refrigerate the mixture, for as long as overnight. Allow it to come up to room temperature before continuing.)

3. Beat the eggs in a large bowl with the sugar until the sugar dissolves and the eggs are foamy. Fold the chocolate mixture into the eggs.

4. Pour the chocolate mixture into the prepared ramekins. Bake for 12 minutes, or until just set—the centers will still be slightly liquid. Let stand for 3 to 4 minutes, then turn them out onto warm plates and serve.

Peppered Peach Tarts
with Ginger-Caramel Sauce

My husband and I used to shun peaches. Ripe peaches are quite fragile—they travel poorly unless properly packaged—and about fifteen years ago, it seemed that almost overnight mealy peach impersonators had supplanted the luscious fruit that had been available in supermarkets. In Europe, peaches are sold either ripe or within a day or two of ripening, but these new hybrids were sold when still quite hard. While it is not true that peaches have to ripen on the tree, not all peaches ripen at home equally well. Many rot before ripening or lose their moisture or just have little taste—all of which seems remarkably similar to the fate of the American tomato. In recent years, however, the growth of farmers' markets has provided an outlet for peaches that don't have to travel. They still aren't sold ripe, so we keep them in a closed shoe box under the kitchen table, letting them ripen almost to the point of collapse before eating them, but they do taste good. New England peaches are smaller than those grown in the South or Southwest, but, like a lot of things in life, size isn't everything. When I can't get farmers' market peaches, I use organic or "tree-ripened" ones.

Peaches and black pepper are a great match, a fact I discovered while grilling them with pork and searing them with rabbit, and I decided to try the same combination in a dessert. Adding black pepper to a classic peach tart gives the dessert an exotic flavor reminiscent of chutney, while the caramel sauce and whipped cream don't let you forget that you're eating a sweet dessert.

MAKES 4 SERVINGS

TARTS
4 ripe peaches
⅓ cup plus 4 teaspoons sugar
4 teaspoons unbleached all-purpose flour, plus extra for rolling out the dough
2 teaspoons freshly ground black pepper
1 recipe Basic Pastry Dough (recipe follows)
4 teaspoons unsalted butter

SAUCE
½ cup sugar
2 tablespoons water
1 tablespoon finely chopped fresh ginger
1 tablespoon unsalted butter
½ cup heavy cream

½ cup heavy cream for whipped cream garnish

1. Bring a large pot of water to a boil. Prepare a large bowl of ice water. Dip the peaches into the boiling water for 10 seconds—no longer. If they cook longer, the flesh will begin to bind with the skin, and peeling the peaches will become a nightmare. Immediately immerse the peaches in the ice water.

2. When they are cool enough to handle, drain and dry the peaches, then peel them. Cut in half and remove the pits. Cut each peach half into 4 slices. Gently toss the peaches with ⅓ cup of the sugar, the flour, and pepper. Set aside.

3. Cut the dough into 4 equal pieces and form into disks. Roll each one into a 6-inch circle about ¼ inch thick. Put the dough on the sheet pans. Arrange 8 peach slices on the dough, spoke-fashion, leaving a border of 1 inch. Pull up the edges of the dough around the peaches, and crimp. Dot each tart with 1 teaspoon of the butter and sprinkle with 1 teaspoon sugar. Chill the tarts for at least 30 minutes and up to 24 hours.

4. Preheat the oven to 400°F.

5. Arrange the tarts on a sheet pan (with sides, in case the juices run out during baking). Bake for 40 minutes, or until the peaches are tender and the crusts are golden and crisp. Allow to cool for 5 minutes on a wire rack.

6. While the tarts are baking, make the sauce: Mix the sugar with the water in a heavy saucepan. Add the ginger and cook over medium heat stirring with a metal spoon, until the sugar is golden and caramelized. Remove the pan from the heat and allow to cool for 30 seconds to avoid the possibility of splattering when you add the butter. Whisk in the butter, making sure it's thoroughly incorporated. Slowly whisk in ½ cup cream—if you add the cream too fast, the caramel may bubble over, and possibly burn you. Strain to remove the ginger, if desired. Set aside.

7. Whip the remaining ½ cup heavy cream in a medium bowl until it stiffens and holds its shape.

8. To serve, place each tart on a plate. Zigzag the caramel sauce over each tart and top with a dollop of whipped cream.

❧ Basic Pastry Dough ❧

I *love a good crust* almost more than whatever it's holding. My favorite part of a pie is the crimped edge of crust and the first inch or so, the top of the pie where the juices have caramelized into the dough. If there's a leftover pie on the kitchen counter when I come home late at night, I'm the one who nibbles at the edges.

Books have been written about pastry, but basically it's a hands-on activity that improves with experience. Even novices can make a decently flaky crust as long as three simple precautions are kept in mind. The chilled butter must be worked into the cold flour quickly so that the butter and flour can form layers; if the butter becomes too soft or (God forbid) melts, then it simply coats the particles of flour instead of forming layers with it. Second, the dough must be manipulated as little as possible so that the gluten fibers remain undeveloped. The more the gluten develops, the chewier the final product (hence, bread dough is kneaded purposely to develop the gluten). Finally, the water should be added as sparingly as possible; the more water, the heavier the dough—and the denser the pastry.

This is a good general-purpose recipe for either sweet or savory dough, depending on whether you use the sugar or not. The dough will keep for a couple of days in the refrigerator, and for several months in the freezer if tightly wrapped in plastic, then in foil.

MAKES ABOUT ¾ POUND; ENOUGH FOR ONE 10- TO 11-INCH PIECRUST OR ONE 11-INCH TART SHELL

1½ cups unbleached all-purpose flour, chilled
¾ teaspoon salt
2 tablespoons sugar (for sweet pastry dough)
9 tablespoons unsalted butter, cut into tablespoon-sized pieces and chilled
3 to 4 tablespoons ice water

1. Pour the flour into a mound on a countertop. Add the salt, and sugar, if you're making sweet pastry, and toss well. Work the butter into the flour with the tips of your fingers until the butter is in small pea-sized pieces. Add the water 2 tablespoons at a time, tossing with your fingers to incorporate the water into the dough. Add more as needed. The dough should be crumbly.

2. Form the dough into a mound and then, using the heel of your hand, gradually push all the dough away from you, flattening out the lumps. Continue until all the dough is flat. Form the dough into a mound and repeat the process one more time. Do not work the butter completely into the mixture—the streaks of butter are what will make the crust flaky.

3. Shape the dough into a disk, wrap in plastic, and refrigerate at least 1 hour to allow it to rest before using.

Blind Baking—
Prebaking Piecrusts and Tart Shells

Prebaking a piecrust or tart shell without the filling is called "blind baking." By baking the crust ahead of time, you avoid the problem of a juicy filling soaking into the raw pastry dough and preventing it from cooking thoroughly.

1 recipe Basic Pastry Dough (page 343)

1. Place the dough on a floured pastry board, countertop, or plastic pastry sheet and roll it out to the desired size. Be sure to roll the dough to an even thickness, or the thinner parts of the crust will burn when baking.

2. Carefully fold the dough in quarters, transfer to the pie plate or tart pan, and unfold. Ease the dough into the corners of the pan; if you stretch it, it will tear. Pull the dough up over the edge of the pie plate or tin so it hangs over by about 1 inch. Then roll it to rest just over the edge and crimp the edge decoratively. The dough will shrink a bit as it bakes, so this slight overhang will help it from falling to the bottom. Put the crust into the fridge for at least 30 min-utes or the freezer for 15 minutes. Chilling will help to keep the dough from shrinking.

3. Preheat the oven to 400°F.

4. Line the dough with baking parchment or foil and then fill with weights. You can use uncooked beans, rice, ball bearings, loose change, or the marble-shaped ceramic pie weights designed specifically for this pur-pose. The point is to fill the pan with some-thing that will keep the dough flat when it bakes.

5. Bake in the center of the oven for 15 minutes. Carefully remove the foil and weights. If the edges of the crust have already started to brown, cover them with foil. Continue baking until the crust is golden brown, about 8 min-utes. Let the crust cool on a wire rack.

Pumpkin and Apple Tart

As soon as a holiday food tradition begins to feel oppressive, it's time to give it a rest, if only temporarily. I love pumpkin pie, but I've grown to prefer it during pumpkin season in late October and early November rather than waiting until Thanksgiving (if I were king, Thanksgiving would be in October, but that's another story). By then, the experience of baking several dozen pies for charity has pretty much blunted whatever appeal a straightforward pumpkin pie might hold for me, and my dessert receptors are looking for a new thrill. This is a New England riff on a traditional Norman apple tart. Instead of the almond cream in the original, the tart uses pumpkin custard; the apples lend a slightly acidic quality, and amaretti crumbs add a little bit of crunch. It's an altogether sharper, lighter dessert that still tastes like comfort food, a necessary element for any holiday tradition.

MAKES ONE 11-INCH TART

2 large baking apples, such as Macoun

¼ cup plus 1 tablespoon granulated sugar

2 teaspoons ground cinnamon

1½ tablespoons freshly squeezed lemon juice

2 tablespoons unsalted butter, melted

3 extra-large eggs, at room temperature

1 cup packed dark brown sugar

2 cups pumpkin purée

1 cup heavy cream, at room temperature

½ teaspoon ground ginger

¼ teaspoon ground allspice

½ teaspoon freshly ground black pepper

1 tablespoon grated fresh ginger

1 teaspoon kosher salt

1 teaspoon vanilla extract

One 11-inch tart shell made with Basic Pastry Dough (page 343) and prebaked in a tin with a removable bottom (see page 344)

4 Italian amaretti macaroons, roughly crumbled

Whipped cream or premium vanilla ice cream (optional)

DO AHEAD: Make the dough and prebake the crust a couple of hours before assembling the tart. Allow time for all of the filling ingredients to come to room temperature before you use them, or the pumpkin custard won't blend properly.

1. Preheat the oven to 400°F.

2. Peel and core the apples, then cut them into ⅛-inch-thick slices. Toss the apple slices in a bowl with ¼ cup of the granulated sugar, ½ teaspoon of the cinnamon, ½ tablespoon of the lemon juice, and the melted butter.

3. Beat the eggs and brown sugar together in a large bowl until the sugar is completely dissolved and the eggs are foamy. Add the pumpkin, cream, the remaining 1½ teaspoons cinnamon, the ground ginger, allspice, pepper, the grated ginger, salt, the remaining 1 tablespoon lemon juice, and the vanilla and beat together until thoroughly mixed. Pour the pumpkin custard into the tart shell. Starting at

the outside of the tart, arrange the apple slices in overlapping concentric rings, covering the custard completely. Sprinkle the apples with the remaining 1 tablespoon sugar.

4. Bake until the custard is set and the apples are tender and caramelized, about 1 hour. Discreetly lift an apple near the center of the tart and insert a knife into the pumpkin custard. When the custard is set, the knife will emerge moist but clean. You can broil the tart briefly if the apples haven't caramelized enough. Cool on a wire rack.

5. When the tart is cool, remove the sides of the tart tin. Just before serving, sprinkle with the amaretti crumbs. Serve with whipped cream or vanilla ice cream, if desired.

NOTE: Tart shells, with their exposed sides, seem much prettier to me than ordinary piecrusts, where the dessert often seems sunken into a pie plate. If you find piecrust easier, or you don't have access to a tart tin with a removable metal ring, you can make this recipe in a prebaked 10-inch piecrust. Add a few minutes to the pie's cooking time because of the greater depth of the custard.

Heather's Cranberry Chocolate Pecan Tart

Heather Miller was my pastry chef for many years, and when she married and moved out of town, I lost a great talent. She invented this revisionist version of a Southern classic for one of our winter menus. The addition of chocolate and cranberries are unexpected accents to this otherwise familiar flavor.

MAKE ONE 11-INCH TART

1 ounce bittersweet chocolate, coarsely chopped

2 cups pecan halves, toasted (see page 16)

½ cup dried cranberries

One 11-inch tart shell made with Basic Pastry Dough (page 343) and prebaked in a tin with removable sides (see page 344)

4 extra-large eggs, at room temperature

1¼ cups packed dark brown sugar

¾ cup light corn syrup

¼ cup molasses

6 tablespoons unsalted butter, melted

1 teaspoon vanilla extract

¼ cup dark rum

½ teaspoon kosher salt

DO AHEAD: Make the dough and prebake the crust a couple of hours before assembling the tart.

1. Preheat the oven to 325°F.

2. Distribute the chocolate, pecans, and cranberries evenly in the tart shell.

3. Beat the eggs in a large bowl until foamy. Add the remaining ingredients and beat until the sugar dissolves and everything is well blended. Pour the mixture into the tart shell.

4. Bake until set, 35 to 40 minutes. Allow to cool for at least 30 minutes on a wire rack.

5. When the tart is cool, remove the sides of the tart tin and serve.

Mascarpone Fig Tart

F igs come into season in August, at the end of our family vacation, when the start of school and return to work loom just around the corner. I associate figs with sun and water and the sadness of saying goodbye. With their honey-like flavor, fresh figs require little enhancement. This is a rustic French-style tart that uses mascarpone as the base of a mild custard rather than cream.

MAKES ONE 11-INCH TART

8 fresh figs (about 1½ ounces each), stems removed and cut in half lengthwise

Grated zest and juice of 1 orange

3 extra-large eggs, at room temperature

¾ cup packed dark brown sugar

8 ounces (1 cup) mascarpone

Juice of 1 lemon

1 tablespoon unbleached all-purpose flour

½ teaspoon kosher salt

One 11-inch prebaked tart shell made with Basic Pastry Dough (page 343) and prebaked in a tin with removable sides (see page 344)

¼ cup hazelnuts, toasted and coarsely chopped (see page 16)

2 tablespoon confectioners' sugar, or as needed

DO AHEAD: Make the dough and prebake the crust a couple of hours before assembling the tart.

1. Toss the figs in a bowl with the orange zest and juice and allow to macerate for 30 minutes.

2. Preheat the oven to 400°F.

3. Beat the eggs in a large bowl with the sugar until the sugar dissolves and the eggs are thick. Add the mascarpone, lemon juice, flour, and salt and mix well.

4. Pour the custard into the tart shell. Remove the figs from the orange juice and drain well; discard or drink the juice. Arrange the figs cut side up in circles on top of the custard. Sprinkle with the hazelnuts.

5. Bake the tart on the lowest oven shelf for 10 minutes. Reduce the oven temperature to 350°F and bake for an additional 30 minutes, or until the custard is just set. It should still wiggle slightly in the middle. Cool on a wire rack for at least 30 minutes.

6. When the tart is cool, remove the sides of the pan, sift a light dusting of confectioners' sugar over the tart, and serve.

Prune Plum and Walnut Butter Cake

I'm a sucker for single-layer butter cakes, especially ones with fruit and nuts. Over the years, I must have tried a hundred different recipes and could never remember which I liked or which I had problems with. Finally I decided to sit down and figure out a recipe I could depend on. This is a great midsummer cake when prune plums (the small narrow plums that are turned into—surprise!—prunes) are available, but you can alter the recipe according to the available fruit—figs, regular plums, or peaches—as long as your choice is soft and ripe.

All the ingredients should be at room temperature except for the butter, which should be a little cooler (about 65°F).

MAKES 8 SERVINGS

9 tablespoons unsalted butter, at room temperature
1 cup plus 1 tablespoon unbleached all-purpose flour
12 prune plums, cut in half and pitted
1¼ cups sugar
¼ cup brandy
1 teaspoon grated lemon zest
½ teaspoon vanilla extract
1 teaspoon baking powder
½ teaspoon kosher salt
2 extra-large eggs, at room temperature
¼ cup ground toasted walnuts (see page 16)

1. Preheat the oven to 350°F. Grease a 9-inch springform pan with 1 tablespoon of the butter and dust it with 1 tablespoon of the flour.

2. Toss the prunes with 2 tablespoons of the sugar and the brandy; set aside.

3. Cream the remaining 8 tablespoons butter in a large bowl with 1 cup of the sugar, the lemon zest, and vanilla until light and fluffy. Sift the remaining 1 cup flour, the baking powder, and salt together and beat into the creamed butter.

4. In a separate bowl, beat the eggs until they start to foam. Do not overbeat, or the cake will be tough. Add the eggs and ground walnuts to the flour and butter mixture. Mix well.

5. Scrape the batter into the prepared pan. Arrange the plums on top in rings. Sprinkle with any remaining brandy-sugar syrup and the remaining 2 tablespoons sugar.

6. Bake for 1 hour, or until the cake is golden brown on top and a toothpick inserted into the cake (not the plums) comes out clean. Let cool for 10 minutes before removing the sides of the springform pan and serving.

Lemon-Almond Butter Cake

From the standpoint of technique, this cake seems almost identical to the Prune Plum and Walnut Butter Cake (page 349), but the substitution of homemade lemon curd for fresh fruit completely transforms its character. The fruit topping in the previous recipe moves it in the direction of a tart; here the lemon curd, cake, and whipped cream begin to operate like a fresher version of trifle, the traditional English dessert of strained fruit folded into ladyfingers or stale cake, where the juice from the fruit (or some sherry) revives the cake.

If you're in a hurry and can't spare 1½ hours for the lemon curd to cool in the refrigerator, you can shave some time from the recipe by chilling a bowl in the freezer. Strain the warm curd into the chilled bowl—it will cool faster.

All the ingredients should be at room temperature except for the butter, which should be a little cooler (about 65°F).

MAKES 8 SERVINGS

LEMON CURD
Grated zest and juice of 2 lemons
¾ cup plus 2 tablespoons sugar
4 extra-large eggs
6 tablespoons unsalted butter, cut into ½-inch cubes

CAKE
9 tablespoons unsalted butter
1 cup plus 1 tablespoon unbleached all-purpose flour
1 cup plus 1 to 2 tablespoons sugar
1 teaspoon baking powder
½ teaspoon kosher salt
2 extra-large eggs
½ cup ground toasted almonds (see page 16)
2 tablespoons sliced almonds, toasted (see page 16)

GARNISH
1 tablespoon almond liqueur (optional)
½ cup heavy cream (optional)
2 tablespoons confectioners' sugar

1. Combine the lemon zest and juice in a nonreactive saucepan with the sugar and eggs and beat well. Add the butter and cook over medium heat, stirring constantly with a rubber spatula or wooden spoon, until the sugar dissolves and the mixture thickens into curd. Be sure to keep scraping the bottom of the pan during the few minutes this takes; you don't want the eggs to scramble before the curd forms. If you're the nervous type, make the curd in a heatproof bowl over a pot of boiling water (the bottom of the bowl shouldn't touch the water). The curd will just take a little longer to thicken, about 5 minutes. Strain the curd into a bowl and press a piece of plastic wrap against the surface so a skin doesn't form. Refrigerate until cool, at least 1½ hours.

2. Preheat the oven to 350°F. Grease a 9-inch springform pan with 1 tablespoon of the butter and dust it with 1 tablespoon of the flour.

3. Cream the remaining 8 tablespoons butter in a large bowl with 1 cup of the sugar until light and fluffy. Sift the remaining 1 cup flour, the baking powder, and salt together and stir into the creamed butter.

4. In a separate bowl, beat the eggs until they start to foam. Do not overbeat, or the cake will be tough. Add the eggs and ground almonds to the flour and butter mixture, mixing well.

5. Scrape the batter into the prepared pan. Drop 8 individual tablespoons of lemon curd evenly around the outside of the cake, leaving a 1-inch border around the edge. Try to place the curd so there is an even amount of cake batter between each dollop of curd. Drop 3 tablespoons curd in the center. Refrigerate any remaining curd for another use (hint: breakfast toast). Sprinkle the top of the cake with the sliced almonds and 1 to 2 tablespoons sugar, according to taste.

6. Bake until the cake is toasty brown on top and a toothpick or knife inserted into the cake comes out clean (be sure not to insert it near the curd), about 40 minutes. Let cool for 10 minutes, then remove the sides of the springform pan and let cool completely on a wire rack.

7. If serving the cake with whipped cream, add the almond liqueur to the heavy cream and beat until the cream is stiff. Sift a thin, even layer of confectioners' sugar over the top of the cake.

8. Present the cake at the table, and offer the almond whipped cream on the side.

Sweet Grape Focaccia

With *focaccia as one of* the standard options in hip sandwich shops, in bread baskets, and even on supermarket bakery shelves, it's difficult to imagine that before the 1980s it was all but unknown outside Italian neighborhoods. Although focaccia is made from yeasted dough, just like pizza, it's generally presented as a flavored flat loaf of bread rather than as a crust with toppings. When I was chef at Michela's, I began experimenting with flatbread and sweet flavorings, especially grapes and chocolate. Not too long ago, someone pointed out a grape focaccia recipe to me in Carol Field's *Celebrating Italy*, which spoke of Tuscan vineyard workers pressing wine grapes into their own focaccia. (There really is nothing new under the sun.) This version makes a great picnic dessert—it's simple to make and travels well.

MAKES 8 TO 10 SERVINGS

2 pounds green and red seedless grapes, stems removed (or wine grapes, for a more intense flavor, if you don't mind the seeds)

¾ cup sugar

¾ teaspoon crushed fennel seeds

¼ teaspoon freshly ground black pepper

1 recipe Basic Pizza Dough (page 123), at room temperature

Flour for rolling out the dough

3 tablespoons extra virgin olive oil

1. Preheat the oven to 450°F.

2. Toss the grapes in a medium bowl with the sugar, fennel seeds, and pepper.

3. Place the dough on a lightly floured surface and roll it out into a rectangle, roughly the size of a 14 × 17-inch sheet pan, and ¼ inch thick. Rub a sheet pan with 1 tablespoon of the olive oil and transfer the dough to the pan. Rub the dough with the remaining 2 tablespoons olive oil. Dimple the dough with your fingertips.

4. Distribute the grapes evenly over the dough and sprinkle with any remaining sugar, fennel, and pepper.

5. Bake for 25 to 30 minutes. The focaccia should be caramelized around the edges and golden brown on the bottom. Allow to cool for 5 minutes before serving.

Ginger Shortbread

Aside from my introduction of ginger, this is a classic shortbread recipe. Because the flavors of butter and ginger are so unadulterated, shortbread is the ideal opportunity to exploit the taste of a fine unsalted European-style butter. The same is true of the ginger. Ground ginger ages rapidly, turning musty after a few months. Buy a small amount of freshly ground ginger at a whole-foods market for a bright sharp flavor. Shortbread will keep for 4 to 5 days in a tightly sealed container at room temperature and up to a month if frozen.

MAKES 4 SERVINGS

8 tablespoons (1 stick) high-quality unsalted butter, at cool room temperature (about 65°F)

⅓ cup sugar

1 teaspoon ground ginger

¼ teaspoon fine sea salt

1 cup unbleached all-purpose flour

1. Preheat the oven to 350°F.

2. Cream the butter in a large bowl with the sugar, ginger, and salt until light and fluffy. Stir in the flour until just combined. The dough will be quite stiff.

3. Press the dough into a 10-inch pie plate and smooth the top. Using the tines of a fork, prick a pattern into the dough, dividing the shortbread into 8 wedges.

4. Bake for 30 minutes, or until a toothpick inserted into the shortbread comes out clean and the shortbread is firm and lightly golden. While still warm, cut the wedges. Allow to cool.

Crema Spessa with Caramelized Raspberry Sauce

*C*rema spessa, literally, "thick cream" in Italian, is a rich baked custard with a silken, quivery texture. This is another recipe I inherited when I became the chef of Michela's, one of their dessert standards whose origins had been lost over the years. Northern Italians have historically had greater access to fresh dairy products than the inhabitants of the poorer South, and they use custard in all kinds of desserts, from the eggless panna cotta of Piedmont to tarts to this simple cream custard. In style, it's similar to a French crème brûlée—with a caramelized raspberry sauce instead of the caramelized sugar on top.

You can prepare the uncooked custard up to a day ahead. Remove from the refrigerator 30 minutes before baking so it comes to room temperature before entering the oven.

MAKES 4 SERVINGS

1 tablespoon unsalted butter for coating the ramekins

CREMA
2 cups heavy cream
¼ cup sugar
Pinch of kosher salt
1 small vanilla bean, split lengthwise in half
6 extra-large egg yolks, at room temperature

SAUCE
1½ cups fresh raspberries
1 cup sugar
2 tablespoons water, or as needed
1 to 2 teaspoons freshly squeezed lemon juice, as needed

GARNISH
¼ cup fresh raspberries
4 sprigs mint

1. Preheat the oven to 350°F. Butter four 4-ounce ramekins.

2. Mix the cream, sugar, and salt together in a large saucepan. Using a paring knife, scrape the sticky mass of tiny vanilla seeds out of the pod and into the pan. Take care to leave as few as possible on the knife blade, or on the sides of the saucepan. Add the pod. Steep over very low heat for 15 minutes. Let cool to room temperature.

3. Beat the egg yolks in a large bowl until smooth, then beat in the room-temperature cream mixture. (If you're making the custard ahead, cover and refrigerate the mixture. Bring up to room temperature before proceeding.)

4. Remove the vanilla pods from the custard, then pour the mixture into the ramekins. Place in a baking pan and add enough hot water to the pan to come halfway up the sides of the ramekins. Cover with aluminum foil and bake for 40 minutes, or until the custards are just set. They should still wiggle a little bit in the center when lightly shaken.

5. Allow to cool in the water bath for about 30 minutes. Then remove from the water bath, cover the cooled cremas with plastic wrap, and refrigerate until chilled, about 2 hours.

6. Meanwhile, purée the raspberries in a food processor and strain into a bowl to remove the seeds.

7. Mix the sugar with the 2 tablespoons water in a heavy saucepan. Cook over medium heat, stirring with a metal spoon to dissolve the sugar, until the sugar melts and the caramel is a light gold color, 5 to 6 minutes. Take care not to let the sugar burn. Remove the pan from the heat and allow to cool for 30 seconds, to avoid the possibility of splattering when you add the raspberry purée, then carefully add the purée and mix well. Allow to cool to room temperature. Add a tablespoon or so of water to the sauce if it seems too thick after cooling. If it seems too sweet, add the lemon juice.

8. To serve, make a small pool of the raspberry sauce on each plate. Dip the ramekins into hot water, then turn the cremas out onto the plates. Garnish each plate with fresh raspberries and a sprig of mint, then serve.

Super-Creamy Rice Pudding with Passion Fruit Sauce

*R*ice pudding is a universal comfort food. Like bread pudding, its appeal has long since elevated it beyond its origins as a poor man's dessert. Mary Higgins, a friend and neighbor from my childhood, gave me a version of this pudding many years ago. I've pushed and prodded it over the years, adding and subtracting elements, until it finally reached the recipe below, but her essential technique of stirring the pudding on top of the stove to produce an exceptionally creamy texture remains unchanged. The passion fruit is a tart foil to the creamy richness of the pudding itself. For a baked version of this dessert, see the instructions following the recipe.

MAKES 4 SERVINGS

½ teaspoon grated lemon zest
½ teaspoon grated orange zest
¼ teaspoon cardamom seeds
5 cups whole milk
¾ cup long-grain white rice
1 cup heavy cream
3 extra-large egg yolks
2 teaspoons vanilla extract
¾ cup sugar
¼ teaspoon kosher salt
2 ripe passion fruit

1. Tie the lemon zest, orange zest, and cardamom seeds in a piece of cheesecloth. Rinse a heavy pot with cold water; do not dry (this will make cleanup easier). Add the milk and bring to a boil over medium heat. Add the rice and cheesecloth bundle and stir until the milk returns to a boil. Lower the heat to a simmer and cook, uncovered, for 50 minutes, or until the rice is tender. Remove from the heat. Discard the cheesecloth bundle.

2. Meanwhile, beat the cream, egg yolks, and vanilla together in a large bowl. As soon as they're blended, add the sugar and salt and continue beating until completely dissolved.

3. Add 1 cup of the hot rice mixture to the egg mixture and stir everything together, then stir this mixture back into the rice remaining in the pot. Return the pot to the heat and cook, stirring constantly, until the custard just comes to the boil. (You should get one large bubble of air out of it.) Immediately remove it from the heat and transfer to a bowl. Put a piece of plastic wrap against the surface to prevent a skin from forming and refrigerate until cool, about 2 hours.

4. To serve, spoon the rice pudding into four bowls. Cut the passion fruit into halves. Scoop out the fruit from half a passion fruit over each portion.

Baked Rice Pudding

My husband and I come down on different sides of the fence regarding rice pudding. I prefer the creamy style that results from stirring the rice in a pot on top of the stove; Ken likes the firmer texture of baked rice pudding. If you prefer the latter as well, here's what to do.

1. Preheat the oven to 350°F.

2. Once you've blended everything together as instructed in Step 3, don't return the pot to the stovetop. Instead, spoon the pudding into four 8-ounce ramekins or heatproof custard cups. Set them in a warm water bath and bake until they're just set, about 50 minutes. They should still have a little wiggle in the middle. Let them cool, then refrigerate until firm.

If you bake the pudding, you also have the option of giving it a brûlée (burnt sugar) topping before serving. To brûlée, sprinkle about 1 tablespoon sugar over the surface of each pudding, enough to coat the top evenly. Run the ramekins under the broiler until the sugar is bubbly and brown. An easier method is to adjust the flame of a small butane kitchen torch to medium and move the flame over the sugar until it caramelizes. Let cool for a few minutes, then serve.

Sources

Farmers' Markets

Most states publish listings of local farmers' markets, available through state agricultural offices. The United States Department of Agriculture also publishes the *National Directory of Farmers' Markets*, updated ever two years in hard copy and continually on the web at www.ams.usda.gov/farmersmarkets. The directory is available by calling (800) 384-8707 or by writing to:

USDA
AMS-T&M-W&AM, Room 2642-S
1400 Independence Avenue, SW
Washington, DC 20250–0267

Spices, Cheeses, and Unusual Ingredients

Formaggio Kitchen
244 Huron Avenue
Cambridge, MA 02138
(888) 212-3224
www.formaggiokitchen.com

Valerie and Ihsan Gurdal's Formaggio Kitchen is an excellent source for cheeses, chickpea flour, chestnut flour, dried flageolets, pomegranate molasses, dried Turkish figs, Hungarian paprika, and other difficult-to-find spices. The mail-order catalogue includes only a partial listing of products, so call if you don't see what you want. Next-day delivery available.

Index

bulgur, phyllo tarts with smoky eggplant, roasted red peppers and, 134–35

butter:

anchovy, 256

anchovy, seared sirloin tips with red wine pan juices and, 254–56

brown, skate wings with capers, anchovies and, 206–7

brown bay, sautéed boneless chicken breasts with, 224–25

cake, lemon-almond, 350–51

cake, prune-plum and walnut, 349

clarified, 111

sage, celery root ravioli with crispy pork confit or, 310–13

simple favas with, 87

buttermilk mashed potatoes, versatile, 107

C

cakes:

lemon-almond butter, 350–51

prune-plum and walnut butter, 349

caper(s):

braised artichokes with anchovies, lemon zest and, 83–84

glazed sweetbreads with smoked ham, pecans and, 326–27

grilled mackerel with eggplant, tomatoes and, 190–91

panzanella—fried bread salad with roasted peppers, toasted garlic and, 71

sauce, green, seared tuna with, 179

skate wings with brown butter, anchovies and, 206–7

smoked salmon pizza with mascarpone and, 130

smoked salmon rolls with arugula, mascarpone, chives and, 9

capocollo, escarole, and Romaine salad with anchovy dressing and fried onions, 67

caramel(ized):

-ginger sauce, peppered peach tarts with, 341–43

onions, five-cheese pizza with truffle oil and, 128–29

onions, tarte flambée with smoked bacon, creamy cheese and, 132–33

pears, gratin with, 115

raspberry sauce, crema spessa with, 354–55

squash, pear, and blue cheese crostata, 138–39

carrots in honey and orange juice with black sesame seeds and mint, glazed, 105

cauliflower, roasted spicy curried broccoli and, 113

celery root:

bay scallops with tangerines and, 204–5

purée, 104

ravioli with sage butter or crispy pork confit, 310–13

salt cod, and artichoke fritters, 299–300

cheese:

creamy, tarte flambée with caramelized onions, smoked bacon and, 132–33

five-, pizza, with caramelized onions and truffle oil, 128–29

herbed, stuffed squash blossoms in fritter batter, 308–9

see also specific cheeses

chestnut(s), 244

buckwheat polenta with figs, Gorgonzola and, 172–73

glazed turnips with prunes and, 116

quail, and farro stew, 245–46

roast Christmas goose stuffed with brandied figs, rye bread and, 320–22

winter vegetable gratin with cranberries and, 114–15

chicken, 231–38

baby (poussin), cooked under a brick with hot-and-spicy ginger sauce, peppered, 231–32

with poppy seeds and pancetta, grilled smoked, 233–34

stew, Oliver's, 52–53

chicken breasts:

with brown bay butter, sautéed boneless, 224–25

stuffed with herbed ricotta, roasted, 226–27

chicken stock, 31

homemade, vs. canned broth, 32

chicken thighs:

with ancho peppers and andouille sausage, braised, 237–38

in mustard with garlic and mascarpone, braised, 235–36

chickpeas, 230

rabbit soup with garlic, peppers and, 58–59

vinegared, thin-sliced calves' liver with greens,
Dijon mustard sauce and, 286–88
gratin:
with caramelized pears, 115
potato gnocchi, 169–70
summer vegetable, salmon marinated in mint and
basil with, 194–95
winter vegetable, with cranberries and chestnuts,
114–15
green beans, warm spring vegetable salad with favas,
peas, radicchio and, 90
greens:
fiery garlicky, 91
many, orzo in chicken broth with Asiago and, 40
roasted spice-rubbed pork with rice, black beans,
lime and, 328–31
thin-sliced calves' liver with Dijon mustard sauce,
vinegared grapes and, 286–88
wilted, fresh and salt cod wrapped in pancetta
with, 314–15
see also specific greens
grill notes, 265
Gruyère cheese, winter vegetable gratin with
cranberries, chestnuts and, 114–15

H

halibut, braised in ginger-lemongrass broth with
cilantro, basil, and mint, 212–13
ham:
Italian, clam and mussel stew with walnuts, leeks
and, 217
smoked, glazed sweetbreads with capers, pecans
and, 326–27
hazelnut(s):
crumb-coated, fried rabbit with peaches, 289–91
goat cheese terrine with dried figs and, 15–16
toasted, roasted pear and radicchio salad with
Gorgonzola cream and, 72
herb(s), herbal, herbed:
cheese, stuffed squash blossoms in fritter batter,
308–9
-fennel stuffing, roasted brined turkey with,
239–41
fresh, roasted vegetables with pomegranate seeds
and, 112
mayonnaise, 14

ricotta, roasted chicken breasts stuffed with,
226–27
and spinach filling, socca crêpes with, 28–29
-stuffed eggs, Bibb lettuce with creamy mustard
dressing and, 64
honey:
braised eggplant and red peppers with spices and,
96–97
fig and Taleggio pizza with sage and, 126–27
glazed carrots in orange juice with black sesame
seeds, mint and, 105
honeyed quince compote, 251
steamed and pan-roasted duck with, 247–51
horseradish, roast cod in terra-cotta, with bacon and,
210–11

I

ice cream, grilled pineapple with rum, lime-ginger
syrup and, 334

L

lamb, 277–85
chops with saffron and roasted garlic pan sauce,
seared loin, 277
with mustard crumbs, roast leg of, 282–83
roast rack of, with Romaine salad and anchovy
dressing, 284–85
shanks, braised rosemary-stuffed, with roasted
fennel and red onions, 279–81
shanks, grilled rosemary, 280–81
steaks with balsamic vinegar and red pepper
marinade, seared, 278
lasagna, 144
with broccoli rabe, brandade, 152–53
leek(s):
artichoke, and fennel strudel, 92–93
clam and mussel stew with Italian ham, walnuts
and, 217
and shiitakes wrapped in pancetta, braised, 79
lemon(s):
-almond butter cake, 350–51
clam and white bean soup with fennel, anchovy
and, 46–47
cream, fazzoletti—"handkerchiefs" with pistachios, spinach, slow-roasted tomatoes and,
164–65

lemons (*continued*)

    fregola—Sardinian pasta with favas, Parmesan, lots of parsley and, 155

    mashed potatoes, 107

    preserved, 268

    preserved, braised veal shanks with flageolets and, 266–68

    Tuscan-style sirloin with Parmesan, truffle oil and, 263–64

lemongrass-ginger broth braised halibut with cilantro, basil, and mint, 212–13

lemon zest, braised artichokes with anchovies, capers and, 83–84

lentils, smoky, seared shad roe with, 192–93

lettuce(s):

    Bibb, with creamy mustard dressing and herb-stuffed eggs, 64

    local, with sherry vinaigrette and edible flowers, 62

    see also Romaine

lime:

    chilled lobster with potato–blood orange salad and, 180–81

    chilled smooth corn soup with tomatoes, avocado and, 36–37

    -ginger syrup, grilled pineapple with rum, ice cream and, 334

    roasted spice-rubbed pork with greens, rice, black beans and, 328–31

linguine:

    braised octopus with paprika and, 215–16

    with salsa cruda, 145

liver:

    duck, and porcini pâté, Venetian, 17–18

    thin-sliced calves', with greens, Dijon mustard sauce, and vinegared grapes, 286–88

lobster:

    chilled, with potato–blood orange salad and lime, 180–81

    corn, and smoked fish chowder, 48

    and corn salad, spicy, chilled grilled tomato soup with, 38–39

    hard-shell vs. soft-shell, 181

    littleneck clam, and andouille sausage stew, 220–21

    stock, 34–35

M

mackerel, grilled, with eggplant, tomatoes, and capers, 190–91

maple-brined grilled pork chops with roasted pear chutney, 272–74

marrowbones, roasted, 168

    semolina gnocchi with red wine mushroom sauce and, 166–68

mascarpone:

    braised chicken in mustard with garlic and, 235-36

    fig tart, 348

    seared quail stuffed with green peppercorns and, 242–43

    smoked salmon pizza with capers and, 130

    smoked salmon rolls with arugula, chives, capers and, 9

mashed potatoes:

    garlic (skordalia), 106

    lemon, 107

    roasted garlic, 107

    versatile buttermilk, 107

mayonnaise:

    herbal, 14

    saffron, spicy mussel salad with black olives, roasted peppers and, 182–83

    —and variations, 13–14

meatballs, little, escarole with mushrooms and, 56–57

mint(ed):

    and basil marinated salmon with summer vegetable gratin, 194–95

    glazed carrots in honey and orange juice with black sesame seeds and, 105

    halibut braised in ginger-lemongrass broth with cilantro, basil and, 212–13

    roasted red saffron peppers with chiles and, 98

    Romaine salad with grapes, ricotta salata, and toasted almonds, 65

monkfish and clam bourride with aïoli and green olive tapenade, 218–19

mozzarella:

    in five-cheese pizza with caramelized onions and truffle oil, 128–29

    in fresh tomato soup with seared eggplant sandwiches, 42–43

peppers, red bell:
>   and eggplant with honey and spices, braised,
>   96–97
>   marinade, seared lamb steaks with balsamic
>   vinegar and, 278
>   rabbit soup with garlic and, 58–59

peppers, roasted red:
>   panzanella—fried bread salad with capers, toasted
>   garlic and, 71
>   phyllo tarts with smoky eggplant, bulgur and,
>   134–35
>   with saffron, mint, and chiles, 98

pesto, 44

phyllo tarts with smoky eggplant, bulgur, and roasted
>   red peppers, 134–35

pineapple, grilled, with rum, lime-ginger syrup, and
>   ice cream, 334

pistachios:
>   fazzoletti—"handkerchiefs" with lemon cream,
>   spinach, slow-roasted tomatoes and, 164–65
>   fresh green pea soup with shaved radicchio and, 41

pizza, 121, 123–31
>   with caramelized onions and truffle oil, five-
>   cheese, 128–29
>   crispy prosciutto and parsley, 131
>   fig and Taleggio, with sage and honey, 126–27
>   smoked salmon, with mascarpone and capers,
>   130

pizza dough, basic, 123–24

plum-prune and walnut butter cake, 349

polenta:
>   with chestnuts, figs, and Gorgonzola, buckwheat,
>   172–73
>   mussel soup over, with saffron, tomatoes, and
>   garlic, 50–51
>   panisse with tomatoes and black olives, 176
>   soft, acquacotta—porcini broth with Taleggio,
>   a poached egg and, 306–7

pomegranate (seeds):
>   glaze, grilled bluefish with cucumber-yogurt sauce
>   and, 184–85
>   grilled onion and parsley salad with black olives
>   and, 73
>   roasted vegetables with fresh herbs and, 112

poppy seeds:
>   grilled smoked chicken with pancetta and, 233–34

ravioli bundles of roasted beets with walnuts,
>   garlic cream and, 160–61

porcini mushrooms:
>   broth with soft polenta, Taleggio, and a poached
>   egg (acquacotta), 306–7
>   dried, braised stuffed veal breast with,
>   269–70
>   dried, preparation of, 271
>   and duck liver pâté, Venetian, 17–18

pork, 272–76
>   chops, grilled maple-braised with roasted pear
>   chutney, 272–74
>   confit, crispy, 313
>   confit, crispy, celery root ravioli with sage butter
>   or, 310–13
>   roasted spice-rubbed, with greens, rice, black
>   beans, and lime, 328–31
>   tenderloin, grilled and roasted, with toasted
>   pumpkin seed sauce, 275–76
>   see also bacon; ham; pancetta; prosciutto

portobella mushroom and arugula salad, 66

potato(es):
>   -basil purée, Reine's, grilled striped bass with,
>   188–89
>   –blood orange salad, chilled lobster with lime and,
>   180–81
>   cakes with crème fraîche, crisp shredded, 110
>   fingerling, fig, and tarragon salad, 70
>   gnocchi gratin, 169–70
>   leek, artichoke, and fennel strudel, 92–93
>   stuffed with wild mushrooms and truffled eggs,
>   roasted, 301–2
>   see also mashed potatoes

poultry, 222–51
>   see also chicken; duck; quail; Rock Cornish game
>   hens; turkey

prosciutto:
>   nidimi—"little nests" stuffed with Fontina, spinach
>   and, 162–63
>   and parsley pizza, crispy, 131

prune(s):
>   glazed turnips with chestnuts and, 116
>   -plum and walnut butter cake, 349

pudding, super-creamy rice, with passion fruit sauce,
>   356–57

pumpkin and apple tart, 345–46

truffled eggs, roasted potatoes stuffed with wild mushrooms and, 301–2

truffle oil:

five-cheese pizza with caramelized onions and, 128–29

Tuscan-style sirloin with Parmesan, lemon and, 263–64

tuna:

with green caper sauce, seared, 179

with romesco sauce, grilled, 186–87

turkey with fennel-herb stuffing, roasted brined, 239–41

turnips, glazed, with chestnuts and prunes, 116

V

veal, 266–71

breast with porcini mushrooms, braised stuffed, 269–70

ground, in escarole soup with mushrooms and little meatballs, 56–57

with Parmesan crust, roast shoulder of, 324–25

shanks with flageolets and preserved lemon, braised, 266–67

vegetable(s), 77–120

crostata, spring, 136–37

gratin, summer, salmon marinated in mint and basil with, 194–95

roasted, with fresh herbs and pomegranate seeds, 112

salad with favas, green beans, peas, and radicchio, warm spring, 90

winter, gratin with cranberries and chestnuts, 114–15

see also specific vegetables

venison, peppered, with sherry sauce and dried fruit chutney, 294–96

vinaigrette:

mustard, tomato and grilled mushroom salad with, 74–75

see also sherry vinaigrette

vinegar:

premium, 63

see also balsamic

vinegared grapes, 288

thin-sliced calves' liver with greens, Dijon mustard sauce and, 286–88

W

walnut(s):

breadsticks, 19

clam and mussel stew with Italian ham, leeks and, 217

and prune-plum butter cake, 349

ravioli bundles of roasted beets with poppy seeds, garlic cream and, 160–61

salmon with dried cranberries and, 200–201

watercress and Stilton soup, 49

wine, red:

braised short ribs of beef with apricots, black olives and, 257–58

mushroom sauce, semolina gnocchi with roasted marrowbones and, 166–68

pan juices, seared sirloin tips with anchovy butter and, 254–56

Y

yogurt-cucumber sauce, grilled bluefish with pomegranate glaze and, 184–85

Z

zabaglione, 5-spice, roasted pears with, 336–37

zucchini flowers, *see* squash blossoms